How to Use This Book

If you're new to programming or just new to REXX [illegible] tool. We designed this book for you to work through the lessons, in order, on a daily basis. Later lessons build on the material presented in earlier lessons. No previous programming experience is required or assumed. Prior experience with another language won't hurt; you'll just be able to learn faster. The book covers some of the rules of programming, as well as teaching you how to program in REXX.

Special Features of This Book

The book contains some special features to help you as you learn REXX.

Syntax Boxes

Syntax boxes show you how to use a specific REXX item. Each box provides concrete examples and fully explains the REXX command or concept.

Another feature of the book is DO/DON'T boxes, which provide tips on real-life usage.

DO	DON'T

DO read this section. It explains what happens in the workshop section at the end of each day.

DON'T skip any of the quiz questions or exercises. If you can finish the workshop exercises, you'll know that you're ready to move on to the next day's material.

We provide numerous examples throughout the book, with explanations that help you learn how to program.

In addition, each day ends with a Q&A session, a quiz, and a set of exercises to help solidify what you've learned in the lesson.

At the end of each week, you'll find "The Week in Review." This section contains a comprehensive program that uses many of the concepts covered in the previous week.

Conventions Used in This Book

This book uses different typefaces to help you differentiate between REXX code and regular English, and also to help you identify important concepts. Actual REXX code is typeset in a special `monospace` font. Placeholders—generic terms that represent the actual names you type within the code—are typeset in an *`italic monospace`* font. Text that you type is set in a **`bold monospace`** font. When a new term is introduced, it is typeset in *italic*.

Teach Yourself REXX in 21 Days

Teach Yourself REXX in 21 Days

William F. Schindler
Esther Schindler

PUBLISHING
201 West 103rd Street, Indianapolis, Indiana 46290

To David and Julie
for increasing the possibilities.

FIRST EDITION

International Standard Book Number: 0-672-30529-1

Library of Congress Catalog Card Number: 94-66268

97 96 95 94 4 3 2 1

Interpretation of the printing code: the rightmost double-digit number is the year of the book's printing; the rightmost single-digit, the number of the book's printing. For example, a printing code of 94-1 shows that the first printing of the book occurred in 1994.

Composed in AGaramond and MCPdigital by Macmillan Computer Publishing

Printed in the United States of America

Trademarks

Publisher
Richard K. Swadley

Associate Publisher
Jordan Gold

Acquisitions Manager
Stacy Hiquet

Managing Editor
Cindy Morrow

Acquisitions Editor
Grace Buechlein

Development Editor
Mark Taber

Production Editor
Charles A. Hutchinson

Editorial Coordinator
Bill Whitmer

Editorial Assistants
Carol Ackerman
Sharon Cox
Lynette Quinn

Technical Reviewer
Brian Proffit

Marketing Manager
Gregg Bushyeager

Cover Designer
Dan Armstrong

Book Designer
Alyssa Yesh

Director of Production and Manufacturing
Jeff Valler

Imprint Manager
Juli Cook

Manufacturing Coordinator
Paul Gilchrist

Production Analysts
Dennis Clay Hager
Mary Beth Wakefield

Graphics Image Specialists
Tim Montgomery
Dennis Sheehan
Susan VandeWalle

Production
Nick Anderson
Troy Barnes
Carol Bowers
Mona Brown
Elaine Brush
Ayrika Bryant
Cheryl Cameron
Elaine Crabtree
Steph Davis
Mike Dietsch
Terri Edwards
Rob Falco
Kimberly K. Hannel
Angela P. Judy
Greg Kemp
Ayanna Lacey
Stephanie J. McComb
Jamie Milazzo
Shelly Palma
Casey Price
Chad Poore
Linda Quigley
Ryan Rader
Kim Scott
Marc Shecter
Susan Shepard
Tonya R. Simpson
SA Springer
Marcella Thompson
Scott Tullis
Dennis R. Wesner

Indexer
Craig A. Small

Overview

Contents

Sams
Learning
Center
SAMS
PUBLISHING

Acknowledgments

Our thanks go to the folks at Sams Publishing who perform the magic of changing thousands of raw words into a finished book. Special thanks go to Grace Buechlein for the tremendous support she gave us from conception to completion. We'd also like to thank our technical editor, Brian Proffit, for all the constructive criticism and program testing.

Bill Schindler

Esther Schindler

About the Authors

William F. (Bill) Schindler

William F. (Bill) Schindler is an independent consultant specializing in system software and optimization. He is coordinator of the OS/2 Special Interest Group of the Phoenix PC Users Group and Sysop of the two 20,000-member OS/2 Vendor Forums on CompuServe.

Esther Schindler

Esther Schindler is a computer consultant and Sysop of the ZiffNet Executives On-Line Forum. She is a contributing editor of *OS/2 Magazine*.

WEEK 1

AT A GLANCE

You are about to begin your first week of learning how to program in REXX. We've written this book assuming that you're going to write REXX programs using the OS/2 operating system. If you don't have OS/2, you can still use this book; you just need to be aware that things may be a little different on your system.

Before you can get started, you're going to need an editor and the REXX interpreter. If you're using OS/2, you should already have both of those items installed on your system. If you're not using OS/2, you need to acquire these items. If you don't have an editor or the REXX interpreter, you can still learn to program in REXX; you may feel like you're learning to swim on dry land, though! Programming is a skill that is best learned by actually doing it. This book contains many REXX programs that give you, the new programmer, a chance to gain hands-on experience.

Each lesson in this book ends with a workshop that contains a quiz and exercises. At the end of each day, you should be able to answer the questions and complete the exercises. For the first few days, we have supplied answers to all of the questions and exercises (see Appendix F, "Answers"). As you progress, we don't supply answers for all the exercises because a variety of correct solutions is possible. Many of the exercises are also designed to produce useful utilities. Take advantage of the exercises and check your answers!

Where You're Going...

The first week covers almost all the material you need to know in order to understand and write simple REXX programs. On Days 1, "Getting Started," and 2, "REXX Ground Rules," you learn how to create a REXX program and how to recognize the basic elements of REXX programs. Day 3, "Variables and Constants," and Day 4, "Instructions, Expressions, and Operators," take the concepts you learned in the first two days and expand on them so that you understand how the various elements covered on Day 2 fit together. Day 5, "Arithmetic," provides information on how to do math in REXX. Day 6, "Executing System Commands," covers using REXX to execute OS/2 system commands and developing REXX programs to replace batch files. Day 7, "Basic Input/Output," wraps up the week with a discussion on writing programs that interact with users.

This information is a lot to cover in just one week, but you shouldn't have any problems if you learn the information one lesson per day.

Getting Started

WEEK 1

Welcome to *Teach Yourself REXX in 21 Days*! This lesson marks the start of your journey in learning to program using the REXX language. Today you learn the following:

- The benefits of using REXX
- How a REXX program is different from a batch file
- The steps involved in creating a REXX program
- How to enter and run a REXX program
- How to read REXX error messages

History of REXX

The REXX language was originally developed in 1979 for IBM's VM mainframe operating system by Mike Cowlishaw. In the early 1980s, REXX became a standard part of the VM system. Non-IBM versions have been implemented for the Atari, UNIX, DEC, Amiga, Windows, and MS-DOS.

REXX became a standard part of OS/2 with the release of OS/2 version 1.3. With the release of OS/2 2.x, REXX has gained considerable popularity.

The design of REXX was based on user feedback. Unlike many programming languages, REXX's design emphasizes the convenience of the user rather than the convenience of the language implementor. Perhaps the only inconvenient part of REXX is its full name under OS/2: Procedures Language2/REstructured eXtended eXecutor.

Note: Over time, REXX programs have been called procedures, commands, execs, scripts, and even batch files. Recent IBM documentation refers to them both as procedures and programs. We settled on calling them REXX programs.

Benefits of Using REXX

REXX has several benefits over most other programming languages. The key benefits to using REXX are as follows:

- It is easy to use.

- It offers a rich selection of built-in functions.
- It comes free with OS/2.
- It can easily customize and extend OS/2.

Ease of Use

The REXX language was designed to be easy to learn and use. Most of the instructions in REXX are common English words, such as SAY and PARSE, rather than abbreviations or jargon. REXX is also a modern structured programming language, so many of the programming techniques that you learn can be used in other programming languages.

REXX has very few rules regarding code formatting, so you have a great deal of freedom to format code as you see fit. REXX does not require line numbers, and you don't need to enter code in specific columns.

REXX is an *interpreted* language. A *compiled* language such as C or Pascal requires the programmer to perform several steps before a program can be run. An interpreted language can be run "as is" without any intervening steps. Therefore, a programmer can write and immediately test several different approaches to solving a programming problem.

Built-In Functions

REXX includes a large number of functions for parsing, manipulating data, reading and writing files, and even debugging. Many functions that, in other languages, you would have to write yourself are supplied with REXX.

Free with OS/2

Every copy of OS/2 2.x includes REXX. You don't have to make a commitment or spend money—it's already there.

Customizes and Extends OS/2

OS/2 provides a collection of REXX extensions that enable you to write programs that can manipulate the Workplace Shell, read and write initialization files, and access file directories. These extensions provide the power to automate and customize the OS/2 desktop.

Comparing REXX Programs to Batch Files

One of the first things you may notice about REXX is that it seems to have a lot in common with batch files. REXX programs are named using a .CMD extension like OS/2 batch files; you can run REXX programs from the OS/2 command line just like you run an OS/2 batch file. And you can use REXX, like an OS/2 batch file, to run a series of OS/2 commands.

REXX isn't just a fancy batch language, however. REXX is a full programming language like BASIC or Pascal. You can convert your batch files to REXX, but you can also develop REXX programs that don't execute a single OS/2 command.

Preparation

You need only a couple of things before you can get started programming in REXX:

- A text editor
- REXX itself

You need a text editor to create and edit REXX programs. Although you can use your favorite word processor, a text editor has a different purpose. Text editors load and save ASCII files, and don't have the primary purpose of doing fancy text formatting. If you want to use a word processor such as DeScribe or Ami Pro, make sure you use the word processor's ASCII, program, or text mode. REXX programs must be saved as ASCII files, not as word processor documents.

If you haven't yet developed any preferences for a text editor, then you should try the Enhanced Editor (called EPM by most programmers). EPM has three big advantages: it is quite powerful, it is configurable, and it is included free with OS/2. See Appendix G for a quick introduction to using the Enhanced Editor.

REXX is included as a standard part of OS/2. If you installed OS/2 with the normal defaults, then you don't need to do anything special. Otherwise, it's possible that you didn't install it, and you must run OS/2's Selective Install application before you can use REXX. See Appendix A for help with using the Selective Install application to install REXX.

Developing REXX Programs

Programming in any computer language is a problem-solving activity more than anything else. A computer language is a *tool* that works well only when the user understands both the tool and the problems that tool is designed to solve.

Most problems are best handled in a step-by-step approach. When you program, you may find that this point is especially true. When you're solving programming problems, you need to perform three steps: design, code, and test and debug. Although these steps may appear to be distinct, they actually overlap and often cycle so that the result of one step is sometimes a return to an earlier step (see fig. 1.1).

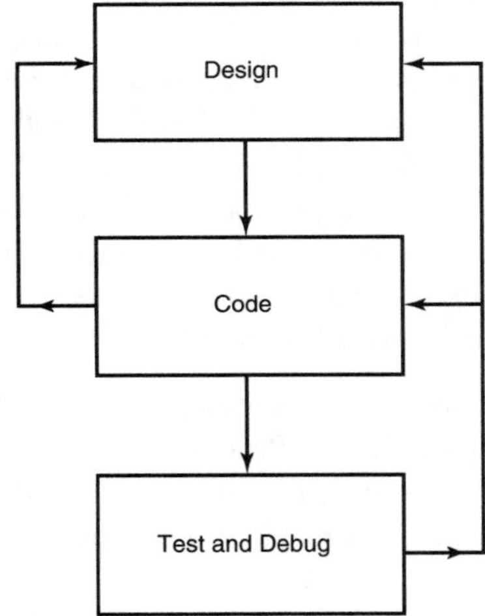

Figure 1.1. *The Program Development Cycle.*

In later lessons, you examine each of these steps in more depth.

Design

The design step is the most important step in creating any program. The process of designing a program includes the following:

- ☐ Understanding the problem
- ☐ Determining the inputs and outputs
- ☐ Breaking large problems into several smaller, more easily solved problems

The first step in creating any program is to determine what the problem is and what you need to do to solve the problem. You need to understand the problem before you can write a program. The problem may be very simple ("display the words 'Hello, world!' on the screen"); or the problem may be complex ("write a word processor that creates .INF files").

A great aid to understanding any programming problem is to determine what inputs and outputs are needed. Almost every program handles some type of input (characters typed by a user, data in files, system information, and so on) and output (messages to a user, data written to files, images, and so on).

Once you know the inputs and outputs, see if you can break the problem into several simpler problems. You might find that you can solve each of these simpler problems easily, whereas the original problem might appear too complex to solve. Solving a big problem by breaking it into several smaller problems is what programmers call *stepwise refinement.* A simple problem (for example, "display 'Hello, world!' on the screen") may not require any refinement. A complex problem (for example, "write a word processor…") may require you to repeatedly break problems into smaller and smaller problems. For instance, on a first pass you may decide that "process user input" is a good stepwise refinement; on the next pass, you may decide that you can break "process user input" into "process normal text" and "process function keys."

You might be tempted to skip over the design step and dive directly into writing the program. But don't skimp on design! Programming is a lot like building a house; you waste a lot of time and energy if you pour concrete and drive nails before you know whether the house is going to be a ranch or a saltbox.

Code

The code step is where the program takes form. During this step, you write the program using a computer language such as REXX. You should write the code for each of the simpler pieces of the problem that you broke out during the design step and the code that is needed to "glue" those pieces together.

You create, edit, and save the code using a text editor. The code you write is called *source code*. Because REXX is an interpreted language, the source code is also the *executable code*, which is the code that the computer runs or executes. (Compiled languages use a process called *compilation* to produce a separate file that contains the executable code.) REXX programs are always named using the .CMD extension.

Test and Debug

Even the most experienced programmers make mistakes or create design errors, commonly called *bugs*. You must test programs in order to discover any such mistakes or errors. You should not test a program to discover if it is correct; you should test it to find the bugs. This point is subtle but important!

Once you find a bug, you need to discover its cause and correct it. A bug can be caused by a typo, by an omission in the code or design, by misunderstanding the programming language, or by misunderstanding some part of the problem during the design step.

Writing Your First REXX Program

Now that you know a little about REXX, you're probably eager to try it. This first demonstration should help you get acquainted with entering and running a REXX program. It's okay if you don't understand everything; for now, your goal is to get comfortable with entering and running programs.

The demonstration program is named HELLO.CMD. This simple program displays a message on the screen and can optionally take a command-line parameter.

Listing 1.1. HELLO.CMD.

```
/* hello.cmd */

IF Arg() >< 0 THEN
  ARG world!

SAY 'Hello,' world!
```

Entering and Running HELLO.CMD

Start your text editor (or your word processor using ASCII mode) and enter the program shown in listing 1.1 exactly as you see it here. Make certain that you enter the `/*` in the first two positions on the first line of the program.

> **Note:** If you are using the Enhanced Editor (EPM), you may discover that when you type **`IF`** and press the Spacebar, EPM inserts some other words.

EPM's automatic code expansion is at work here. For now, you may find that automatic expansion is a greater distraction than a help. To shut it off, open the Command dialog by pressing Ctrl+I, type **expand off**, and press Enter. See Appendix G for more help on using EPM.

After you enter the program, save it as HELLO.CMD and then start an OS/2 command prompt. Change directories to where you saved HELLO.CMD. Type **hello** at the command prompt and press Enter.

If you entered and saved the program correctly, you should see the following:

```
Hello, WORLD!
```

Type **hello bill** at the command prompt and press Enter. The output will be slightly different this time:

```
Hello, BILL
```

Congratulations! You've just entered and run your first REXX program!

Note: Later lessons include an analysis section following the output from the program. Because this program is just a demonstration, we don't do an analysis here.

Understanding Errors

Sometimes you may have a typo or some other error in a REXX program, and REXX produces an error message and stops running. You then need to edit the program to fix the error that REXX discovered.

You may soon find that REXX is very literal-minded. If you type **SEY** instead of **SAY**, REXX complains. It doesn't try to guess at what you really meant; it only attempts to process the exact characters and words that you type into your text editor.

To see what a REXX error message looks like, you're going to deliberately create an error in HELLO.CMD. Load HELLO.CMD into your editor and move the cursor to the line that ends with THEN. Delete the word THEN and save the file. HELLO.CMD should now look like listing 1.2.

Tip: If you run EPM from the command line, try using the command **`START EPM HELLO.CMD`** instead. You can then edit the file, and try running it from the command line without closing the editor.

Listing 1.2. HELLO.CMD with a syntax error.

```
/* hello.cmd */

IF Arg() >< 0
  ARG world!

SAY 'Hello,' world!
```

Start an OS/2 command line. Type **`hello`** and press Enter. What you should see is a typical REXX error message:

```
     4 +++   Arg world!;
REX0018: Error 18 running R:\REXX\HELLO.CMD, line 4: THEN expected
```

REXX shows you the line number in your source code on which the error occurred, followed by the text of the statement that caused the error. The next part of the error message shows the REXX error number, REX0018, and the error message itself.

Notice that the line shown in the error message is not the line on which you would expect the error to be, but the next line. REXX had to look at the third line before it could be certain that `THEN` really is missing, so the third line is the one that gets flagged as being in error. This occurrence is common, and you should be aware that you may need to look back one line in order to find the real cause of the error.

To learn more about this error message, type **`help REX0018`** at an OS/2 command prompt and press Enter. You then see the following:

```
REX0018: ***THEN expected***

EXPLANATION: All IF clauses and WHEN clauses in REXX must be followed
             by a THEN clause.  Some other clause was found when a
             THEN was expected.
```

The explanation clarifies the original error message—REXX expected to see the word `THEN` following `IF Arg() >< 0` but found something else instead. To fix the error, you must replace the `THEN`, which you deleted earlier.

To get additional information on any REXX error message, type `help` followed by the error number. Doing so always produces a longer message that should aid you in determining the cause of the error.

Summary

In this lesson, you learned some of the key benefits of using REXX. Ease of use and a rich selection of functions, combined with REXX being a standard part of OS/2, make REXX hard to beat.

You learned the steps for developing a REXX program—design, code, and test and debug. Programming is a problem-solving activity, and design is the most important step in writing a program; understanding the problem, determining the inputs and outputs, and stepwise refinement are all required to produce a program that works.

You also learned about REXX error messages. You should know how to use the OS/2 help command to get more detail on a REXX error. Remember that REXX often reports an error one line after the actual location of the error.

Q&A

Q If I want to share my program with someone else, does he or she need to have REXX, too?

A Anyone who wants to run a REXX program must have REXX installed on his or her computer. Installing REXX usually isn't a problem if the other person is running OS/2. If he or she isn't running OS/2, then that user will need to purchase a REXX interpreter for his or her computer.

Q Why does my REXX program run faster the second time I run it?

A The first time you run a REXX program, REXX needs to translate it into the compressed format that REXX uses internally. REXX then stores the compressed format in your program's extended attributes (we'll spend some time on extended attributes on Day 16). The next time you run the program, REXX uses the information in the extended attributes instead of translating the program again. Whenever you change your program, REXX recompresses it and stores the changed version in the extended attributes.

Q If REXX knows that `THEN` is needed, why doesn't it fix my code for me?

A The `IF` could be in error (that is, you accidentally inserted `IF`). REXX's error messages tell you what REXX expects to find, but that may not be what you intended.

Workshop

The Workshop provides quiz questions to help strengthen your understanding of the material covered and exercises to provide you with experience in using what you've learned. You should understand the quiz and exercise answers before continuing to the next lesson. Answers are provided in Appendix F, "Answers."

Quiz

1. Name three benefits of using REXX.
2. What are the steps in developing programs?
3. What is stepwise refinement?
4. How do you get additional information on an error message?
5. What extension should you use for REXX programs?

Exercises

1. Enter the following program and run it. What does this program do?

```
/* Ex1-1.cmd */

DO i = 1 TO SourceLine()
  SAY SourceLine(i)
END
EXIT
```

2. Enter the following program and run it. What does this program do?

```
/* Ex1-2.cmd */

target = Random(1, 10)
SAY "I'm thinking of a number between 1 and 10. Can you guess it?"
```

```
DO UNTIL guess = target
  SAY "Enter your guess:"
  PULL guess
  IF guess < target THEN
    SAY "That was too low"
  IF guess > target THEN
    SAY "That was too high"
END
SAY "That's right!"

EXIT
```

3. The following program has a problem. Enter it and run it. What error message is produced? What additional information can you get on the error?

```
/* Ex1-3.cmd */
SAY "You'll see an error when you run this
EXIT
```

REXX Ground Rules

A REXX program consists of several elements that can be combined in specific ways. A large part of this book is devoted to explaining these program elements and the various ways you can use them. The first step is to get an overall understanding of the elements of a REXX program. So today you do the following:

- ☐ Examine the structure of a simple REXX program
- ☐ Learn the purpose of each of the program elements identified

A Simple REXX Program

The REXX program WHERE.CMD is shown in listing 2.1. This simple program searches the current disk drive for all files that match a given name. You tell WHERE.CMD what file to search for, either by entering the filename as a command-line parameter (such as **`where config.sys`**) or by responding to the program's prompt for the filename. You can also use wildcards, such as `where *.txt`, to search for several files at once. It's a handy utility to have when you remember the name of a file but forget where you hid it.

Don't worry if you don't understand how the program works. Your purpose today is to become familiar with the parts of a REXX program so that it will be easier to understand programs presented later in this book. By the way, the number and colon at the beginning of each line in listing 2.1 are not part of the WHERE.CMD program—they were added to help you find the lines as they're discussed in later sections.

Type **Listing 2.1. WHERE.CMD.**

```
 1: /* Find all files matching a file name */
 2:
 3: IF Arg() >< 0 THEN /* Any command line arguments? */
 4:   PARSE ARG filename
 5: ELSE
 6:   DO
 7:   SAY "Enter name of file to find:"
 8:   PULL filename
 9:   END
10:
11: CALL CheckName
12:
13: 'dir' filename '/B /S'
14:
15: EXIT
16:
17: /* Ensure search starts in root directory */
18: CheckName: PROCEDURE EXPOSE filename
19:   IF Left(filename, 1) >< '\' THEN
20:     filename = '\' || filename
21:   RETURN
```

The output from running `where config.sys` on an OS/2 boot drive is as follows:

```
C:\CONFIG.SYS
C:\OS2\INSTALL\CONFIG.SYS
```

Structure of a REXX Program

The following sections discuss each of the elements of the REXX program shown in listing 2.1. The line numbers following each heading are included to help you find the element being discussed.

Program Comments (Lines 1, 3, 15)

In a REXX program, text enclosed between `/*` and `*/` is called a *comment*. Every REXX program must begin with a comment beginning with `/*` in column one on the first line. This comment is required because it tells the OS/2 command interpreter that the .CMD file is a REXX program and not a command or batch file.

Comments have no effect on how your program runs; they are ignored by the REXX interpreter. You use comments in a program to explain and document the program code. Because comments are ignored by REXX, you are free to write anything you want in a comment.

Comments can take part of a line, an entire line, or several lines. For example,

```
/* This comment is on a line by itself */
SAY "Hi, there!" /* Comment on part of a line */

/* This comment takes
more than one line. It
could even go on for pages! */

/* This /* comment contains
/* nested */ comments. */
*/
```

Because comments are ignored by REXX, you may be tempted to ignore the comments yourself and not bother putting any in your programs. Don't succumb to this temptation! For the simplest programs, a line of text in the opening comment may suffice. However, you should always use comments in longer programs. You should document what each part of your program does so that the next person who looks at your program (who may be you) can easily understand it.

Comments can be *nested* (that is, they can contain other comments), but nesting comments is often a sure path to confusion. Look at the last comment in the preceding example, and you can see how confusing nested comments can be.

The only part of a REXX program that must exist is the comment on line one. One of the most common errors for a beginning REXX programmer is to forget this comment. If you forget this comment, OS/2 produces an error like the following:

```
SYS1041: The name specified is not recognized as an
internal or external command, operable program or batch file.
```

You may get additional errors or a different error message with a number following the letters `SYS`. These messages are caused by the OS/2 command interpreter attempting to execute your REXX program as an OS/2 batch file. If you get an `SYS` error, carefully check your REXX program to ensure that it begins with a comment.

DO | **DON'T**

DO add plenty of comments to your code. You should comment any line of code that might not be immediately understood by you or someone who might have to change your code later. You may understand a program when you write it, but will you understand it next month when you want to change it?

DON'T leave an empty comment at the beginning of a REXX program. Although it is legal to use just `/* */` at the beginning of a REXX program, doing so is poor form. Use the required opening comment to document the purpose of the program.

DON'T use nested comments.

DON'T use redundant comments. Almost worse than no comments are comments such as the following:

```
SAY "Hi!" /* Display "Hi!" */
```

Your comments should explain and clarify, not repeat what is already obvious.

DO work on creating a consistent comment style that's aimed at helping anyone who might read your code.

DO use blank lines to break your program into logical sections.

Instructions (Lines 3–9, 11, 15, 18–21)

An *instruction* is a part of the REXX language that tells REXX to do something. You include REXX instructions to perform a variety of actions, such as displaying information on the screen, getting user input, performing mathematical calculations, reading

and writing disk files, making decisions, and other operations necessary to create a useful program.

Several different types of instructions are used in the example program. The following sections briefly describe these instructions; all of these instructions are covered in depth later in the book.

2

IF...THEN...ELSE (Lines 3, 5, 19)

The `IF`, `THEN`, and `ELSE` instructions allow the program to make a decision based on a comparison. If the comparison is true, the instruction following `THEN` is executed; if the comparison is false, the instruction following the `ELSE` is executed. The `ELSE` part of the instruction is optional and is omitted when it isn't needed. The `IF`, `THEN`, and `ELSE` instructions are discussed in detail on Day 8.

PARSE ARG (Line 4)

The `PARSE ARG` instruction gets any command-line arguments and saves them in the *variable* `filename`. A variable is a place to store data within a program; variables are covered in detail on Day 3.

DO...END (Lines 6, 9)

The `DO` and `END` instructions are used here (lines 6 to 9) to create a group of instructions called a *block*. You use blocks to tell REXX to execute a group of instructions where REXX would normally execute only one instruction, such as following `THEN` or `ELSE`.

The `DO` and `END` instructions are also used to create *loops*, or groups of instructions that are executed more than once. Although this program doesn't contain any loops, you will encounter (and write) many programs that do. To see examples of two programs that contain loops, look at exercises 1 and 2 in the lesson for Day 1.

SAY (Line 7)

The `SAY` instruction displays information on the screen. You can use `SAY` to display information appearing in quotation marks (called *strings*) and a variety of other program information.

PULL (Line 8)

You use the `PULL` instruction to get information from the user. In this case, whatever the user types at the keyboard is saved in the variable `filename`. When the `PULL` instruction is encountered, the program stops until the user presses Enter.

CALL (Line 11)

You use the `CALL` instruction to cause a *procedure* (that is, code elsewhere in your program or outside your program), to execute. The procedure finishes executing when it encounters a `RETURN` instruction, and the program continues with the next instruction following `CALL`.

EXIT (Line 15)

The `EXIT` instruction tells REXX that the program has ended. When REXX encounters the `EXIT` instruction, it quits executing your program and returns to OS/2.

A Procedure (Lines 18–21)

A procedure consists of one or more instructions that have a *label* at the beginning and a `RETURN` instruction at the end. A label in a REXX program is a word immediately followed by a colon; a label at the beginning of a procedure is the name of that procedure.

The `RETURN` instruction (see listing 2.1, line 21) marks the end of a procedure. This instruction causes REXX to return to the point that the procedure was called and to continue execution from there.

You execute a procedure by using the `CALL` instruction followed by the name of the procedure. For example, to call a procedure named `CopyFiles`, you use the instruction `CALL CopyFiles`. In figure 2.1, you can see what happens when you call a procedure. Notice that the same procedure can be called many times; you can reuse code without rewriting it.

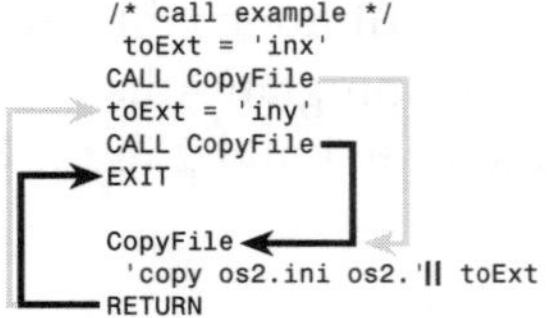

Figure 2.1. *Calling a REXX procedure.*

There's also a special kind of procedure called a *function*. A function is a procedure that returns a value. You can distinguish a function from a procedure by looking at the `RETURN`. If `RETURN` is followed by some value, such as `RETURN 5`, then you're looking at a function. You call functions by placing parentheses immediately after the name of the function; the `CALL` instruction isn't used in this case. In the following example, `SAY` displays the value returned by the function `FreeDiskSpace`:

```
SAY 'There are' FreeDiskSpace() 'bytes free.'
```

Assuming that `FreeDiskSpace` returns the amount of free disk space on the current disk drive, the result of running this instruction might be

```
There are 4096 bytes free.
```

The program in listing 2.1 contains two functions. `Arg` is used on line 3 and `Left` is used on line 19. Both of these functions are supplied by REXX, so it isn't necessary to define them within the program.

2

Commands (Line 13)

A *command* is anything that is not a REXX instruction or label. REXX passes commands back to the *invoking environment* (the program that started REXX, such as the OS/2 command processor), and that program executes the command, rather than REXX.

You can use any OS/2 command (such as `copy`, `backup`, or `delete`) in a REXX program. In WHERE.CMD, the `dir` command is used to display matching filenames on the hard drive. The `dir` command is not executed by REXX; REXX passes the `dir` command back to the OS/2 command processor, which executes the `dir` command and prints the results on the screen.

It isn't always necessary to put quotation marks around a command. However, it is a good habit to develop, because without the quotes, REXX attempts to process the command as an instruction, and it may occasionally confuse a command (or part of a command) with an instruction.

Indenting, Formatting, and Style

When you look at REXX programs written by others, you may see a variety of programming styles. REXX doesn't care about indenting, spacing, or the case of words (that is, UPPER, lower, or Mixed case), so programmers are free to develop and use almost any style imaginable.

We've written the code throughout this book employing a style that uses two spaces for indenting; we've written instructions in uppercase. Some programmers may indent four spaces and use mixed case for instructions; others may indent three spaces and use lowercase instructions. None of these styles are right or wrong as long as they're *consistent*.

Note: Some programmers feel very strongly that their particular programming style is the One Right Way. They may give you several complicated reasons why their way is right. (We were once blessed with a 30-minute explanation of why `DO` must be put on the same line as `THEN`.) Listen to the reasons, but apply salt liberally afterward.

No style is perfect. Each programming style has pluses and minuses. The best you can hope for is to find a style that you feel comfortable with and that doesn't distress others unduly.

An inconsistent programming style creates code that is hard to read and hard to change. Poorly formatted code often hides errors that would stand out otherwise. For example, here are lines 3 through 9 from listing 2.1, rewritten using poor formatting and an inconsistent style:

```
IF ARG() >< 0 then
 /* Any command line arguments? */
        parse ARG filename; Else
  do
SAY "Enter name of file to find:"
    pull filename; End
```

Compare this example with the same code in listing 2.1. This code seems hard to understand because the formatting doesn't give any hints about the structure of the program. It is impossible to tell at a glance if the code is correct or if an error is hidden by the programmer's sloppy style. (By the way, the semicolons in this example are valid. Semicolons allow more than one REXX instruction to be put on the same line.)

Developing a consistent programming style is as important as properly commenting your code. When you look at a REXX program, pay attention to both the function of the program and the formatting. Try out different programming styles, but above all, be consistent within each program!

Entering and Running the Program

You should enter and run WHERE.CMD. As you enter the program, try to identify each of the elements discussed in this lesson. If you have trouble with the following steps, you may want to review the lesson from Day 1.

1. Start your programming editor.
2. Enter the code for WHERE.CMD, as shown in listing 2.1. (Remember to *not* enter the line numbers, though!)
3. Save the file to your programming directory.
4. Start an OS/2 command-line session.
5. Make your programming directory the current directory.
6. Type `where where.*` and observe the output.
7. If you receive an error message, try to determine what caused it. If you need help understanding an error message, review the section on understanding errors in the lesson on Day 1.

After the program runs, load it back into your editor and look at the code again. Add a few comments of your own, save the program, and run it again. If you entered your comments correctly, the program should run the same as it did before. If you have an error, double-check that each comment begins with `/*` and ends with `*/`.

Summary

This lesson introduced the major elements of REXX programs. You learned that every REXX program must start with a comment. You also learned that you should add additional comments to your REXX programs so that you, and others, can later understand what the code does and why you wrote it that way. You learned why a consistent programming style is important.

This lesson introduced you to commands and instructions. It also acquainted you with some general programming concepts, such as variables, blocks, loops, and procedures. You should now be able to look at REXX code written by others and gain a general concept of how the program does what it does.

Q&A

Q Do comments affect the execution speed of my program?

A Comments affect the execution speed of your program only the first time you run it. This difference in speed is another effect of REXX compressing your program (see the Q&A for Day 1)—comments aren't kept in the compressed code, so they don't affect the speed of your program.

Q What happens when I put a REXX instruction in a comment?

A REXX ignores everything between the comment delimiters (/* and */), so any instructions or commands that are inside a comment are also ignored. You can put comment delimiters around code to remove the code from a program temporarily without deleting it from the file. Many programmers refer to this process as "commenting out code."

Q How do I find out what functions are predefined by REXX?

A You can find a quick reference of all the predefined functions in Appendix H. For more than a quick reference, look in the Information folder on your OS/2 desktop. One of the objects in that folder is the online reference for REXX, the `REXX Information` book. Open the book by double-clicking on it. Then click the plus sign next to `Functions` (the second-to-last item in the `Contents`), and you will see a list of the built-in REXX functions.

Workshop

The Workshop provides quiz questions to help strengthen your understanding of the material covered and exercises to provide you with experience in using what you've learned.

Quiz

1. What is the first thing that must be included in a REXX program?
2. How is an instruction different from a command?
3. How do you add comments to a program?
4. Why should you add comments to a program?
5. What does the `EXIT` instruction do?
6. List two problems caused by an inconsistent programming style.
7. Can a comment appear within another comment?
8. What is a procedure?
9. What is the difference between a procedure and a function?

Exercises

1. Write the shortest REXX program possible.
2. Add a comment to the program that you wrote in exercise 1. Include the name of the program, your name, and the date the program was written.
3. Examine the following program. For each line of the program, determine if it is

   a. a comment
   b. an instruction
   c. a command

```
/* Backup config.sys */
'copy config.sys \backup'
IF rc >< 0 THEN /* Error in copying? */
  SAY "Couldn't copy config.sys -- rc =" rc

EXIT
```

4. Enter the following program. Which lines contain labels? Instructions? Comments? Function calls? Run the program. What does it do?

```
/* Ex2-4.cmd */

ARG filename                  /* Get the command line argument */
IF filename = '' THEN         /* If no argument ... */
  DO                          /* ... show proper usage and exit */
  SAY 'Usage: number <file name>'
  SIGNAL OuttaHere
  END

SIGNAL ON NotReady            /* So the following loop ends */

lineNum = 1
DO FOREVER                    /* Read the file, add line numbers */
  SAY Right(lineNum, 3, ' ')':' LineIn(filename)
  lineNum = lineNum + 1
END

NotReady:
  IF lineNum = 1 THEN
    SAY 'Could not open "' || filename || '"'
```

```
OuttaHere:
  EXIT
```

5. Enter the following program and run it. What does it do?

```
/* Ex2-5.cmd */
SAY 'What is your first name?'
firstName = GetName()
SAY 'What is your last name?'
lastName = GetName()
SAY
SAY Copies('*', 60)
SAY '*' Center(firstName lastName, 56) '*'
SAY Copies('*', 60)
EXIT

GetName: PROCEDURE
  PARSE PULL nm
  RETURN nm
```

Variables and Constants

WEEK 1

A REXX program uses computer memory to store various values that are used while the program runs. Programmers use variables and constants to access values within a program, and variables are the primary way programmers have for manipulating computer memory. Today you learn the following:

- ☐ How a REXX program uses memory
- ☐ What a constant is
- ☐ What a variable is
- ☐ How REXX manipulates numbers and strings
- ☐ What a data type is and how to use data types in REXX programs

Using Computer Memory

All computer programs make some use of computer memory. Because your programs use memory, you should have at least a rudimentary knowledge of what memory is and how it is accessed.

The *random-access memory* (RAM) in a computer stores data and programs while a computer is running. The computer's RAM is actually a set of integrated circuits (usually called *chips*) that are part of the computer system. RAM is volatile; data stored in RAM can be changed, erased, and replaced. The data stored in RAM exists only as long as the computer is turned on—shut off the power and the data is lost.

The amount of data that RAM can hold is measured in *bytes*. One byte is equivalent to a single character. RAM is measured in *kilobytes* (K) and *megabytes* (M or Mb). One kilobyte of memory is 1,024 bytes. One megabyte is 1,024 kilobytes. A computer with 8M of RAM has 8,388,608 bytes of RAM. To get a feel for how many bytes it takes to store various data in REXX, look at table 3.1.

Table 3.1. Memory usage for REXX data.

Data	Memory Used
The character *S*	1 byte
A space	1 byte
The number 1,024	4 bytes
The text *Using Computer Memory*	21 bytes

Data	Memory Used
One page of this book	Approximately 1,000 bytes
This entire book	Approximately 600 kilobytes

Every byte of RAM has a unique address. Addresses are assigned numerically beginning at zero and increase up to the maximum that your computer can access. Each byte has its own unique address so that the computer can easily find and access the data stored at that location. REXX takes care of manipulating memory addresses behind the scenes; you don't need to worry about the mechanics of using addresses to access memory.

REXX uses memory for several purposes. When a program is run, the program code is first loaded into memory. Then, as the program runs, memory is used to store and manipulate data. The data may be your name, the current price of IBM stock, the balance of your checkbook, a sound file, or a wide variety of other things. No matter what it is, all data is stored in memory while a program is manipulating it.

Now that you understand what memory is and how REXX uses it, you're ready to learn how you can use memory in your own programs.

Strings

A *string* is any type of text surrounded by quotation marks. REXX allows both single and double quotation marks, but the same type of mark must be used at the beginning and end of a string. This type of string is called a *literal string* because REXX stores the characters between the quotation marks exactly as they are typed.

Literal strings are also called *constants* because a program can't change the contents of the string.

Syntax

Strings

```
" [characters] "
' [characters] '
```

A string consists of a group of characters surrounded by single or double quotation marks. The beginning and ending quotation marks must be the same type of mark. The REXX interpreter uses the characters between the quotation marks exactly as they were typed. Any character may appear in a string. A string containing no characters, called an *empty string* or *null string*, is also valid. The surrounding quotation marks are removed from the string by the REXX interpreter.

Strings containing single or double quotation marks should be surrounded by the other type of quotation mark. Alternatively, you can double the mark in the string to produce a single quotation mark in the result.

The following are examples of strings:

Example 1

```
"Four score and seven years ago"
```

Result

```
Four score and seven years ago
```

Example 2

```
"""He's a jolly good fellow"""
```

Result

```
"He's a jolly good fellow"
```

Example 3

```
'"It''s nice to meet you," said Harry.'
```

Result

```
"It's nice to meet you," said Harry.
```

Numbers

A number is a special type of REXX string. Because a number is a string, you can manipulate it exactly like you manipulate any other string. You also can use a number as an operand in a math operation.

Another way that numbers are special is that they don't have to be quoted. In other words, `'100'` is equal to `100`.

The rules for numbers are as follows:

- A number must include one or more decimal digits (`0` to `9`).
- An optional decimal point can be included. The decimal point can be between digits, or it can appear as a suffix or prefix to the number.
- A number can have leading or trailing blanks.

- A sign (+ or -) is optional. If you include a sign, you must place it before any digits or decimal point. The sign itself can have leading and trailing blanks.
- If a number includes any leading or trailing blanks, the number must be quoted.

REXX recognizes three different types of numbers:

- Integers are whole numbers; they do not have a fractional part. REXX internally treats all integers as signed values; integers are positive, negative, or zero. Examples of integers are `-1`, `35`, `0`, and `-835542`.
- Floating point numbers are numbers that contain a decimal point (in other words, they have a fractional part). Examples of floating point numbers are `3.141596`, `-69.5`, and `1.4142`.
- Exponential notation is like floating point, except that the value is raised to a power of 10. You indicate the power of 10 by adding a suffix of `e` (or `E`) followed by the power. Examples of exponential notation are `1.024e3`, `2.78E9`, and `3.141596e11`.

3

Here are some examples of valid numbers:

```
25              /* integer */
'-100'          /* signed integer */
'- 2 '          /* signed integer, embedded spaces */
27.50           /* floating point */
'+ 2e3'         /* exponential notation */
3.3333E-2       /* exponential notation */
.25             /* floating point */
```

Variables

A program often must work with data that changes or that isn't known by the programmer when the program is written. Values such as a user's name, the number of files on a diskette, and the current time are examples of *variable data*. You can tell REXX to reserve a place to store this type of information by creating a *variable*.

A variable is a place to store a value within a program. Variables have names, and although the value of the variable can change, the name cannot. You can think of a variable as being something like the hall closet—the contents of the closet may change, but it's still called the hall closet.

A value is stored in a variable by using an assignment. A simple assignment to a variable named `myVariable` might look like the following:

```
myVariable = 25
```

This instruction assigns the value `25` to `myVariable`. The variable contains the value `25` until the next assignment to it. Unlike the hall closet, a variable can hold only one thing at a time. If you assign `99` to `myVariable`, the prior value (`25` in this case) is lost.

Variable Names

To create REXX variables, you need to know how to create valid variable names. REXX has specific rules for naming variables:

- The first character of a variable name must be a letter, an underscore (_), an exclamation point (`!`), or a question mark (`?`).
- The remaining characters of a variable name can be letters, numbers, underscores, exclamation points, or question marks.
- Uppercase and lowercase have no effect. The variable names `person`, `Person`, and `PERSON` all refer to the same variable.
- REXX instructions can be used as variable names. REXX usually can figure out what is meant from the context. Using REXX instructions as variables is not a recommended practice, however!

Here are some legal and illegal REXX variable names:

```
test1               /* legal */
myVeryOwnVariable   /* legal */
1A                  /* illegal -- starts with a number */
if                  /* not recommended (REXX instruction) */
clean_up            /* legal */
chocolate!          /* legal */
SayWhat?            /* legal */
big#                /* illegal -- contains # */
```

A variable that is *uninitialized* (has not been assigned a value) has the uppercase value of its own name. If you forget to put quotation marks around a string, REXX often accepts the words in the string as uninitialized variables. When those variables are displayed, they appear in uppercase. Listing 3.1 demonstrates how forgetting to use quotation marks can affect a program's output.

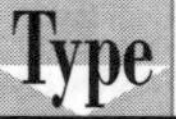

Listing 3.1. Uninitialized variables are uppercased.

```
/* Demonstrate the use of uninitialized variables */
SAY "hello world!"
SAY hello world!
hello = 'goodbye'
SAY hello world!
EXIT
```

```
[D:\]list0301
hello world!
HELLO WORLD!
goodbye WORLD!
```

The program first displays the string `"hello world!"` with results that you expect—the string is displayed exactly as entered. Next, two uninitialized variables, `hello` and `world!`, are displayed. Because the variables are uninitialized, the variable names appear in all capital letters. Finally, the variable `hello` is initialized, and the same two variables appear again. This time, `hello` displays the value that was stored in it (`'goodbye'`); `world!` is still uninitialized, so its name is displayed in uppercase.

When you create variable names, strive to make them meaningful. Variable names such as `x1` and `cc` are easy to type but hard to understand. Variable names such as `userName` and `weeklySalary` convey their use and purpose immediately. Following are two major naming conventions used for creating variable names:

1. Use an underline between each word in the variable name. This convention produces variable names such as `interest_on_loan` and `input_is_valid`.
2. Use an uppercase letter to start each word in the variable name. This convention produces variable names such as `interestOnLoan` and `inputIsValid`. You may prefer to make the initial letter uppercase, too.

We use the second naming style throughout this book (and throughout our own code). This particular style is sometimes called *camel notation* because the uppercase letters look something like humps on a camel. Whichever style you choose, remember to be consistent!

DO	DON'T

DO use variable names that describe their purpose and use.

DO develop a consistent variable-naming style.

DON'T start variable names with a special character (for example, an underscore, exclamation point, or question mark) unless it's absolutely necessary.

Types of Data

The *data type* of a variable or constant indicates the kind of data that is stored in that location. Possible data types include integer, alphabetic, binary, and so forth.

Many programming languages are strict about what you can store in different types of variables. In REXX, however, all variables and constants are strings. Therefore, a variable in REXX has only one type, no matter what kind of data you've stored in it. Variables' having only one type makes it easier for you to begin programming in REXX than in a language that has stricter rules. But because REXX treats all values as character strings, it's often necessary for you to determine exactly what type of data has been stored in a variable.

The built-in function `Datatype` enables you to test a variable's contents to determine the type of data stored there.

Syntax

The *Datatype* Function

`Datatype( string[ , type] )`

You can use the `Datatype` function to perform either a simple type check to determine whether *`string`* is numeric, or you can use `Datatype` to check *`string`* for a specific data type.

When *`type`* is not specified, the `Datatype` function determines whether the data represented by *`string`* is a valid REXX number. If *`string`* contains a valid REXX number, `Datatype` returns `NUM`; otherwise, `Datatype` returns `CHAR`.

When *`type`* is specified, `Datatype` returns `1` if *`string`* is that data type; `Datatype` returns `0` if *`string`* is not the *`type`* specified.

See table 3.1 for a list of valid types. You can specify the type using either the entire type name or the single letter shown in the table as the short form.

Table 3.2. Valid types for the `Datatype` function.

Type Name	Short Form	Returns 1 When String Contains
`Alphanumeric`	`A`	Only uppercase and lowercase letters and digits (a to `z`, `A` to `Z`, and `0` to `9`)
`Bits`	`B`	Only the digits `0` or `1`
`C`	`C`	Mixed SBCS and DBCS (Single Byte Character Set and Double Byte Character Set—used for representing international characters)
`Dbcs`	`D`	Pure DBCS
`Lowercase`	`L`	Only lowercase letters (`a` to `z`)

Type Name	Short Form	Returns 1 When String Contains
Mixed case	M	Only alphabetic characters (a to z and A to Z)
Number	N	A valid REXX number
Symbol	S	Only characters that are valid in REXX symbols (a to z, A to Z, 0 to 9, ?, _, ., and !)
Uppercase	U	Only uppercase letters (A to Z)
Whole number	W	A REXX whole number
Hexadecimal	X	Only hexadecimal digits or an empty string (a to f, A to F, and 0 to 9)

Example 1

```
DataType('25')              /* returns 'NUM' */
```

Example 2

```
DataType('Kermit')          /* returns 'CHAR' */
```

Example 3

```
DataType('testing', 'Lowercase')
                           /* returns 1 */
```

Example 4

```
DataType('Testing', 'L')  /* same as 'Lowercase' */
                          /* returns 0 */
```

Using *Datatype*

Listing 3.2 shows an example of `Datatype` being used in its simplest form. In this form, `Datatype` returns `NUM` when the value is a valid REXX number; otherwise, it returns `CHAR`.

Type **Listing 3.2. Using the simple form of `Datatype`.**

```
/* Demonstrate the simple form of the Datatype function */

is = 'is type'

val = 25
SAY val is Datatype(val)
val = '$25'
```

continues

Listing 3.2. continued

```
SAY val is Datatype(val)
val = '   - 100.25'
SAY val is Datatype(val)
val = 2.5e3
SAY val is Datatype(val)
val = 'Earth'
SAY val is Datatype(val)

EXIT
```

```
[D:\]list0302
25 is type NUM
$25 is type CHAR
   - 100.25 is type NUM
2.5E3 is type NUM
Earth is type CHAR
```

The result of calling `Datatype` with different values is displayed. You might want to review the section on numbers to see the rules `Datatype` used to determine whether each value is a number.

When `Datatype` is asked to test for a specific type, its return values are limited to `0` (the value is not of that type) and `1` (the value is of that type). Listing 3.3 uses `Datatype` to test a string against all of the types that `Datatype` recognizes.

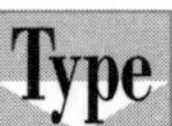

Listing 3.3. `Datatype` function used with a type.

```
/* Demonstrate the use of the Datatype function */

is = "isn't is"

SAY 'Enter a value to test:'
PARSE PULL val

SAY val Word(is, Datatype(val, 'A') + 1) 'Alphanumeric'
SAY val Word(is, Datatype(val, 'B') + 1) 'Bits'
SAY val Word(is, Datatype(val, 'C') + 1) 'Mixed SBCS/DBCS'
SAY val Word(is, Datatype(val, 'D') + 1) 'DBCS'
SAY val Word(is, Datatype(val, 'L') + 1) 'Lowercase'
SAY val Word(is, Datatype(val, 'M') + 1) 'Mixed case'
SAY val Word(is, Datatype(val, 'N') + 1) 'Number'
SAY val Word(is, Datatype(val, 'S') + 1) 'Symbol'
SAY val Word(is, Datatype(val, 'U') + 1) 'Uppercase'
SAY val Word(is, Datatype(val, 'W') + 1) 'Whole number'
SAY val Word(is, Datatype(val, 'X') + 1) 'Hexadecimal'

EXIT
```

```
[D:\]list0303
Enter a value to test:
beef
beef is Alphanumeric
beef isn't Bits
beef is Mixed SBCS/DBCS
beef is DBCS
beef is Lowercase
beef is Mixed case
beef isn't Number
beef is Symbol
beef isn't Uppercase
beef isn't Whole number
beef is Hexadecimal

[D:\]list0303
Enter a value to test:
2.5e3
2.5e3 isn't Alphanumeric
2.5e3 isn't Bits
2.5e3 isn't Mixed SBCS/DBCS
2.5e3 isn't DBCS
2.5e3 isn't Lowercase
2.5e3 isn't Mixed case
2.5e3 is Number
2.5e3 is Symbol
2.5e3 isn't Uppercase
2.5e3 is Whole number
2.5e3 isn't Hexadecimal
```

The program prompts the user for a value and then tests that value against each type. It displays the results of each type test. Although the short form of the type name was used in this program, you can use the long form to achieve the same results (but more typing). You should run the program several times with various values to see the results.

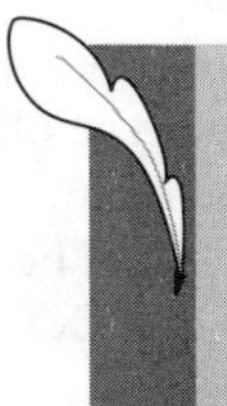

Note: We used a technique here to display `is` or `isn't` depending on the value returned by `Datatype`. The `Word` function selects and returns a single word from a string, based on a word number that we give it. `Word` counts the first word as one (the second word as two, and so on). Because `Datatype` returns a zero or one, it's a simple matter of adding one to `Datatype`'s result and using that value as the word number we want `Word` to select. The string we pass to `Word` contains two words—`isn't` and `is`. So, when `Datatype` returns `0` (the string is not the type), we add one and request `Word` to give us the first word from the string `"isn't is"`. The first word is `isn't`, so that word appears. When `Datatype` returns `1` (the string is the type), we add one and request Word to give us the second word from the string `"isn't is"`.

Summary

This lesson discussed REXX's one data type, the string. It also explored the special type of string that REXX recognizes as a number. You learned how to create strings, and you learned about the three different types of numbers that REXX recognizes: integers, floating point numbers, and exponential notation.

The lesson also explored variables. A variable is used to hold information that is not known when the program is written or that may change while the program is running. You learned the rules for creating variable names.

The concept of the type of a data was introduced. You learned how to use the `Datatype` function to determine what type of information is stored in a REXX string. You can use `Datatype` simply to determine if data is a number, or you can use it to test extensively for specific types of data.

Q&A

Q Why doesn't anything happen when I assign a value to a variable?

A Many beginning programmers expect an assignment to do something, well, interesting. All an assignment does is move data from one place in RAM to another. It doesn't have any other effect. Moving data is a very large percentage of what programs do, though.

Q Which is better, the strict types in other programming languages or typeless variables like REXX has?

A One of REXX's basic purposes is to provide an easy-to-use programming language. Strict types make the programmer do more work when writing a program; all variables must be defined before they're used, and only one type of data can be stored in a variable. The benefit of strict types is that the compiler can catch many of the programmer's errors before the program is ever run. The philosophy in REXX is that a single type requires less work and, because REXX is interpreted, it's easy to run the program and correct errors as they appear.

Each way is better for different types of programming. Strict typing is great for large, complex programs such as a spreadsheet or a word processor. When you're writing small or simple programs and extending batch files, REXX's way is faster and simpler.

Workshop

The Workshop provides quiz questions to help strengthen your understanding of the material covered and exercises to provide you with experience in using what you've learned.

Quiz

1. What is the difference between an integer, a floating point number, and exponential notation?
2. What are the rules for putting quotation marks within a string?
3. What is the value of an uninitialized variable?
4. What is a variable?
5. What's the difference between a variable and a constant?
6. What are the possible values returned by the `Datatype` function when it's called without a type parameter?
7. What characters can you use when creating a variable name?
8. What characters can appear inside a string?
9. What does assignment do?

Exercises

1. Which of the following variable names are valid?

   a. `x123`
   b. `???`
   c. `@AllTimes`
   d. `yes_or_no_answer_from_the_user`
   e. `!OK!`
   f. `Mr&Mrs`
   g. `currentDirectory`
   h. `then`
   i. `as-expected`
   j. `i`
   k. `23skiddoo!`

2. Create a variable name to hold the name of a city and assign the name of the town you live in to the variable.
3. Write a REXX string that holds the value `"I've got a bad feeling about this," said Han.`
4. Write the code necessary to determine whether the variable `testValue` contains a valid REXX number.
5. Write the code necessary to determine whether the variable `lastName` contains only uppercase letters.
6. Which of the following are valid REXX numbers?
   a. `'   -   1.125'`
   b. `7.727E-2`
   c. `' 0 '`
   d. `"5e5"`
   e. `'1 2'`
   f. `.e3`
7. Which of the following are valid REXX strings?
   a. `""`
   b. `'Hi!"`
   c. `'What's this mean?'`
   d. `'Twinkle, twinkle'`
   e. `"!@3(&'""(^$"`

Instructions, Expressions, and Operators

WEEK
1

Programmers must follow specific rules when writing any program. REXX doesn't have a lot of rules, but breaking any of them keeps your program from running correctly, or running at all. This lesson explains what those rules are. Today you learn the following:

- What a clause is
- What an expression is
- What different types of assignment are
- How to create and use labels

Instructions and Expressions

Learning a programming language is a lot like learning a new "human" language. When you start to learn a programming language, most of what you must do is learn the rules of that language. Even though most of the words are familiar, you may feel as though you're learning a foreign language. In both human and programming languages, you must follow specific rules for combining words and using punctuation. These rules are called *syntax* or *grammar*.

Syntax rules cover only the structure of the language, not the meaning. For example, the syntax of English includes rules such as "sentences must contain a verb," "prepositions must be followed by a noun phrase," and "questions must end with a question mark." Thus, the sentence "Colorless green ideas sleep furiously" has legal English syntax—even if it lacks meaning!

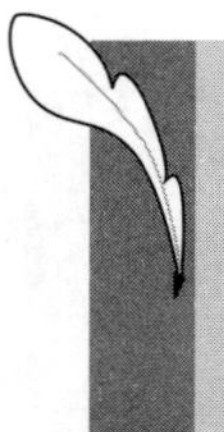

Note: "Colorless green ideas ..." was originally used by linguists to show how the syntax of a language is separate from the *semantics*, or meaning, of a language. If you've read Lewis Carroll's *Alice in Wonderland* or *Through the Looking Glass*, then you may already be familiar with the concept of syntax being separate from semantics.

In a few important ways, programming languages are not at all like human languages. First, programming languages are always designed so that each word has a very exact meaning in any given context. Second, programming languages are very strict about punctuation.

You can be rather inexact when using a human language. If you're trying to find the restroom in a foreign country, you may break all of the syntax rules, but you can still get directions. Even with poor syntax, you can still get your meaning across. However, in programming, syntax must be correct before your code can have any meaning to the computer. If you break the syntax rules in REXX, it cannot understand what you're telling it.

REXX, like all programming languages, demands that you always follow its rules. Many of the error messages that you will see are caused by syntax errors in your programs.

Keyword Instructions

The preceding section introduced the notion of syntax and semantics. The syntax of the REXX language is made up of many parts that work together. Beginning with this section, we concentrate on the individual parts of the syntax and show you how parts go together to accomplish specific things.

An *instruction* is a part of the REXX language that tells REXX to do something. Examples of instructions are `IF` (which tests a condition), `SAY` (which displays something), and `EXIT` (which stops interpreting a program). These words are called *keywords*; they have a special meaning to REXX. As you can see in table 4.1, most REXX keywords are English verbs.

Table 4.1. REXX keyword instructions.

ADDRESS	END	LEAVE	PULL	THEN
ARG	EXIT	NOP	PUSH	TO
BY	EXPOSE	NUMERIC	QUEUE	TRACE
CALL	FOR	OPTIONS	RETURN	UNTIL
DO	IF	OTHERWISE	SAY	WHEN
DROP	INTERPRET	PARSE	SELECT	WHILE
ELSE	ITERATE	PROCEDURE	SIGNAL	

Clauses

A REXX program is made up of one or more *clauses*. A clause is a complete instruction, including any necessary information and options. The REXX interpreter reads and processes one clause at a time.

Following are the five types of clauses in REXX:

- *Null clauses* consist only of blanks or comments. REXX ignores null clauses.
- *Keyword instructions* begin with a keyword (see table 4.1) and may include other information required by the particular instruction.
- *Assignments* give a variable a value. Assignments are discussed in more detail later in this lesson.
- *Labels* are single words followed by a colon. Labels are also discussed in more detail later in this lesson.
- *Commands* are clauses that are not a keyword, assignment, or label. You examine commands in depth on Day 6.

Clauses always end with a semicolon. However, REXX implies a semicolon at the end of a line, following certain keywords, and after a label. You therefore don't need to use semicolons except under certain conditions.

Usually, you write a REXX program with one clause on each line. Because this structure satisfies one of the conditions under which a semicolon is not required (at the end of a line), most programmers don't put semicolons in their code. Having one clause per line is not, however, a requirement. You can put more than one clause on a line by separating the clauses with a semicolon:

```
SAY "Hello!"; SAY "My name is REXX"; SAY "What's your name?"
```

The preceding example has three clauses on the same line. This example produces the same result as if the code had been written on separate lines:

```
SAY "Hello!"
SAY "My name is REXX"
SAY "What's your name?"
```

Each of the lines in this example could end with a semicolon. Because REXX automatically implies a semicolon at the end of a line, however, you can save a little typing by letting REXX do the work. Also, notice how much clearer the second example is when compared to the first example.

A clause can also extend over two or more lines. To have a clause span more than one line, you need to tell REXX that the clause is continued on the next line by putting a comma at the end of the current line. For example,

```
SAY "Now is the time",
    "for all good men"
```

When the SAY instruction in this example is executed, it displays a single line:

```
Now is the time for all good men
```

When REXX encounters a comma at the end of a line, REXX treats the comma like a space and doesn't insert an implied semicolon on that line.

In one other case, REXX doesn't imply a semicolon at the end of a line. This case is best explained with an example:

```
SAY "Now is the time" /* This comment is
on two lines */ "for all good men"
```

Notice that the comment in this example extends over two lines. The code following the comment is treated as though it's on the same line as the code preceding the comment. In other words, this instruction produces the same result as if you had used a comma to extend the clause.

Using a comment to extend a clause can create problems in two different ways:

- When you want a clause to extend over two lines and you use a comment to extend the clause (as in the preceding example). It's entirely too easy to introduce an error later by reformatting the comment.
- When you do not want the clause to extend, yet you add a comment that wraps from the end of the line to the beginning of the next line. The comment accidentally causes the clause to be extended.

The best rule, in most cases, is never to have code on the right side of a comment; use a comma when you want to extend a clause.

Expressions

Clauses can include *expressions*. An expression consists of strings, symbols, and function calls, interspersed with operators and parentheses.

> **Note:** The technical jargon for "strings, symbols, and function calls" is *term*. To be technically accurate (or to impress your friends), you can say that an expression consists of terms, operators, and parentheses.

Strings are anything surrounded by quotation marks. See the lesson for Day 3 if you have any questions about strings.

Symbols are groups of characters that aren't surrounded by quotation marks or comment delimiters. The characters that you can use in a symbol are `a` to `z`, `A` to `Z`, `0` to `9`, the underscore (_), the question mark (`?`), the period (`.`), and the exclamation point (`!`). If a symbol is a variable, then it is replaced by the value of the variable. If the symbol is something else, such as a number or an uninitialized variable, REXX treats it as though it is a literal string.

A function call looks like a word immediately followed by a parenthesis. Functions are a special type of procedure that returns a value. Functions were introduced on Day 2 and are covered in depth on Day 14.

Expressions can be a single string, symbol, or function call. Or expressions can be many strings, symbols, and function calls combined with operators and parentheses. Following are all valid expressions:

```
'dir a:'
x - 2
Square(side)
(3 + 218) - 7
```

Operators

You're probably familiar with operators from math. For example, some basic math operations in REXX are addition (`+`), subtraction (`-`), multiplication (`*`), and division (`/`). The operator is the symbol that is used in REXX to perform the operation. Each operator requires one or two *operands*—the values that are operated on. For the expression `a + 1`, the operator is the plus (`+`) and the operands are `a` and `1`. Operations produce results, which may be used in further operations or assigned to a variable.

All operators in REXX are special characters such as `+`, `-`, `¦`, `\`, `/`, and `<`.

REXX's full set of math operators is covered in the next lesson. The string operators are covered on Day 9.

Putting It All Together

Programs contain one or more clauses. Clauses consist of one or more expressions. Expressions are made up of strings, symbols, function calls, operators, and parentheses. The REXX program in listing 4.1 is an example of how all these pieces fit together.

Listing 4.1. Get the square of a number.

```
 1: /* list0401.cmd */
 2:
 3: SAY "Enter a number:"; PULL number
 4: IF Datatype(number) = 'NUM' THEN
 5:   answer = "The square of" number "is",
 6:       (number * number)
 7: ELSE
 8:   answer = number "is not a number"
 9: SAY answer
10: EXIT
```

```
[D:\]list0401
Enter a number:
5
The square of 5 is 25

[D:\]list0401
Enter a number:
zero
ZERO is not a number
```

The following bullets give a line-by-line analysis of how REXX interprets the program in listing 4.1.

- Lines 1 and 2 are null clauses. Line 1 is a comment that REXX ignores. Line 2 is a null clause because it is blank.
- Line 3 has two clauses, separated by a semicolon. Both clauses are keyword instructions. The `SAY` instruction is followed by an expression that is a single string. The `PULL` instruction is followed by an expression that is a single symbol. REXX implies a semicolon at the end of line 3, which ends the clause beginning with `PULL`.
- On line 4, the `IF` instruction is followed by an expression that consists of the function call `Datatype(number)`, the operator `=`, and the string `'NUM'`. The keyword `THEN` gets special handling by REXX; an implied semicolon is inserted before and after `THEN`. The `IF` expression on this line is used to determine whether the user entered a valid REXX number.
- Lines 5 and 6 contain one clause; a comma is used at the end of line 5 to continue the clause to line 6. The expression within the parentheses calculates the square of the value stored in `number`. The result of the entire expression on the right side of the equal sign is assigned to the variable `answer`. REXX inserts an implied semicolon at the end of line 6.

- Line 7 contains a single keyword instruction. REXX inserts an implied semicolon following `ELSE`.
- On line 8, the result of the expression on the right of the equal sign is assigned to the variable `answer`. REXX inserts an implied semicolon at the end of the line. This clause is executed only when the value stored in `number` is not a valid REXX number.
- The clause on line 9 is the keyword instruction `SAY` followed by the expression `answer`. This instruction displays the contents of the variable `answer`. REXX inserts an implied semicolon at the end of the line.
- The clause on line 10 consists of the single keyword `EXIT`. REXX inserts an implied semicolon at the end of the line.

Assignments

An assignment copies a value into a variable. The simplest form of assignment was introduced on Day 3. Here, you look at an assignment in all of its forms.

Syntax

Assignment

`variable = expression`

The equal sign indicates an assignment operation. The assignment `x = 5` is not read as "x equals 5" but as "5 is assigned (or stored) to x," or simply "x gets 5."

The *`expression`* is evaluated and the result is assigned to *`variable`*.

Example 1

```
count = 1
```

Example 2

```
pay = hourlyRate * hours
```

Example 3

```
type = Datatype(userInput)
```

Another type of assignment is performed by certain keywords such as `PULL`. The result of executing the keyword is that a new value is stored in a variable. In the following example, `PULL` assigns a value to a variable:

```
PULL userInput
```

The PULL instruction waits for the user to enter some data and press Enter. PULL then stores that data in variable userInput. The PULL instruction is covered in detail in the lesson for Day 7.

Labels

A label is a symbol followed by a colon. To be recognized as a label, the symbol and colon cannot appear within quotation marks or inside a comment.

Labels mark locations in a program. Function calls and the CALL and SIGNAL keyword instructions are all followed by a label name (that is, the symbol without the colon). When REXX sees one of these instructions, it searches through the program, looking for the label. After REXX finds the label, it starts executing code at that location.

One use of a label is to mark the beginning of a procedure. A label at the beginning of a procedure also names that procedure. The CALL instruction and function calls both tell REXX to go to a label. The procedure ends with a RETURN instruction, which tells REXX to go back to the next instruction following the call.

The SIGNAL instruction tells REXX to go to a label. Unlike a procedure, REXX never returns to execute the code following the SIGNAL. In listing 4.1, you examine how using labels and SIGNAL can affect the execution of a REXX program.

Listing 4.2. Using labels with SIGNAL.

```
/* list0402.cmd */
SAY "Start of program"
SIGNAL Gettysburg
SAY "Great minds think alike"
Quantity:
SAY "Billions and billions"
SIGNAL ByeBye
Gettysburg:
SAY "Four score and seven years ago"
SIGNAL Quantity
ByeBye:
SAY "I'm done"
EXIT
```

```
[D:\]list0402
Start of program
Four score and seven years ago
Billions and billions
I'm done
```

The program in listing 4.2 executes the first `SAY` instruction and then uses `SIGNAL` to go to the label `Gettysburg`. It executes the `SAY` instruction on the line following `Gettysburg` and then uses `SIGNAL` to go to the label `Quantity`. The `SAY` instruction following `Quantity` is executed, and then `SIGNAL` causes REXX to go to the label `ByeBye`. At `ByeBye`, `SAY` is executed and then `EXIT` finishes the program. Notice that the instruction `SAY "Great minds think alike"` is never executed because the `SIGNAL` instruction skips over it.

The program in listing 4.2 is written in a form that is called *spaghetti code*. If you draw a line from each `SIGNAL` to the label that `SIGNAL` goes to, you see why code like this is called spaghetti. The lines crisscross in a tangled knot like a plate of spaghetti. Code written in this style is very hard to understand, and even harder to change.

Summary

In this lesson, you learned that REXX programs consist of one or more clauses. The five types of clauses are null clauses, keyword instructions, assignments, labels, and commands. Clauses contain expressions that are made up of symbols, strings, function calls, operators, and parentheses.

This lesson taught you how to use a comma to extend a clause over more than one line. It also showed you how to use the semicolon to put more than one clause on a single line. You learned how to create a label and use the `SIGNAL` instruction to go to a label.

Q&A

Q When I use `SAY` with the two strings `"Hi" "there"`, REXX always displays the instruction as though I had typed `"Hi there"`. Why?

A A space between two strings is actually a REXX operator. REXX joins, or *concatenates*, the two strings with a space inserted between the last word of the first string and the first word of the second string. REXX does the same thing with two variables, or a variable and a string. This operation is used several times in listing 4.1. We cover all the string operators in depth on Day 9.

Q When I assign the value in one variable to another (for example, `result = oldValue`), what happens to the original value?

A When you use assignment, the value is copied. Therefore, the original value is not affected by the assignment. In the example, `oldValue` and `result` contain

the same value after the assignment. An assignment affects only the variable on the left side of the equal sign.

Q If code can't be executed because a `SIGNAL` skips over it, does REXX do anything with the skipped code?

A No, if your program has legal syntax, REXX doesn't try to determine whether it makes sense. It's up to you to notice that your program contains clauses that cannot be executed. This kind of programming error is called a *logic error* because it is usually caused by a mistake in the design of the program.

Workshop

The Workshop provides quiz questions to help strengthen your understanding of the material covered and exercises to provide you with experience in using what you've learned.

Quiz

1. What is a clause?
2. How can you write more than one clause on a single line?
3. Name two ways that you can extend a clause over more than one line.
4. What is the purpose of an operator?
5. What is the difference between a `CALL` and a `SIGNAL`?
6. Name three different operators.
7. What is spaghetti code?
8. How is a label created?
9. What is an expression?

Exercises

1. The following program prompts the user for two numbers and shows the sum. Rewrite the program so that it has just one clause on each line. Run the program to make sure it works.

```
/* Ex4-1.cmd */
SAY 'This program adds',
    'two numbers.'
SAY 'Enter the first number:'; PULL num1
SAY 'Enter the second number:'; PULL num2
answer = /* Now we add the two numbers
    together */ num1 + num2
SAY 'The sum of' num1,
    'plus' num2,
    'is' answer; EXIT
```

2. The following program has been written using spaghetti code. Rewrite the code so that it executes without using any `SIGNAL` instructions. (The result of running the program should remain the same.)

```
/* Ex4-2.cmd */
SAY 'Enter a number:'
SIGNAL GetANumber
ShowIt:
SAY "You entered" number
EXIT
GetANumber:
PULL number
SIGNAL ShowIt
```

3. Which of the following are valid labels?
   a. `test:`
   b. `HandleError  :`
   c. `'usage:'`
   d. `AbsoluteZero:`
   e. `/* NextLocation: */`
   f. `25:`

4. The following program contains errors. Find and fix the errors. (You should enter and run the program to ensure that you fixed the errors.)

```
/* Ex4-4.cmd */
SAY "This is a test", SAY "This is only a test"
SAY "Now starting the test"; 'dir';
'*.cmd'
EXIT
```

5. The following program contains errors. Find and fix the errors.

```
/* Ex4-5.cmd */
SAY "Please enter your full name:"
CALL GetName
SAY "There are"
    Length(name) "characters in your name."
EXIT
GetName
  PULL name
  RETURN
```

Arithmetic

REXX includes arithmetic operators that perform operations such as addition and division. Today you learn the following:

- How to create arithmetic expressions
- REXX's arithmetic operators
- What operator precedence is
- How to use parentheses to change the order of evaluation

Arithmetic Operators

REXX uses the characters `+`, `-`, `*`, `/`, and `%` to define the basic set of arithmetic operators. Two of the arithmetic operators use more than one character; operators constructed from more than one character may have blanks (and comments) between the characters. The following expressions all produce the same result:

```
3**2
3 ** 2
3 * * 2
3 /* calculate three squared */ ** 2
3 * /* calculate three squared */ * 2
```

Note: Although all the expressions in the preceding example are equivalent, the last two are confusing and should not be used in a program.

In REXX, arithmetic operations are either unary or binary. A unary operation has a single operand. A binary operation has two operands. Unary operators are also called prefix operators because the operator precedes its operand.

All operands used with the arithmetic operators must be valid REXX numbers. If an operand is not a valid REXX number, REXX displays an error message. Look at the following example:

```
/* Demonstrate arithmetic error */
a = 10
c = a + b
EXIT
```

When you run the code in the preceding example, it produces the following error message:

```
     3 +++   c = a + b;
REX0041: Error 41 running R:\ERR.CMD, line 3: Bad arithmetic conversion
```

Because b does not contain a valid numeric value, REXX cannot perform the operation. If your REXX program generates this error message, make certain that you have assigned a numeric value to each of the variables you're using in the arithmetic expression.

Addition

In REXX, addition is performed using the + operator. This operation is a binary operation—the + operator requires two operands. Neither operand is affected; the operation produces a result that should be used in further operations, or it produces an assignment. For example,

```
a = 10
b = 15
c = a + b
```

The values stored in the variables a and b are added together and stored in c. Prior to performing the addition, a has the value 10, b has the value 15, and c has the value C. Following the addition, a has the value 10, b has the value 15, and c has the value 25.

One of the most common forms of addition done in a program is to increment, to add one to, a value. To increment any variable, you need to add one to its current value and store the result back to the same variable. In the following example, the value in count is added to 1 and the result is stored in count:

```
count = count + 1
```

5

More than one addition operation can be performed in a single expression. Addition is performed left to right, with the result from the addition of the leftmost values being used as the left operand to the next addition operation. The following example should help clarify this process:

```
quarter = jan + feb + mar
```

The value in jan is added to the value in feb. The result is then added to the value in mar. The final result then is stored in quarter.

Subtraction

In REXX, subtraction is performed using the - operator. Subtraction is a binary operation. The right operand is subtracted from the left operand without affecting the values stored in either operand.

Several subtraction operations can be performed in a single expression. Subtraction is performed left to right, with the result from the leftmost subtraction being used as the left operand to the next subtraction operation. Note that reordering the operands in subtraction often produces a different result. Look at the following example:

```
takeHome1 = gross - fedTaxes - stateTaxes
takeHome2 = fedTaxes - stateTaxes - gross
```

The value for `takeHome1` is calculated by subtracting `fedTaxes` from `gross` and then subtracting `stateTaxes` from the result. The value for `takeHome2` is calculated by subtracting `stateTaxes` from `fedTaxes` and then subtracting `gross` from the result. The results of these two expressions are obviously quite different!

One of the common uses of subtraction is to *decrement*, or count down, a value. Decrementing is related to incrementing—they just count in opposite directions.

Negation

Negation changes the sign of a value, unless the value is zero. Negation uses the unary - operator.

REXX also allows a unary + operation, but this operation has no real effect. The unary + operation is equivalent to adding zero to a value.

Here are some examples of these operations:

```
outlook = - attitude
outlook = + attitude
```

In the first example, `attitude` is negated and the result is assigned to `outlook`. In the second example, the value of `attitude` is not affected by the prefix + operator, so `outlook` is assigned the value of `attitude`.

Multiplication

In REXX, the `*` operator is used to perform multiplication. The right and left operands of `*` are multiplied without affecting the values stored in either operand. A series of multiplication operations may be done in one expression. Multiplication is performed left to right, with the result from the multiplication of the leftmost values being used as the left operand to the next multiplication operation. The result of multiplication is unaffected by the ordering of the operands. For example,

```
seconds = minutes * 60
hours = weeks * 7 * 24
```

The result of multiplying `minutes` by `60` is assigned to `seconds`. In the second example, the result of multiplying `weeks` by `7` is then multiplied by `24`, and the result of that calculation is assigned to `hours`.

Division

REXX utilizes three division operators. All three division operators are binary; the left operand is always divided by the right operand.

- Regular division is performed using the `/` operator. This division operator produces the same result that you would expect to get using the division key on a calculator. For example, the expression `25 / 2` produces the result `12.5`.
- The `%` operator is used to perform division and return only the integer part of the result. The result is not rounded; any value following the decimal point is simply truncated. For example, the expression `25 % 2` produces the result `12`.
- The `//` operator is used to perform division and return the remainder from the division. The result may be negative. For example, the expression `25 // 2` produces the result `1`; the expression `25 // 10` produces the result `5`; the expression `-25 // 10` produces the result `-5`.

In listing 5.1, the mean of one or more numbers is calculated.

5

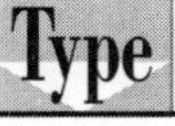

Listing 5.1. Computing the mean of several numbers.

```
/* List0501.cmd */

SAY "This program calculates the mean of 1 or more numbers"

total = 0
count = 0

GetAnother:
SAY "Enter a number, or press [Enter] to end the list:"
PULL number
IF number = "" THEN
  SIGNAL ShowResult
total = total + number
count = count + 1
SIGNAL GetAnother

ShowResult:
SAY "The arithmetic mean is" total / count

EXIT
```

```
[D:\]list0501
This program calculates the mean of 1 or more numbers
Enter a number, or press [Enter] to end the list:
20
Enter a number, or press [Enter] to end the list:
11
Enter a number, or press [Enter] to end the list:
16
Enter a number, or press [Enter] to end the list:

The arithmetic mean is 15.6666667
```

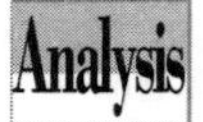

The program prompts for values until the user presses the Enter key without entering a number. As numbers are entered, the program keeps a running total in `total` and keeps track of how many numbers were entered by incrementing `count`. When the user is done entering numbers, the program calculates the mean by dividing `total` by `count`.

If the program in listing 5.1 had used the `%` operator instead, the mean would not have a fractional part. The result in the output would be `15` instead of `15.6666667`.

Power

The `**` operator raises a value to an integer power (that is, performs exponentiation). Raising a value to a power is shorthand for multiplying a value by itself one or more times. For instance, `3 ** 2` produces the same result as `3 * 3`; `4 ** 5` produces the same result as `4 * 4 * 4 * 4 * 4`.

In the following example, `val` is assigned the value `8`:

```
val = 2 ** 3
```

Order of Evaluation

The order of evaluation, or operator *precedence*, controls the order in which operations are performed. REXX follows the same arithmetic precedence rules that you probably learned (and forgot) in school. The following example illustrates how precedence affects the order of evaluation:

```
val = 10 + 7 * 6
```

If the addition is performed before the multiplication, then `val` is assigned the value `102` (the result of `17 * 6`). On the other hand, if the multiplication is performed first (`10 + 42`), then `val` is assigned the value `52`.

Obviously, the order of evaluation for this example is important. Without operator precedence rules to guide you, you have no way of determining exactly what the result of this expression is going to be.

REXX has a set of specific rules that govern the precedence of operators. The relative precedence of REXX's arithmetic operators is shown in table 5.1.

Table 5.1. Precedence of REXX's arithmetic operators.

Operator Group	Operators	Relative Precedence
Unary operators	`-, +`	Highest
Power	`**`	
Multiply and divide	`*, /, %, //`	
Add and subtract	`+, -`	Lowest

The operators with the highest precedence are evaluated first. Operators that have the same precedence (such as multiply and divide) are evaluated in left-to-right order.

Using REXX's precedence rules, you can see that the result in the earlier example, `val = 10 + 7 * 6`, is `52` because multiplication has higher precedence than addition.

Now look at a more complex example:

```
percentRemaining = 100 - 20 * 100 % 75
```

The result of this expression is `74`. The multiplication and the integer division are evaluated left to right. Both have a higher precedence than the subtraction, so the subtraction is performed last. Thus, the multiplication is done first (`20 * 100`), followed by the integer division, and then the subtraction.

Operator precedence often does not match the order of evaluation that you want. You can change the order of evaluation by using parentheses. Therefore, you can write the first example as follows:

```
val = (10 + 7) * 6
```

When you put an expression in parentheses, it is evaluated first. In the preceding example, `10 + 7` is evaluated before the multiplication. Using parentheses changes the result assigned to `val` to `102`.

You also can use multiple and nested parentheses in an expression. When parentheses are nested, the expression is evaluated from the innermost parentheses out. Look at the following expression:

```
val = (99 - (( 3 + 4) * (8 + 3))) / 11
```

REXX evaluates this expression in the following order:

1. Of the two innermost parenthesized expressions, the left one, `3 + 4`, is evaluated first with a result of `7`.

   ```
   val = (99 - (7 * (8 + 3))) / 11
   ```

2. The next innermost expression is `8 + 3`, which evaluates to `11`.

   ```
   val = (99 - (7 * 11)) / 11
   ```

3. The innermost expression is now `7 * 11`. This expression evaluates to `77`.

   ```
   val = (99 - 77) / 11
   ```

4. The final parenthesized expression is `99 - 77`, which evaluates to `22`.

   ```
   val = 22 / 11
   ```

5. The final expression is evaluated, and `2` is assigned to `val`.

DO | **DON'T**

DO use parentheses to help clarify complex expressions even if precedence makes parentheses unnecessary.

DON'T make an expression extremely complex. You should break long or complex expressions into several smaller expressions.

The program in listing 5.2 implements a method of calculating the day of the week from a date. The method used is called *Zeller's Congruence.* The day of the week is calculated as a value in the range of `0` to `6`. Sunday is represented by `0`, Monday by `1`, Tuesday by `2`, and so forth. You build on Zeller's Congruence in later lessons.

Listing 5.2. Calculating the day of the week.

```
/* List0502.cmd */

SAY "Enter date as mm dd yyyy:"
PULL month day year

SAY month'-'day'-'year "is weekday number" Zeller()

EXIT
```

```
/* Zeller's Congruence
 * This function takes month, day, and year as input.
 * It returns a number that represents the day of the week
 * for the given date; 0 = Sunday ... 6 = Saturday.
 */
Zeller:
  IF month > 2 THEN
    DO
    adjMonth = month - 2
    adjYear = year
    END
  ELSE
    DO
    adjMonth = month + 10
    adjYear = year - 1
    END

  century = adjYear % 100
  yearInCentury = adjYear - 100 * century
  dayOfWeek = ((13 * adjMonth - 1) % 5 + day + yearInCentury + ,
        yearInCentury % 4 + century % 4 - century - century + 77) ,
        // 7
  RETURN dayOfWeek
```

```
[D:\]list0502
Enter date as mm dd yyyy:
1 1 1995
1-1-1995 is weekday number 0

[D:\]list0502
Enter date as mm dd yyyy:
3 1 2000
3-1-2000 is weekday number 3

[D:\]list0502
Enter date as mm dd yyyy:
5 13 1994
5-13-1994 is weekday number 5
```

The user is prompted for a date, and the function `Zeller` is called to calculate the day-of-week number. The `Zeller` function implements *Zeller's Congruence*. The heart of the routine is in the single expression that computes the `dayOfWeek` value. This expression is evaluated in the following order:

1. The innermost expression `13 * adjMonth - 1` is evaluated first. Because multiplication has precedence over subtraction, the multiplication is performed first.

2. Division has precedence over addition and subtraction, so all of the division operations within the next level of parentheses are performed next. The various division operators have the same precedence, so they're evaluated left to right.

The result of step 1 is divided by `5`, then `yearInCentury % 4` is evaluated, and finally `century % 4` is evaluated.

3. All of the subtraction and addition is then performed left to right.
4. The last step is to calculate the remainder using the `//` operator.

This overly complex expression should be broken into several expressions. We've included it here to illustrate how precedence works and to show you *why* you should not write expressions that are this complex. Compare the following rewritten expression to the expression in `Zeller`:

```
adjYr = yearInCentury + (yearInCentury % 4) + (century % 4)
adjYr = adjYr - century - century + 77
dayOfWeek = ((13 * adjMonth - 1) % 5) + day + adjYr
dayOfWeek = dayOfWeek // 7
```

Summary

This lesson discussed the arithmetic operations that are defined by REXX. You learned about the arithmetic operators for addition (`+`), subtraction (`-`), multiplication (`*`), division (`/`), integer division (`%`), remainder (`//`), power (`**`), and negation (prefix `-`).

This lesson also discussed operator precedence and the effect of precedence on the order that operators are evaluated. REXX has specific rules that define operator precedence and the order in which expressions are evaluated.

Q&A

Q Because they both use the same operator, how does REXX tell the difference between subtraction and negation?

A REXX uses the context to determine which operation is intended. Most of the time, determining the use is a fairly simple thing to do. Negation is often performed as a single statement:

```
a = -b
```

Sometimes, though, negation is performed as part of a more complex expression. In the following example, it may not be quite so obvious which operator is which:

```
a = b - - c
```

REXX evaluates this expression as though it was written `a = b - (-c)`. It's usually best to parenthesize a negation in this way rather than have a confusing expression like the one in the preceding example.

Q How are binary operators related to the binary of ones and zeros?

A In both cases, *binary* means "consisting of two things." Binary operators have two operands; binary numbers have ones and zeros. Other than having this one point in common, binary operators and binary numbers are not related.

Workshop

The Workshop provides quiz questions to help strengthen your understanding of the material covered and exercises to provide you with experience in using what you've learned.

Quiz

1. What is operator precedence?
2. How do spaces and comments affect arithmetic operators?
3. What does the `**` operator do?
4. What operator do you use to get the remainder from a division?
5. What is the difference between unary and binary operators?
6. What is the order of evaluation for operators of equal precedence?
7. Which operators produce a different result when the order of their operands is changed?
8. What operation is required to increment a variable?
9. What does the `%` operator do?
10. How can you change the order of evaluation?

Exercises

1. Evaluate the following expressions to determine their resulting value.
   a. `5 + 6 * 3`
   b. `100 * 2 % 5`

c. `(3 - 5) * -2`
d. `2 ** 3 * 2`
e. `(5 + 3 * 4) * 2`
f. `15 // 7 + 1`

2. The following program has an error in its calculation for Celsius degrees. The `fahrenheit` variable should have 32 subtracted from it before it is multiplied by `5 / 9`. Enter the program, fix it, and run it to make sure that it works correctly. (**Hint:** Remember that 32 degrees Fahrenheit is 0 degrees Celsius, and 212 degrees Fahrenheit is 100 degrees Celsius.)

```
/* Ex5-2.cmd */
SAY "Enter a Fahrenheit temperature to convert:"
PULL fahrenheit
celsius = 5 / 9 * fahrenheit - 32
SAY fahrenheit "degrees Farenheit =" celsius "degrees Celsius"
EXIT
```

3. The following program has several errors. Enter the program and find and fix the errors. The program should prompt for and add five numbers and then display the sum of those five numbers.

```
/* Ex5-3.cmd */
SAY "This program adds 5 numbers"

GetANumber:
IF count = 0 THEN
  SIGNAL Done
count = count - 1
SAY "Enter a number:"
PULL number
total = number + count
SIGNAL GetANumber

SAY "The sum is" total
EXIT
```

Executing System Commands

WEEK 1

You may be using the OS/2 batch language to automate and control some of the tasks you perform under OS/2. REXX can perform the same tasks as the batch language; with the addition of variables, math, and the power of a full programming language, REXX far surpasses the capabilities of the batch language. Today you learn the following:

- How to execute OS/2 system commands from a REXX program
- How to use REXX variables with OS/2 system commands
- REXX equivalents for some OS/2 system commands
- How to convert simple OS/2 batch files to REXX
- How to check return codes from OS/2 system commands

Accessing OS/2's Commands

An OS/2 system command is any command that you type at the OS/2 command prompt, such as `del`, `dir`, `copy`, and `chkdsk`.

The most direct way to run an OS/2 command from a REXX program is to put the command directly into the REXX program. In listing 6.1, for example, a REXX program executes the `dir` command.

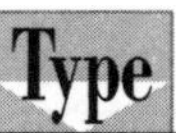

Listing 6.1. Using a simple `dir` command.

```
/* d.cmd */
dir
EXIT
```

```
[C:\OS2\BOOK]d

 The volume label in drive C is OS2 SYSTEM.
 The Volume Serial Number is A66D:DC14
 Directory of C:\os2\book

 3-31-94  12:33p     <DIR>           0  .
 3-31-94  12:33p     <DIR>           0  ..
 4-29-93   9:43p    415378           0  CMDREF.INF
12-01-93   1:39a    194417           0  DESKMAN.INF
 5-26-93   6:43p    359879           0  EPMTECH.INF
 4-20-93   7:35p    273087           0  EPMUSERS.INF
 4-29-93  10:03p    201920           0  REXX.INF
         7 file(s)    1444681 bytes used
                     61082624 bytes free
```

The OS/2 command dir is executed. The output is identical to entering the same command at an OS/2 command prompt. REXX recognizes dir as a valid REXX symbol. Because the program doesn't assign a value to dir, it contains the string DIR—the uppercase value of its own name. Because the string DIR is not a keyword instruction, assignment, or label, REXX assumes the string is a command and passes DIR to the OS/2 command processor. The command processor executes the dir command and displays the output.

Note: The output shown for the dir command is the default for an HPFS formatted drive. If you're using a FAT formatted drive, the output for the dir command will not look the same as what is shown here.

When you use OS/2 commands in a REXX program, you often need to use characters that have a special meaning to REXX. For instance, if you want dir to display a wide listing, you use dir /w. REXX recognizes dir and w as valid symbols, and the / is the REXX operator for division. When REXX processes dir /w, it attempts to divide dir by w and generates an error message.

To prevent REXX from misinterpreting commands as instructions, you must change the command into a string. REXX does not attempt to interpret the characters between quotation marks, so 'dir /w' is passed directly to the command processor.

Quoting a command is *always* safe. Using an unquoted command can introduce errors, even when the command doesn't use special characters. Some commands and program names are also REXX keyword instructions. It's also possible that you may have inadvertently used a command name as a REXX variable. For example, the following code may produce some surprising results if you have a STARTUP.CMD file on your boot drive:

```
dir = "C:\STARTUP"
dir
```

In this example, dir is assigned the value 'C:\STARTUP'. When REXX encounters dir by itself on a line, the variable is replaced by its value, and REXX passes that value (C:\STARTUP) to the command processor. If a STARTUP.CMD (or STARTUP.EXE) exists in the root directory of drive C:, then the command processor executes that command.

The following code passes the dir command to the command processor:

```
dir = 'C:\STARTUP'
'dir'
```

Using Variables with Commands

You can use variables to simplify and enhance the use of commands in a REXX program. You can use a variable with a command by including the variable in the same clause as the command. For example,

```
fileSpec = "*.sys"
'dir' fileSpec
```

When REXX interprets the line `'dir' fileSpec`, the variable `fileSpec` is replaced by the value `*.sys`, and the resulting command (`dir *.sys`) is passed to the command processor.

You also can use variables to hold an entire command. For instance, the following code deletes all the files ending with .BAK in the current directory:

```
delBackups = "del *.bak"
delBackups
```

Replacing Commands with REXX Instructions

REXX includes instructions and functions that perform an equivalent function to some OS/2 commands. For example, the `SAY` instruction displays text much like the `ECHO` command does.

The following sections discuss a few of the REXX instructions and functions that can replace commands. Later lessons in this book explore other instructions and functions that expand on the ones discussed here.

The *Directory* Function

The `Directory` function works like the `cd` (or `chdir`) command to change the current directory. Unlike the `cd` command, `Directory` can change to a different drive, too. The `Directory` function returns a string that is the name of the current drive and directory, after optionally changing to a new drive and directory.

Syntax

The *Directory* Function

`Directory([`*`newdirectory`*`])`

The `Directory` function changes to *`newdirectory`* and then returns the name of the current directory. If *`newdirectory`* is not supplied, `Directory` returns the name of the current directory.

If *newdirectory* is supplied and it names a directory that does not exist, `Directory` returns an empty string. If *newdirectory* starts with a drive letter and a colon, `Directory` makes that drive the current drive before changing directories.

The directory name returned by `Directory` always begins with the current drive letter followed by a colon (unless *newdirectory* is not a valid directory name).

Example 1

```
curDir = Directory()     /* get the current directory */
```

Example 2

```
newDir = Directory('C:\Desktop')
```

Example 3

```
CALL Directory '\TMP'
```

The *SAY* Instruction

The `SAY` instruction can directly replace the `ECHO` command when `ECHO` is used to display text. You should place the text that `ECHO` displays within quotation marks when you use `SAY`.

Some differences in usage exist between `SAY` and `ECHO`. Most differences are caused by limitations of the `ECHO` command.

- When `ECHO` is used to display a blank line, it is often used as `ECHO .`(`ECHO` followed by a single period). You can use the `SAY` instruction by itself to display a blank line.
- One use of `ECHO` is to turn command echoing on (`ECHO ON`) or off (`ECHO OFF`). For this use of `ECHO`, you should place the command in quotation marks (that is, `'ECHO OFF'`) rather than change it to a `SAY` instruction.
- `ECHO` has trouble with many special characters, such as <, >, and ¦. These characters have special meaning to the command processor. `SAY` does not have any trouble displaying these characters if they are within quotation marks.

The *SetLocal* and *EndLocal* Functions

The `SetLocal` and `EndLocal` functions replace the `SETLOCAL` and `ENDLOCAL` commands. The `SetLocal` function saves the current drive and directory names, and the current values of the OS/2 environment. The `EndLocal` function restores the values saved by the most recent `SetLocal` function within the same program.

You can nest the SetLocal and EndLocal functions, unlike the commands of the same name. The program in listing 6.2 demonstrates the effect of nested SetLocal and EndLocal functions.

Listing 6.2. Using nested SetLocal and EndLocal functions.

```
/* list0602.cmd */
SAY "Starting directory:" Directory()
CALL SetLocal
CALL Directory 'C:\OS2'
SAY "Directory is now:" Directory()
CALL SetLocal
SAY "Directory is now:" Directory('C:\OS2\APPS')
CALL EndLocal
SAY "EndLocal, directory is now:" Directory()
CALL EndLocal
SAY "EndLocal, directory is now:" Directory()
EXIT
```

```
[D:\]list0602
Starting directory: D:\
Directory is now: C:\OS2
Directory is now: C:\OS2\APPS
EndLocal, directory is now: C:\OS2
EndLocal, directory is now: D:\
```

The program in listing 6.2 displays the current directory. The SetLocal function is called, and the directory is changed to C:\OS2. The new current directory is displayed. SetLocal is called once again, the directory is changed to C:\OS2\APPS, and the current directory is displayed. The EndLocal function is called, and the current directory is displayed; because EndLocal has restored the drive and directory that was saved by the last SetLocal call, the current directory is now C:\OS2. Finally, EndLocal is called again to restore the drive and directory saved by the first SetLocal call, and the current drive and directory are displayed.

Note: If your system has OS/2 installed on a drive other than C:, listing 6.2 doesn't work. You must change the drive letter used by Directory to the drive on which OS/2 is installed.

The *PULL* Instruction

In REXX programs, you can use the PULL instruction to wait for the user to press Enter. The PULL instruction can do much more than just wait for Enter, but we wait until Day 7 to cover the other uses.

The OS/2 PAUSE command displays a message and waits for the user to press a key. When you use PAUSE, it defaults to displaying the following message:

```
Press any key when ready . . .
```

The following code shows how you can use the REXX SAY and PULL instructions to simulate the PAUSE command:

```
SAY "Press Enter when ready . . ."
PULL .
```

The period following the PULL instruction tells REXX that you want to throw away anything the user may have typed before pressing Enter.

Converting Existing Batch Files

You can quickly convert many OS/2 batch files to REXX by adding a REXX comment at the beginning of the file and putting quotation marks around each command.

After you convert a batch file, you can begin exploring ways of enhancing it. This section presents two different batch files and steps through converting them to REXX and then performing some simple enhancements. You explore further enhancements and extensions in later lessons.

The OS/2 batch file in listing 6.3 copies several OS/2 system files to a backup directory. It keeps three generations of each file, in case one of the files becomes corrupted.

Type

Listing 6.3. BACKSYS.CMD OS/2 batch file.

```
@echo off
c:
cd \backup
del *.??2
ren *.??1 *.??2
ren *.sys *.sy1
ren *.ini *.in1
copy C:\config.sys
copy C:\OS2\os2*.ini
attrib *.ini -R
```

```
[D:\]backsys
        1 file(s) copied.
C:\OS2\OS2.INI
C:\OS2\OS2SYS.INI
        2 file(s) copied.

[C:\BACKUP]
```

To run this batch file, you'll need to create a C:\BACKUP directory. The output may be different the first three times that you run the batch file because the second and third generations of the file don't exist.

This batch file changes to the backup directory on drive C:, deletes all files in that directory with filenames ending with `2`, renames the current files, copies the CONFIG.SYS and OS2*.INI file, and then clears the read-only attribute on the .INI files.

Note: If your system has OS/2 installed on a drive other than C:, listing 6.3 doesn't work. You must change the drive letter used to the drive on which OS/2 is installed.

A direct conversion of this batch file to REXX requires the following steps:

1. Add a comment at the beginning of the program.
2. Put quotation marks around each of the commands.
3. Although it isn't required, it's good practice to end a REXX program with the `EXIT` keyword.

After you make these changes, you should have the program shown in listing 6.4.

Listing 6.4. Direct conversion of BACKSYS.CMD.

```
/* List0604.cmd */
'@echo off'
'c:'
'cd \backup'
'del *.??2'
'ren *.??1 *.??2'
'ren *.sys *.sy1'
'ren *.ini *.in1'
'copy C:\config.sys'
'copy C:\OS2\os2*.ini'
'attrib *.ini -R'
EXIT
```

```
[D:\]backsys
        1 file(s) copied.
C:\OS2\OS2.INI
C:\OS2\OS2SYS.INI
        2 file(s) copied.

[C:\BACKUP]
```

The program in listing 6.4 exactly duplicates the function of the batch file in listing 6.3.

The version of BACKSYS.CMD shown in listing 6.4 works fine as it is currently written. However, you can fix a couple minor problems. First, the program ends with the user in a different directory from the one in which the program was started. Second, as a side effect of the OS/2 commands executing, some "noise" is displayed on the screen. Lines like `1 file(s) copied` do not supply any useful information for the user.

To fix these two problems, you can make the following changes:

1. Use the `Directory` function to capture the user's current directory. You also use the `Directory` function in place of the `cd` command to change directories.
2. Redirect the output from the commands to the `NUL` device. This step effectively throws away any of the text these commands were putting on the screen. The redirection `> NUL` is stored in a variable to simplify adding it to each command.

After you make these changes, the BACKSYS.CMD program should now look like listing 6.5.

Listing 6.5. Improving BACKSYS.CMD with the `Directory` function.

```
/* List0605.cmd */
'@echo off'
toNul = '> NUL'
currentDir = Directory()      /* Get the current directory */
CALL Directory 'C:\backup'   /* Change to the Backup directory */
'del *.??2' toNul
'ren *.??1 *.??2' toNul
'ren *.sys *.sy1' toNul
'ren *.ini *.in1' toNul
'copy C:\config.sys' toNul
'copy C:\OS2\os2*.ini' toNul
'attrib *.ini -R' toNul
CALL Directory currentDir  /* Return to the starting directory */
EXIT
```

```
[D:\]backsys

[D:\]
```

The string used for redirection to `NUL` is assigned to the `toNul` variable. The `Directory` function is called to get the current directory, and the result is stored in `currentDir`. The `Directory` function is called as a procedure to change to the C:\BACKUP directory. The `toNul` variable is appended to each of the OS/2 commands, so those commands no longer display their output on the screen. Finally, the `Directory` function is called again to change back to the user's original directory, and the program exits.

You could have written the program in listing 6.5 without the `toNul` variable. You can append the string `'> NUL'` to each of the commands. The `toNul` variable adds a small amount of programming elegance, however. If you suspect that there is a problem with one of the commands, you can change the assignment to `toNul = '> logfile'` and the output from all the commands is stored in the file `logfile` for later analysis.

You also can use the `SetLocal` and `EndLocal` functions instead of the `Directory` function to save and restore the current directory. Both methods are equally effective, so the choice of one over the other is simply a matter of personal style.

Now look at converting another batch file. The BKCHNG.CMD batch file in listing 6.6 backs up only the files in the OS/2 directory that have changed.

Listing 6.6. BKCHNG.CMD OS/2 batch file.

```
@echo off
echo Insert a blank formatted disk in drive A:
pause
xcopy C:\OS2\* A:\ /M /T
```

```
[D:\]bkchng
Insert a blank formatted disk in drive A:
Press any key when ready...

Source files are being read...

C:\OS2\EPM.INI
C:\OS2\OS2.INI
C:\OS2\OS2SYS.INI
C:\OS2\REXXTRY.CMD

4 file(s) copied.
```

The batch file in listing 6.6 prompts the user to insert a diskette in drive A: and then waits for a key press. Following the key press, the `XCOPY` command is executed with flags set so that it copies only modified files in the C:\OS2 directory.

This time, you convert the batch file to the final REXX program in one editing session. You make the following changes as part of the conversion:

1. You add a REXX comment as the first line of the program.

2. You replace the ECHO command with a SAY instruction. You put quotation marks around the text so that it isn't converted to uppercase or so that it doesn't cause an error.
3. You replace the PAUSE command with a SAY instruction followed by a PULL instruction. This technique was shown earlier in this lesson.
4. You put the XCOPY command in quotation marks.

These changes are reflected in the program in listing 6.7.

Listing 6.7. BKCHNG.CMD converted to REXX.

```
/* list0607.cmd */
SAY "Insert a blank formatted disk in drive A:"
SAY "Press Enter to continue..."
PULL .
'xcopy C:\OS2\* A:\ /M /T'
EXIT
```

```
[D:\]list0607
Insert a blank formatted disk in drive A:
Press Enter to continue...


Source files are being read...

C:\OS2\EPM.INI
C:\OS2\OS2.INI
C:\OS2\OS2SYS.INI
C:\OS2\REXXTRY.CMD

4 file(s) copied.
```

The program in listing 6.7 displays a message prompting the user for a blank diskette in drive A:. It then displays a message telling the user to press Enter to continue and then waits by using the PULL instruction. After the user presses Enter, the XCOPY command is run to copy changed files from the C:\OS2 directory to drive A:.

Return Codes

Every program and nearly every command that you run sets a *return code*. A return code is a value that is set by a command to indicate the success of that command. The convention of using a return code of zero to indicate success was established in the dim past of the computing industry. (You can remember the zero as "nothing went wrong.") The meaning of any other values is left entirely up to each program.

REXX has a predefined variable that is automatically set to the return code from the last command executed. You can use this variable, rc, exactly like any other variable. On Day 8, you look at how to make a REXX program respond differently when rc isn't zero. In this section, you look at some of the values that are returned by common commands.

The program in listing 6.8 deliberately runs several commands that should fail.

Listing 6.8. Return codes from various commands.

```
/* list0608.cmd */
'@echo off'
SAY '>>>Copy a non-existent file:'
'copy realjunk.txt z:\'
SAY "copy RC =" rc
SAY
SAY ">>>Dir of a bad directory name:"
'dir C:\NotARealDirName'
SAY "dir RC =" rc
SAY
SAY ">>>Try to remove a full directory:"
'rd C:\OS2'
SAY "rd RC =" rc
SAY
SAY ">>>Bad switch for ver:"
'ver /w'
SAY "ver RC =" rc
EXIT
```

```
[OS/2]list0608
>>>Copy a non-existent file:
realjunk.txt
SYS0002: The system cannot find the file specified.
        0 file(s) copied.
copy RC = 1

>>>Dir of a bad directory name:

 The volume label in drive C is OS2 SYSTEM.
 The Volume Serial Number is A66D:DC14
 Directory of C:\

SYS0002: The system cannot find the file specified.
dir RC = 18

>>>Try to remove a full directory:
SYS0016: The directory cannot be removed.
rd RC = 1

>>>Bad parameter for ver:
SYS1003: The syntax of the command is incorrect.
ver RC = 1
```

Note: Your output may be different from what you see here. Which error OS/2 generates for each command depends on the format of your hard drive (FAT or HPFS), whether your system is connected to a network, what drive OS/2 is installed on, and what version of OS/2 you are running. As long as you see errors, the program is working correctly.

The program in listing 6.8 executes several commands to generate nonzero return codes deliberately. REXX sets the predefined variable `rc` to the return code of each command. The value of `rc` appears after each command is executed. It should be obvious that each command uses return codes that may not correspond to the return codes from any other command.

Generating a Return Code

Your REXX programs can generate their own return codes. To generate a return code, you need to put a number after the `EXIT` instruction. For example,

```
EXIT 3
```

REXX sets the return code to the value following `EXIT`. The value then can be checked by other programs. REXX also accepts a variable or expression after `EXIT`.

For the OS/2 command processor, the return code set by `EXIT` should be a whole number in the range –32,768 to 32,767. If the number is outside that range, REXX quietly returns zero. REXX also returns zero when `EXIT` is used alone or if the program "runs off the end" (has no `EXIT` instruction).

Summary

This lesson covered the basics of writing and converting OS/2 batch files to REXX programs. You learned that you can use OS/2 commands in REXX programs in much the same way you use commands in OS/2 batch files. To ensure that the command is not misinterpreted by REXX, you should place it in quotation marks. You also learned how to combine REXX variables with commands.

Some commands have equivalent REXX instructions or functions. Part of the process of converting a batch file to a REXX program is recognizing when and how to replace a command with a REXX instruction.

Commands set a return code that REXX stores in the predefined variable `rc`. REXX programs can also set a return code if you place a value or an expression following the `EXIT` instruction.

Q&A

Q When a command and a REXX instruction both do the same thing, which should I use?

A You should use the REXX instruction. REXX must pass commands to OS/2, and this transfer takes longer than processing an instruction. REXX instructions allow you more control over their output and usually offer more functionality than commands.

Q What is redirection?

A Redirection is used to change where a program sends its output and where a program gets its input. By default, a program gets its input from the computer's standard input (usually the keyboard) and sends its output to the computer's standard output (usually the screen).

For example, you use the redirection symbol > to send standard output to a place other than the screen. If you type **`dir > mydir`** at the command prompt, no data appears on the screen, and a file named MYDIR is created. The file MYDIR contains the directory listing.

For more information on redirection, open the `Glossary` book that's on your OS/2 desktop. Scroll to the `redirecting` subject and double-click on the `input and output` subtopic.

Workshop

The Workshop provides quiz questions to help strengthen your understanding of the material covered and exercises to provide you with experience in using what you've learned.

Quiz

1. Why should OS/2 commands be enclosed in quotation marks when you use them in a REXX program?

2. What is the difference between the `cd` command and the `Directory` function?
3. When do you use `ECHO` rather than `SAY`?
4. What effect does using a period after the `PULL` instruction have?
5. What does the `NUL` device do?
6. What do the `SetLocal` and `EndLocal` functions do?
7. What is a return code?
8. What does REXX store in the predefined variable `rc`?
9. What are the steps for converting an OS/2 batch file directly to a REXX program?
10. What return code indicates that a command was successful?

Exercises

1. Convert the following OS/2 batch file to a REXX program.

```
@echo off
echo Put the diskette to be checked in Drive A:
pause
chkdsk A: /F
```

2. Convert the following OS/2 batch file to a REXX program.

```
@echo off
cls
echo Making a copy of the desktop EAs
eautil C:\Desktop C:\desktop.eas /S /R /P
echo All done!
```

3. The following program contains errors. Enter the program, fix it, and run it.

```
/* Ex6-3.cmd */
/* Format a diskette in drive A: */
SAY "Put the diskette to be formatted in Drive A:"
SAY "Press Enter when ready..."
POLL
format A: /ONCE
EXIT rc
```

Basic Input/Output

WEEK
1

All computer programs are made up of three basic operations: input, process, and output. *Input* may come from a variety of sources, such as a keyboard, a file on disk, another program, a modem, or a joystick. *Process* is the manipulation of the input data. *Output* may go to a variety of destinations, such as the screen, a printer, a file, or a modem.

The most basic input and output are keyboard- and screen-oriented—a "conversation" with the user. Today you learn the following:

- ☐ How to display text and numbers
- ☐ How to get input from a user
- ☐ How to create help and usage messages

Displaying Text and Numbers

You've used the SAY instruction in every lesson up to this one, so you should be quite familiar with it. You may not be aware of a few intricacies, however, so now we'll take a close look at how you can use SAY.

The SAY instruction displays text on *standard output*. Standard output (also called *stdout*) is the computer screen unless you have redirected output using > or ¦ at the command prompt. You can use SAY to display literal strings, variables, and the results from expressions. Here are some examples:

```
SAY 'Hello, world!'             /* a literal string */
SAY message                     /* a variable */
SAY 'You are' age 'years old.'  /* literal string and variable */
SAY '2 ** 3 =' 2 ** 3           /* expression */
```

When you're using the SAY instruction, remember that you're writing text on the screen. The usual screen is 80 characters wide and 25 rows high. You need to format your program's output to fit into this space.

If the text for a single SAY instruction is longer than 80 characters, the text is displayed on two lines. The text isn't word wrapped; the text appears to be cut at the end of the first line and continues with the next character on the following line.

If you display more than 25 lines of text at a time, the top line scrolls off the screen. The user then cannot read that line.

You can use several REXX functions with SAY to produce nicely formatted output. The two functions discussed in this section enable you to center a string and to create multiple copies of a string.

The `Center` (or `Centre`) function returns a string centered in a given length. If you want to center `HELLO!` on the screen, for example, you can use the following:

```
SAY Center('HELLO!', 79)
```

In this example, `Center` returns a string 79 characters long, containing `HELLO!` centered in it. If you don't tell `Center` what character to fill the new string with, `Center` defaults to spaces. To fill the string with something else, you use a third parameter. Look at the following example:

```
SAY Center(' Hello ', 79, '*')
```

This example displays `' Hello '` centered with 36 asterisks on either side.

Sometimes you need a character repeated several times. The `Copies` function does exactly that. If you need to draw a separator line or draw a box, using `Copies` can save you a lot of typing and counting. In the following example, `Copies` produces a single line of asterisks:

```
SAY Copies('*', 79)
```

The `Copies` function isn't limited to repeating a single character. In the following example, `Copies` duplicates a string:

```
SAY Copies('Hello? ', 10)
```

The use of the `Center` and `Copies` functions is demonstrated in listing 7.1. Notice how the functions reduce the amount of work the programmer would otherwise have to do.

Listing 7.1. Demonstration of the `Center` and `Copies` functions.

```
/* list0701.cmd */
SAY Copies('*', 65)
SAY
SAY Center('Computers are useless.', 65)
SAY Center('They can only give you answers.', 65)
SAY
SAY Center(' Pablo Picasso ', 65, '-')
SAY Copies('*', 65)
EXIT
```

7

```
[OS/2]list0701
*****************************************************************

                     Computers are useless.
                 They can only give you answers.

------------------------- Pablo Picasso -------------------------
*****************************************************************
```

Analysis

When this program executes, it does the following in order:

1. Displays a line of 65 asterisks using the `Copies` function
2. Displays a blank line using a `SAY` instruction by itself on a line
3. Displays each line of the quote, centered in 65 spaces, by using the `Center` function
4. Displays a second blank line
5. Displays the author of the quote, centered between dashes
6. Displays a final line of 65 asterisks

Formatting Numbers

REXX uses a set of default rules for formatting numbers. Any number that you enter as a literal string in your program is displayed exactly as you entered it. A number that is the result of an expression is formatted as follows:

- If necessary, the number is rounded. The number of digits displayed is controlled by the `NUMERIC DIGITS` instruction. The default number of digits is nine.
- Leading zeros are removed. If there is no digit to the left of the decimal point, one zero is supplied.
- If the value is zero, it is always expressed as a single digit.

The default formatting rules don't create aligned columns of numbers or display dollar amounts with exactly two decimal places. To display a number with a different format from the default, you must use the `Format` function.

The `Format` function rounds a number and formats it with the number of integer and decimal places requested. This function is handy for displaying dollar amounts or keeping decimal points aligned when displaying a column of numbers.

Syntax

The *Format* Function

`Format(number [,[before][,[after][,[expp][,expt]]]])`

The `Format` function returns *`number`* rounded and formatted. The *`before`* and *`after`* values specify the size of the integer and decimal parts of the formatted value. The *`expp`* and *`expt`* values control the formatting of exponential notation. The *`expp`* specifies the number of places for the exponent, and *`expt`* specifies the size that the integer portion of *`number`* must exceed before exponential notation is used.

If *before* is not large enough to contain the integer portion of *number*, an error results. If *before* is larger, the result is padded on the left with spaces.

When *expt* is zero, *number* is always formatted using exponential notation, unless *number* contains only one integer digit. When the length of the decimal part of *number* is greater than twice *expt*, *number* is formatted using exponential notation; exponential notation is used even if the integer part of *number* fits within *expt* digits.

The *expp* parameter controls the number of digits used in the exponent (that is, the number following `E`). If exponential notation is not used and *expp* is given, then trailing spaces sufficient to hold *expp* digits are added to the result.

Example 1

```
Format(25.33333, 6, 2)
```

Example 2

```
Format(value, , , , 0)
```

Example 3

```
Format(value, 2, 4, 2, 0)
```

In listing 7.2, you use the `Format` function to format the same value in several different ways. After you enter and run this program, try changing the parameters passed to `Format` to see what effect they have.

Type

Listing 7.2. Formatting numbers with the `Format` function.

```
/* list0702.cmd */

value = 22 / 7 * 100
SAY Format(value, 4, 4) Format(value, 6, 2) Format(value, 6, 0) ,
    Format(value, 3, 2, 4, 0) Format(value, 3,,, 0) value
value = 5
SAY Format(value, 4, 4) Format(value, 6, 2) Format(value, 6, 0) ,
    Format(value, 3, 2, 4, 0) Format(value, 3,,, 0) value
value = 85.555
SAY Format(value, 4, 4) Format(value, 6, 2) Format(value, 6, 0) ,
    Format(value, 3, 2, 4, 0) Format(value, 3,,, 0) value

EXIT
```

```
[D:\]list0702
 314.2857    314.29    314   3.14E+0002    3.14285714E+2 314.285714
   5.0000      5.00      5   5.00          5 5
  85.5550     85.56     86   8.56E+0001    8.5555E+1 85.555
```

7

Three different values are formatted and displayed in listing 7.2. You use the same formats in the three `SAY` instructions to show how different values are handled. EACH `SAY` has five `Format` calls, followed by the unformatted value. Table 7.1 explains each call of `Format`.

Table 7.1. Effect of different parameters with the `Format` function.

Format Call	Format Action
`Format(value, 4, 4)`	`value` is formatted with four spaces for integer digits, and four places for decimal digits (`' 314.2857'`).
`Format(value, 6, 2)`	`value` is formatted with six spaces for integer digits, and two places for decimal digits (`'   314.29'`).
`Format(value, 6, 0)`	`value` is formatted with six spaces for integer digits, and no decimal digits (`'   314'`).
`Format(value, 3, 2, 4, 0)`	`value` is formatted in exponential notation, except when `value` has only one digit to the left of the decimal point. The integer part is formatted with three spaces for integer digits, two places for decimal digits, and four places for the exponent (`'  3.14E+0002'`).
`Format(value, 3,,, 0)`	`value` is formatted in exponential notation, except when `value` has only one digit to the left of the decimal point. The integer part is formatted to fit in three spaces (`'  3.14285714E+2'`).

The result returned by `Format` is always affected by the current `NUMERIC DIGITS` setting. The default setting of `NUMERIC DIGITS` is nine, so the following `Format` call returns the number formatted in exponential notation:

```
Format('1234567890', 11)
```

To keep exponential notation from being used, you need to change the `NUMERIC DIGITS` setting. The following example displays the value as a whole number:

```
NUMERIC DIGITS 12
SAY Format('12345678901', 15)
```

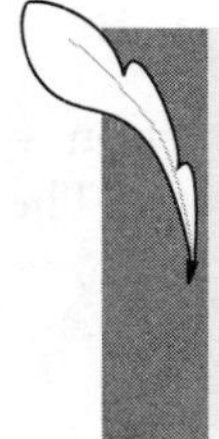

Note: The `NUMERIC DIGITS` setting controls the *precision*, or number of digits used, for all arithmetic operations. Although you can set the `NUMERIC DIGITS` setting to a very large number, increasing the precision has an adverse impact on the speed of arithmetic operations. Don't change the setting to a value higher than necessary.

When you format a number using exponential notation, you can change the formatting used for exponential notation using the `NUMERIC FORM` instruction. You can set `NUMERIC FORM` to either `SCIENTIFIC` (the default) or `ENGINEERING`. For example,

```
NUMERIC FORM ENGINEERING
```

The `ENGINEERING` form uses two digits to the left of the decimal point when exponential notation is used.

Getting Input

Input from the user normally comes from *standard input*. Standard input (also called *stdin*) is the keyboard, unless redirected using < or ¦ at the command prompt. Although a mouse is a normal part of an OS/2 system, input from the mouse is not considered part of standard input.

REXX provides several ways of getting data from standard input. The following sections look at a few variations on the `PULL` instruction. You also learn about the `ARG` instruction for getting user input from the command line.

The *PULL* Instruction

You can use the `PULL` instruction to get input from standard input. In the following example, `PULL` gets a response from the user:

```
PULL response
```

The `PULL` instruction always converts user input to uppercase. In the preceding example, if the user had typed **`Gondola`**, the value assigned to `response` would be `GONDOLA`.

You may want to save the exact characters that the user typed, including upper- and lowercase. The `PARSE PULL` instruction gets and stores the user's response without any conversion. Here's an example of using `PARSE PULL`:

```
PARSE PULL response
```

Actually, the PULL instruction is shorthand for a variant of the PARSE PULL instruction—PARSE UPPER PULL. The keyword UPPER tells PARSE to convert the data to uppercase. The following example is equivalent to using the PULL instruction by itself:

```
PARSE UPPER PULL response
```

You can use a single PULL or PARSE PULL instruction to assign values to more than one variable. The first word the user types (including any punctuation, such as a trailing comma) is assigned to the first variable; the second word, to the second variable; and so forth. The last variable is assigned all the remaining text. If there are more variables than words, the extra variables are assigned empty strings.

In listing 7.3, you use PARSE PULL to get two values from the user. Run the program and try giving it a variety of different inputs.

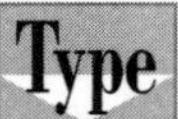

Listing 7.3. Using PARSE PULL with more than one variable.

```
/* list0703.cmd */

SAY "Enter your first and last name:"
PARSE PULL firstName lastName
SAY 'Your last name is' lastName
SAY 'Your first name is' firstName
EXIT
```

```
[D:\]list0703
Enter your first and last name:
Frodo Baggins
Your last name is Baggins
Your first name is Frodo

[D:\]list0703
Enter your first and last name:
Madonna
Your last name is
Your first name is Madonna

[D:\]list0703
Enter your first and last name:
Wrong Way Corrigan
Your last name is Way Corrigan
Your first name is Wrong
```

The program in listing 7.3 prompts for a first name and last name. It then gets the user's response and displays the last name and then the first name. As long as the input is what was expected (two words), the output is sensible.

The *ARG* Instruction

The ARG instruction is used to read parameters that the user typed at the command prompt when the program was started. Command-line parameters can be switches, filenames, or any other type of information that your program allows. Command-line parameters are also called *arguments*.

ARG has the same forms as PULL. Here are examples of all three forms:

```
ARG param
PARSE ARG param
PARSE UPPER ARG param
```

The first and simplest form of ARG in the preceding example always uppercases the command-line parameters before assigning them to the variable. PARSE ARG assigns the command-line parameters to the variable without any change. PARSE UPPER ARG is the long form of ARG and works just the same.

Like PULL, the ARG instruction can also assign values to more than one variable.

You can use the ARG instruction to give your REXX programs the same feel as OS/2 system commands. The program in listing 7.4 can be used as a command to change to a different drive and directory in one step. If you name the program something short, such as DD.CMD, you may find it handy for navigating your system from the command line.

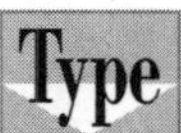

Listing 7.4. Using ARG to implement a new command.

```
/* list0704.cmd */

ARG newDir
SAY Directory(newDir)
EXIT
```

```
[D:\]list0704 C:\OS2
C:\OS2

[C:\OS2]list0704 apps
C:\OS2\APPS

[C:\OS2\APPS]list0704
C:\OS2\APPS

[C:\OS2\APPS]list0704 D:\
D:\
```

Using the ARG instruction, the program in listing 7.4 stores any command-line arguments in the variable newDir. The Directory function is called with the newDir variable. The result of the Directory function appears. If newDir contains a valid directory name, the current directory is changed and the new directory name is displayed. If `newDir` is an empty string (that is, the user didn't type any command-line arguments), then the current directory is displayed.

Usage and Help Messages

When you write a program, you should never assume that the way your program works will be obvious to a user. Always give the user some way of getting help on how to use your program.

Utilities are programs that perform a single function, usually from the command prompt. Utilities usually produce a type of help message that is called a *usage message*, which describes the use of the utility. The message should describe the syntax necessary to run the utility and explain each of the parameters.

An established convention is to use the command-line switch `/?` or `-?` as a request for the usage message. Most OS/2 commands follow this convention. Here's an example of a usage message:

```
[D:\]del /?
Use the ERASE or DEL command to delete one or more files.

SYNTAX:  ERASE [drive:][path]filename [/P]
         DEL   [drive:][path]filename [/P]

Where:
  [drive:][path]filename Specifies the file to delete.  The
                         global file name characters * and ? can
                         be used in the file name specified.
  /P                     Prompts for confirmation before deleting
                         each file.
```

This example is a good format to follow for writing usage messages. The first line tells the purpose of the command in a single sentence. The next part of the message describes the syntax. The last part describes each of the parameters.

A good way to start writing a program is to write the usage message. Explaining the purpose of your program in one sentence forces you to understand clearly what the program does. Describing the syntax and parameters can help clarify how the program works. If the purpose isn't clear or the syntax is complex, then you need to spend more time thinking about your program's design.

Look at the program in listing 7.4. Although the program is quite simple, a usage message would still enhance it. The lesson for Day 8 explains how to test for the `/?` command-line parameter, so we leave that part until later. For now, the program always displays the usage message. Listing 7.5 shows the program with a usage message included.

Listing 7.5. Adding a usage message.

```
/* list0705.cmd */
/* The DD.CMD with a usage message */

SAY 'Use the DD command to change the current drive and'
SAY 'directory or display the current ones.'
SAY
SAY 'SYNTAX:  DD [drive:][directory]'
SAY
SAY 'Where:'
SAY '  [drive:][directory]  Specifies the drive and'
SAY '                       directory you want to change to'
SAY
ARG newDir
SAY Directory(newDir)
EXIT
```

```
[D:\]list0705
Use the DD command to change the current drive and
directory or display the current ones.

SYNTAX:  DD [drive:][directory]

Where:
  [drive:][directory]  Specifies the drive and
                       directory you want to change to

D:\
```

The program in listing 7.5 still works the same as the program in listing 7.4, except that a usage message always appears.

The program in listing 7.5 mimics the usage message from the OS/2 commands. You have some good reasons for mimicking the OS/2 usage messages, the most important of which is to keep from violating the *principle of least astonishment*. Programs should not astonish users by being different; a program should work the way the user expects it to work. There's no good reason to invent a different style of usage message, and a different style isn't what a user would expect.

7

DO | **DON'T**

DO include usage and help messages in your programs.

DON'T violate the principle of least astonishment. Make your program fit in the environment in which it runs.

Summary

This lesson covered several topics related to displaying information and getting input. You learned about standard input and standard output. The lesson also explained how to enhance output using the `Copies` and `Center` functions. You saw how to use the `Format` function to display numbers formatted for specific requirements.

The lesson also introduced the `PULL` and `ARG` instructions. You learned how to use the `PULL` and `PARSE PULL` instructions to get data from the user, and you learned how to get data entered on the command line by using the `ARG` and `PARSE ARG` instructions.

Finally, the lesson discussed creating usage messages. You learned that a usage message helps the user determine how to use a program. Creating the usage message first can also aid in writing the program.

Q&A

Q My program displays 80 characters on a line, but a blank line always appears following each 80-character line. What causes this blank line?

A When a line is displayed, two invisible characters are always added at the end of the line: the carriage return and the line feed. The carriage return sends the cursor back to the left side of the screen. The line feed moves the cursor to the next line. When 80 visible characters (*visible* includes the space character) are displayed, the cursor is forced to the next line. The carriage return has no effect (the cursor is already at the left edge), but the new line still advances one line. If you limit your lines to 79 characters, you don't get this double-spacing effect.

Q What happens if I don't use the `ARG` instruction until late in my program? Does the data on the command line go away?

A The command-line arguments are available as long as your program runs. Although it's normal to use `ARG` as one of the first lines in your program, it doesn't hurt to wait until late in the program, either.

Workshop

The Workshop provides quiz questions to help strengthen your understanding of the material covered and exercises to provide you with experience in using what you've learned.

Quiz

1. What is stdin?
2. What is stdout?
3. What does the `Copies` function do?
4. What does the `PARSE ARG` instruction do?
5. How is `PULL` different from `PARSE PULL`?
6. What instructions do you use to display a string centered on the screen?
7. How can you ensure that a number is displayed with two decimal places?
8. What is the effect of using the `NUMERIC DIGITS` instruction?
9. What is a usage message?
10. What is the principle of least astonishment?

Exercises

Note: Beginning with this lesson, the exercises ask you to design and write programs on your own. Your program may not match the answer we've provided in Appendix F. Having another answer does not mean your program is wrong—there is no one right way to write a program. If your program performs correctly, then your answer is correct.

1. What is the result from each of these `Format` function calls?

   a. `Format('12.1', 3, 2)`
   b. `Format('995', 2, , , 0)`
   c. `Format('0.9', 2, 0)`
   d. `Format('1000', 2, 3, 3, 0)`

2. A program is executed with the following command:

   ```
   [D:\]myprog Cogito Ergo Sum
   ```

   Determine what values are assigned to the variables for each of the following `ARG` instructions:

a. `ARG arg1`
b. `PARSE ARG arg1`
c. `PARSE ARG arg1 arg2`
d. `ARG arg1 arg2 arg3`
e. `PARSE ARG arg1 arg2 arg3 arg4 arg5`

3. Design and write a program that echoes a user's input. Specifically, the program should do the following:

    a. Prompt the user for a line of text.
    b. Accept a line of text from the user.
    c. Display the line of text exactly as entered by the user.

4. Design and write a program that echoes its command-line parameters.

5. Add a usage message to the program in exercise 4. Be sure to follow the guidelines given in this lesson.

6. Modify the program in exercise 3 so that the output is centered with a line of dashes above and below it.

7. Design and write a program that displays a wide directory listing for the user's choice of directory. **Hint:** The `dir /w` OS/2 command displays wide directory listings.

8. Design and write a program that does the following:

    a. Prompts for three dollar amounts.
    b. Gets the user's input.
    c. Calculates the sum of the three amounts.
    d. Displays the three amounts and the sum in a column with the decimal points aligned. The sum should be separated from the three amounts by a line of 12 equal signs.

9. The following program has an error. The user wants the program to display the result as dollar values (that is, with two decimal digits). Determine what the error is and fix the program.

```
/* Ex7-9.cmd */
val1 = 974532.39
val2 = 31000.25
val3 = 5.01
theResult = (val1 * val2) / val3
SAY 'The result is' theResult
EXIT
```

10. The following program contains errors. Find the errors and fix the program.

```
/* Ex7-10.cmd */
cmPerInch = 2.54
SAY "Give your height in inches:"
PULL heightInInches
heightInCm = heightInInces * cmPerInch
heightInMeters = heightInCm / 100
SAY 'You are' Format(heightInCm, 1, 2) 'centimeters'
SAY 'which is' Format(heightInMeters, 1, 2) 'meters.'
EXIT
```

7

1

The Week in Review—Week 1

You now have finished the first week of learning how to program with REXX. At this point, you should be comfortable with using an editor, creating simple programs, and running those programs. The following program pulls together several of the topics covered in the past week.

WEEK IN REVIEW

Note: The numbers to the left of the line numbers indicate the lesson (that is, DAY02 indicates the lesson for Day 2) that first explains the material represented by that line of code. If you don't understand the line of code or it seems confusing, refer to the indicated lesson.

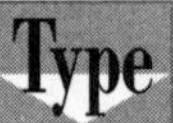

Listing WR1.1. Week 1 review listing.

```
DAY02  /*********************************************************/
       /* File: listr101.cmd                                    */
       /* Creates a copy of OS/2 diskette 1, and then modifies  */
       /* the diskette so that OS/2 can perform an automated    */
       /* installation.                                         */
       /*********************************************************/

DAY06  '@echo off'
DAY06  CALL SetLocal
DAY04  pressEnter = 'Press Enter to continue;' ,
              'Ctrl+Break, Enter to exit.'

DAY07  SAY 'This program copies Diskette 1 of the OS/2 diskettes'
       SAY 'and modifies the copy so that OS/2 installs without'
       SAY 'prompting you.'
       SAY
       SAY 'You need a blank diskette and Diskette 1 from your'
       SAY 'original OS/2 diskettes.'
       SAY
       SAY 'Put OS/2 Diskette 1 in drive A:'
       SAY
       SAY pressEnter
DAY07  PULL .

       'cls'
       SAY 'The diskcopy program is run to copy the diskette.'
       SAY ' * The "source diskette" is the OS/2 Diskette 1.'
       SAY ' * The "target diskette" is the blank diskette.'
       SAY ' * When the copy is complete, respond N to the'
       SAY '   prompt "Copy another diskette (Y/N)?"'
       SAY
       'diskcopy a: a:'

       'cls'
       SAY 'You can now put OS/2 Diskette 1 in a safe place.'
       SAY
       SAY 'The new copy will be modified. Ensure that it is'
       SAY 'in drive A:.'
       SAY
       SAY pressEnter
       PULL .

       SAY
       SAY 'What drive is OS/2 installed on (i.e. C:)?'
```

```
DAY07  PULL drive
DAY06  CALL Directory drive
       CALL Directory '\OS2\INSTALL'

       SAY
       SAY 'Modifying diskette...'

DAY06  'del a:\sysinst2.exe > NUL'
       'del a:\mouse.sys > NUL'
       'copy rspinst.exe A:\ > NUL'
       'copy user.rsp A:\OS2SE20.RSP > NUL'
DAY04  line1 = 'SET OS2_SHELL=RSPINST.EXE A:\OS2SE20.RSP'
       line2 = 'REM Delete any lines beginning with:'
       line3 = 'REM   set os2_shell=sysinst2.exe'
       line4 = 'REM Also delete the line:'
       line5 = 'REM   device=\mouse.sys'
       line6 = 'REM ***delete these remarks when done***'
       'echo' line1 '> config.rx1'
       'echo' line6 '>> config.rx1'
       'echo' line2 '>> config.rx1'
       'echo' line3 '>> config.rx1'
       'echo' line4 '>> config.rx1'
       'echo' line5 '>> config.rx1'
       'echo' line6 '>> config.rx1'
       'copy config.rx1+A:\config.sys config.rxx > NUL'
       'del A:\config.sys > NUL'
       'del config.rx1 > NUL'
       'copy config.rxx A:\config.sys > NUL'
       'del config.rxx > NUL'

       'cls'
       SAY 'You need to edit A:\config.sys to remove any'
       SAY 'lines that start with'
       SAY '  set os2_shell=sysinst2.exe'
       SAY 'and you also need to remove the line'
       SAY '  device=\mouse.sys'
       SAY
       SAY 'The System Editor is started automatically so'
       SAY 'you can edit A:\config.sys.'
       SAY
       SAY pressEnter
DAY07  PULL .

DAY06  'e a:\config.sys'

       'cls'
       SAY 'That completes the modifications.'
       SAY
       SAY 'For further information, see the OS/2 Installation'
       SAY 'Guide, Chapter 5, Using a Response File to Install.'

DAY06  CALL EndLocal
DAY02  EXIT
```

Using the skills you acquired on Day 1, “Getting Started,” and Day 2, “REXX Ground Rules,” you should be able to enter and run this program. This program begins with a longer comment than any of the other listings that you’ve seen so far, and the messages it displays are also considerably longer. This program looks more like what a real program should look like (as contrasted to the examples in the lessons).

This program creates a copy of the OS/2 Diskette 1 and modifies the copy to create an automated installation. For the program to work successfully, you must have installed OS/2 using a choice other than `Install preselected features`, and you must have installed the `Installation Utilities`. The program still runs in any case, but the diskette that it creates isn’t of use. (See the *OS/2 Installation Guide*, Chapter 5, “Using a Response File to Install,” for instructions on how to set up your system or for information on how the automated installation works.) The program copies a response file and a program file to the diskette and adds some lines to the CONFIG.SYS file on the diskette.

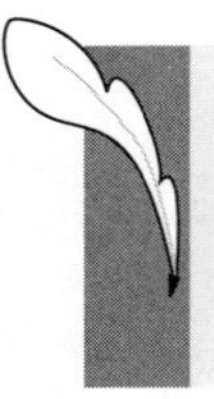

Note: This program was tested with OS/2 2.1. Later versions of OS/2 may require some modifications to the program. Be sure to test the diskette created by the program to ensure that the program worked properly with your system.

The opening comment on line 1 tells OS/2 that this is a REXX program. The comments on lines 2 to 5 give some general information about the program. Notice how the comment forms a box; it helps separate the comment from the code and makes it stand out.

Line 8 is a command. The `echo off` command keeps further commands from being echoed (displayed). The `@` preceding the command keeps the current command from being echoed.

A call to `SetLocal` is performed on line 9 because the program changes directories. The call to `EndLocal` on line 96 restores the user’s environment without any other special attention from the program.

On lines 13 to 22, the user is informed of the purpose of the program and what he or she needs to supply. The program then waits for the user to press Enter.

The `cls` command clears the screen on line 25, and instructions for responding to the diskcopy program are displayed on lines 26 to 31. The `diskcopy` command is run on line 32.

Lines 34 to 41 again clear the screen and display additional information following the completion of the `diskcopy` command. When the user presses Enter, the program prompts for the drive on which OS/2 is installed and then assigns the user input to `drive` (line 45). The variable `drive` is used with the `Directory` function to change to the OS/2 installation drive. The `Directory` function is called again (line 47) to change to the \OS2\INSTALL directory.

Some space is created on the diskette by deleting two files that are not needed (lines 52 and 53), and RSPINST.EXE and the response file are copied to the diskette (lines 54 and 55). Lines 56 to 61 set up the data that is added at the beginning of the CONFIG.SYS file in lines 62 to 69. The new CONFIG.SYS file is copied to the diskette, and the program deletes its work files in lines 71 to 73.

In lines 75 to 85, the user is told what changes need to be made to CONFIG.SYS. When the user presses Enter (line 86), the System Editor is started using the `e` command.

Finally, on lines 90 to 94, the program clears the screen and displays some final information for the user. The call to `EndLocal` on line 96 restores the user's original directory, and the `EXIT` instruction ends the program.

This program uses most of what you learned in your first week of teaching yourself REXX to replace what you might have once done using an OS/2 batch file. If you use everything you have learned in this first week, you should be able to start enhancing your OS/2 system using REXX programs. But what you can do is still limited; week 2 will increase your knowledge of REXX so that you can solve a wide variety of programming problems.

WEEK 2 AT A GLANCE

8

9

10

11

12

13

14

You have finished your first week of learning how to program in REXX. By now, you should feel comfortable entering simple programs.

Where You're Going...

The second week covers a large amount of material. Now that you have the basics under your belt, you learn to use many of the features that make REXX powerful. You learn about REXX's powerful string handling and stem variables, and you also spend a day learning how to debug your programs effectively.

You spend part of this week learning how to control program flow. On Day 8, you learn how your program can make decisions. Day 11, "Using Loops," teaches you how REXX programs can repeat instructions. On Day 14, "Using Subroutines," you learn another way to control the operation of your programs.

By the end of the first week, you were able to write simple REXX programs. By the end of Week 2, you should be able to write complex programs that can accomplish nearly any task.

2

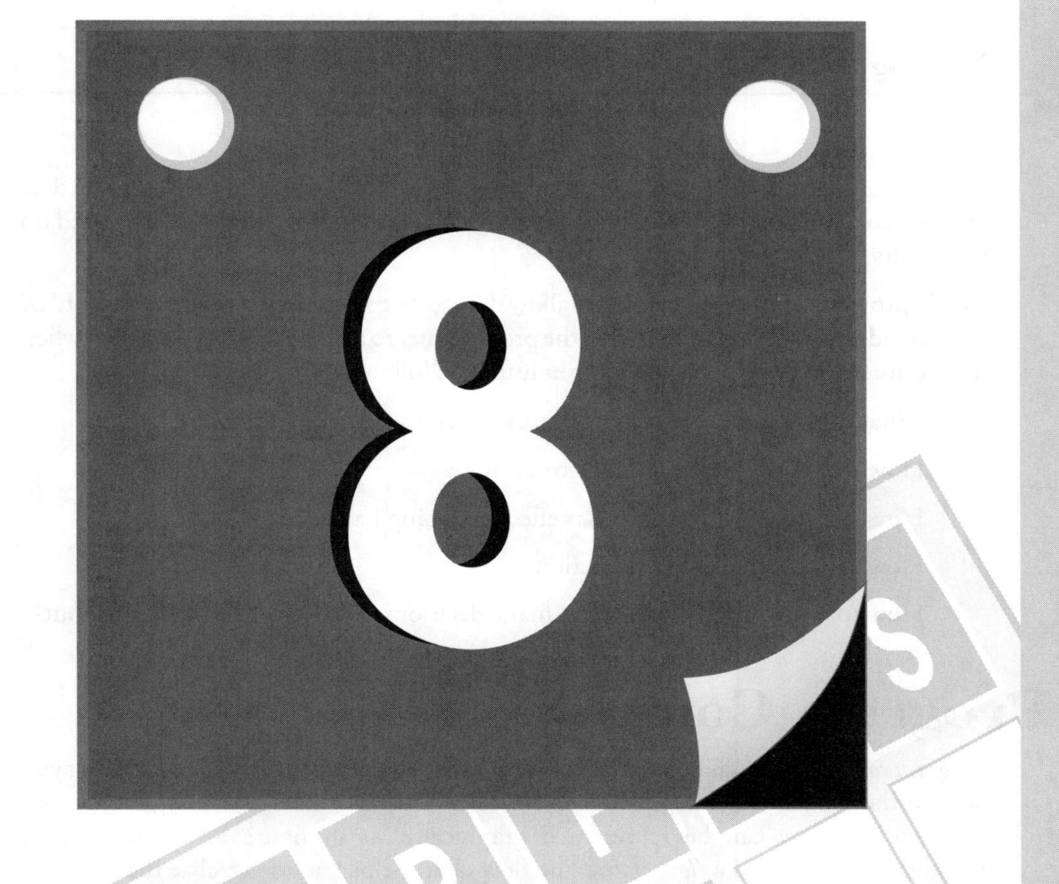

Making Decisions

WEEK

2

Most computer programs are required to make decisions based on input data. The data must be compared to other data, and the program must be able to take action based on the results of the comparison.

REXX provides a set of operators that allow data to be compared in various ways. REXX also provides instructions that enable the programmer to alter what a program does when it encounters different data. Today you learn the following:

- What logical and relational operators are and how they are used
- How to use the `IF` and `ELSE` instructions
- How to group clauses and what effect grouping has
- How to use the `SELECT` instruction
- How to write programs that can make decisions based on the program's input

Program Control

Program control clauses change the order of program execution. Most of the code that you have worked with so far has executed each REXX clause in order. This straight-through, or sequence, flow can be represented graphically, as in figure 8.1. This graphic representation is called a *flow chart*. The flow chart helps you to visualize the flow of a program.

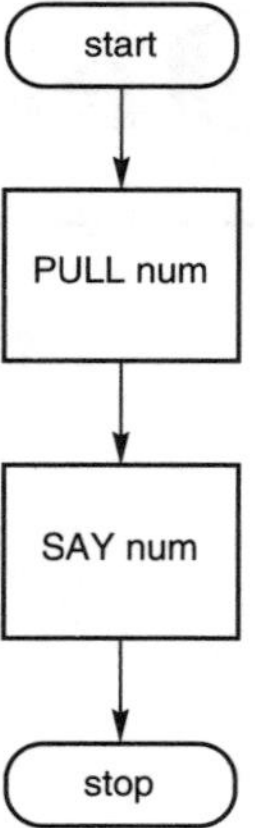

Figure 8.1. *A diagram of straight-through program flow.*

This lesson introduces the use of conditions to test the relationship of values in a program. A condition always has a result of *true* or *false*. Although truth may be a vague concept in human affairs, REXX has an exacting definition of both true and false: true is equal to `1`, and false is equal to `0`.

8

A condition is an operation that produces a true or false (`1` or `0`) result. A condition can be as simple as the value `1`, or it can be quite complex. Most conditions are comparisons that test for equality (such as `a = b`) or magnitude (such as `age > 21`).

The program flow created using a condition to make a decision can be shown graphically. In figure 8.2, the condition is evaluated, and the program flow changes based on the result. The clause is executed only when the condition is true. If the condition is false, the clause is skipped.

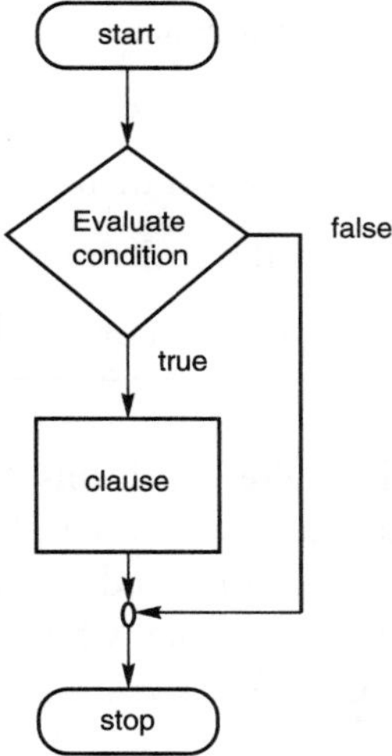

Figure 8.2. *A diagram of the effect of testing a condition.*

The following sections introduce operations for creating conditions and discuss two instructions that alter program flow based on the result of testing a condition.

Using Relational and Logical Operators

You can use a relational operator to create a condition by comparing two values. Relational operators produce a result of either true or false (`1` or `0`).

The relational operators perform the equivalent of asking a question about the relation of two values. For instance, you might ask, "Is Joe's age greater than 30?" The equivalent question expressed as a REXX condition is `joesAge > 30`.

Table 8.1. lists the relational operators.

Table 8.1. The relational operators.

Operator	Meaning	Example
=	equals	`a = b`
>	greater than	`a > b`
<	less than	`a < b`
>< or <> or \= or ¬=	not equal	`a >< b`
\> or ¬>	not greater than	`a ¬> b`
\< or ¬<	not less than	`a \< b`
>=	greater than or equal	`a >= b`
<=	less than or equal	`a <= b`

Some relational operators have alternate forms. For instance, the *not equal* operator has three forms. Two characters can represent *not*: \ and ¬. Because you cannot find the ¬ character on most keyboards, you may find the backslash (\) more convenient. You can type ¬ by pressing and holding the Alt key while typing **170** on the numeric keypad. (Or, if you're using EPM, press Ctrl+6.)

You can use relational operators in expressions in the same way that you use arithmetic operators. All relational operations produce a `1` or a `0` as a result. The result can be assigned to a variable or used in a further calculation.

The program in listing 8.1 demonstrates the use of some of the relational operators.

Listing 8.1. Using the relational operators.

```
/* list0801.cmd */
SAY 'Enter a number:'
PULL num
SAY num '= 10 result:' (num = 10)
SAY num '< (2 ** 32 - 1) result:' (num < (2 ** 32 - 1))
SAY num '> 0 result:' (num > 0)
SAY 'Enter a city name:'
PARSE PULL city
```

```
isNewYork = (city = 'New York')
SAY 'isNewYork is' isNewYork
SAY city '=' city 'result:' (city = city)
EXIT
```

```
[D:\]list0801
Enter a number:
-1
-1 = 10 result: 0
-1 < (2 ** 32 - 1) result: 1
-1 > 0 result: 0
Enter a city name:
Austin
isNewYork is 0
Austin = Austin result: 1
```

The program in listing 8.1 displays the result of comparing user input to various values. The result of each comparison is `0` when the comparison is false, and `1` when the comparison is true.

Logical Operators

More than one comparison operation can be performed in a single expression if you join the comparison operations using the `&` (*and*), `¦` (*or*), or `&&` (*xor* or *exclusive or*) logical operators. You also can invert the result of a comparison by using the prefix *not* (\ or ¬) logical operator. Table 8.2 shows how the logical operators affect the evaluation of conditions.

Table 8.2. Effect of using the ¬, &, ¦, and && operators.

Expression	Meaning	Expression Is True When
cond1 & cond2	*cond1* and *cond2*	Both conditions are true.
cond1 ¦ cond2	*cond1* or *cond2*	Either or both conditions are true.
cond1 && cond2	*cond1* xor *cond2*	One, and only one, condition is true.
¬ *cond* or \ *cond*	not *cond*	The condition is false.

The following example shows how you use the `&` operator to combine conditions. Notice how you use parentheses to help clarify the expression.

```
potentialPlayer = (age < 30) & (height > 78)
```

A *truth table* precisely shows the result of a logical operation. Because each operand of a logical operator can have only one of two values (true or false), four possible combinations exist for each of the binary operators.

The truth table for the & operator is shown in table 8.3. This operator produces a true result only when both of its operands are true. For example,

```
isDebutante = (gown = 'white') & (age = 16)
```

Table 8.3. Truth table for the & operator.

When *Cond1* Is	And *Cond2* Is	& Result Is
false (0)	false (0)	false (0)
true (0)	false (1)	false (0)
false (0)	true (1)	false (0)
true (1)	true (1)	true (1)

The truth table for the ¦ operator is shown in table 8.4. The result of the ¦ operator is true when either of its operands is true. For example,

```
isStarWars = (movie = 'Empire Strikes Back') ,
           ¦ (movie = 'Return of the Jedi')
```

Table 8.4. Truth table for the ¦ operator.

When *Cond1* Is	And *Cond2* Is	¦ Result Is
false (0)	false (0)	false (0)
true (1)	false (0)	true (1)
false (0)	true (1)	true (1)
true (1)	true (1)	true (1)

The truth table for the && operator is shown in table 8.5. The result of the && operator is true when one, but not both, of its operands is true. For example,

```
isTasty = (ingredient1 = 'chocolate') && (ingredient2 = 'garlic')
```

Table 8.5. Truth table for the && operator.

When *Cond1* Is	And *Cond2* Is	&& Result Is
false (0)	false (0)	false (0)
true (1)	false (0)	true (1)
false (0)	true (1)	true (1)
true (1)	true (1)	false (0)

The truth table for the \ (or ¬) operator is in table 8.6. This operator inverts the result of the following condition—the operator result is false when the condition is true, and the result is true when the condition is false.

Table 8.6. Truth table for the ¬ operator.

When *Cond* Is	¬ Result Is
true (1)	false (0)
false (0)	true (1)

Relational and Logical Operator Precedence

On Day 5, you learned about the concept of operator precedence, or order of evaluation. The logical and relational operators also have a place in the operator precedence hierarchy. Operator precedence, including the relational and logical operators, is shown in table 8.7.

Table 8.7. Precedence of REXX operators.

Operator Group	Operators	Relative Precedence
Unary operators	`- + \ ¬`	Highest
Power	`**`	
Multiply and divide	`* / % //`	

continues

Table 8.7. continued

Operator Group	Operators	Relative Precedence
Add and subtract	`+ -`	
Comparisons	`= \= >< <> > < \> \< >= <=`	
And	`&`	
Or and exclusive or	`¦ &&`	Lowest

You use parentheses to change the order of evaluation for the relational and logical operators. Because the order of evaluation for `&`, `¦`, and `&&` can be confusing, you should always use parentheses when an expression contains two or more of these operators.

The precedence of the arithmetic operators is higher than the precedence of the relational operators. Arithmetic is performed before any comparisons. In the following example, all of the math is performed before the `<` operator is evaluated:

```
aIsLess = a < 1 + 5 * 4
```

Even though REXX evaluates this expression correctly, it takes some study for you to understand what the expression does. If you need to mix arithmetic expressions with relational operators, use parentheses to delineate the operations.

The *IF* Instruction

The relational and logical operators are used most often in conditional expressions that are tested by the `IF` instruction to make decisions. The `IF` instruction uses the outcome of the condition to alter the flow of the program. A clause is attached to the `IF` instruction by the keyword `THEN`. `IF` tests the condition, and when it's true, the clause following `THEN` is executed. If the condition is false, the clause is not executed. Now look at an example:

```
IF modemResult = 'BUSY' THEN
  SAY 'The phone number is busy.'
```

Compare this example to the diagram in figure 8.2. The expression `modemResult = 'BUSY'` is the condition to be evaluated. The clause beginning with `SAY` is executed when the condition is true. In other words, if the variable `modemResult` is equal to `'BUSY'`, the `SAY` instruction is executed. When `modemResult` is not equal to `'BUSY'`, the `SAY` instruction isn't executed.

Nesting *IF* Instructions

A nested `IF` instruction is when the clause contained in an `IF` instruction is another `IF` instruction. The following example should help clarify the concept of nested `IF` instructions:

```
IF time >= '09:00' THEN
  IF time <= '17:00' THEN
    SAY 'Normal working hours.'
```

When the condition for the first `IF` instruction is true, the second, nested `IF` instruction is evaluated. The `SAY` clause for the nested `IF` instruction is executed only when the conditions for both `IF` instructions are true.

The effect of nesting `IF` instructions is the same as using the `&` logical operator. The following example produces the same result as the previous example:

```
IF time >= '09:00' & time <= '17:00' THEN
  SAY 'Normal working hours.'
```

Formatting and Style Using *IF*

All of the examples of `IF` instructions follow a rather rigorous indentation scheme. You always indent the clause following the `IF` instruction two spaces. When `IF` instructions are nested, you indent each `IF` instruction an additional two spaces.

The indentation does not mean a thing to REXX; REXX accepts and executes the code even if it is all lined up at the left margin. The indentation is a visual clue for the programmer. It highlights the structure of the program and aids the programmer in following the logic of the program.

Remember to indent your code to follow the logic of the program. If you don't use indentation, your programs will be incomprehensible within days. Indent your code!

The *ELSE* Instruction

The `ELSE` instruction works with the `IF` instruction. When the condition in the `IF` instruction is false, program control is passed to the `ELSE` instruction.

In the following example, `ELSE` is executed when `currentTime` is greater than or equal to `'07:00'`:

```
IF currentTime < '07:00' THEN
  SAY 'Go back to sleep.'
ELSE
  SAY 'Get up! Get up!'
```

The preceding example is equivalent to writing the following two IF instructions:

```
IF currentTime < '07:00' THEN
  SAY 'Go back to sleep.'
IF currentTime \< '07:00' THEN
  SAY 'Get up! Get up!'
```

Using ELSE is both easier to understand and simpler to write. Figure 8.3 illustrates how the ELSE instruction affects program flow.

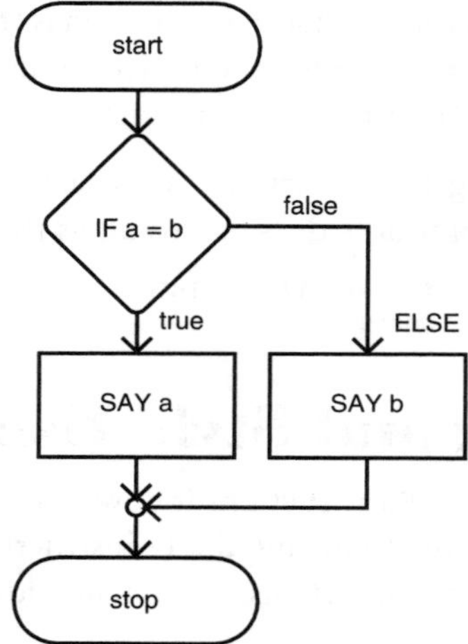

Figure 8.3. *Program flow using the* IF *and* ELSE *instructions.*

Nesting with the *ELSE* Instruction

You can use the ELSE instruction with nested IF instructions. When you use ELSE with nesting, however, you must be careful that the code does what you think it does. ELSE always binds with the nearest IF at the same level. For example,

```
IF a = b THEN
  IF c = d THEN
    SAY 'Gotcha.'
ELSE
  SAY 'Nope.'
```

The indentation in this example indicates that the programmer wants the ELSE to be executed when the expression a = b is false. However, the ELSE will bind to the second IF instruction rather than the first, so it will execute only when the first IF is true and the second IF is false.

You can fix this problem by introducing a second ELSE followed by a NOP instruction. The NOP instruction is a special "do nothing" instruction that means *no operation*. The fixed example looks like this:

```
IF a = b THEN
  IF c = d THEN
    SAY 'Gotcha.'
  ELSE
    NOP
ELSE
  SAY 'Nope.'
```

Notice that the ELSE with the NOP instruction acts as a placeholder. These instructions do nothing but force the following ELSE to bind with the correct IF.

The program in listing 8.2 illustrates the use of the IF and ELSE instructions.

Listing 8.2. Using the IF and ELSE instructions.

```
/* list0802.cmd */
SAY "Enter a value for a:"
PULL a
SAY "Enter a value for b:"
PULL b
SAY

IF a = b THEN
  SAY 'a equals b'
ELSE IF a < b THEN
  SAY 'a is less than b'
ELSE
  SAY 'a is greater than b'

IF a < 0 & b < 0 THEN
  SAY 'Both a and b are negative'
ELSE IF a < 0 THEN
  SAY 'Only a is negative'
ELSE IF b < 0 THEN
  SAY 'Only b is negative'
ELSE
  SAY 'Neither a nor b is negative'

EXIT
```

```
[D:\]list0802
Enter a value for a:
25
Enter a value for b:
-3

a is greater than b
Only b is negative
```

```
[D:\]list0802
Enter a value for a:
1
Enter a value for b:
1

a equals b
Neither a nor b is negative

[D:\]list0802
Enter a value for a:
-200
Enter a value for b:
-100

a is less than b
Both a and b are negative
```

The program in listing 8.2 uses `IF` instructions to display information about the two input values. Most of the code in this program should be familiar by now. The program prompts for each input value, and it assigns the values to variables `a` and `b` using the `PULL` instruction. The first set of `IF` instructions tests to determine if `a` is equal to `b` or less than `b`. The final `ELSE` catches the only remaining condition—a is greater than `b`. The next set of `IF` instructions tests to determine if both `a` and `b` are negative, if only `a` is negative, or if only `b` is negative. Failing those tests, the `ELSE` displays a message that neither `a` nor `b` is negative.

Syntax

The *IF* ... *THEN* ... *ELSE* Instruction

```
IF condition [;] THEN [;]
  clause
[ELSE [;]
  clause]
```

The `IF` instruction alters program flow based on the result of *`condition`*. The *`clause`* after the `THEN` is processed when *`condition`* evaluates to true (`1`).

The `ELSE` instruction is optional. It is executed when *`condition`* evaluates to false (`0`).

You cannot add a null clause after `THEN` or `ELSE`. The `NOP` (*no operation*) instruction is provided for the cases where you want a null clause.

An implied semicolon follows both the `THEN` and `ELSE` keywords. The clause can immediately follow the keyword; no semicolon is required between the keyword and the clause. If `ELSE` is to follow on the same line as the prior clause, a semicolon must separate the clause from the `ELSE`.

Example 1

```
IF overtimeHours > 0 THEN
  overtimePay = overtimeHours * rate * 1.5
```

Example 2

```
IF response = 'YES' THEN
  SAY 'Great!'
ELSE
  SAY 'Sorry.'
```

Example 3

```
IF file = '' THEN SAY 'No files.'; ELSE SAY 'File is' file
```

Grouping Instructions

You often need to execute more than one clause following a THEN or ELSE instruction. To do so, you can use DO and END to group one or more clauses so that they act like a single clause. The DO and END instructions allow more than one clause to be attached to a THEN or ELSE. Look at the following example:

```
IF today = birthday THEN
  DO
  SAY "You're one year older!"
  SAY "Happy birthday!"
  END
```

The DO and END create a *block* of code. You can use a block anywhere that you would normally use a single clause.

In the section on ELSE, you learned about a problem with using ELSE with nested IF instructions. You can use grouping as another way to fix this problem. Instead of adding an additional ELSE followed by NOP, you can put the nested IF in a block. Doing so has the effect of "hiding" the IF instruction, so the ELSE binds with the outer IF instruction. Here's the earlier example, fixed by using DO and END:

```
IF a = b THEN
  DO
  IF c = d THEN
    SAY 'Gotcha.'
  END
ELSE
  SAY 'Nope.'
```

The program in listing 8.3 shows how you can use the DO and END instructions to group code.

Listing 8.3. Calculating the greatest common divisor.

```
/* list0803.cmd */
SAY "Enter two positive integers:"
PULL val1 val2

u = val1
v = val2

gcd:
IF u > 0 THEN
  DO
  IF u < v THEN
    DO
    tmp = u
    u = v
    v = tmp
    END
  u = u - v
  SIGNAL gcd
  END

SAY
SAY "The greatest common divisor of" val1 "and" val2 "is" v
EXIT
```

```
[D:\]list0803
Enter two positive integers:
35 25

The greatest common divisor of 35 and 25 is 5

[D:\]list0803
Enter two positive integers:
555 102

The greatest common divisor of 555 and 102 is 3

[D:\]list0803
Enter two positive integers:
209 231

The greatest common divisor of 209 and 231 is 11
```

This program in listing 8.3 calculates the greatest common divisor of two positive integer values. It prompts the user for two positive integer values, and it stores those values in `val1` and `val2`. The values are then copied to `u` and `v`. The two nested `IF` instructions do the bulk of the work. The outer `IF` checks whether `u` is greater than zero; when `u` is less than or equal to zero, the calculation is complete. The inner `IF` compares `u` to `v` and exchanges the values (in the block following the `IF`) if `u` is less than `v`. The value in `v` is then subtracted from `u`. The program then goes to the `gcd` label just prior to the first `IF`. Once `u` is less than or equal to zero, the result is displayed and the program exits.

The *SELECT* Instruction

Sometimes a program needs to check for several possible values and perform a different action for each value. If you use the `IF` instruction to perform a different action for each letter of the alphabet, you need to create a long string of `IF ... ELSE IF` instructions, as follows:

```
IF userInput = 'A' THEN
  SAY 'apple'
ELSE IF userInput = 'B' THEN
  SAY 'banana'
ELSE IF userInput = 'C' THEN
  SAY 'cat'
ELSE IF userInput = 'D' THEN
  SAY 'dog'
ELSE
  SAY '???'
```

Obviously, using the `IF` instruction to test each of these values is cumbersome and requires a great deal of typing.

You can easily rewrite the preceding example using the `SELECT` instruction. The `SELECT` instruction works just like a series of `IF ... ELSE IF` instructions. The difference is that `SELECT` is easier to write and easier to understand. Here's the example rewritten using `SELECT`:

```
SELECT
WHEN userInput = 'A' THEN
  SAY 'apple'
WHEN userInput = 'B' THEN
  SAY 'banana'
WHEN userInput = 'C' THEN
  SAY 'cat'
WHEN userInput = 'D' THEN
  SAY 'dog'
OTHERWISE
  SAY '???'
END
```

The `SELECT` instruction starts with `SELECT` and ends with `END`. REXX tests each `WHEN` condition and executes the `THEN` clause for the first one that is true. If none of the `WHEN` conditions are true, then REXX executes the `OTHERWISE` clause.

`SELECT` doesn't require you to test the same variable in every `WHEN` clause. In each `WHEN`, you can test conditions that are completely unrelated; the first `WHEN` that produces a true result will be executed, and then REXX skips to the `END` instruction. This example shows how different variables can be tested in a single `SELECT` instruction:

```
SELECT
WHEN firstName = 'Bill' THEN
  SAY 'Nice book!'
WHEN lastName = 'Schindler' THEN
  SAY 'Nice list!'
OTHERWISE
  SAY 'Nice try!'
END
```

Listing 8.4 illustrates the use of the `SELECT` instruction. The `Zeller` function, which was first introduced on Day 5 (see listing 5.2), is used to determine the day of the week on which you were born.

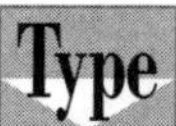

Listing 8.4. Using `SELECT` with the `Zeller` function.

```
/* list0804.cmd */

SAY "Enter your birth date as mm dd yyyy:"
SAY "(like 11 17 1975)"
PULL month day year

dow = Zeller()

SELECT
WHEN dow = 0 THEN
  birthday = "Sunday"
WHEN dow = 1 THEN
  birthday = "Monday"
WHEN dow = 2 THEN
  birthday = "Tuesday"
WHEN dow = 3 THEN
  birthday = "Wednesday"
WHEN dow = 4 THEN
  birthday = "Thursday"
WHEN dow = 5 THEN
  birthday = "Friday"
OTHERWISE
  birthday = "Saturday"
END

SAY "You were born on a" birthday

EXIT

/* Zeller's Congruence
 * This function takes month, day, and year as input.
 * It returns a number that represents the day of the week
 * for the given date; 0 = Sunday ... 6 = Saturday.
 */
Zeller:
  IF month > 2 THEN
    DO
    adjMonth = month - 2
    adjYear = year
    END
```

```
ELSE
  DO
  adjMonth = month + 10
  adjYear = year - 1
  END

century = adjYear % 100
yearInCentury = adjYear - 100 * century
dayOfWeek = ((13 * adjMonth - 1) % 5 + day + yearInCentury + ,
      yearInCentury % 4 + century % 4 - century - century + 77) ,
      // 7
RETURN dayOfWeek
```

```
[D:\]list0804
Enter your birth date as mm dd yyyy:
(like 11 17 1975)
1 10 1958

You were born on a Friday
```

The program in listing 8.4 uses Zeller's Congruence to calculate the day of week for a birth date. First, the user is prompted to enter his or her date of birth. The birth date is stored in the variables `month`, `day`, and `year`. The `Zeller` function is called, and the returned day-of-week number is assigned to `dow`. A `SELECT` instruction is then used to compare `dow` to the seven possible values that it can have (0 through 6). The name of the corresponding day name is assigned to `birthday`. Finally, the weekday on which the user was born is displayed.

You should now understand all of the lines in the `Zeller` function. Notice how the `IF` instruction at the beginning of `Zeller` uses blocks to control the assignments to `adjMonth` and `adjYear`.

Syntax

The *SELECT* Instruction

```
SELECT
WHEN condition [;] THEN [;]
  clause
[[WHEN condition [;] THEN [;]
  clause] ...]
OTHERWISE [;]
  [clause]
END
```

The `SELECT` instruction conditionally executes one of several alternative instructions.

Each *`condition`* is evaluated in turn until one evaluates as true (`1`). When a *`condition`* evaluates as true, the *`clause`* following the associated `THEN` is executed, and control passes to the instruction following `END`. If none of the conditions evaluate as true, then the clause following `OTHERWISE` is executed.

Example

```
SELECT
WHEN taxesOwed = 0 THEN
  SAY 'No taxes owed!'
WHEN taxesOwed < 0 THEN
  SAY 'Refund due!'
WHEN taxesOwed <= bankBalance THEN
  DO
  SAY 'After you pay your taxes,'
  SAY 'You will have' (bankBalance - taxesOwed) 'left.'
  END
OTHERWISE
  SAY 'WARNING:'
  SAY 'Taxes exceed bank balance!'
END
```

Summary

This lesson introduced conditions and the relational and logical operators. You learned that REXX defines true as `1` and false as `0`. The relational and logical operators always produce a result of `0` and `1`. You use the relational operators to compare two values. The logical operators operate on the true and false values that result from the use of the relational operators. The order of evaluation for relational and logical operators is defined as part of the hierarchy of operator precedence.

The lesson also discussed the `IF` and `ELSE` instructions and showed how you use them to change the flow of a program. You learned that `IF` is used to test a condition and execute code when the condition is true. `ELSE` conditionally executes code when the condition tested by `IF` is false. You learned how to use `DO` and `END` to group clauses so that `IF`, `ELSE`, and `WHEN` can conditionally execute more than one clause.

The lesson also introduced the `SELECT` instruction. You saw how you can use the `SELECT` instruction to replace a series of `IF ... ELSE IF` instructions.

Q&A

Q How does REXX distinguish an assignment from a comparison using equals?

A REXX uses the context to determine whether the = operator is an assignment or a comparison. A clause that begins with a variable followed by the = operator is always treated as an assignment. All other uses of = are treated as comparisons.

Q Is it better to use the `&` operator or nested `IF` instructions?

A Neither one is best in all situations. The choice of one over the other depends on what your program needs to accomplish, which method seems easier to understand, and (to a lesser degree) on personal style. Sometimes an `ELSE` is required because you cannot write the instruction correctly using one method or the other. You need to analyze each situation and decide on the best method. You may want to write the code both ways to see which works best for you.

Workshop

The Workshop provides quiz questions to help strengthen your understanding of the material covered and exercises to provide you with experience in using what you've learned.

Quiz

1. What does a program control clause do?
2. How does REXX define true and false?
3. What is a relational operator?
4. What is a logical operator?
5. What does the `IF` instruction do?
6. Which operators have higher precedence?

    a. `<` or `+`
    b. `\` or `**`
    c. `&&` or `&`
    d. `\>` or `><`

7. What instructions are used to create a block?
8. What is the purpose of the `ELSE` instruction?
9. What does the `SELECT` instruction do?
10. When is the clause following `OTHERWISE` executed?

Exercises

1. What is the result of each of the following expressions?

    a. `5 > 1`
    b. `'A' = 'z'`
    c. `9 <= 7 | 1 <= 3`
    d. `17 \> 17`
    e. `50 < 55 && 2 < 3`
    f. `(2 * 10) > (3 * 5) & 1`

2. Rewrite the following code fragment using the `SELECT` instruction.

```
IF song = "oldie" THEN
  SAY 'Woolie Bullie'
ELSE IF song = "classical" THEN
  SAY 'Symphony No. 4 in D minor'
ELSE IF song = "rock" THEN
  SAY 'One of These Days'
ELSE IF song = "big band" THEN
  SAY 'In The Mood'
ELSE
  SAY 'Poisoning Pigeons In The Park'
```

3. Design and write a program that does the following:

    a. Prompts the user for two numbers.
    b. Determines which number is the largest.
    c. Displays the largest number and then the smallest number.
    d. Displays the difference between the largest and smallest numbers.

4. Modify the following program (DD.CMD from the lesson for Day 7) so that the usage message is displayed only when the user starts the program with a command-line argument of `/?` or `-?`. The program should exit after displaying the usage message rather than call the `Directory` function.

```
/* DD.CMD — change drive and directory */

SAY 'Use the DD command to change the current drive and'
SAY 'directory or display the current ones.'
SAY
SAY 'SYNTAX:  DD [drive:][directory]'
SAY
SAY 'Where:'
```

```
SAY '  [drive:][directory]  Specifies the drive and'
SAY '                       directory you want to change to'
SAY
ARG newDir
SAY Directory(newDir)
EXIT
```

5. The following program contains errors. Find the errors, fix them, and run the program.

```
/* Ex8-5.cmd */
SAY 'Insert diskette for backup in Drive A:'
SAY 'Press Enter when ready.'
PULL .

xcopy C:\OS2\*.ini A:\ > NUL
IF rc >< 0 THEN
  SAY 'Error encountered while copying files.'
  SAY 'Disk in Drive A: may be full.'

EXIT
```

Manipulating Strings

WEEK 2

Because REXX views all data as strings, it provides a rich selection of built-in functions for manipulating strings. Today you learn the following:

- How to get the length of a string
- How to change and edit the contents of a string
- How to concatenate strings
- How to compare strings
- How to cut strings and create substrings
- How to search strings for characters
- How to interpret parts of a string using the `PARSE` instruction

Getting the Length

REXX supplies built-in functions to determine the length of a string in both characters and words. You can use the `Length` function to determine the length of a string in characters. Here's an example:

```
whyCry = "It's my party"
len = Length(whyCry)
```

The value `13` is assigned to `len`. The `Length` function counts all of the characters in `whyCry`, including the spaces.

The `Words` function counts the number of words in a string. For all of the word-based functions, a word is any group of characters delimited by one or more spaces. In the following example, `SAY` displays `6`:

```
SAY Words("History is more or less bunk.")
```

The `WordLength` function determines the length of a single word in a string. The function is passed both the string and a number indicating which word to examine. Following are some examples of `WordLength`:

```
SAY WordLength("I came, I saw, I conquered.", 3)  /* displays 1 */
SAY WordLength("I came, I saw, I conquered.", 6)  /* displays 10 */
```

Notice that, because only spaces are used to delimit words, punctuation is included in the length of the word.

The program in listing 9.1 calculates the grade level required to read a sentence, making good use of both the `Length` and `Words` functions.

Listing 9.1. Using `Length` and `Words` in calculating readability.

```
/* list0901.cmd */

SAY 'Enter a single sentence:'
PULL sentence

len = Length(sentence)
words = Words(sentence)
avgWordLen = (len - (words - 1)) / words
syllables = avgWordLen / 3  /* guesstimate! */

gradeLevel = (0.39 * words) + (11.8 * syllables) - 15.59

SAY
SAY "Words:           " Format(words, 3, 0)
SAY "Avg word length:" Format(avgWordLen, 3, 2)
SAY "Avg syllables:  " Format(syllables, 3, 2)
SAY
SAY "Grade level required is" Format(gradeLevel, , 2)
EXIT
```

```
[D:\]list0901
Enter a single sentence:
Incorporation of additional constraints requires analysis.

Words:             6
Avg word length:   8.83
Avg syllables:     2.94

Grade level required is 21.49

[D:\]list0901
Enter a single sentence:
Run, Dick, run!

Words:             3
Avg word length:   4.33
Avg syllables:     1.44

Grade level required is 2.62
```

The program in listing 9.1 uses the Flesch-Kincaid grade-level calculation to determine the grade level required to read an input sentence. The program determines the character and word lengths of the sentence. The average length of each word is calculated by dividing the character length by the number of words. This calculation subtracts `(words - 1)` from `len` to adjust for the spaces between words. The average number of syllables per word is estimated by dividing the average word length by three. Finally, the grade level is calculated, and the results are displayed.

Making Conversions

Converting data from one form to another is one of the common activities that programs must perform. You may need data to be all uppercase, to have leading and trailing spaces removed, or to have characters displayed as hexadecimal or decimal codes.

Using the *Translate* Function

The `Translate` function can perform a variety of conversions on strings. The simplest use of `Translate` is to convert a string to uppercase. For example,

```
newString = Translate("don't shout")
```

The value assigned to `newString` is `"DON'T SHOUT"`.

You can also use the `Translate` function to perform other conversions. For this purpose, you need to give `Translate` two conversion tables. The input table tells `Translate` which characters are to be converted, and the output table tells `Translate` what to convert those characters to. This example shows how the tables are used:

```
inputTbl = 'ABCDEF'
outputTbl = 'abcdef'
converted = Translate('COPACETIC', outputTbl, inputTbl)
```

The result that is assigned to `converted` is `cOPaceTIc`. As you can see from this example, the characters that aren't in the input table are copied to the result unchanged.

Creating tables of any size can be time consuming and tedious. You can use the `XRange` function to make this job a great deal easier. `XRange` creates a string that contains all values between and including a starting character value and an ending character value. The following example uses `XRange` and `Translate` to convert a string to lowercase:

```
inputTbl = XRange('A', 'Z')  /* all uppercase characters */
outputTbl = XRange('a', 'z') /* all lowercase characters */
lower = Translate('COPACETIC', outputTbl, inputTbl)
```

Syntax

The *Translate* Function

```
Translate( string [, tableo [, tablei [, pad]]] )
```

The `Translate` function returns *`string`* with each character either translated to another character or unchanged. The result string is always the same length as *`string`*.

The `Translate` function searches the input table, *`tablei`*, for each character in *`string`*. For each character found, the corresponding character in the output table, *`tableo`*, is

placed in the result. If a character from *string* is not found, the original character is used. If *tablei* contains duplicate characters, the first occurrence of a character is used.

When both translation tables are omitted, *string* is translated to uppercase. If *tablei* is omitted, it defaults to the full character set. If *tableo* is omitted, it defaults to an empty string and is padded with *pad* or truncated as necessary. The default value of *pad* is the space character.

Example 1

```
SAY Translate('this is a test')
```

Example 2

```
SAY Translate('This is a test', '-', ' ')
```

Example 3

```
SAY Translate('password', , , '*')
```

The program in listing 9.2 uses the `Translate` function to convert a text phone number (like 1-800-BUYMICE) to all digits.

Listing 9.2. Using the `Translate` function.

```
/* list0902.cmd */
SAY "Enter the phone number:"
PULL number

phoneLetters = 'ABCDEFGHIJKLMNOPRSTUVWXY'
phoneNumbers = '222333444555666777888999'

SAY number 'is' Translate(number, phoneNumbers, phoneLetters)

EXIT
```

```
[D:\]list0902
Enter the phone number:
1-800-3ibmos2
1-800-3IBMOS2 is 1-800-3426672
```

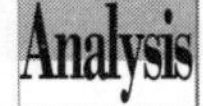

In listing 9.2, the `Translate` function converts a text-based telephone number to a numeric telephone number. The user is prompted for a number. An input table and an output table are created; they map from the letters on a telephone keypad to the numbers. The `Translate` function is called with the number the user entered, and the result is displayed.

Using the *Strip* Function

You may occasionally encounter strings that have extra space characters at the beginning or end. The `Strip` function is handy for removing these extra spaces.

`Strip` can remove leading spaces, trailing spaces, or spaces from both ends. `Strip` removes spaces from both ends by default. For example,

```
SAY Strip('   Spacy    ', 'Leading') 'string.'  /* "Spacy    string." */
SAY Strip('   Spacy    ', 'Trailing') 'string.' /* "   Spacy string." */
SAY Strip('   Spacy    ') 'string.'             /* "Spacy string."    */
```

The string displayed by each `SAY` instruction is shown in the comment on the right of each example. The preceding example could also use the `Both` option with the same result. You can shorten the words `Leading`, `Both`, and `Trailing` to just `L`, `B`, and `T`.

`Strip` takes an optional third parameter that determines what character (other than spaces) is removed. The full syntax for `Strip` is as follows:

```
result = Strip(string [, [option] [, character])
```

Using the *Reverse* Function

The `Reverse` function reverses the characters in a string. Although this function may sound rather strange, it can prove useful in a surprising number of ways. The most obvious use is to display palindromes:

```
word = 'live'
SAY 'Remember,' word 'is' Reverse(word) 'spelled backwards!'
```

The `Reverse` function can also help when you need to work primarily with the last characters in a string. You use `Reverse` to help solve some sorting and formatting problems in later lessons.

Decimal and Hexadecimal Conversions

Your computer stores all data, including characters, in numeric form. Each character is assigned a numeric code. The code used by almost all PCs is called the ASCII code, or the ASCII character set. (ASCII means American Standard Code for Information Interchange.)

You can type a character using its numeric code by pressing the Alt key while typing a number on the numeric keypad. For example, typing Alt+65 produces the letter *A*. The decimal code for *A* is 65.

Several built-in REXX functions enable you to convert from and to the numeric code. For instance, you can use the `D2C` function to convert from decimal to character, so you can display `H e l l o` this way:

```
SAY D2C(72) D2C(101) D2C(108) D2C(108) D2C(111)
```

REXX also includes built-in functions that convert from and to the hexadecimal value. Decimal is base 10 (10 digits are used: 0 through 9); hexadecimal is base 16 (16 digits are used: 0 through 9, A, B, C, D, E, and F). Hexadecimal is convenient because it represents all values for a single byte using no more than two digits.

For now, don't worry about trying to understand how hexadecimal works. The days when programmers had to read and understand hexadecimal are largely gone.

Table 9.1 shows the conversion functions, with examples of how they are used. The decimal functions convert only a single character (`C2D` can also convert a hexadecimal string); the hexadecimal functions can convert complete strings with one call.

Table 9.1. Conversion functions.

Conversion	Function	Example	Result
Character to decimal code	`C2D`	`C2D('a')`	`97`
Decimal code to character	`D2C`	`D2C(88)`	`X`
Character to hexadecimal	`C2X`	`C2X('a')`	`61`
Hexadecimal to character	`X2C`	`X2C('AA')`	`¬`

The program in listing 9.3 demonstrates using `C2D` and `C2X` to display the decimal and hexadecimal codes for a character.

Listing 9.3. Getting the decimal and hexadecimal codes for a character.

```
/* list0903.cmd */
PARSE ARG char
IF char = '' THEN
  DO
  SAY "Usage: list0903 <character>"
  EXIT
  END

SAY char "is decimal" C2D(char) "or hexadecimal" C2X(char)
EXIT
```

```
[D:\]list0903 r
r is decimal 114 or hexadecimal 72

[D:\]list0903 R
R is decimal 82 or hexadecimal 52

[D:\]list0903 1
1 is decimal 49 or hexadecimal 31

[D:\]list0903 @
@ is decimal 64 or hexadecimal 40
```

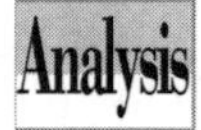

In listing 9.3, the character typed on the command line is converted to its decimal and hexadecimal values. This program displays a simple usage statement when the user doesn't type a letter on the command line.

Concatenation

Concatenation is an operation that joins two or more strings into a single string. You can use concatenation to join strings with a single space or with no intervening spaces.

The first concatenation operator is one you already know. When two strings are next to each other in a clause with one or more spaces in between, REXX joins the strings with a single space between them. A space between two strings is actually a special kind of concatenation operator. For example,

```
hello1 = 'Hello' 'world'
hello2 = 'Hello'          'world'
```

Both variables, `hello1` and `hello2`, have the value `Hello world`. REXX concatenates the strings `'Hello'` and `'world'` with a single space between them. Putting more than one space between the strings has no effect on the result.

Two operators concatenate strings without an intervening space:

- Abuttal. You achieve abuttal by putting two or more terms (a string, symbol, or function call—see the lesson for Day 4) next to each other without any intervening spaces. REXX must recognize the terms as separate, so abuttal does not work for two consecutive strings or symbols.
- The `||` (concatenation) operator.

The abuttal operator produces code that can sometimes seem confusing; the code can look messy and the intent of the abuttal may not always be obvious. Because the `||` operator makes the concatenation operation obvious, you may prefer this operator to abuttal.

Table 9.2 shows some examples of concatenation and the results from each operation.

Table 9.2. Examples of concatenation operations and their results.

Concatenation Operation	Result	Comment
`'REXX'    'program'`	`REXX program`	Intervening space
`'REXX''program'`	`REXX'program`	Abuttal creates a single string.
`'REXX' ¦¦ 'program'`	`REXXprogram`	Concatenation
`rexx = 'REXX'`		
`rexx'program'`	`REXXprogram`	Abuttal
rexx = 'REXX'		
`pgm = 'program'`		
`rexxpgm`	`REXXPGM`	Abuttal creates a new symbol.
`(1 ¦¦ 2) / 3`	`4`	Numbers are strings.

Using Relational Operators with Strings

The normal comparison operators ignore leading spaces when two strings are compared. The shorter string is also padded on the right with spaces until both strings are the same length. Thus, the following code evaluates to `1` (true):

```
'yes' = '   yes  '
```

REXX ignores the leading spaces in the right operand and begins by comparing `'yes'` to `'yes  '`. The left operand is shorter; it will be padded on the right with spaces so that both operands are the same length. The values that REXX actually compares will be `'yes  '` and `'yes  '`.

After ignoring leading spaces and padding the shorter operand, REXX compares the operands character by character from left to right. Uppercase and lowercase characters are not equal, so if you need to test an input value, you need to account for case. You can test for all possible combinations of uppercase and lowercase, as follows:

```
IF val = 'OK' ¦ val = 'ok' ¦ val = 'Ok' ¦ val = 'oK' THEN
  /* body of IF */
```

Or you can use the `Translate` function to force the input to uppercase and code only one comparison, as follows:

```
IF Translate(val) = 'OK' THEN
  /* body of IF */
```

If you want to test for an exact match, you need to use the strict comparison operators. Strict comparison forces REXX to compare the strings exactly as they are. For instance, when the previous example is tested for strict equality, as follows, the result is `0` (false):

```
'yes' == '   yes  '
```

The strict comparison operators look mostly like the regular comparison operators doubled. Table 9.3 lists each of the strict comparison operators and what operation each performs.

Table 9.3. The strict comparison operators.

Operation Performed	Operator	Example
Strictly equal	==	`a == b`
Not strictly equal	\== or ¬==	`a \== b`
Strictly greater than	>>	`a >> b`
Not strictly greater than	\>> or ¬>>	`a ¬>> b`
Strictly less than	<<	`a << b`
Not strictly less than	\<< or ¬<<	`a \<< b`
Strictly greater than or equal	>>=	`a >>= b`
Strictly less than or equal	<<=	`a <<= b`

Listing 9.4 displays the results from comparing two strings using regular comparison and strict comparison.

Listing 9.4. Strict and regular comparisons.

```
/* list0904.cmd */

SAY "Enter the first string:"
PARSE PULL str1
SAY "Enter the second string:"
PARSE PULL str2
```

```
SAY
SAY 'Comparing "' || str1 || '" to "' || str2 || '"'

equality = (str1 = str2)
strictEquality = (str1 == str2)
less = (str1 < str2)
strictLess = (str1 << str2)
greater = (str1 > str2)
strictGreater = (str1 >> str2)

SAY "Comparison    Regular   Strict"
SAY "equal        " Center(equality, 9) ,
    Center(strictEquality, 9)
SAY "less than    " Center(less, 9) ,
    Center(strictLess, 9)
SAY "greater than" Center(greater, 9) ,
    Center(strictGreater, 9)

EXIT
```


Output

```
[D:\]list0904
Enter the first string:
Rexx
Enter the second string:
REXX

Comparing "Rexx" to "REXX"
Comparison    Regular   Strict
equal            0         0
less than        0         0
greater than     1         1

[D:\]list0904
Enter the first string:
 REXX
Enter the second string:
  REXX

Comparing " REXX" to "  REXX"
Comparison    Regular   Strict
equal            1         0
less than        0         0
greater than     0         1

[D:\]list0904
Enter the first string:
  REXX
Enter the second string:
REXX

Comparing "  REXX" to "REXX"
Comparison    Regular   Strict
equal            1         0
less than        0         1
greater than     0         0
```

Analysis In listing 9.4, six different comparisons are done on two strings and the results are shown in a table. The results show how a regular comparison ignores leading spaces. The strict comparisons compare all characters in the strings, including any leading and trailing spaces. Strings that spell the same words but use different cases are not equal. Also, notice how the program uses concatenation to help show the exact contents of the two strings, including spaces.

A Last Word on Operator Precedence

By now, you've probably guessed that the concatenation operators and the strict comparison operators have a place in REXX's operator precedence hierarchy. Table 9.4 lists this hierarchy, which now includes all of the REXX operators.

Table 9.4. Precedence of all REXX operators.

Operator Group	Operators	Relative Precedence
Unary operators	`- + \ ¬`	Highest
Power	`**`	
Multiply and divide	`* / % //`	
Add and subtract	`+ -`	
Concatenation	`" " ¦¦`	abuttal
Comparisons	`= \= >< <> > < \> \< >= <=` `== \== >> << \>> \<< >>= <<=`	
And	`&`	
Or and Exclusive or	`¦ &&`	Lowest

Cutting Strings

Cutting strings is the opposite of concatenation. The result of cutting a string is called a substring. REXX supplies several built-in functions for getting substrings. One set of functions creates substrings based on characters; another set of functions creates substrings based on words.

Character-Based Substrings

The `SubStr` function gets a piece of a string based on position. You can, for instance, get a substring that begins with the fifth character and ends with the eighth character. For example,

```
SAY SubStr("I'm a frayed knot", 7, 4)
```

`SubStr` returns a substring beginning at the seventh character in the string and having a length of four characters. Thus, the string `fray` is displayed.

When you don't include length, the remainder of the string is included in the substring:

```
SAY SubStr("I'm a frayed knot", 14)
```

This example displays `knot`.

If the length is greater than the remaining length of the string, then the substring is padded on the right. The default padding character is a space, but you can use a different character. For example,

```
SAY SubStr("Fun with REX", 10, 6, 'X')
```

This example displays `REXXXX`.

The `Left` and `Right` functions are close relatives of the `SubStr` function. The `Left` function returns a substring that is the leftmost part of a string. The `Right` function returns a substring that is the rightmost part of a string. Both functions are passed a number that determines the length of the substring. If the number of characters requested is greater than the length of the original string, the substring is padded to the requested length with spaces on the left (when using the `Right` function) or the right (when using the `Left` function). Both `Left` and `Right` take an optional third parameter that is used to pad the resulting string. Here are some examples:

```
Left("the sinister right", 4)    /* returns 'the ' */
Right("the sinister right", 4)   /* returns 'ight' */
Left("Bill", 6)                  /* returns 'Bill  ' */
Right("Bill", 6)                 /* returns '  Bill' */
```

Word-Based Substrings

The `SubWord` function gets a substring beginning with a given word. `SubWord` is the word-based equivalent of the `SubStr` function. You must give `SubWord` a string and a starting word number. You can also tell `SubWord` how many words you want it to return. For example,

```
SAY SubWord("To be or not to be", 4)    /* displays 'not to be' */
SAY SubWord("To be or not to be", 2, 3) /* displays 'be or not' */
```

The Word function gets a single word from a string based on position. Word is equivalent to using SubWord with a length of one. The Word and SubWord calls in the following example return the same values:

```
SubWord("alpha beta gamma", 2, 1)
Word("alpha beta gamma", 2)
```

Using the Substring Functions

The program in listing 9.5 combines several of the functions introduced in this lesson in order to format dollar amounts. Solving this problem is more complex than you might first realize. The number needs to be formatted with two decimal places, the dollar part of the number needs to have commas inserted where necessary, and negative amounts must be handled properly.

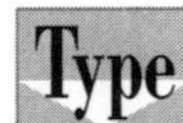

Listing 9.5. Using substrings and concatenation to format a number.

```
/* list0905.cmd */

SAY "Enter number to be formatted as dollars:"
PULL number

rawBucks = Format(number,, 2)
cents = Right(rawBucks, 3) /* decimal part plus decimal point */
rawDollars = Left(rawBucks, Length(rawBucks) - 3) /* remove cents */
fmtDollars = '$'

IF Left(rawDollars, 1) = '-' THEN /* negative? */
  DO
  fmtDollars = fmtDollars'-'
  rawDollars = Right(rawDollars, Length(rawDollars) - 1)
  END

IF Length(rawDollars) >= 7 THEN   /* millions */
  DO
  leadPiece = Length(rawDollars) - 6
  fmtDollars = fmtDollars ¦¦ Left(rawDollars, leadPiece)','
  rawDollars = Right(rawDollars, 6)
  END

IF Length(rawDollars) >= 4 THEN   /* thousands */
  DO
  leadPiece = Length(rawDollars) - 3
  fmtDollars = fmtDollars ¦¦ Left(rawDollars, leadPiece)','
  rawDollars = Right(rawDollars, 3)
  END

fmtDollars = fmtDollars ¦¦ rawDollars ¦¦ cents
```

```
SAY
SAY "The formatted amount is" fmtDollars

EXIT
```

```
[D:/]list0905
Enter number to be formatted as dollars:
-1000

The formatted amount is $-1,000.00

[D:\]list0905
Enter number to be formatted as dollars:
7500000

The formatted amount is $7,500,000.00

[D:\]list0905
Enter number to be formatted as dollars:
5

The formatted amount is $5.00
```

After prompting for and getting a number from the user, the program in listing 9.5 formats the number to begin with a dollar sign, have two decimal places, and have commas delineating the thousands.

Searching

You can use the `Pos` and `LastPos` functions to search a string for a given substring. The `Pos` function searches from left to right, and the `LastPos` function searches from right to left. Both functions return the position of the substring within the string being searched, or zero if the substring is not found.

The parameters for both functions are identical. The first parameter is the substring to search for, and the second parameter is the string to search. Look at the following examples:

```
Pos('\', "C:\OS2\APPS\klondike.exe")     /* returns 3  */
Pos('APPS', "C:\OS2\APPS\klondike.exe")  /* returns 8  */
Pos('HELP', "C:\OS2\APPS\klondike.exe")  /* returns 0  */
LastPos('\', "C:\OS2\APPS\klondike.exe") /* returns 12 */
LastPos('be', "To be or not to be.")     /* returns 17 */
```

You also can control the position at which the search begins by adding a third parameter that indicates the position to start the search. For example,

```
LastPos('be', "To be or not to be.", 15) /* returns 4 */
Pos('o', "To be or not to be.", 3)       /* returns 7 */
```

Parsing Strings

Perhaps the most powerful of REXX's string manipulation capabilities is the PARSE instruction. You learned about the PARSE instruction on Day 7. In that lesson, you used PARSE ARG and PARSE PULL to get data from a user.

This section adds PARSE VALUE and PARSE VAR to your repertoire. It also introduces the use of templates with PARSE. Both PARSE VAR and PARSE VALUE enable you to perform the equivalent of several SubStr function calls in a single step.

PARSE VAR parses the contents of a variable according to a template. The results of parsing are stored in one or more variables that are part of the template. Following is the syntax:

```
PARSE [UPPER] VAR variable template-list
```

PARSE VALUE parses the result of an expression. The results of parsing the expression are stored in one or more variables that are part of the template. The syntax for the PARSE VALUE instruction is as follows:

```
PARSE [UPPER] VALUE expression WITH template-list
```

The `variable` for PARSE VAR and the `expression` for PARSE VALUE are called the *source string*. The source string is the data to parse. Parsing divides the data in the source string into pieces and assigns those pieces to variables named in the `template-list`.

The `template-list` that you use with both of these instructions tells PARSE how you want the source string parsed. The simplest template is just a list of variable names:

```
variableNameOne variableNameTwo variableNameThree
```

This template tells PARSE to cut the source string into space-delimited words and assign the words to the variables. You used this type of template on Day 7 to split the user input into several words.

The template can include patterns, which tell PARSE how to split the source string. Following are the two general classes of patterns:

- *String patterns* match characters in the source string and tell PARSE where to cut the string.
- *Positional patterns* tell PARSE the character positions to cut the source string.

Here's an example of PARSE VAR using string patterns:

```
file = 'C:\OS2\BACKUP.EXE'
PARSE VAR file drive ':\' path '\' fileName '.' extension
```

The literal strings in this template are the string patterns. PARSE first divides the source string into substrings using the patterns. It then parses each substring into space-delimited words, as necessary.

- PARSE scans the source string `file` for the patterns. After this parsing step is complete, the substrings that will be used for the next parsing step are as follows:

  ```
  C
  OS2
  BACKUP
  EXE
  ```

- Each of the substrings is assigned to a variable so that the final result is the equivalent of the following assignments:

  ```
  drive = 'C'
  path = 'OS2'
  fileName = 'BACKUP'
  extension = 'EXE'
  ```

The characters in the string patterns (that is, `:\`, `\`, and `.`) are not stored in a variable. They are matched by the pattern and removed in the process of parsing the string into substrings.

You can combine patterns and space-delimited words in a single parse:

```
fullName = "Baggins, Bilbo Mr"
PARSE VAR fullName lastName ', ' firstName title
```

The source string is first split into two substrings by the pattern `', '`, and then the second substring `'Bilbo Mr'` is parsed into two words.

If there are more variables than substrings, the excess variables are assigned an empty string. In the following example, `title` is assigned an empty string:

```
fullName = "Baggins, Bilbo"
PARSE VAR fullName lastName ', ' firstName title
```

You can use a period in the template to indicate that you want to ignore the corresponding word from the source string. If, for instance, you need only the last name and the title in the previous example, you can use a template like this:

```
fullName = "Baggins, Bilbo Mr"
PARSE VAR fullName lastName ', ' . title
```

The template can also contain positional patterns. Positional patterns are numbers rather than literal strings. For example,

```
PARSE VALUE 'Rosebud' WITH var1 5 var2
```

Here, PARSE begins with the first character in the source string. The substring consisting of the first four characters (Rose) is assigned to var1, and the substring consisting of characters five through the end of the source string (bud) is assigned to var2.

Using positional patterns, you can back up to an earlier position in the source string. The following example displays Red Rose:

```
PARSE VALUE 'Rosebud' WITH first 5 1 second 2 4 third 5 7 fourth
SAY second || third || fourth first
```

As you can see from this example, more than one positional pattern can appear between variables. The first pattern determines the end of the substring assigned to the prior variable. The second pattern indicates where the beginning of the next substring will be located.

The pattern can specify a relative position by prefixing the positional number with + or -. The + moves the position forward, and the - moves the position backward. You can rewrite the preceding example using relative positional patterns:

```
PARSE VALUE 'Rosebud' WITH first +4 -4 second +1 +2 third +1 +2 fourth
SAY second || third || fourth first
```

You can combine the different types of patterns in a single template to handle almost any parsing situation that you can imagine.

Note: The PARSE ARG and PARSE PULL instructions also use templates in the same way as PARSE VAR and PARSE VALUE.

The program in listing 9.6 creates a copy of a file with a .BAK extension. The PARSE instruction removes the current file extension. PARSE also removes any quotation marks that may be surrounding the filename. The Reverse function simplifies parsing the file extension. If you run the program on an HPFS formatted hard drive, the filename may contain more than one period, and you want only the last one.

Listing 9.6. Creating a .BAK file.

```
/* list0906.cmd */

PARSE ARG file

IF file = '' | file = '/?' | file = '-?' THEN
  DO
  SAY "Use the BAK command to create a .BAK version of a file."
```

```
  SAY
  SAY "SYNTAX:  BAK [drive:][path]filename"
  SAY
  SAY "Where:"
  SAY "   [drive:][path]filename Specifies the file to copy to"
  SAY "                          a .BAK file."
  EXIT
  END

IF Left(file, 1) = '"' THEN
  PARSE VAR file '"' file '"' /* remove optional quotes */

backFile = Reverse(file)
IF Pos('.', backFile) <= 4 THEN /* check for extension */
  PARSE VAR backFile extension '.' backFile

backFile = Reverse(backFile) || '.bak'

IF Translate(file) = Translate(backFile) THEN /* uppercase compare */
  DO
  SAY 'File already has a .BAK extension.'
  EXIT
  END

'@copy' '"'file'"' '"'backFile'"' '> NUL'

IF rc >< 0 THEN
  SAY "Error making backup file."

EXIT
```

```
[D:\]bak /?
Use the BAK command to create a .BAK version of a file.

SYNTAX:  BAK [drive:][path]filename

Where:
  [drive:][path]filename Specifies the file to copy to
                         a .BAK file.

[D:\]bak list0903.cmd

[D:\]bak list0903.bak
File already has a .BAK extension.
```

In listing 9.6, a file is copied to a file of the same name with a .BAK extension. If the user entered the filename within double quotation marks, a `PARSE` instruction strips the quotation marks. The filename is reversed and stored in the `backFile` variable. If the name has an extension (that is, a period appears within the last four characters of the name), the extension is removed from the name by a `PARSE` instruction. The `backFile` is reversed again—it's now back to the correct order—and the .BAK extension is concatenated to it. The backup filename is compared to the original filename to ensure that the file isn't being copied to itself. If all is well, the file is copied to the backup.

This program is designed to handle both HPFS and FAT filenames. Both file systems allow periods in directory names, so the program must reverse the string to find the file extension (the last period in the filename). HPFS filenames can contain spaces, so the filenames must be quoted when they're passed to the OS/2 `COPY` command.

Summary

This lesson introduced several functions and operators that manipulate strings in a variety of ways. You learned how to get the length of a string in both words and characters. You saw how to perform various conversions on strings using the `Translate`, `Reverse`, and `Strip` functions. You also learned about character codes, and the lesson showed how to convert between characters and their hexadecimal or decimal codes.

This lesson showed you how to use the space, abuttal, and `¦¦` operators to concatenate strings. You learned how REXX compares strings, and the strict comparison operators were introduced. Several functions for getting a substring were covered, including the `SubStr`, `Left`, and `Right` functions for character substrings and the `SubWord` and `Word` functions for word substrings.

The lesson also presented more information on using the `PARSE` instruction. You saw how `PARSE` uses a template to control the parsing process. Finally, you learned how to use string patterns and positional patterns to create templates to perform a variety of parsing actions.

Q&A

Q How can I display the binary value of a character?

A REXX provides a built-in function to convert a hexadecimal value to a binary value: the `X2B` function. Because there is no function to go directly from a character to a binary representation, you must perform the conversion in two steps. First, use `C2X` to convert to hexadecimal; then use `X2B` to convert to binary. You should look in Appendix H and browse the `REXX Information` book in the `Information` folder on your OS/2 desktop for additional conversion functions that aren't covered in this lesson.

Workshop

The Workshop provides quiz questions to help strengthen your understanding of the material covered and exercises to provide you with experience in using what you've learned.

Quiz

1. What function determines how many characters are in a string?
2. What does the `WordLength` function do?
3. Name two ways to uppercase a string.
4. What function do you use to get the decimal code for the letter *m*?
5. What is abuttal?
6. How does the `||` operator differ from the space operator?
7. How is strict comparison different from regular comparison?
8. What does the `SubStr` function do?
9. What function should you use to find the last occurrence of a comma in a string?
10. What is the effect of a pattern in a `PARSE` template?

Exercises

1. What is the result of each of the following expressions?

    a. `'moon' || 'light'`
    b. `val = 'hope'; val'chest'`
    c. `'This'      'time'      'tomorrow'`
    d. `"This         time " || 'tomorrow'`

2. Assume that this assignment has been executed:

    ```
    str = "/* This, is a test! */"
    ```

    What is assigned to each of the variables in the following expressions?

    a. `PARSE UPPER VAR str saveIt`
    b. `PARSE VAR str a b c`

c. `PARSE VALUE Reverse(str) WITH a b`
d. `PARSE VAR str a ', ' b c`
e. `PARSE VAR str a '* ' b '! *' c`
f. `PARSE VAR str a 'is' b`
g. `PARSE VAR str 4 a +15 2 b +19`

3. Design and write a program that displays your name and address right-justified on the screen.

4. Design and write a program that parses a date into its respective month, day, and year values. Assume that the user will always enter the date with dashes as separators—for example, `12-25-79`. Do not assume that the month and day numbers will always be two digits. Your program should properly parse a date in the form `3-1-85`.

5. Design and write a program that accepts a decimal character code as input and displays the corresponding character as output.

6. The following program contains errors. Find and fix the errors.

```
/* Ex9-6.cmd
 * Create a skeletal REXX program.
 */

PARSE ARG pgmName '"' author '"' .

IF pgmName = '' & author = '' THEN
  DO
  SAY "Use SKEL to create a REXX program skeleton."
  SAY
  SAY 'SYNTAX:  SKEL programname "authorname"'
  EXIT
  END

progLine = Left('Program:', 7) ¦¦ pgmName
authLine = Left('Author:', 11) ¦¦ author
dateLine = Left('Created:', 11) ¦¦ Date()

SAY '/* ' ¦¦ D2C(218) ¦¦ Copies(D2C(196), 70) ¦¦ D2C(191)
SAY ' * ' ¦¦ D2C(179) progLine ¦¦ D2C(179)
SAY ' * ' ¦¦ D2C(179) authLine ¦¦ D2C(179)
SAY ' * ' ¦¦ D2C(179) dateLine ¦¦ D2C(179)
```

```
SAY ' * ' ¦¦ D2C(192) ¦¦ Copies(D2C(196), 70) ¦¦ D2C(217)
SAY ' */'
SAY
SAY
SAY 'EXIT'

EXIT
```

Testing and Debugging

WEEK
2

Testing and debugging are activities that occupy, on average, about half of a programmer's time. Even the simplest one-line program needs to be tested—and debugged if an error is discovered. Today you learn the following:

- The purpose of testing
- How to create useful tests
- The process of debugging a program
- How to use the `TRACE` instruction as an aid to debugging
- How to trap errors using the `SIGNAL` instruction
- How to use PMREXX as a debugging environment

Techniques and Tools

Anyone who has used a computer for more than a couple of weeks has encountered the term *bug*. Many users and even some programmers believe that bugs "just happen." In almost all cases, bugs are caused by programmers! Because of this misconception, we use the terms *error* and *program defect* instead of bug.

We use the words *testing* and *debugging* throughout this lesson. These words are used with rather precise meanings:

- *Testing* is the process of executing a program with the intention of finding errors.
- *Debugging* is the process of diagnosing the exact nature of a known error and then correcting that error.

Testing encompasses all the tools and techniques that you use to discover errors in a program. Debugging requires a different set of tools and techniques to find the cause of an error and determine how you can fix the error.

Program testing is, more than anything else, an intellectual activity. The primary testing tool that you have is your own analytical ability. You must do detective work, think about how the program works, and try different approaches to find any errors.

Once you find the errors, you can then begin debugging. Sometimes the source of an error is obvious. Other times you need to do more detective work to find the cause of an error. REXX provides tools to help you debug your programs. You should become comfortable with your debugging tools before you need them. Debugging a program is sometimes frustrating, and the additional frustration of learning a new tool at the same time can be overwhelming.

Testing

The first law of testing is: *every program contains defects.*

Many novice programmers assume that the reason they need to test a program is to prove that the program works. This approach can be ego-inflating, but it can also produce embarrassing and humbling results the first time someone else uses the program.

A good test case is one that has a very good chance of discovering a previously unknown defect. The worst test case is one that is designed to prove that a program has no defects.

Exhaustive testing is impossible. Even simple programs can require thousands of tests to check every possibility. Instead of trying to devise an exhaustive set of tests, look in the program for code that is complex or hard to understand. Create test cases that exercise that code first.

You should keep in mind that it's very hard to do a good job of testing your own programs. When you design and write a program, you work from a set of assumptions. Those assumptions are fertile ground for testing, but because they are *your* assumptions, they may be hard to recognize. Test your code, but whenever possible, have someone else test your code, too.

Finally, testing isn't the most effective way to find program defects. The most effective ways to improve code quality require two or three other programmers, a few hours of training, and lots of commitment from everyone involved. This lesson can teach you only some basic testing techniques. If you're interested in learning more than that, you should visit your local library or bookstore and pick up a couple books on software quality assurance and the software development process.

Fertile Areas for Testing

Some types of tests produce better results (that is, discover more defects) than others. At a minimum, your tests should answer each of these questions:

- Does the program accept valid input data? Try several different valid inputs.
- Is the program output valid and formatted correctly? Inspect the program's output to ensure that the program is performing calculations correctly and that the results are being presented properly.
- Does the program refuse to accept invalid input data? What happens when you enter no data, or too much data? Does the program accept letters when only numbers should be allowed?

- ☐ Does the program work correctly with boundary conditions? *Boundary conditions* are values that are at the edge of a program's operating tolerances. For example, if a program accepts one to fifty values, the boundary conditions are one value and fifty values. For this example, you should try testing with zero, one, fifty, and fifty-one values.

Finally, when you think you've found and fixed a defect, run your tests again. Occasionally, a change that fixes an error introduces another error.

DO	DON'T

DO test your programs to find the defects.

DON'T test your programs to prove they run correctly.

DO pay special attention to testing the more complex parts of a program.

The *TRACE* Instruction

When you're trying to find the cause of a bug, being able to trace the actions and results of each line of REXX code is useful. The `TRACE` instruction controls the tracing action of the REXX interpreter. `TRACE` has a terse syntax, which is an advantage, because it is not uncommon to enter `TRACE` instructions manually during an interactive debugging session.

You control what is traced by following the `TRACE` keyword with an action. The `TRACE` actions are shown in table 10.1. Although the actions are shown as full words, you can use just the first letter of the action name. For example, the following two `TRACE` clauses are equivalent:

```
TRACE Results
TRACE R
```

Table 10.1. The `TRACE` actions.

Action	Description
`All`	Traces (that is, displays) all clauses before execution
`Commands`	Traces all commands before execution. Any nonzero (error) return code from the command is displayed.

Action	Description
`Error`	After execution, traces commands that result in an error or failure
`Failure`	After execution, traces commands that result in a failure (that is, the command cannot be found or cannot be executed)
`Intermediates`	Traces all clauses before execution; traces intermediate results of expression evaluation
`Labels`	Traces labels passed during execution
`Normal`	Traces any failing command after execution (same as `Failure`)
`Off`	Nothing is traced.
`Results`	Traces all clauses before execution; traces final results of expression evaluation and `PULL`, `PARSE`, and `ARG` statements

Tip: Putting the action name in quotation marks is a good idea, just in case the same word has been used as a variable name in the program.

The recommended `TRACE` action for most debugging is `Results`. Listing 10.1 shows the effect of using the `TRACE R` instruction in a short program.

Type

Listing 10.1. Using the `TRACE Results` instruction.

```
/* list1001.cmd */
TRACE 'R'
SAY "Enter three values:"
PARSE PULL a . b
c = a || b
d = 25 * 3
EXIT
```

```
[D:\]list1001
     3 *-*   Say 'Enter three values:';
       >>>     "Enter three values:"
Enter three values:
     4 *-*   Parse Pull a . b;
1 2 3
       >>>     "1"
       >.>     "2"
       >>>     "3"
```

```
5 *-*   c = a || b;
  >>>     "13"
6 *-*   d = 25 * 3;
  >>>     "75"
7 *-*   Exit;
```

In listing 10.1, the `TRACE Results` instruction traces the execution of a simple REXX program. The output shows each clause just prior to execution and the result of each clause immediately after it has executed.

All of the output from the `TRACE` instruction is prefixed by three characters that indicate the source or meaning of the traced output (see table 10.2).

Table 10.2. Meaning of `TRACE` output prefixes.

Prefix	Meaning
`*-*`	Source clause from the program
`+++`	A trace message. Trace messages include command error return codes, the interactive debug prompt message, and clauses displayed after a syntax error.
`>.>`	The value assigned to a placeholder (that is, a period) during parsing
`>>>`	The result of an expression, the value assigned to a variable by `PARSE`, or the return value from a function
`>C>`	(`TRACE Intermediates`) A traced compound (or stem) variable (stem variables are covered on Day 12)
`>F>`	(`TRACE Intermediates`) The traced result of a function call
`>L>`	(`TRACE Intermediates`) A traced literal
`>O>`	(`TRACE Intermediates`) The traced result of an operation
`>P>`	(`TRACE Intermediates`) The traced result of a prefix operation
`>V>`	(`TRACE Intermediates`) The traced contents of a variable

The normal action of `TRACE` is to trace the running program without any intervention from the programmer. If you want to single-step through a program or interactively display and change variables, you need to use the prefix `?` option. The following instruction turns on interactive debug, with results traced:

```
TRACE ?R
```

When interactive debugging is on, TRACE halts the program after each clause. While the program is halted, you can enter one or more REXX clauses, or you can press Enter to execute the next clause in the program. You can also use = to run the last clause again.

The prefix ? acts like an on-off switch for the interactive debug mode. If interactive debug is active, you can turn it off using a TRACE instruction with a prefix ? or by entering TRACE Off.

If you want to run several clauses without interactively tracing them, you can enter a number following the TRACE instruction. The number tells TRACE to suspend interactive debug for that many clauses. Tracing information is still displayed. If you want TRACE to suspend interactive debug for the next three clauses, you use the following:

```
TRACE 3
```

You can shut off both interactive debug and tracing for a number of clauses by using a negative number. To stop tracing for the next 15 clauses, you enter the following:

```
TRACE -15
```

Listing 10.2 is essentially the same program as listing 10.1, except that the TRACE uses interactive debugging and the Intermediates action. Notice how the program is interactively controlled in the output sample.

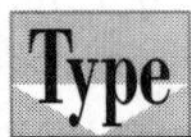

Listing 10.2. Interactive debugging using the TRACE instruction.

```
/* list1002.cmd */
TRACE '?I'
SAY "Enter three values:"
PARSE PULL a . b
c = a || b
d = 25 * 3
EXIT
```

```
[D:\]list1002
     3 *-*   Say 'Enter three values:';
       >L>     "Enter three values:"
       >>>     "Enter three values:"
Enter three values:
```

Enter pressed

```
       +++   Interactive trace. "Trace Off" to end debug, ENTER to Continue.

     4 *-*   Parse Pull a . b;
5 3 1000
       >>>     "5"
       >.>     "3"
       >>>     "1000"
```

Enter pressed

```
     5 *-*   c = a || b;
       >V>     "5"
       >V>     "1000"
       >O>     "51000"
       >>>     "51000"
SAY a
5
SAY b
1000
TRACE 'R'
```

Enter pressed

```
     6 *-*   d = 25 * 3;
       >>>     "75"
```

Enter pressed

```
     7 *-*   Exit;
```

In listing 10.2, an interactive debug session is started using the prefix `?` with the `TRACE` instruction. The `Intermediates` action causes more data to be traced than the `Results` action used in listing 10.1. Two variables are interactively displayed during the debug session, and the tracing action is changed to `Results`.

You should run the program in listing 10.2 several times and do different things during each interactive debug session to see the effect of different actions. Try assigning a different value to `a` or `b` before the assignment to `c`. Try different `TRACE` actions to determine how the traced information changes for each action. You should also try using the numeric options with `TRACE` to see what their effects are.

Don't use `TRACE` for debugging alone. Running a program using interactive debug can be very instructive when you don't understand how the program works. Even when you do think you understand how a program works, watching each clause execute can often produce some surprises.

Trapping Errors with *SIGNAL*

You can use a special form of the `SIGNAL` instruction to trap error conditions within a REXX program. The syntax for this form of `SIGNAL` is as follows:

```
SIGNAL ON condition-name [NAME trapname]
SIGNAL OFF condition-name
```

The *`condition-name`* indicates the condition to be trapped. Conditions are raised in response to specific events (see table 10.3). A condition trap is either enabled (`ON`) or disabled (`OFF`). REXX disables all condition traps by default.

When the condition occurs and the condition trap is enabled, REXX transfers control to a label matching *condition-name*, or *trapname* if the optional NAME *trapname* is used.

Table 10.3. Conditions and corresponding events.

Condition	Event Raising the Condition
`Error`	A command returns an error. If the `Failure` condition is not set, the `Error` condition also traps that event.
`Failure`	A command indicates a failure condition on return.
`Halt`	An attempt is made to interrupt and terminate the program. This condition is normally raised when the user presses Ctrl+Break. However, the event is not trapped if Ctrl+Break is pressed while a command or other external function is running.
`NotReady`	An error occurred during an input or output operation. Use of the `NotReady` condition is covered on Day 15.
`NoValue`	An uninitialized variable is used in an expression as the name following `PARSE VAR` or as a variable reference in a parsing template.
`Syntax`	A language-processing error. This condition includes true syntax errors as well as an attempt to perform an arithmetic operation on a nonnumeric value.

You can use any of several predefined variables and functions to determine the source and cause of a condition trap. When an `Error` or `Failure` condition is trapped, the predefined variable `rc` is set to the command return code. When a `Syntax` condition is trapped, `rc` contains the syntax error number.

The `ErrorText` function returns the text for a given REXX error number. You can use `ErrorText` with `rc` to display the REXX error message when a `Syntax` condition is trapped. For example,

```
SAY ErrorText(rc)
```

The predefined variable `sigl` contains the line number of the clause that was executing when the condition was raised. You can use `sigl` to help find the line in your program that is causing problems.

The SourceLine function can either return the number of lines in the program or the text on a given line in the program. The syntax for SourceLine is as follows:

```
SourceLine([number])
```

The parameter *number* is the line number that you want to retrieve. In a condition trap, you can use sigl with SourceLine to get the text for the program line that caused the trap. For example,

```
SAY 'Error in line' sigl || ':' SourceLine(sigl)
```

The Condition function returns information about the current trapped condition. This function is most useful when you have several conditions that trap to the same location in the program. For example, the beginning of your program might contain the following:

```
SIGNAL ON Syntax
SIGNAL ON Halt
SIGNAL ON Error
```

You then put the code for the trapped conditions at the end of your program (the C option for Condition is explained in table 10.4):

```
Syntax:
Halt:
Error:
SAY Condition('C') "was raised!"
```

Instead of just displaying the condition, you can use the Condition function to test for which condition was raised. Then your code can respond differently for each condition trap. The benefit to having all conditions trap to one common location is that each trap usually has a common core of code. You can deal with the slight variations using a SELECT instruction, and you don't need to duplicate the common code across three or more condition traps.

The Condition function can return information other than the condition name. Table 10.4 lists the valid options for Condition. You can use the first character of an option in place of the entire word.

Table 10.4. Options for the Condition function.

Condition Option	Condition Returns
Condition	The name of the current trapped condition
Description	A description of the current trapped condition. If no description is available, an empty string is returned.

`Instruction`	Either `CALL` or `SIGNAL`—the instruction that enabled the current trap condition. Use of the `CALL` instruction with condition traps is covered on Day 14.
`Status`	The status of the current trapped condition (`ON`, `OFF`, or `DELAY`)

Listing 10.3 demonstrates trapping a syntax error using the `SIGNAL` instruction. Notice how the `TRACE` instruction is followed by a `NOP` instruction. The `NOP` allows `TRACE` to pause without immediately falling into the `EXIT` instruction and exiting the program.

10

Type

Listing 10.3. Using `SIGNAL` to trap a syntax error.

```
/* list1003.cmd */
SIGNAL ON Syntax

SAY "This demonstrates trapping a syntax error."
SAY "Please enter an invalid number:"
PULL val
val = val + 1

EXIT

Syntax:
  SAY "Syntax error" rc "occurred on line" sigl":"
  SAY ErrorText(rc)
  SAY SourceLine(sigl)
  SAY
  TRACE ?R; NOP;
  EXIT
```

```
[D:\]list1002
This demonstrates trapping a syntax error.
Please enter an invalid number:
No way!
Bad arithmetic conversion occurred on line 7:
val = val + 1

    15 *-*   Nop;
       +++   Interactive trace. "Trace Off" to end debug, ENTER to Continue.
SAY val
NO WAY!

    16 *-*   Exit;
```

The program in listing 10.3 sets a trap for `Syntax` and then prompts for an invalid number. When the user enters an invalid number in the following arithmetic expression, REXX raises the `Syntax` condition. Control is transferred to the code beginning at the `Syntax` label. A message is displayed, showing the syntax error, the line number of the error, and the line of code in which the error occurred. Interactive tracing is then turned on so that the user can determine the exact cause of the error.

Syntax Trapping as a Programming Aid

The first kind of program error that you usually encounter is a syntax error. The normal process of finding and fixing syntax errors is as follows:

1. Run the program and get a syntax error message.
2. Examine the syntax error message for the line in error.
3. Load the program in an editor and find the line in error.
4. Fix the error.

Because you can trap syntax errors in your program, you can make your program help you find and fix syntax errors. Your program can actually load itself into the editor and position the cursor on the line that contains the syntax error.

First, the program must get its own filename to tell the editor which file to edit. The `PARSE SOURCE` instruction gets the operating system, environment, and program filename. Here's an example:

```
PARSE SOURCE os environ pgmName
```

When REXX is running under OS/2, the `os` variable is set to `OS/2`. The `environ` variable is `COMMAND` when the program is run from an OS/2 command prompt. The `pgmName` variable is the full pathname of the program file. (Because all you need is the program name, you could use `PARSE SOURCE . . pgmName`.)

The program in listing 10.4 starts the Enhanced Editor whenever a syntax error is encountered. You can use this program as a template for your own programs—just remember to remove the line that deliberately creates a syntax error!

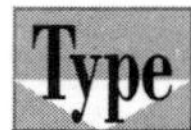

Listing 10.4. Automatically starting an editor on a syntax error.

```
/* list1004.cmd */
SIGNAL ON Syntax

PARSE PUUL val
EXIT

Syntax:
```

```
PARSE SOURCE os environ pgmName
errorMsg = "'messagebox" ErrorText(rc)"'"
errorLine = "'" || sigl || "'"
"EPM" pgmName errorLine errorMsg
EXIT
```

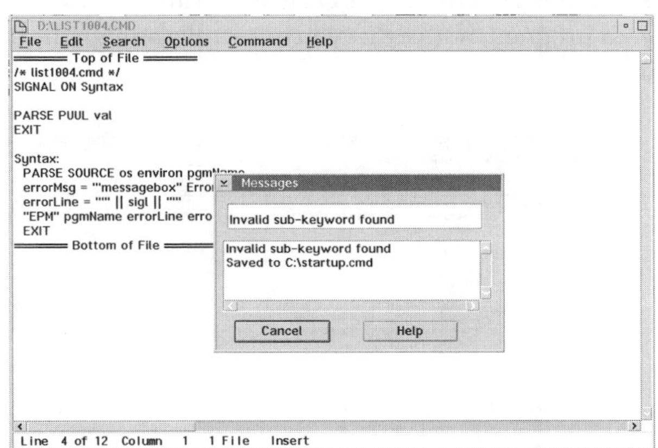

Figure 10.1. *The result of running the program in listing 10.4.*

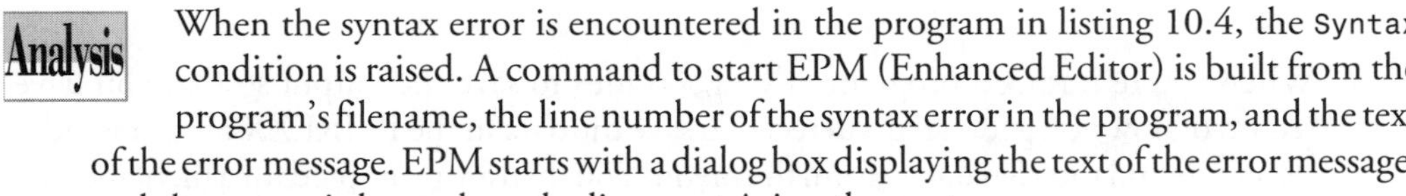

When the syntax error is encountered in the program in listing 10.4, the `Syntax` condition is raised. A command to start EPM (Enhanced Editor) is built from the program's filename, the line number of the syntax error in the program, and the text of the error message. EPM starts with a dialog box displaying the text of the error message, and the cursor is located on the line containing the syntax error.

Using PMREXX

The PMREXX program is designed to run a REXX program interactively in the OS/2 PM environment. From PMREXX, you can scroll through the output of a REXX program, interactively debug a program, save the output of a program to a file, and copy and paste the output and input of a program.

To start PMREXX, start an OS/2 command prompt and type **`PMREXX`** ***`program-name`***. The *`program-name`* is the name of any REXX program that you want to run. PMREXX opens an OS/2 window and displays the output of the REXX program within the window.

If your program contains a `TRACE` instruction, tracing data appears in the PMREXX window (see fig. 10.2). You can also set interactive trace on from the menu, as follows:

1. Select Options from the menu.
2. Select Interactive trace on. A check mark should appear next to the menu item.

Once interactive tracing has started, you can control tracing using the Action menu. You can trace the next clause, rerun the last clause, or turn tracing off from this menu. Also, as you trace your program, notice that you can scroll through the trace information using the scroll bar.

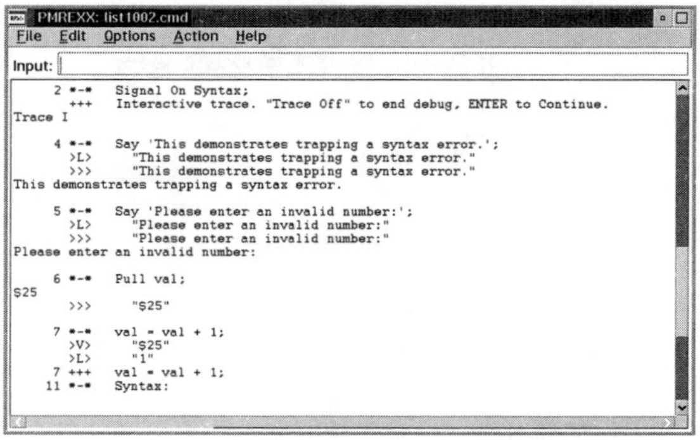

```
PMREXX: list1002.cmd
File  Edit  Options  Action  Help
Input:
     2 *-*   Signal On Syntax;
       +++   Interactive trace. "Trace Off" to end debug, ENTER to Continue.
Trace I

     4 *-*   Say 'This demonstrates trapping a syntax error.';
       >L>     "This demonstrates trapping a syntax error."
       >>>     "This demonstrates trapping a syntax error."
This demonstrates trapping a syntax error.

     5 *-*   Say 'Please enter an invalid number:';
       >L>     "Please enter an invalid number:"
       >>>     "Please enter an invalid number:"
Please enter an invalid number:

     6 *-*   Pull val;
$25
       >>>     "$25"

     7 *-*   val = val + 1;
       >V>     "$25"
       >L>     "1"
     7 +++   val = val + 1;
    11 *-*   Syntax:
```

Figure 10.2. *Tracing using the PMREXX program.*

When you're testing a program, it's a good idea to save the output so that you have a record of how you generated a defect. To save the data in the PMREXX output window, select File and then Save as… from the menu. You then are prompted for a filename. After you save the output, you can update the file by selecting File and then Save. The output filename will appear on the menu next to the word Save.

Summary

This lesson discussed testing and debugging and some of the issues involved in ensuring that a program works correctly. You learned that the purpose of testing is to discover program defects; the purpose of debugging is to fix program defects.

This lesson also introduced some tools to help debug a program. You saw how you can use the `TRACE` instruction to trace clauses and different types of data in a program. You can also use the `TRACE` instruction to interactively debug a program.

Error conditions are trapped using the `SIGNAL ON` instruction. You learned how to trap several types of conditions and how to gather and display information about a condition trap.

Finally, the lesson showed you how to use PMREXX as a REXX debugging environment. PMREXX enables you to save the output from a REXX program and paste data from other programs.

Q&A

Q Is there a way to start an interactive debug session without editing my program and adding a `TRACE` instruction?

A When REXX starts running a program, it always checks for the `RXTRACE` OS/2 environment variable. When `RXTRACE` is set to `ON`, REXX runs the program as though the first line were `TRACE '?R'`. To start an interactive debug without editing your program, type the following at the OS/2 command prompt:

```
SET RXTRACE=ON
```

Run and debug your program. When you're finished, you should set `RXTRACE` to `OFF` so that other REXX programs will run normally.

Q Every time I fix one error, another one appears in the same area. What's the best way to *really* fix this program?

A This problem is almost certainly caused by an error in the design of the program. No amount of code debugging is going to fix the program. Research has shown that it almost always takes less time to redesign and recode than it does to fix an error-infested block of code. It's time to step back from the details of the code and think about the design again.

Workshop

The Workshop provides quiz questions to help strengthen your understanding of the material covered and exercises to provide you with experience in using what you've learned.

Quiz

1. What is the purpose of testing?
2. What is the purpose of debugging?
3. What is a good test case?
4. What does `TRACE Results` do?

5. How can you turn on the interactive debug mode?
6. What does the `SIGNAL ON` instruction do?
7. What instruction do you use to trap an error from an OS/2 `dir` command?
8. What is the predefined variable `sigl` used for?
9. How can you display the text for a REXX error message?
10. What does the `SourceLine` function do?

Exercises

1. Enter and run the following program. Modify it so that it automatically loads into your editor when the syntax error is encountered.

```
/* Ex10-1.cmd */
SAY "Enter your first and last name:"
PARSE PULL firstName lastName
fullName = lastName ¦ ',' firstName
SAY fullName
EXIT
```

2. Using the following program as a base, add the code necessary to trap the `Halt` condition. When the condition is trapped, have the program display the following message and exit:

```
User requested halt. Exiting.
```

Test your program by pressing Ctrl+Break. **Note:** You may need to press Enter after pressing Ctrl+Break. This is a side effect of using the `PARSE PULL` instruction.

```
/* Ex10-2.cmd */
SAY 'Enter some text:'
PARSE PULL text
SAY 'You entered:' text
EXIT
```

3. The following program tests a string to see whether it is a palindrome (that is, a word that spells the same thing forward and backward). Spaces and case are ignored when determining whether a given text is a palindrome. This program contains several errors. Test and debug the program using the tools that you've

learned about in this lesson. (To get started, two valid inputs are "Poor Dan is in a droop" and "Madam, I'm Adam.")

```
/* Ex10-3.cmd */

SAY 'What is the potential palindrome?'
PARSE PULL palindrome

forwards = Translate(Space(palindrome, 0))
forwards = Reverse(forwards)
backwards = Translate(forwards, ",'", "',")

IF forwards = backwards THEN
  SAY '"'palindrome'" is a palindrome'
ELSE
  SAY '"'palindrome'" is not a palindrome'

EXIT
```

Using Loops

WEEK
2

In REXX, you use loops to create programs that can perform the same actions more than once. Today you learn the following:

- ☐ What a loop is
- ☐ How to use loops for counting
- ☐ How to create loops that exit based on a condition
- ☐ What an infinite loop is and how to create one
- ☐ How to exit loops and how to go to the next repetition of a loop

Repeating a Group of Instructions

You know that the `DO` and `END` instructions are used to group together several clauses. The clauses in the group are executed once. For example,

```
DO
  val = val + 1
  SAY val
END
```

You also use the `DO` and `END` instructions to define a *loop*, or a block of instructions that is executed more than once. The act of repeatedly executing a group of instructions is called *iteration.*

Types of Loops

Figure 11.1 graphically depicts a simple loop. Notice how a loop creates something very much like a circle in the code.

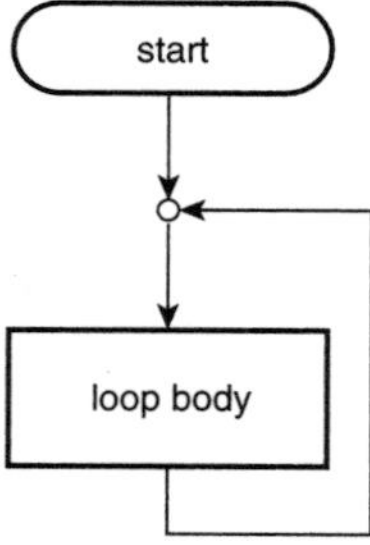

Figure 11.1. *A simple loop.*

Most loops are controlled by a condition that is used to determine when the loop is exited. The most common form of loop tests the condition at the beginning of each iteration. This type of loop is called a *do-while* loop because the loop is executed while the condition is true (see fig. 11.2).

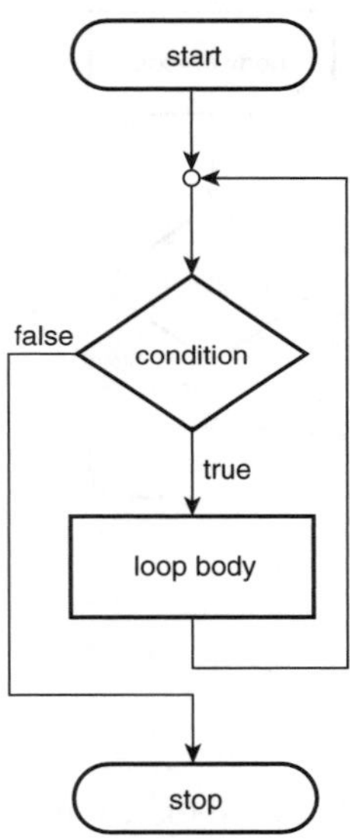

Figure 11.2. *A do-while loop.*

Another form of loop tests the condition at the end of each iteration. This type of loop is called a *do-until* loop because the loop is executed until the condition is true (see fig. 11.3).

Some programmers call do-until loops *one-trip* loops because the code in the loop is always executed at least once—the program makes at least one trip through the loop. The do-while loop is sometimes called a *zero-trip* loop because the program may not execute the loop at all. If you examine figures 11.2 and 11.3, you should be able to see why the code may not be executed in a do-while loop.

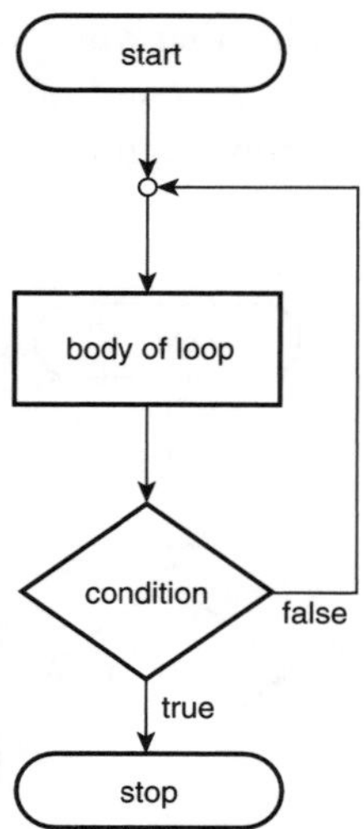

Figure 11.3. *A do-until loop.*

A Basic Loop

The first kind of REXX loop that we'll look at uses an expression to indicate the number of iterations for the loop. The expression must evaluate to a positive whole number; it isn't possible to loop a negative or fractional number of times.

The expression immediately follows the `DO` keyword. Here's an example:

```
DO 3
  SAY 'Again!'
END
```

Here, the digit `3` tells `DO` how many times to execute the code within the loop. The result of executing this loop is as follows:

```
Again!
Again!
Again!
```

The expression can be based on a variable. Using a variable allows the number of iterations to be changed by the user or by other conditions in the program. Here's an example of allowing the user to control the number of iterations:

```
PULL number
DO number
  SAY 'Again!'
END
```

This loop is best for situations when the user knows how many times he or she wants an action repeated. One example is getting the sum or average of a list of numbers (see listing 11.1). If the user knows how long the list is, the program can get the length of the list and then prompt for each value.

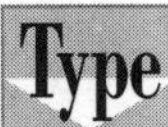

Listing 11.1. Looping a variable number of times.

```
/* list1101.cmd */
SAY "How many numbers do you want to average?"
PULL howMany
total = 0

DO howMany
  SAY "Enter a number:"
  PULL number
  total = total + number
END

SAY "Average =" (total / howMany)
EXIT
```

11

```
[D:\]list1101
How many numbers do you want to average?
4
Enter a number:
35
Enter a number:
40
Enter a number:
27
Enter a number:
29
Average = 32.75
```

In listing 11.1, the user is prompted for how many numbers are to be averaged. The number that the user enters sets the number of iterations for the loop. The program loops, prompting for each number. The values entered are added to the total on each pass through the loop. When the loop ends, the average of the numbers is displayed.

Using *WHILE* and *UNTIL*

REXX directly implements both the do-while and do-until forms of loops using the `DO WHILE` and `DO UNTIL` instructions.

The `WHILE` loop evaluates its condition at the top of the loop. If the condition is false the first time, the loop isn't executed. Otherwise, the loop is executed until the condition is false. Here's an example of a `DO WHILE` loop:

```
DO WHILE count < 100
  count = count + count
END
```

Here, this loop is executed as long as count is less than 100.

The UNTIL loop evaluates its condition at the bottom of the loop. The loop executes once before the condition is evaluated. Otherwise, the loop executes until the condition is true. Here's an example of a DO UNTIL loop:

```
DO UNTIL count >= 100
  count = count + count
END
```

Here, this loop is executed until count is greater than or equal to 100. Except for the case where count isn't less than 100 when the loop is first executed, the effect of this loop is the same as the previous example using WHILE. If count is not less than 100 when the UNTIL loop is first executed, count is doubled once before being tested.

The program in listing 11.2 uses the DO UNTIL instruction to help implement a checkbook balancing program.

Listing 11.2. A checkbook balancing program.

```
/* list1102.cmd */
SAY "Checkbook Balancing Program"
SAY
SAY "Enter starting balance:"
PULL balance
SAY "Enter transactions as:  code amount"
SAY "Codes are:  C - check, D - deposit, O - other"
SAY "Enter a blank line to end the program."
SAY

DO UNTIL code = ''
  SAY Right('Balance:', 20) '$'Format(balance,, 2)
  PARSE UPPER PULL code amount
  SELECT
  WHEN code = 'C' THEN
    balance = balance - amount
  WHEN code = 'D' THEN
    balance = balance + amount
  WHEN code = 'O' THEN
    balance = balance - amount
  OTHERWISE
    NOP;
  END
END

EXIT
```

```
[D:\]list1102
Checkbook Balancing Program

Enter starting balance:
100
Enter transactions as:  code amount
Codes are:  C - check, D - deposit, O - other
Enter a blank line to end the program.

            Balance: $100.00
c 15.35
            Balance: $84.65
c 4.25
            Balance: $80.40
o 3.00
            Balance: $77.40
d 225
            Balance: $302.40
c 125.50
            Balance: $176.90
```

In the program in listing 11.2, the loop drives the program. User input is accepted and processed until the user enters an empty line. The program gets the initial balance before the loop begins. Each entry is processed by the SELECT instruction, depending on the code the user enters. Invalid entries are ignored. The current balance is displayed at the start of each iteration of the loop.

Counting Through a Loop

One of the most common uses of a loop is to count. If you needed to write a loop that counts from one to five, for example, it might look like this:

```
i = 1
DO WHILE i <= 5
  SAY i
  i = i + 1
END
```

Because counting is such a common function for a loop, REXX includes a form of the DO instruction that performs the counting work. The variable, starting value, and ending value are all part of the DO instruction. The following loop does the same thing as the preceding example:

```
DO i = 1 TO 5
  SAY i
END
```

Although the preceding example may not look like a do-while loop, it actually is a specialized form of it. The TO 5 part of the DO instruction performs the same function as the WHILE i <= 5 in the earlier example. The variable i is initialized to 1 on the first execution of the loop and is tested at the beginning of each iteration. The variable is incremented by one on each pass through the loop. When the value of the variable is greater than the value following TO, the loop is exited.

The variable is called a *control variable* because it is used to control the execution of the loop. The loop itself is called a *controlled loop*.

If you need a different value added to the control variable, you can use the sub-keyword BY followed by the amount you want added on each iteration. For example,

```
DO i = 1 TO 9 BY 3
  SAY "i is" i
END
```

This example adds 3 to i on each iteration, so the loop displays the following:

```
i is 1
i is 4
i is 7
```

The number following BY is called a *step value*. The step value can be any type of numeric value—positive, negative, even a fraction. If you use a negative step value, the loop counts down. For example, the following code counts from 10 to 1:

```
DO j = 10 TO 1 BY -1
  SAY j
END
```

Another variation is to use the sub-keyword FOR to limit the number of loop iterations. The value following FOR indicates how many times the loop should be executed. For example,

```
DO k = 1 BY 2 FOR 5
  SAY "k =' k
END
```

Here, the loop executes five times, displaying the odd numbers 1, 3, 5, 7, and 9. You can use a combination of TO and FOR—the loop exits when either condition is met.

You can specify the control variable name as part of the END clause for the loop. REXX produces a syntax error if the name following END does not match the control variable name. This setup is particularly useful with nested loops because it allows REXX to check the nesting automatically. Look at the following example:

```
DO count = 1 TO 10
  DO mult = 2 TO 8 BY 2
    SAY count * mult
  END mult
END count
```

If count had followed the first END in this example, a syntax error would be generated. Nested loops can become quite complex, so using the control variable after END can help you quickly find errors in your code that could have disastrous results otherwise.

Infinite Loops

An *infinite loop* is a loop that can potentially execute forever. The loop shown in figure 11.1 is an infinite loop. You may create an infinite loop unintentionally by using a condition that never becomes true. Here's an example of this type of infinite loop:

```
count = 1
DO WHILE count < 5
  SAY count
END
```

The loop is exited when the value of count is greater than or equal to five. However, the value of count never changes within the loop, so the loop executes forever—or until the user presses Ctrl+Break.

Another way to create an infinite loop is to use a control variable without a TO or FOR to limit the execution of the loop. Because there's no limit, the control variable is incremented forever. In the following example, all of the odd numbers beginning with 1 are displayed.

```
DO i = 1 BY 2
  SAY i
END
```

Infinite loops are occasionally very useful. A program may need to process a random number of events that could conceptually be infinite in number. Consider a program editor that processes characters as they are typed. The core part of the editor might be a loop that performs the following steps:

1. Get a keystroke.
2. Process the keystroke.
3. Go to step 1.

This loop is exited only when the program is exited.

The need to create an infinite loop happens often enough that REXX provides the subkeyword FOREVER. Here's an example:

```
DO FOREVER
  SAY "I'm stuck!"
END
```

Listing 11.3 illustrates the use of an infinite loop for collecting some user input. This program actually works like many early program editors. Also, notice that, even though the program uses an infinite loop, there is a way to exit the loop.

Note: The program in listing 11.3 adds the end-of-line characters to each line the user types. These characters are the carriage return and the line feed. A string that has an `x` immediately following the closing quotation mark is interpreted as a hexadecimal value. The decimal value of a carriage return is 13, which is hexadecimal `D`. The decimal value of a line feed is 10, which is hexadecimal `A`. Thus, the code `'0D'x || '0A'x` creates the end-of-line characters.

Listing 11.3. A rudimentary text editor.

```
/* list1103.cmd */
SAY "Enter each line of text."
SAY "Use /EXIT to quit, /TYPE to display"
text = ''
crlf = '0D'x || '0A'x  /* carriage return + line feed */

DO FOREVER
  PARSE PULL thisLine
  firstWord = Translate(Word(thisLine, 1))
  SELECT
  WHEN firstWord = '/EXIT' THEN
    EXIT
  WHEN firstWord = '/TYPE' THEN
    SAY text
  OTHERWISE
    text = text || thisLine || crlf
  END
END

EXIT
```

```
[D:\]list1103
Enter each line of text.
Use /EXIT to quit, /TYPE to display
/* test program */
SAY "Hello, world!"
/TYPE
/* test program */
SAY "Hello, world!"
```

```
EXIT
/TYPE
/* test program */
SAY "Hello, world!"
EXIT

/exit
```

The program in listing 11.3 loops, accepting text and commands from the user. Two commands are accepted: /TYPE to display the lines typed and /EXIT to exit the program. When the user enters a line of text, that line plus a carriage return and line feed are concatenated to all the text entered previously. The loop is an infinite loop that is exited only when the program is exited. Commands are recognized by uppercasing and examining the first word entered. If the first word does not match a command, the program assumes the entry is text.

DO	DON'T

DON'T create loops that cannot be exited. Even an infinite loop should have some way of exiting.

DO use infinite loops when they solve the programming problem.

Exiting and Continuing Loops

Sometimes you need to exit a loop early, or you may need to exit a loop to go immediately to the next iteration. Two REXX instructions, LEAVE and ITERATE, answer both needs.

You use the LEAVE instruction to exit a loop. LEAVE ends the current iteration of the immediate loop and exits the loop. Look at the following example:

```
DO FOREVER
  PULL command
  IF command = 'STOP' THEN
    LEAVE
END
```

If the user types **STOP**, the IF instruction executes LEAVE and the loop ends.

When you nest loops, you can use LEAVE to exit several levels of loops by using the control variable's name after LEAVE. Here's an example:

```
DO i = 1 TO 25
  DO j = 1 TO 10
    IF i * j > 100 THEN
      LEAVE i
  END j
END i
```

Here, the `LEAVE i` clause exits both the inner and outer loops.

The `ITERATE` instruction tells REXX to begin the next iteration of the loop immediately. Code within the loop following `ITERATE` is not executed. `ITERATE` is almost always used in an `IF` or `SELECT` instruction. In the following example, `ITERATE` skips over the last `SAY` clause in the loop as long as the user does not answer `YES`:

```
DO 1000
  SAY "Had enough?"
  PULL answer
  IF answer >< 'YES' THEN
    ITERATE
  SAY "No you haven't!"
END
```

DO **DON'T**

DON'T use `LEAVE` unless it simplifies the code.

DO try to use loop conditions instead of `IF` statements to control when a loop exits.

Syntax

The *DO* Instruction

```
DO [repetitor] [conditional] [;]
  [clause]
END [name]
```

Repetitor is

`name = expri [TO exprt] [BY exprb] [FOR exprf]`

or

`FOREVER`

or

exprr

Conditional is:

`WHILE exprw`

or

`UNTIL expru`

You use the DO and END instructions to group instructions together as a block of code, optionally executing the block repetitively.

All of the expressions *expri*, *exprt*, *exprb*, *exprf*, and *exprr* must evaluate to a number. The expressions *exprw* and *expru* must evaluate to either 1 or 0 (true or false).

The *repetitor* steps the control variable *name* through a range of values. The first value in the range is *expri*. You can express the upper bound of the range using the TO phrase, or you can set the total number of iterations using the FOR phrase. If the step value *exprb* is not given, it defaults to 1. The TO, FOR, and BY phrases can appear in any order.

When *repetitor* is FOREVER, the loop is executed until *conditional* is satisfied or some REXX instruction (such as LEAVE or EXIT) ends the loop.

When *repetitor* is *exprr*, the expression is evaluated and the loop is then executed that number of times.

The *conditional* causes the termination of the loop based on a condition. The WHILE phrase is evaluated at the beginning of each loop iteration, and the loop terminates if *exprw* evaluates to 0. The UNTIL phrase is evaluated at the end of each loop iteration, and the loop is terminated if *expru* evaluates to 1.

A *conditional* may follow any of the forms of *repetitor*. The loop exits when either the *conditional* or the *repetitor* is satisfied.

Example 1

```
DO 5
  SAY "Testing"
END
```

Example 2

```
DO i = 5 TO 105 BY 5 UNTIL ans = 'Y'
  SAY "Are you younger than" i "years? (Y/N)"
  PULL ans
END
```

Example 3

```
DO WHILE DataType(response) >< num
  SAY "Enter a number:"
  PULL response
END
```

Example 4

```
DO FOREVER
  PULL input
  string = string || input
END
```

In listing 11.4, you bring the `Zeller` function back to help create a calendar for any month you want. The program isn't perfect—it ignores leap years—but it does use several loops to generate and display the calendar.

Listing 11.4. Creating a calendar for a single month.

```
/* list1104.cmd */

SAY "Enter the month and year:"
PULL month year

day = 1
dow = Zeller() + 1

/* space over days before first of month */
week = ''
DO dow - 1
  week = week || '   '
END

/* get number of days for month (ignores leap years) */
SELECT
WHEN month = 2 THEN
  mthLen = 28
WHEN month = 4 | month = 6 | month = 9 | month = 11 THEN
  mthLen = 30
OTHERWISE
  mthLen = 31
END

/* display the heading */
SAY
SAY Center(month || '/' || year, 21)
SAY '  S  M  T  W  T  F  S'

/* build each week and display it */
DO wk = 1 TO 6 UNTIL day > mthLen
  DO dow = dow TO 7 UNTIL day > mthLen
    week = week Format(day, 2)
    day = day + 1
  END
  dow = 1
  SAY week
  week = ''
END

EXIT

/* Zeller's Congruence */
Zeller:
  IF month > 2 THEN
    DO
    adjMonth = month - 2
    adjYear = year
    END
```

```
ELSE
  DO
  adjMonth = month + 10
  adjYear = year - 1
  END

century = adjYear % 100
yearInCentury = adjYear - 100 * century
dayOfWeek = ((13 * adjMonth - 1) % 5 + day + yearInCentury + ,
      yearInCentury % 4 + century % 4 - century - century + 77) ,
      // 7
RETURN dayOfWeek
```

```
[D:\]list11000
Enter the month and year:
12 1995

       12/1995
  S  M  T  W  T  F  S
                 1  2
  3  4  5  6  7  8  9
 10 11 12 13 14 15 16
 17 18 19 20 21 22 23
 24 25 26 27 28 29 30
 31
```

The program in listing 11.4 generates a calendar for any month and year you want. The Zeller function determines the day of the week for the first day of the month. Following are the steps used to create the calendar:

1. The user is prompted for the month and year.
2. The `Zeller` function is called to calculate the day of the week for the first day of the month.
3. If the day of the week for the first day of the month isn't Sunday, spaces are added to `week` to move to the correct position. This loop may be executed zero times.
4. A `SELECT` instruction gets the number of days for the month.
5. The heading is printed for the month and year and the first letters of each day of the week.
6. A maximum of six weeks is processed by the outer loop, depending on when all days in the month have been processed. Because variable `wk` isn't used in the loop, the instruction could also be `DO 6 UNTIL day > mthLen`. The variable `wk` helps document what the loop is doing.
7. The inner loop formats each day number and concatenates the result to the `week` string.

8. The outer loop finishes by resetting the day of week to `1`, displaying the week, and setting `week` to an empty string.

Summary

This lesson introduced loops and the various forms of loops that REXX defines. You learned about the do-while and do-until forms of loops, and you saw how REXX uses `WHILE` and `UNTIL` to implement those loops.

The lesson also showed you how to count in a loop using a control variable and `TO`, `BY`, and `FOR`. You learned how you can create an infinite loop in error and how you can deliberately create an infinite loop using `FOREVER`.

Finally, the lesson discussed how a loop can be exited using the `LEAVE` instruction and how a loop can be repeated using the `ITERATE` instruction.

Q&A

Q How do I decide whether to use `UNTIL` or `WHILE`?

A First, you need to decide whether the loop must execute before or after the condition is tested. If you can write the loop either way, writing the loop using `WHILE` is usually better. Sometimes you need to initialize any variables used in a `WHILE` loop before the loop starts. Initializing variables may create duplicate code inside and outside the loop, but it is often the only way to get the loop "primed." In some cases, using an `UNTIL` loop eliminates the duplicate code and simplifies the loop. You may need to try writing the code both ways and then pick the one that is simpler.

Q Why doesn't the loop `DO i = 1 TO 10 BY -1` do anything?

A REXX looks at the step value following `BY` to determine which direction to count. If the value is positive, the loop is counting up, and if the value is negative, the loop is counting down. The control variable is compared to the `TO` value based on the sign of the step value. If the step value is positive, the control variable must be less than or equal to the `TO` value. If the step value is negative, the control variable must be greater than or equal to the `TO` value.

Workshop

The Workshop provides quiz questions to help strengthen your understanding of the material covered and exercises to provide you with experience in using what you've learned.

Quiz

1. What is a loop?
2. What is the difference between a do-while loop and a do-until loop?
3. What does the instruction `DO 15` do?
4. What is an infinite loop?
5. What instructions would you use to create a loop that counts from `3` to `12`?
6. What instructions do you use to display even numbers from `2` to `20`?
7. What kind of loop does `DO FOREVER` create?
8. What effect does the `ITERATE` instruction have?
9. What instructions do you use to create a loop that exits when `response` is `yes`?
10. When is the condition following `UNTIL` tested?
11. When is the condition following `WHILE` tested?
12. What is a control variable?
13. What is the effect of putting a variable name after `END`?
14. How does `FOR` affect the execution of a loop?

Exercises

1. The following program creates a triangle of asterisks. Rewrite the loop so that the base of the triangle is on top and the point is on the bottom.

```
/* Ex11-1.cmd */
ast = "*********"
DO i = 1 TO Length(ast) BY 2
  SAY Center(Left(ast, i), Length(ast))
END
EXIT
```

2. Design and write a program that prompts the user for a number and keeps trying until the user enters a valid number. Your program should reject empty strings and nonnumeric entries. (**Hint:** Use `Datatype` to check the input.)
3. Design and write a program that counts the number of vowels (the letters *a*, *e*, *i*, *o*, *u*, and *y*) in a string. The program should prompt for the string and display the count of vowels when complete.
4. The following program contains errors. Test it, determine what the errors are, and fix the program. You may need to use `TRACE` to discover why the program isn't working correctly.

```
/* Ex11-4.cmd */
SAY "Enter the first name and last name:"
DO WHILE firstName = '' ¦ lastName = ''
  PARSE PULL firstName lastName
END

DO WHILE areacode = '' ¦ prefix = '' ¦ number = ''
  SAY "Enter the phone number as ###-###-####:"
  PARSE PULL areacode '-' prefix '-' number
END

SAY lastName',' firstName '  (' ¦¦ areacode ¦¦ ')' prefix'-'number
EXIT
```

Compound Variables

WEEK 2

One of the basic jobs that any computer program has to manage is structuring, manipulating, and controlling data. Almost every programming language provides some way of collecting and structuring data so that it can be manipulated logically. REXX uses a single general-purpose construct, the compound variable, to implement almost any data grouping scheme needed. Today you learn the following:

- What a compound variable is
- What an array is and how to use arrays in REXX
- What a structure is and how structures are used in REXX

Introducing Compound Variables

A *compound variable* (or *compound symbol*) is a special kind of symbol that can group several different values. Compound variables simplify managing large amounts of data by adding another level of organization. You can think of a compound variable as a sort of file folder for variables—it keeps the variables in one place, and you can add to the folder whenever you need to.

Any variable name that contains a period is treated as a compound symbol. Here are some examples of compound symbols:

```
name.last
files.4
chapter.page.line
screen.row
```

The part of a compound symbol that leads up to and includes the first period is called the *stem*. The stem is always a valid variable name followed immediately by a period.

The remainder of the compound symbol is called the *tail*. The tail is made up of one or more valid symbols, separated by periods. The symbols can be constants or variable names.

Note: Most programmers refer to compound symbols as stems, or stem variables. Although it's technically inaccurate, *stem* is definitely easier to say than *compound symbol*. However, it's hard to determine whether the programmer is referring to the stem or the entire compound variable, so we use the more exact terminology here.

A compound variable, like a simple variable, has the default value of its own name in uppercase. You can assign a value to all the compound variables accessed through a common stem through a single assignment to the stem. For example,

```
mailbox. = 'empty'
```

Any compound variable based on the stem `mailbox.` now has the value `empty`. In other words, the value `empty` is now the default for all compound variables based on the stem `mailbox.`, even if those variable names haven't been used yet. When the compound variable is displayed, as follows:

```
SAY mailbox.2 mailbox.jim mailbox.i
```

the result is `empty empty empty`. You can find what value was stored in the stem by checking the stem the same way that you check a simple variable. For example, the following `SAY` instruction displays `empty`:

```
SAY mailbox.
```

Notice that the `SAY` instruction displays the default value only for `mailbox.`, not the values of all compound variables based on `mailbox.`.

REXX substitutes values for any simple variables in the tail of a compound variable. Here's an example to help explain how this works:

```
i = 3
person.i = "Cornelius"
```

12

The value of `i` is substituted in `person.i` before the assignment. Thus, `Cornelius` is assigned to the derived name `PERSON.3`.

REXX only substitutes the values of simple variables. If you need to use a value from a compound variable, you must copy the value to a simple variable and use that instead of the compound variable.

The result of a substitution does not have to be a numeric value. The substitution can produce variable names that you could not create otherwise. For example,

```
name = 'Smith, John'
password.name = 'top secret'
```

The derived name used in this example is `PASSWORD.Smith, John`. This example is a valid compound variable name, even though you can only create it using tail substitution.

You can use this feature in many ways, but be careful: unlike simple variables, the derived name is case sensitive. The following code doesn't produce the output you might first expect:

```
name = 'Smith'
password.name = 'mutter'
SAY password.smith
```

The SAY instruction displays PASSWORD.SMITH. Because REXX converts all variable names to uppercase, the compound variable used with SAY does not match the derived name of PASSWORD.Smith used in the assignment. To make this example work, you need to ensure that the derived name exactly matches the way REXX sees the variable name:

```
name = 'SMITH'
password.name = 'mutter'
SAY password.smith
```

The SAY instruction now displays mutter.

Arrays

An *array* is a group of values that can be accessed using an index value (a whole number). The values in an array are usually visualized as being next to each other, somewhat like cells in a spreadsheet. A single value in an array is called an *element.*

Unlike most other programming languages, REXX doesn't need you to tell it how big the array is going to be. In reality, an array in REXX is not a special construct; it is simply a way of viewing a compound variable. However, the concept of an array is useful for solving some kinds of programming problems.

You set up an array in REXX by using a whole number in the tail of a compound variable. The convention is to start with one and increment the number for each new element in the array. Here's an array of historic proportions:

```
wives.1 = 'Catherine of Aragon'
wives.2 = 'Anne Boleyn'
wives.3 = 'Jane Seymour'
wives.4 = 'Anne of Cleves'
wives.5 = 'Catherine Howard'
wives.6 = 'Catherine Parr'
```

Remember that REXX substitutes the values of any simple variables in the tail of a compound variable. So, following the assignment in the preceding example, the values can be displayed using a variable and a loop:

```
DO j = 1 TO 6
  SAY wives.j
END
```

REXX does not have a built-in method to determine the size of an array. Because REXX doesn't care how many elements you keep in an array, you and your program are responsible for tracking the array size. Most programmers follow the convention of using

element zero to keep track of how many elements are in the array. Here's an example using the wives compound variable:

```
wives.0 = 6
```

The loop that prints the values from the array changes to look like this:

```
DO j = 1 TO wives.0
  SAY wives.j
END
```

There is a definite advantage to this approach—only one point in the code needs to change when the array size changes. Note that you don't have to keep the array size in element zero; you can store that array size in `wives.length` or use some other convention in your programs. However, most external libraries (discussed on Day 16) use the convention of storing the array size in element zero.

Some arrays have an inherent fixed size. If you store month names in an array, you know that the array always holds 12 values. You don't need to keep the size of the array in this case because you are always working with a fixed value.

Arrays are compound variables, so you initialize all values in an array by assigning a single value to the stem (see listing 12.1).

Type **Listing 12.1. Using an array.**

```
/* list1201.cmd */

th.   = 'th' /* default to 'th' */
th.1  = 'st' /* for '1st' */
th.2  = 'nd' /* for '2nd' */
th.3  = 'rd' /* for '3rd' */
th.21 = 'st' /* for '21st' */
th.22 = 'nd' /* for '22nd' */
th.23 = 'rd' /* for '23rd' */
th.31 = 'st' /* for '31st' */

PARSE VALUE Date() WITH day month year
SAY "Today is the" day ¦¦ th.day "of" month"."

EXIT
```

```
[D:\]list1201
Today is the 21st day of May.
```

In the program in listing 12.1, a stem variable is initialized with the suffix characters to concatenate to a day of the month. A default value of `th` is set by assigning to the stem (`th. = 'th'`). The special cases are then initialized. The current date is parsed, and the day is concatenated with a suffix. The value of the variable `day` is substituted in the compound variable `th.day`, and the result is used to determine which element of `th.` should be used.

Multidimensional Arrays

Arrays can have more than one dimension. A two-dimensional array is called a *table*. Multidimensional arrays are accessed using indexes, just like one-dimensional arrays. To access all the elements in a multidimensional array, you need to use nested loops, as follows:

```
DO i = 1 TO 10
  DO j = 1 TO 10
    multTable.i.j = i * j
  END
END
```

This example sets up a ten-by-ten multiplication table. You can visualize the contents of `multTable.` like this:

```
  1   2   3   4   5   6   7   8   9  10
  2   4   6   8  10  12  14  16  18  20
  3   6   9  12  15  18  21  24  27  30
  4   8  12  16  20  24  28  32  36  40
  5  10  15  20  25  30  35  40  45  50
  6  12  18  24  30  36  42  48  54  60
  7  14  21  28  35  42  49  56  63  70
  8  16  24  32  40  48  56  64  72  80
  9  18  27  36  45  54  63  72  81  90
 10  20  30  40  50  60  70  80  90 100
```

As you can see, using two indexes enables you to create a two-dimensional array. By the way, you can print the preceding table using the following code:

```
DO i = 1 TO 10
  line = ''
  DO j = 1 TO 10
    line = line || Format(multTable.i.j, 4)
  END
  SAY line
END
```

You can add more dimensions to an array by adding more indexes. It may be hard for you to visualize arrays with four or more indexes (little less find a use for them), but REXX is capable of easily supporting such arrays if you do find a need for them.

Structures

In REXX, you use a *structure* to group unlike, but related, data. Structures are also called *records* because they act like a single record in a file folder. The values in a structure are accessed using *field names*. For instance, a structure can contain the name, size, and date of a file:

```
file.name = 'C:\CONFIG.SYS'
file.size = 4096
file.date = '3 May 1994'
```

The information about the file is now conveniently held in one location. You can see that structures are implemented using compound variables.

You can use structures in a variety of programming situations. Some of the more common uses include names and addresses, date and time, and information about an object on the OS/2 desktop. Listing 12.2 shows how a structure groups related information.

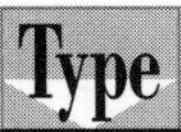

Listing 12.2. Using a structure to group related information.

```
/* list1202.cmd */
SAY "Please supply the following information."
SAY
SAY "Your first and last name:"
PARSE PULL info.firstName info.lastName
SAY "Your current age in years:"
PULL info.age
SAY "Your height in inches:"
PULL info.height
SAY "Your sex (M/F):"
PULL info.sex
SAY

IF info.sex = 'F' THEN
  info.title = 'Ms'
ELSE
  info.title = 'Mr'

SAY 'Thank you,' info.title info.lastName'.'
SAY 'You are' info.age 'years old, and' ,
      (info.height % 12)"'" (info.height // 12)'" tall.'
EXIT
```

```
[D:\]list1202
Please supply the following information.

Your first and last name:
Alfred Neuman
Your current age in years:
53
```

12

```
Your height in inches:
63
Your sex (M/F):
m

Thank you, Mr Neuman.
You are 53 years old, and 5' 3" tall.
```

The program in listing 12.2 prompts for and stores personal information in a structure. The user's title is determined from the sex. The data stored in the structure is then displayed.

Arrays and Structures

You can combine the two concepts of arrays and structures to produce arrays of structures (such as a name and address database) or structures containing arrays (such as an insurance record with the first names of children). Here's an example of a structure containing an array:

```
student.name = 'John Smith'
student.classes.0 = 2
student.classes.1 = 'English 102'
student.classes.2 = 'Metallurgy 101'
```

A student may take any number of classes, so the array allows the structure to be extended as necessary. The size of the array is always kept in the structure so that the array can be easily traversed by a loop.

An array of structures enables you to create a simple database in memory. You can extend the preceding example to allow all student records to be kept in an array:

```
student.1.name = 'John Smith'
student.2.name = 'Jane Smythe'
student.3.name = 'Jean Schmidt'
```

You can access any of the structures in the array using a loop. An array of structures is just like a simple array, except the index value isn't the last symbol in the compound variable's tail. This code displays all the students in the `student.` array:

```
DO j = 1 TO student.0
  SAY student.j.name
END
```

A structure containing an array can be an element of an array of structures. The code to manipulate this construct is very much like the code for multidimensional arrays:

```
DO i = 1 TO student.0
  SAY student.i.name
  DO j = 1 TO student.i.classes.0
    SAY '   'student.i.classes.j
  END
END
```

The name of each student is displayed with the classes that student is taking.

Associative Memory

Associative memory is a cross between the concepts of an array and a structure. Instead of using a number as an index, you use a value contained in one or more variables. Let's work through an example to see how to use associative memory:

```
memNum = 1000
memName = 'Beethoven'
member.5.id = memNum
member.5.name = memName
```

The stem `member.` holds an array of member names and identification numbers. To find any member by number, the array must be searched sequentially:

```
DO i = 1 TO member.0
  IF member.i.id = memNum THEN
    DO
    SAY member.i.id 'is' member.i.name
    LEAVE
    END
END
```

If you want to find a member by name rather than number, you must write a loop that compares `member.i.name` with a search value. The sequential search can be slow because the code has to check each value in the array. If the array contains 1,000 elements, the code may have to check all 1,000 elements to find the desired record.

Associative memory gives you the ability to take a shortcut to the desired record. First, you need to add a few extra fields to the compound variable:

```
member.ids.memNum = 5
memName = Translate(memName) /* to uppercase */
member.names.memName = 5
```

The array index is stored in two compound variables. One variable uses the member number in the tail; the other variable uses the member name in the tail. Notice that the member name is translated to uppercase to ensure that the derived variable name is always in uppercase. Assuming that `memNum` and `memName` still have the values assigned in the first example, the derived variable names are as follows:

```
MEMBER.IDS.1000
MEMBER.NAMES.BEETHOVEN
```

The member number and member name serve the same function as an index for an array. In the example, both compound variables contain the value 5, which is an index for the associated array of structures. Thus, the member number or member name can be used like an array index to get the real array index for the associated structure. So, if you have the member number, you can display the member name like this:

```
index = member.ids.1000 /* member number 1000 */
SAY member.index.name   /* displays Beethoven */
```

Now, instead of using a loop, you can find the record you want in a single step. You use the name or number to look up the correct array index, and then you use that value to get the rest of the member's information:

```
/* by name */
memName = Translate(memName)
i = member.names.memName
SAY member.i.name 'has ID #' || member.i.id
/* by number */
i = member.ids.memNum
SAY member.i.id 'is' member.i.name
```

The program looks up the array index by using the member name or member number in the tail of the compound variable. The index that was stored in that location earlier is retrieved and then used to display the record you want. Of course, if the name or number is not valid, the index isn't valid. Checking the index value before using it is always a good idea.

Associative memory is a powerful concept, but beware of painting yourself into a design corner. Always remember to design a way to get data back out of a structure. If you didn't store the data in this example in a normal array, you couldn't quickly display all the records using a simple loop. For example,

```
memName = 'SMITH, JOHN'
member.memName.id = '1100'
member.memName.expiration = '1998-01-01'
```

As long as you know the member's name, you can find the record. But what happens when the name isn't available to the program? The design in the preceding example does not allow for getting the data back out of the record.

You can use associative memory to simplify tasks that would require a considerable amount of code otherwise. The program in listing 12.3 uses associative memory to count the vowels in a sentence. To write the same program without associative memory would require either a complex `IF` instruction, or a `SELECT` instruction with a `WHEN` for each vowel.

Listing 12.3. Using associative memory to count vowels.

```
/* list1203.cmd */

isVowel. = 0 /* default to false */
isVowel.A = 1 /* set vowels to true */
isVowel.E = 1
isVowel.I = 1
isVowel.O = 1
isVowel.U = 1
isVowel.Y = 1

SAY "Enter some text:"
PULL text
totalVowels = 0
DO i = 1 TO Length(text)
  letter = SubStr(text, i, 1)
  IF isVowel.letter THEN
    totalVowels = totalVowels + 1
END

SAY "That text contains" totalVowels "vowels."
EXIT
```

```
[D:\]list1203
Enter some text:
Where id was, there shall ego be. --Freud
That text contains 12 vowels.
```

In the program in listing 12.3, the compound variable `isVowel.` is initialized to `0` (false). Each vowel is used as a tail, and each resulting variable is initialized to `1` (true). The user is prompted for some text, and then each character in the input is used as a tail with `isVowel.`. If the character is a vowel (has a value of `1` in the compound variable), then `totalVowels` is incremented. The count of vowels is displayed after all characters in the input have been processed.

You can use arrays, structures, and associative memory together to solve many programming problems. The program in listing 12.4 combines all three to enable the user to choose the order in which fields are displayed in a small database.

Listing 12.4. Dynamically accessing fields in a structure.

```
/* list1204.cmd */

info.1 = 'FIRSTNAME'
info.2 = 'LASTNAME'
info.3 = 'PHONE'
```

continues

Listing 12.4. continued

```
SAY 'Column choices are:'
DO i = 1 TO 3
  SAY ' ' i info.i
END
SAY
DO i = 1 TO 3
  SAY 'Select a field for column' i' (1,2,3):'
  PULL fld
  column.i = info.fld
END

folks.0 = 4
folks.1.firstName  = 'Bilbo'
folks.1.lastName  = 'Baggins'
folks.1.phone = '919-555-1211'
folks.2.firstName  = 'Deb'
folks.2.lastName  = 'Xyzzy'
folks.2.phone = '214-555-2345'
folks.3.firstName  = 'Grant'
folks.3.lastName  = 'Lee'
folks.3.phone = '708-555-2121'
folks.4.firstName  = 'A. Jean'
folks.4.lastName  = 'Hibi'
folks.4.phone = '602-555-1000'

DO i = 1 TO folks.0
  line = ''
  DO j = 1 TO 3
    col = column.j
    line = line || Left(folks.i.col, 15)
  END
  SAY line
END

EXIT
```

```
[D:\]list1204
Column choices are:
  1 FIRSTNAME
  2 LASTNAME
  3 PHONE

Select a field for column 1 (1,2,3):
2
Select a field for column 2 (1,2,3):
1
Select a field for column 3 (1,2,3):
3
Baggins        Bilbo          919-555-1211
Xyzzy          Deb            214-555-2345
Lee            Grant          708-555-2121
Hibi           A. Jean        602-555-1000
```

```
[D:\]list1204
Column choices are:
  1 FIRSTNAME
  2 LASTNAME
  3 PHONE

Select a field for column 1 (1,2,3):
3
Select a field for column 2 (1,2,3):
1
Select a field for column 3 (1,2,3):
2
919-555-1211    Bilbo          Baggins
214-555-2345    Deb            Xyzzy
708-555-2121    Grant          Lee
602-555-1000    A. Jean        Hibi
```

In the program in listing 12.4, associative memory is used to enable the user to select the order in which columns are displayed. First, a menu listing the columns appears, and the user enters the desired column order in response to the prompts. The desired column order is stored as an array in the `column.` compound variable. The "database" is then initialized with four records. A loop iterates over each record, and a nested loop processes each column. The inner loop gets the index of each column and concatenates the data for that column to the variable `line`. The `SAY` instruction in the outer loop then displays the result.

12

Summary

This lesson introduced you to compound variables. You learned that a compound variable is made up of a stem and a tail. The stem is any valid variable name ending with a period. The tail can be one or more constants or simple variables, separated by periods. You also learned that REXX creates a derived variable name by replacing the simple variables in the tail with the values of those variables.

The lesson showed you how to use compound variables to create arrays, or groups of values that are accessed by an index. You also learned how to use compound variables to create structures, or groups of related values that are accessed by field names.

Finally, the lesson discussed using compound variables to implement a type of associative memory. You saw how you can use data as a tail in a compound variable to establish a relationship between two records or perform a fast lookup.

Q&A

Q If I don't know what is stored in a compound variable, is there a way to find out?

A It is your responsibility to keep track of the values stored in a compound variable. If your program doesn't keep or can't re-create the value used to create a derived name, then any value stored in that derived name is inaccessible.

Workshop

The Workshop provides quiz questions to help strengthen your understanding of the material covered and exercises to provide you with experience in using what you've learned.

Quiz

1. What is a compound variable?
2. What is a stem?
3. What is a tail?
4. How is a value found in an array?
5. What is a structure?
6. What is a derived name?

Exercises

1. Change the program in listing 8.4 in the lesson for Day 8 to use an array rather than a `SELECT` instruction to get the day of the week that the user was born.
2. Design and write a program that counts the number of times each letter is used in user input. It's okay to convert the input to uppercase. The output should look something like this:

```
'A' is used 3 times     'B' is used 1 time
'C' is used 0 times     'D' is used 2 times
'E' is used 5 times     'F' is used 0 times
```

   The output should continue through the letter `Z`. Don't display a count for any characters other than letters.

Dealing with User Input

WEEK
2

The user interface is the part of a program that directly interacts with the user; it's how the user and the computer communicate with each other. The user interface includes prompts, messages, menus, and input.

User interface design is one of the most heavily researched areas in the computer industry; no one has learned yet how to design the perfect user interface. The subject is still an art, which means that there are no hard and fast rules. However, several conventions have evolved over time, based on research done with "real users." This lesson discusses those conventions. Today you learn the following:

- How to write prompts and messages that help the user
- How to use sound and color to enhance the user interface
- How to check user input to ensure that it's correct
- How to use defensive programming to make your programs "bulletproof"

Using Prompts

A program's prompts, explanations, and error messages play a critical role in a user's acceptance of the program. The wording and presentation of all messages are important to making the program accessible to any user.

A prompt tells the user what action or information is needed. If a prompt is unclear or confusing, the user may respond incorrectly. Try to make the prompt clear but also keep it short. Most people don't read a long prompt; almost anyone can be overwhelmed by a screen packed with text. If additional information can be presented, give the user the option of seeing the information but don't require that the user read all of it every time the prompt appears.

A prompt also can be too short. If the first prompt a program displays is `Name:`, the user may be hard pressed to guess what the program needs. Should it be the company name, the user's name, or something else? A better prompt might be `Your first name:`.

The user must determine from the prompts what information the program needs. Quietly watch someone use your program. Notice where he or she seems confused or where he or she spends an inordinate amount of time reading the screen. When you wrote the program, you knew what you intended, but the prompts may not communicate your intent to the user.

Here are some guidelines to help you when you're creating prompts and other messages:

- Messages should never refer to the program or the computer as though it is a person.

  Research has shown that programs that use *anthropomorphic messages* (that is, refer to themselves as though they are humans) reduce the user's efficiency. Anthropomorphic programs either tend to be too cute for day-to-day use, or they fool the user into believing that the computer has an independent will and intelligence.

  Here's an example of an anthropomorphic message:

  ```
  Hello! I'm here to help you balance your checkbook!
  ```

  Here's a better form of the same message:

  ```
  Use this program to help you balance your checkbook.
  ```

- Error messages should be clear and should educate or guide the user in the use of the program. Most errors should result in a help message.

  Error messages have a strong effect on the user's opinion of a program. Many otherwise well-written programs produce error messages that are incomprehensible or that blame the user for the error. Errors often occur because the user is confused; error numbers and vague messages such as `invalid input` tend to increase the confusion. If the user could possibly ask, "So, what do I do *now*?" when faced with an error message, you should revise the message text.

  Here's an error message that makes the user responsible for the error and does not help the user understand or correct the problem:

  ```
  ERROR: Invalid value in State field. Re-enter.
  ```

  Here's an improved response to the same error:

  ```
  State is limited to Post Office two-character state abbreviations.
  Press ? [Enter] to see a list of recognized abbreviations.
  ```

Help and Hand-Holding

Most of your first REXX programs will be fairly simple. You probably won't need to supply more help than a usage message. However, if your program needs in-depth instructions for each prompt, you may need to consider how to implement a rudimentary help system.

The program in listing 13.1 shows one way of implementing a simple help system. The user can enter a question mark at any prompt to receive additional information.

Listing 13.1. Implementing a simple help system.

```
/* list1301.cmd */

DO FOREVER
  SAY "First name:"
  PARSE PULL firstName
  SELECT
  WHEN firstName = '?' THEN
    SAY "The applicant's first, or given, name."
  WHEN firstName = '' THEN
    SAY "The first name is required information."
  OTHERWISE
    LEAVE
  END
END

EXIT
```

```
[D:\]list1301
First name:

The first name is required information.
First name:
?
The applicant's first, or given, name.
First name:
Bill
```

In the program in listing 13.1, the user is prompted until he or she enters a first name. A question mark gets additional information about the expected input. Entering no data causes the program to inform the user that an entry is required.

Using Sound

Sound is a good way to get someone's attention. You can use it to signal the end of a long operation, to call attention to an error, to act as an alarm tone, or to play music. REXX's `Beep` function sounds the computer's speaker at a specific tone for a given duration. The syntax for `Beep` is fairly simple:

```
Beep(frequency, duration)
```

The *`frequency`* is in cycles per second (hertz), and the *`duration`* is length of time in milliseconds to make the sound. You may want to play with the `Beep` function a bit to get a feel for different styles of beeps. The following example plays a two-tone error beep:

```
CALL Beep 262, 250
CALL Beep 131, 500
```

Sound is particularly effective at getting a user's attention. You should, however, be cautious about using sound too much in a program. If your program beeps at every prompt, users may ask for some way to shut off the sound. Noisy programs are particularly obnoxious in an office environment. Unless you're writing a game, you should reserve beeps for errors and other unusual situations that require the user's attention. Otherwise, the beeps become a background noise that is either cursed or ignored.

Using Color

In REXX programs, you can use color to give a visual cue of the type of information that is being displayed. Errors may be displayed in red; prompts, in bright white; and general information, in green.

Color, like sound, can become annoying when overused. You should introduce color with some degree of caution. Programs that were otherwise professionally done have fallen out of use because of garish or tasteless color combinations.

REXX doesn't have any special functions to control the color of output. However, OS/2 command sessions do allow a certain amount of color control. By default, OS/2 has ANSI terminal emulation turned on. The terminal emulation is controlled by "displaying" special ANSI control strings. The ANSI control strings can clear the screen, position the cursor, and set the foreground and background colors.

All the ANSI strings begin with an escape character (decimal 27 or hexadecimal 1B) and a left square bracket. Those two characters are followed by other characters that make up the actual command. For example, you can clear the screen with the following:

```
SAY '1B'x || '[2J'
```

Because the ANSI commands don't mean much to humans, it's better to assign them to variables with names that indicate the function of the command. For instance, if you assign the ANSI command in the preceding example to `clearScreen`, it's easy to see what the command does whenever you use it.

Here's the syntax for the ANSI clear screen command:

```
ESC[2J
```

The *ESC* is the escape character. The letter `J` must be uppercase. The clear screen command clears the screen using the current color setting.

The ANSI command to set the color is a little more complex:

```
ESC[attribute;attribute;...m
```

Each *attribute* is a number representing a foreground or background color (see table 13.1). If the command does not contain any *attribute* or an *attribute* is 0, the color is reset to the default of white foreground and black background. An *attribute* of 1 sets the foreground color to bright. When several *attributes* are combined in a single command string, their effect is cumulative.

Table 13.1. ANSI color attributes.

Color	Foreground	Background
Black	30	40
Red	31	41
Green	32	42
Yellow	33	43
Blue	34	44
Magenta	35	45
Cyan	36	46
White	37	47

Several ANSI commands are available for moving the cursor. We only use one of them because of the side effect of cursor positioning with the SAY instruction. The SAY instruction always moves the cursor to the beginning of the line, so you have to be careful when and how you use the ANSI cursor-positioning command. The ANSI command to position the cursor is

```
ESC[row;columnH
```

Here, the command ends with the capital letter H. The upper-left corner of the screen is row 1, column 1.

The best way to understand how the ANSI commands work is to see them in use. Listing 13.2 uses the ANSI command strings to clear the screen and set the prompts and heading to bright white.

Listing 13.2. Using ANSI command strings.

```
/* list1302.cmd */
book. = ''
clrScr = '1B'x || '[2J'
whiteOnBlue = '1B'x || '[37;44m'
redOnBlue = '1B'x || '[31;44m'
bright = '1B'x || '[1m'
normal = '1B'x || '[0m' || whiteOnBlue
helpLoc = '1B'x || '[3;1H' /* help prompter line location */
firstNameLoc = '1B'x || '[5;1H' /* first name location */
lastNameLoc = '1B'x || '[7;1H'  /* last name location */
addrLoc = '1B'x || '[9;1H'      /* address location */
cityLoc = '1B'x || '[11;1H'     /* city, state location */
clearHelp = helpLoc || Copies(' ', 60) || helpLoc

i = 0
DO FOREVER
  SAY whiteOnBlue || clrScr  /* clear the screen */
  SAY bright || Center('Add to Address Book', 60) || normal
  SAY clearHelp || Center('(First name or "quit" to exit)', 60)

  SAY firstNameLoc || bright || 'First name:' || normal
  PARSE PULL nm
  IF Translate(nm) = 'QUIT' THEN
    LEAVE
  i = i + 1 /* next record */
  book.i.firstName = nm
  SAY clearHelp || Center('(Last name)', 60)
  SAY lastNameLoc || bright || 'Last name:' || normal
  PARSE PULL book.i.lastName
  name = book.i.firstName book.i.lastName
  SAY clearHelp || Center('(Address for' name || ')', 60)
  SAY addrLoc || bright || 'Address:' || normal
  PARSE PULL book.i.address
  SAY clearHelp || Center('(City, State, and Zipcode)', 60)
  SAY cityLoc || bright || 'City, ST Zipcode:' || normal
  PARSE PULL book.i.city ',' book.i.state book.i.zipcode
  book.i.state = Translate(book.i.state)
END
book.0 = i

SAY normal || clrScr
DO i = 1 to book.0
  SAY
  SAY book.i.firstName book.i.lastName
  SAY book.i.address
  SAY book.i.city',' book.i.state book.i.zipcode
END

EXIT
```

```
[D:\]list1302

                         Add to Address Book
                      (City, State, and Zipcode)

First name:
Belladonna
Last name:
Took
Address:
Bag End
City, ST Zipcode:
Underhill, SH 11111

                         Add to Address Book
                    (First name or "quit" to exit)

First name:
quit


Belladonna Took
Bag End
Underhill, SH 11111
```

In the program in listing 13.2, you use a few ANSI commands to clear the screen and set colors. After the user has entered a record, the screen is cleared, and the user is prompted for the next name and address. If the user enters **`quit`** at the `First name:` prompt, the program exits. Notice how the program displays a help prompt just below the title on the screen. The help prompt changes as the user moves to each field. To display the help prompt, the program must position the cursor at the correct line, display spaces to erase the old help prompt, reposition the cursor to the beginning of the line, display the help prompt, and then position the cursor on the correct line for the input prompt. When the user quits, the program displays all the records that were entered.

With careful design work, you can add an information line (or help prompt) at the bottom of the screen. The information line can give additional data about the current field without forcing the user to always read that data. To add the line, you need to use the ANSI command to position the cursor. You also need to display the information line and the prompt using a single `SAY` instruction. Here's how to do it for one prompt:

```
infoPos = '1B'x || '[24;1H'
pmptPos = '1B'x || '[5;1H'
info = "First name of person to add to the address book"
SAY infoPos || info || pmptPos || 'First name:'
```

The cursor must be moved off the last line of the screen immediately after writing `info`; otherwise, the `SAY` instruction causes the screen to scroll. If the user has used the OS/2 `MODE` command to change the number of lines on the screen, your program may not format the screen in the way that you expect. You may want to start your program by using the `MODE` command to force the screen to a known number of lines.

DO	DON'T

DO try to make prompts as clear as possible.

DON'T make the program refer to itself as "I." A program is a tool, not a person.

DON'T beep the speaker at every prompt. Use sound to get the user's attention for errors and unusual situations.

DO use color to make the purpose of on-screen information obvious at a glance.

Using Arguments

An *argument* is a parameter that is passed to a program from the command line. An argument can be almost any kind of data, but it is limited in length by the command processor.

Many programs that run from the command line accept a special kind of optional argument called a *switch*. A switch is a value that changes the operation of the program. For example, the OS/2 command `dir` displays a single column of files, but `dir /w` displays several columns. The `/w` is a switch.

You can use switches in your programs by parsing the command-line arguments. The first character of a switch is either a dash (-) or a forward slash (`/`). The best approach is to accept either character. The remainder of the switch is usually a single character, but it can be a combination of characters, or even whole words. The case of the switch characters usually doesn't affect the meaning of the switch, but some programs are case sensitive due to the large number of switches they have to support.

The code needed to process and recognize switches is more or less the same from one program to the next. Listing 13.3 is a program skeleton for recognizing switches and other command-line arguments. One of the useful things that this program does is correctly handle quoted command-line arguments.

Listing 13.3. A skeleton for recognizing arguments and switches.

```
/* list1303.cmd */

PARSE ARG commandLine

switches.0 = 0
arguments.0 = 0

DO WHILE commandLine >< ''
  PARSE VAR commandLine thisArg commandLine /* get next argument */
  IF Left(thisArg, 1) = '/' ¦ Left(thisArg, 1) = '-' THEN /* switch? */
    DO
    j = switches.0 + 1
    switches.j = SubStr(thisArg, 2) /* remove '-' or '/' */
    SELECT
     WHEN switches.j = '?' ¦ switches.j = 'h' THEN
       SAY 'This program parses and displays switches'
     OTHERWISE
       NOP
    END
    switches.0 = j
    END
  ELSE /* not a switch */
    DO
    j = arguments.0 + 1
    IF Left(thisArg, 1) = '"' THEN /* quoted argument */
      DO
      commandLine = thisArg commandLine /* reassemble command line */
      PARSE VAR commandLine '"' thisArg '"' commandLine /* parse for quotes */
      END
    arguments.j = thisArg
    arguments.0 = j
    END
END

SAY 'Switches:'
IF switches.0 = 0 THEN
  SAY '  No switches on command line.'
ELSE
  DO i = 1 TO switches.0
    SAY "  Switch" i':' switches.i
  END

SAY 'Arguments:'
IF arguments.0 = 0 THEN
  SAY '  No non-switch arguments on command line.'
ELSE
  DO i = 1 TO arguments.0
    SAY "  Argument" i':' arguments.i
  END

EXIT
```

```
[D:\]list1303 -Dx "Big   file name" /a test.txt
Switches:
  Switch 1: Dx
  Switch 2: a
Arguments:
  Argument 1: Big   file name
  Argument 2: test.txt
```

Analysis The program in listing 13.3 is skeleton code for recognizing switches and arguments on the command line. The `DO WHILE` loop does all the processing to parse the command line into individual words and check each word to determine whether it is a switch. You add code to the `SELECT` instruction for the switches that are in your program. The `SELECT` instruction checks for a request for help (`/?` or `/h`) and prints a short help message. Special handling is given to arguments that are in double quotation marks. The word is concatenated back to the command line, and then the command line is parsed again to get the complete string. This process handles strings that may contain embedded spaces (such as HPFS filenames), or strings that begin with a slash or a dash but should not be seen as a switch. Finally, the program displays the switches and arguments found. The final two loops are for testing and are not included in a full program.

Checking Input

Here's an old rule of computing that you should use as a mantra whenever you need to handle user input: *garbage in, garbage out.* If a program accepts bad data, it will produce bad data.

A common programming mistake is to assume that the user entered the correct data. Users seldom deliberately enter incorrect data, but people have bad days and they make mistakes. They make typos, they press Ctrl instead of Shift, and they press Enter without entering data. Your program must be prepared to compensate for, and recover from, user errors. Once bad data gets into your program, it's almost impossible to produce a good result. If your program doesn't check its input, it can even crash.

It's especially important to ensure that nonnumeric characters don't end up in numeric input. You can easily check the input using the `Datatype` function (see the lesson for Day 3). If your program needs whole numbers, check to ensure that none of the numbers contain fractions.

Although you should rigorously check the input, beware of going to extremes. For instance, the only thing you can guarantee about a person's name is that it contains at least one character. City names can be made up of multiple words, and product names may have odd capitalization and contain special characters. You can only ensure that this type of input fits within rather loose guidelines and then accept it.

If you are comparing user input against fixed values, remember to check for both uppercase and lowercase. It's usually easier to use `Translate` to convert the input to uppercase and compare against an uppercase value.

When an input value needs to be in uppercase, the program should just convert the input to uppercase rather than force the user to type all uppercase.

You can offer the user some flexibility by accepting abbreviations for some responses. The most common place to do so is when the program needs a yes or no response. A `y` or `n` is enough to tell the program what it needs to know, but some users prefer to type the entire word. The `Abbrev` function simplifies checking the input for an abbreviation. The syntax for `Abbrev` is as follows:

```
Abbrev(information, info [, length])
```

If *`info`* is equal to the leading characters of *`information`*, `Abbrev` returns `1`; otherwise, `Abbrev` returns `0`. If *`length`* is specified, *`info`* must contain at least *`length`* characters. Abbrev is case sensitive, so the characters in *`info`* must exactly match the leading characters of *`information`*.

The program in listing 13.4 uses `Abbrev` to check the user's response to a yes/no question.

Listing 13.4. Using Datatype and Abbrev to validate user input.

```
/* list1304.cmd */

SAY 'Enter 3 numbers to be averaged:'
PULL num.1 num.2 num.3

DO i = 1 TO 3
  DO WHILE Datatype(num.i) >< 'NUM'
    SAY 'The value "' ¦¦ num.i ¦¦ '" is not a number.'
    DO FOREVER
      SAY 'Would you like to re-enter it (y/n)?'
      PULL ans
      SELECT
      WHEN Abbrev('YES', ans, 1) THEN
        DO
        SAY 'Enter new value:'
        PULL num.i
        LEAVE
        END
      WHEN Abbrev('NO', ans, 1) THEN
        DO
        SAY 'Exiting...'
        EXIT
        END
      OTHERWISE
        SAY 'Only a "y" or an "n" is expected.'
```

```
      END
    END
  END
END

SAY 'The average is' ((num.1 + num.2 + num.3) / 3)

EXIT
```

```
[D:\]list1304
Enter 3 numbers to be averaged:
3 5 a
The value "A" is not a number.
Would you like to re-enter it (y/n)?
y
Enter new value:
1
The average is 3

[D:\]list1304
Enter 3 numbers to be averaged:
10 2o 12
The value "2o" is not a number.
Would you like to re-enter it (y/n)?
n
Exiting...

[D:\]list1304
Enter 3 numbers to be averaged:
90 75
The value "" is not a number.
Would you like to re-enter it (y/n)?
y
Enter new value:
&*
The value "&*" is not a number.
Would you like to re-enter it (y/n)?
y
Enter new value:
78
The average is 81
```

13

The program in listing 13.4 prompts for and averages three numbers. The core part of the program ensures that the user input is valid and gives the user a chance to recover from any input errors. The `Abbrev` function validates the `yes` and `no` responses. The user can validly respond with `y`, `ye`, `yes`, `n`, and `no` in uppercase, lowercase, or mixed case. If this program were "real," it would need to test any invalid input further and produce better error messages (such as `No value entered`).

Defensive Programming

Defensive programming is like defensive driving—you must always expect the unexpected, and you never trust that the other guy is going to act intelligently. In programming, "the other guy" is most often the user.

Most programs work well when they are given correct data and when external routines and commands respond as expected. However, a good program must be able to recover when things don't happen as expected. You learned about checking the user input in the preceding section, but your program should be prepared for other situations.

- When a REXX program receives a Ctrl+Break or a Ctrl+C keypress, the program is exited unless a `SIGNAL ON Halt` is active. Your program should trap the `Halt` condition to provide a graceful exit.
- A command may fail. Your program should check `rc` after each command. If it doesn't check `rc`, the results could potentially be disastrous in some cases. For instance, a `copy` followed by a `delete` can create trouble if `copy` fails. The safest way is to use `delete` only when `copy` is successful:

```
'copy' importantFile backupDir
IF rc = 0 THEN
'del' importantFile
```

Even if your program can't do anything about an external problem, it should always display a message and exit gracefully. A program crash is *almost* the worst possible response to a problem; inadvertently deleting a file is *the* worst response.

If the program can retry a failing operation, give the user that option. If your program retries an operation automatically, beware of getting the program stuck in a retry loop. It's usually best to let the user know a problem exists and let the user decide whether to retry the operation or exit the program.

To make your programs truly "bulletproof," you must always be on the lookout for possible problems. Check return codes and use the `SIGNAL ON` instruction to trap any possible errors.

Summary

This lesson covered many of the aspects of dealing with user input and other user interface issues. You learned how to add sound and color to your programs. You also learned some guidelines for creating prompts and messages that can help the user use your programs.

The lesson discussed using the command line and how to parse command-line arguments. You learned how to write a program that can recognize switches on the command line.

Guidelines for checking user input were introduced. The lesson also showed you how to use the `Datatype` and `Abbrev` functions to help validate user input.

Finally, the lesson introduced the concept of defensive programming. Your programs must be able to either recover from an error or exit gracefully.

Q&A

Q What is CUA?

A CUA stands for Common User Access. In the CUA, IBM has defined a set of guidelines for creating a user interface. One implementation of the CUA interface is OS/2's Workplace Shell (the OS/2 desktop).

Q How do I turn on ANSI if it's off?

A You use the `ANSI` command to turn the ANSI mode on or off. The `ANSI` command without any parameters displays the current state. To turn ANSI on, use the following command in your REXX program:

```
'ANSI on > NUL'
```

Q How much of my program should be devoted to error checking?

A The answer depends on how much user input your program needs to deal with. A well-written program that gets all of its input from command-line arguments has about 10 to 20 percent of its code devoted to error checking. A program that is highly interactive, with a great deal of user input, may have anywhere from 60 to 90 percent of its code devoted to error trapping and recovery.

Workshop

The Workshop provides quiz questions to help strengthen your understanding of the material covered and exercises to provide you with experience in using what you've learned.

Quiz

1. What is a user interface?
2. When should a program beep?
3. What are ANSI commands?
4. What is defensive programming?
5. Give three reasons why a program should check user input for validity.
6. What does the `Abbrev` function do?
7. How can you verify that the user has entered a whole number?
8. What is a program argument?

Exercises

1. Design and write a program that adds a list of numbers and displays the result. The program should accept numbers from the user until he or she enters an equal sign (=). Ensure that each number is a whole number and allow the user to correct the entry when it's in error.
2. Rewrite and improve the following program.
   a. Follow the guidelines set out in this lesson to fix the prompts.
   b. Add some rudimentary help.
   c. Check the user input for validity.
   d. Allow the user to quit early.
   e. Exit gracefully if the user presses Ctrl+Break.
   f. Allow the user to play again without restarting the program.

```
/* Ex13-2.cmd */
target = Random(1, 10)
SAY "I'm thinking of a number between 1 and 10."
SAY "Can you guess it?"
DO FOREVER
  SAY "Enter your guess:"
  PULL guess
  SELECT
  WHEN guess = target THEN
    LEAVE
```

```
    WHEN guess < target THEN
      SAY "That guess is too low."
    OTHERWISE
      SAY "That guess is too high."
    END
  END
  SAY "You guessed it!"
  EXIT
```

13

Using Subroutines

WEEK
2

A *subroutine* (also called a *procedure* or *function*) is program code that can be called from more than one place in a program. Subroutines can be within the current program or located in an external file. Today you learn the following:

- What a subroutine is and how to create subroutines
- How to control the visibility of variables within a subroutine
- How to create functions
- What recursion is and how to solve certain programming problems using recursion
- How to create external REXX procedures
- How REXX searches for a procedure name

Introducing Subroutines

A subroutine is program code that is separate from the main part of a program. To use a subroutine, you *call* it. The program flow of control transfers to the subroutine, the code in the subroutine is executed, and flow of control returns to the instruction immediately following the subroutine call. Subroutines in REXX are called *procedures* or *functions*. Functions are a special type of subroutine that returns a value; they are covered in detail later in this lesson.

A REXX procedure begins with a label and ends with a `RETURN` instruction. The label is the name of the procedure; you use the label with the `CALL` instruction to tell REXX which procedure to execute. For example,

```
CALL TrackIt
EXIT
TrackIt:
  SAY 'Procedure TrackIt was called.'
  RETURN
```

The procedure in the preceding example is named `TrackIt`. The procedure is called by the clause `CALL TrackIt`. When REXX encounters the `CALL` instruction, it looks for a label that matches the name following `CALL`. In this case, `TrackIt` is found, and control is transferred to the first clause following the label. The `SAY` instruction is executed, and the `RETURN` instruction causes REXX to continue with the clause immediately following the `CALL` instruction.

In listing 14.1, you see how to call a procedure. The program begins with `TRACE 'R'` so that you can see the effect of the `CALL` and `RETURN` instructions.

Listing 14.1. Tracing the `CALL` and `RETURN` instructions.

```
/* list1401.cmd */
TRACE 'R'
CALL TestOne
SAY 'Back from TestOne'
CALL TestTwo
SAY 'Back from TestTwo'
CALL TestOne
SAY 'Back from TestOne (again)'
EXIT

TestOne:
  SAY 'In TestOne'
  RETURN

TestTwo:
  SAY 'In TestTwo'
  RETURN
```

```
[D:\]list1401
     3 *-*   Call TestOne;
    11 *-*     TestOne:
    12 *-*     Say 'In TestOne';
       >>>       "In TestOne"
In TestOne
    13 *-*     Return;
     4 *-*   Say 'Back from TestOne';
       >>>     "Back from TestOne"
Back from TestOne
     5 *-*   Call TestTwo;
    15 *-*     TestTwo:
    16 *-*     Say 'In TestTwo';
       >>>       "In TestTwo"
In TestTwo
    17 *-*     Return;
     6 *-*   Say 'Back from TestTwo';
       >>>     "Back from TestTwo"
Back from TestTwo
     7 *-*   Call TestOne;
    11 *-*     TestOne:
    12 *-*     Say 'In TestOne';
       >>>       "In TestOne"
In TestOne
    13 *-*     Return;
     8 *-*   Say 'Back from TestOne (again)';
       >>>     "Back from TestOne (again)"
Back from TestOne (again)
     9 *-*   Exit;
```

The program in listing 14.1 calls two procedures; each displays a message. Tracing is turned on so that you can see the action performed by `CALL` and `RETURN`.

A procedure has access to all the caller's variables unless you specify otherwise (see "Controlling Visibility" later in this lesson). Also, variables that you introduce in a procedure are accessible by the caller. For example, if you create a variable named `mumble` in the main part of your program, the procedures in your program can all access and modify `mumble`. If a procedure creates a variable named `deepPurple`, the main part of your program and all other procedures can access and modify `deepPurple`.

Listing 14.2 uses a procedure to test and update main program variables.

Listing 14.2. Getting a list of valid drive letters.

```
/* list1402.cmd */
CALL SetLocal

validDrives = ''
DO driveIdx = C2D('C') TO C2D('Z')
  drive = D2C(driveIdx) || ':'
  CALL TestForValidDrive
END

SAY 'Valid drive letters are:'
SAY validDrives

CALL EndLocal
EXIT

TestForValidDrive:
  IF Directory(drive'\') = drive'\' THEN
    validDrives = validDrives drive
  RETURN
```

```
[D:\]list1402
Valid drive letters are:
 C: D: E: F: G: H: L: M: P: R: U: V: W: Z:
```

The program in listing 14.2 illustrates how a procedure has access to all of a program's variables. The loop in the main program loops through each letter from `C` to `Z` and calls `TestForValidDrive` for each letter. `TestForValidDrive` determines whether the drive is valid by attempting to change to the root directory of the drive. If the directory change is successful, the procedure adds the drive to the list of valid drives in the `validDrives` variable. When the loop in the main program exits, the list of drives is displayed.

Using Arguments

An *argument* is data supplied to a subroutine when that subroutine is called. The data is available to the subroutine by using the ARG or PARSE ARG instructions or the Arg built-in function.

You use the ARG and PARSE ARG instructions the same way with subroutine arguments as you use them with command-line arguments. The single difference is that subroutines can have more than one argument, each separated by a comma. For subroutines that have two or more arguments, you use the ARG or PARSE ARG instruction with a comma between each variable. If a subroutine is called like this:

```
CALL ShowIt 5, "orange apple peach", 'D:\'
```

then ShowIt can retrieve each of its three arguments using PARSE ARG:

```
ShowIt:
  PARSE ARG number, string, drive
```

The arguments are assigned to the variables so that number contains 5, string contains orange apple peach, and drive contains D:\. If each of the values assigned to string is needed in separate variables, you can use the normal PARSE syntax to parse the argument:

```
ShowIt:
  PARSE ARG number, fruit1 fruit2 fruit3, drive
```

The words in the string passed as the second argument are parsed into the three variables fruit1, fruit2, and fruit3.

The Arg function retrieves a single argument or determines how many arguments were passed to the subroutine. You can retrieve the three arguments passed to ShowIt like this:

```
ShowIt:
  number = Arg(1)
  string = Arg(2)
  drive = Arg(3)
```

If Arg is called without any parameters, it returns the number of arguments passed to the subroutine.

The program in listing 14.3 uses a procedure to multiply two numbers passed as arguments to the procedure.

Type **Listing 14.3. Calling a procedure with arguments.**

```
/* list1403.cmd */

DO value = 1 TO 10
  CALL Multiply value, value + 1
  SAY value 'times' (value + 1) 'is' answer
END

EXIT

Multiply:
  ARG first, second
  answer = first * second
  RETURN
```

```
[D:\]list1403
1 times 2 is 2
2 times 3 is 6
3 times 4 is 12
4 times 5 is 20
5 times 6 is 30
6 times 7 is 42
7 times 8 is 56
8 times 9 is 72
9 times 10 is 90
10 times 11 is 110
```

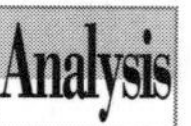

The program in listing 14.3 loops, calling `Multiply` each time with a value and one plus that value. The `Multiply` procedure multiplies its two arguments and stores the result in `answer`. The loop then displays `answer`.

Syntax

The *CALL* Instruction

`CALL` *`procedure-name [argument1, argument2, ... argument20]`*

The *`procedure-name`* can be any legal REXX symbol. Each argument is an expression that is evaluated before *`procedure-name`* is called. Arguments are evaluated left to right, and a maximum of 20 arguments is allowed under OS/2.

Example 1

```
CALL GotoHomeDir
```

Example 2

```
CALL CheckFilename filename
```

Designing for Subroutines

Subroutines are a natural way of implementing the result of stepwise refinement (introduced on Day 1). After you break a programming problem into several parts, you can implement each part as a subroutine.

One common method for using subroutines is to break the overall program into three major sections: initialization, process, and cleanup. A program designed this way has a main code section that looks like the following:

```
PARSE ARG cmdArgs
CALL InitializeEverything cmdArgs
CALL DoWhateverThisProgramDoes
CALL Cleanup
EXIT
```

This particular design method forces you to break the problem into three parts from the beginning. You then break apart each one of these pieces using stepwise refinement until you can easily and logically write the program.

You should design each procedure to perform one logically distinct action. Because the `CALL` and `RETURN` instructions require a small amount of time to execute, most procedures should contain several clauses. If your program must call a procedure to perform only one or two clauses, then you might want to consider replacing the procedure call with the one or two clauses contained in the procedure.

While you're developing a program, you can put in subroutine calls as placeholders and add the subroutine as just a label and a `RETURN` instruction. Then, as you write each subroutine, you can test the program to ensure that the subroutine works correctly. If each subroutine works correctly, then you have a much better chance of making the whole program work correctly.

Creating Your Own Subroutines

After you have a design that logically breaks up a large programming problem, you can begin creating procedures. You can follow several guidelines to make your program easier to write and easier to understand.

First, carefully consider the name for each procedure. The name should describe succinctly the purpose of the procedure. One naming convention that works well is to name all procedures using a verb-noun pair. Examples of procedure names that follow this convention are `SortFilenames`, `CalculateHourlyWages`, and `CountVowels`. Notice that it is easy to guess what the procedure does from the procedure's name.

You should place all the procedures for a program after the EXIT instruction. This way, the main code for the program is at the top of the file, and all procedures are toward the end of the file. If you leave out the EXIT instruction before the first procedure, your program will execute the first procedure just before exiting (a RETURN at the outer level of a program has the same effect as the EXIT instruction).

After you have a name for the procedure, you write the procedure code in exactly the same way that you write any REXX program code. The procedure must end with a RETURN instruction.

Finally, you should add at least a one-line comment at the beginning of the subroutine. The comment should describe the purpose of the subroutine, with notes on arguments and any special requirements for calling the subroutine.

Controlling Visibility

As your programs grow in size, you will begin to encounter problems created by procedures having access to all variables in the program. Look at the following program fragment:

```
DO i = 1 TO 5
  CALL DoOneRow i
END
EXIT
DoOneRow:
  ARG multiplier
  row = multiplier
  DO i = 1 TO 9
    row = row Right(i * multiplier, 2)
  END
  SAY row
  RETURN
```

The variable i is used in a loop within DoOneRow and by the code that calls DoOneRow. The result is that the program executes the first loop only once because the value of i is greater than five when DoOneRow returns. You can change the name of the variable in DoOneRow, but if the procedure is called from several places in the program, solving this problem may become tedious.

A better way to fix this problem is by using the PROCEDURE instruction. PROCEDURE makes all the variables outside the procedure invisible within the procedure. In the preceding example, adding the PROCEDURE instruction makes DoOneRow get its own copy of the variable i, and the variable row is not visible outside DoOneRow.

Note: The technical term *scope* is used when discussing the visibility of a variable. For instance, the scope of `row` is `DoOneRow`.

The `PROCEDURE` instruction immediately follows the label for the procedure. Here's the preceding example corrected by using the `PROCEDURE` instruction:

```
DO i = 1 TO 5
  CALL DoOneRow i
END
EXIT
DoOneRow: PROCEDURE
  ARG multiplier
  row = multiplier
  DO i = 1 TO 9
    row = row Right(i * multiplier, 2)
  END
  SAY row
  RETURN
```

This example works correctly, and it produces five rows of a multiplication table.

In many cases, a procedure needs access to an external variable, but you may want to limit the access to *only* that variable. For instance, a procedure may need access to a compound variable. A compound variable cannot be passed as an argument, so the simplest solution is to give the procedure access to the compound variable.

In REXX, you can make certain variables visible within a procedure by using the `EXPOSE` option with the `PROCEDURE` instruction. You follow `EXPOSE` with a list of variables that you want to be visible within the procedure. Variables not in the `EXPOSE` list will not be visible. The syntax is straightforward:

```
PROCEDURE EXPOSE name [name [...]]
```

If you use simple variables with `PROCEDURE EXPOSE`, then only the simple variables are exposed. If you use a stem, then all possible compound variable names beginning with that stem are visible. For example,

```
PrintAccount: PROCEDURE EXPOSE index addr. balance
```

The variables `index` and `balance` are visible both outside and within `PrintAccount`. Also, the stem variable `addr.` and any compound variables beginning with `addr.` (such as `addr.25` or `addr.index`) are visible.

Listing 14.4 uses two procedures to input numbers from the user and graph those numbers. The procedures are designed to limit the number of variables that are visible to the whole program.

Type

Listing 14.4. Creating a graph.

```
/* list1404.cmd */

SAY 'Graph a series of numbers.'
SAY 'Enter each number at the prompt.'
SAY 'Press Enter alone to quit.'
SAY

biggest = 0
CALL GetNumbers

DO i = 1 TO numbers.0
  CALL GraphOneLine numbers.i
END

EXIT

/* Get the list of numbers */
GetNumbers: PROCEDURE EXPOSE biggest numbers.
  DO i = 1 UNTIL input = ''
    SAY 'Number:'
    PULL input
    IF input >< '' THEN
      DO
      numbers.i = input
      biggest = Max(input, biggest)
      END
  END
  numbers.0 = i - 1
  RETURN

/* Create one line for the graph */
GraphOneLine: PROCEDURE EXPOSE biggest
  ARG value
  i = (value * 100) % biggest % 2 /* each '*' is 2 percent */
  SAY Right(value, 5) Copies('*', i)
  RETURN
```

Output

```
[D:\]list1404
Graph a series of numbers.
Enter each number at the prompt.
Press Enter alone to quit.

Number:
550
Number:
823
Number:
738
Number:
601
Number:
```

```
550 *********************************
823 **************************************************
738 ********************************************
601 ************************************
```

Analysis The program in listing 14.4 uses a subroutine to get a list of numbers from the user. The subroutine stores the numbers in a compound variable (`numbers.`) and tracks the largest number that the user enters. The variables `biggest` and `numbers.` are both exposed so that they can be used by the rest of the program. The main program then loops over each value in `numbers.` and calls `GraphOneLine` to create the graph. `GraphOneLine` calculates the number of asterisks to use for the graph line and displays the number with its graph.

Functions

A *function* is a special kind of subroutine that returns a value. Functions use a different call format than procedures use. A function is called by placing parentheses immediately after the function name, instead of preceding the name with `CALL`. Here's the syntax for a function call:

```
function-name([argument1, argument2, ..., argument20])
```

You can use the function anywhere in an expression that you can use a constant. At this point, you have used several built-in functions, so you are already familiar with how to use a function.

You create a function the same way you create a procedure. The function begins with a label and ends with the `RETURN` instruction. Functions are different from procedures in that the `RETURN` instruction must be followed by an expression. The expression is evaluated, and the function returns the result. For example,

```
Square: PROCEDURE
  ARG num
  RETURN num * num
```

Sometimes you don't need the result from a function. The function may do more than just return a value, so you may be interested only in the function's side effects rather than its returned value. You can call the function like a procedure and thereby ignore any returned value:

```
CALL HardWorkingFunction filename
```

Even if you call a function without saving the result, the value that would be returned is still available. REXX always sets the special variable `result` to the result of the function.

You can use `result` to simplify some code that would be much more complex otherwise. For example, if you want to count the spaces in a string, you might create a loop like this:

```
ix = Pos(' ', string)
DO WHILE ix >< 0
  count = count + 1
  ix = Pos(' ', string, ix + 1)
END
```

If you use `result`, you can modify the loop so that it works like this:

```
ix = 0
DO WHILE Pos(' ', string, ix + 1) >< 0
  ix = result
  count = count + 1
END
```

Although the second example produces the same number of lines of code, it is both easier to understand and easier to modify. If you need to change the call to `Pos`, you need to change the call in only one place in the second example.

Listing 14.5 uses a simple function to convert temperatures from Fahrenheit to Celsius.

Listing 14.5. Using a function to convert temperatures.

```
/* list1405.cmd */

SAY "What is the current Fahrenheit temperature?"
PULL degrees
SAY "That's" Celsius(degrees) "degrees celsius."

EXIT

Celsius: PROCEDURE
  ARG fahrenheit
  degrees = 5 / 9 * (fahrenheit - 32)
  RETURN Format(degrees,, 2)
```

```
[D:\]list1405
What is the current Fahrenheit temperature?
105
That's 40.56 degrees celsius.
```

In the program in listing 14.5, a function converts degrees Fahrenheit to degrees Celsius. The `Celsius` function converts its argument and returns the result formatted to two decimal places.

Using Recursion

You can simplify some types of programming problems by using *recursion*. Recursion is the process of a subroutine calling itself. For recursion to be useful, the subroutine can't simply call itself forever; a recursive subroutine must have some condition that allows the recursion to terminate.

Another way of thinking of recursion is as a way of solving a problem by solving smaller versions of the same problem. For instance, the method for finding the greatest common divisor for two numbers (also called *Euclid's Algorithm*) is to find the greatest common divisor of the smaller number and the result of subtracting the smaller number from the larger number. The process is repeated until the smaller number is zero; the larger number is the greatest common divisor. Because division is the equivalent of repeated subtraction, you can use division instead of subtraction to save some time. The following example shows how to use recursion to solve smaller versions of the same problem:

```
gcd: PROCEDURE
  ARG u, v
  IF v = 0 THEN
    RETURN u
  ELSE
    RETURN gcd(v, u // v)
```

Notice how the `gcd` function calls itself to solve a smaller version of the same problem. Also notice that the test `IF v = 0` gives the function a way of exiting. If this exit condition did not exist, the function would infinitely recurse until either REXX ran out of resources or you pressed Ctrl+Break.

An example of using recursion to solve a programming problem is calculating the factorial of a number. The factorial of a number is calculated by computing `1 * 2 * 3 * ... * number`. Thus, 2! is 2, 3! is 6, 4! is 24, and so forth. (The exclamation point is read as "factorial.") One of the ways of defining factorial is itself recursive:

```
n! = (n - 1)! * n
```

With a little thought, you can directly convert this definition of factorial to a function. The program in listing 14.6 uses a recursive function to calculate the factorial of a number entered by the user.

Listing 14.6. Calculating factorial using a recursive function.

```
/* list1406.cmd */

SAY 'Enter a number:'
PULL number
SAY number || '! is' Factorial(number)
EXIT

Factorial: PROCEDURE
  num = Arg(1)
  IF num = 1 THEN
    RETURN num
  RETURN Factorial(num - 1) * num
```

```
[D:\]list1406
Enter a number:
5
5! is 120

[D:\]list1406
Enter a number:
10
10! is 3628800

[D:\]list1406
Enter a number:
3
3! is 6
```

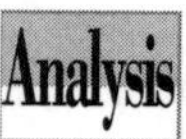

In the program in listing 14.6, the factorial of a number is calculated by using recursion.

Although recursive subroutines are usually functions, they can also be procedures. Listing 14.7 uses recursion to implement a sorting routine.

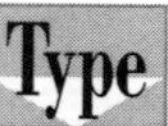

Listing 14.7. Using recursion to implement a sorting routine.

```
/* list1407.cmd */

SAY 'Starting array:'
list.0 = 10
DO i = 1 TO list.0
  list.i = Random(1, 100)
  SAY Format(i, 3)':' Format(list.i, 3)
END

CALL QuickSort 1, list.0

SAY; SAY 'Sorted array:'
DO i = 1 TO list.0
```

```
  SAY Format(i, 3)':' Format(list.i, 3)
END

EXIT

QuickSort: PROCEDURE EXPOSE list.
  ARG lower, upper
  choose = list.lower
  center = lower
  large = upper + 1
  DO WHILE (center + 1 < large)
    next = center + 1
    IF list.next <= choose THEN
      DO
      list.center = list.next
      center = center + 1
      list.next = choose
      END
    ELSE
      DO
      large = large - 1
      temp = list.large
      list.large = list.next
      list.next = temp
      END
  END
  IF center - 1 > lower THEN
    CALL QuickSort lower, center - 1
  IF center + 1 < upper THEN
    CALL QuickSort center + 1, upper
  RETURN
```

Output

```
[D:\]list1407
Starting array:
  1:  14
  2:  73
  3:  41
  4:  55
  5:   8
  6:  99
  7:  32
  8:  49
  9:  75
 10:  68

Sorted array:
  1:   8
  2:  14
  3:  32
  4:  41
  5:  49
  6:  55
  7:  68
  8:  73
  9:  75
 10:  99
```

The program in listing 14.7 creates a list of 10 random numbers between 1 and 100. The `QuickSort` procedure is called to sort the list. `QuickSort` sorts the list by subdividing it and recursing in order to sort each smaller list. To see how `QuickSort` reorders the list, try running the program with tracing turned on. The `QuickSort` procedure is written so that you can reuse it in your own programs.

Sorting is a highly technical subject, and an in-depth explanation of how `QuickSort` works is beyond the scope of this book. After you have a working sort procedure, it's usually best to treat it as a black box and simply use the procedure.

External REXX Procedures

An external REXX procedure is located in a file that is separate from the current program. An external procedure does not have access to any of the program's variables. This limitation is exactly like an internal procedure that uses the `PROCEDURE` instruction without `EXPOSE`.

The external procedure's name is the same as the name of the file that contains the procedure, minus the extension. Thus, if the filename is GETDIR.CMD, then the external procedure name is `GETDIR`.

Note: OS/2 supports two file systems: FAT and the High Performance File System (HPFS). Under FAT, all external procedure names are limited to a maximum of eight characters. HPFS allows long filenames (up to 254 characters); if your REXX external procedure must run on a variety of OS/2 systems, then you should limit the procedure name to eight characters so that it can run on either file system.

You can explicitly tell REXX to use an external procedure by using the procedure name and file extension in quotation marks. You can also use the full pathname of the procedure. If GETDIR.CMD is in your D:\COMMAND directory, then all the following examples would execute the `GETDIR` function:

```
SAY GetDir()
SAY GetDir.cmd()
SAY 'GetDir.cmd'()
SAY 'D:\COMMAND\GETDIR.CMD'()
```

If your program is installed on several machines, you should consider how to install external procedures so that REXX can find them. The procedure must either be in the current directory, in a directory on the path, or in the directory explicitly referenced by the procedure call.

Procedure Search Order

It's important to know how REXX searches for a procedure name so that you can control the result of the search. It's also hard to debug a program if you don't know how or why REXX found a particular procedure.

REXX normally searches first for a procedure name in the current program file, then searches for a matching built-in function, and then searches for an external procedure. If you need REXX to skip some part of this search, you can either put the procedure name in quotation marks or (if it's an external procedure) use the procedure's filename.

If you put the procedure name in quotation marks, REXX skips searching the current program file for a matching label. You can replace built-in functions by creating a function in your program that uses the built-in function name. You can then call the built-in function from your new function by quoting the function name. For example,

```
Translate: PROCEDURE
  PARSE ARG inString, oTable, iTable
  IF oTable = '' & iTable = '' THEN
    DO
    oTable = XRange('a', 'z')
    iTable = XRange('A', 'Z')
    END
  string = 'TRANSLATE'(inString, oTable, iTable)
  RETURN string
```

In this example, the default action of `Translate` is changed so that it translates a string to lowercase rather than uppercase. The built-in `Translate` is called by quoting the function name. Notice that the built-in function name is in uppercase; because the name is in quotation marks, it must be in the same form that REXX uses it internally, which is all uppercase.

The following steps list the order that REXX searches for a procedure name:

1. The current program is searched for a label matching the procedure name. If the procedure name is in quotation marks, REXX skips this step.
2. REXX checks for a matching built-in function.
3. External function libraries are searched for a matching name (using external function libraries is covered on Day 16).

4. REXX searches for a file with the procedure name and a file extension matching the current program's file extension.
5. REXX searches for a file with the procedure name and a file extension matching the default extension (that is, .CMD).
6. If the previous steps fail to find the procedure, REXX generates an error message.

Summary

This lesson discussed creating and using subroutines, which are pieces of program code that are executed by being called. A procedure is a subroutine that is executed using the `CALL` instruction. A function is a subroutine that is executed by immediately following the function name with parentheses. Functions return values; procedures do not return values.

Procedures and functions can optionally take arguments, which are passed to the subroutine when it is called. You use the `Arg` function and the `ARG` and `PARSE ARG` instructions to access the arguments.

Subroutines can be located within the same file that the subroutine is called or in a separate file. REXX searches the local file first, built-in REXX functions next, and then searches for an external procedure.

Q&A

Q How can a function return more than one value?

A Depending on your requirements, you can use one of the several different methods to return multiple values from a function. One method is to concatenate all the values into a single string and return the string. Another method is to use `PROCEDURE EXPOSE` to make one or more variables visible outside the function and return additional values in that variable.

Workshop

The Workshop provides quiz questions to help strengthen your understanding of the material covered and exercises to provide you with experience in using what you've learned.

Quiz

1. What is a function?
2. What is the difference between a function and a procedure?
3. How do you control a procedure's access to variables outside the procedure?
4. How are procedure arguments accessed?
5. What is recursion?
6. What rules does REXX use when searching for a procedure?
7. What are the rules for naming a function?
8. How can you use subroutines with stepwise refinement?
9. How do you pass a compound variable as an argument?

Exercises

1. Design and write a program that takes an integer `N` as input and computes:

   a. The sum of the integers from 1 to `N`
   b. The sum of the squares of the integers from 1 to `N`

   Use functions to perform these two calculations and display the results.

2. The following program contains errors. Test and debug the program and fix the errors.

```
/* Ex14-2.cmd */

DO UNTIL GetYesNoResponse('Roll again?') = 'Y'
  SAY 'You rolled a' D6() 'and a' D6()
END

/* Get a yes/no response from the user */
GetYesNoResponse: PROCEDURE
  PARSE ARG prompt
  DO FOREVER
    SAY prompt
    PULL answer
```

```
      SELECT
        WHEN Abbrev(answer, 'YES', 1) THEN
          DO
          answer = 'Y'
          LEAVE
          END
        WHEN Abbrev(answer, 'NO', 1) THEN
          DO
          answer = 'N'
          LEAVE
          END
        OTHERWISE
          CALL Beep 226, 250
      END
    END
    RETURN

  /* Roll a simulated 6-sided die */
  D6: PROCEDURE
    roll = Random(1, 6)
    RETURN roll
```

3. Redesign and rewrite the `Zeller` function (see listing 8.4 in the lesson for Day 8) so that it runs as an external procedure. At a minimum, you need to pass the month, day, and year as arguments.

2

WEEK

IN REVIEW

8

9

10

11

12

13

14

The Week in Review—Week 2

You now have completed your second week of learning how to program in REXX. At this point, you have covered almost all of the basics, and you should be able to write some fairly complex programs. The following program uses most of the material covered in the past week.

Note: The numbers to the left of the line numbers indicate the lesson (that is, DAY09 indicates the lesson for Day 9) that first explains the material represented by that line of code. If you don't understand the line of code or it seems confusing, refer to the indicated lesson.

Type Listing WR2.1. Week 2 review listing.

```
       /**********************************************************/
       /* File: chexx.cmd                                          */
       /* An implementation of the game of checkers. The user      */
       /* plays against the computer. The checkerboard and         */
       /* pieces are drawn using ANSI command strings.             */
       /**********************************************************/

       CALL Initialization
DAY11  DO FOREVER
         CALL DrawBoard
DAY08    IF PromptUser() THEN
DAY11      LEAVE
DAY12    you = move.1
DAY11    DO mv = 1 TO (move.0 - 1)
           mvTo = mv + 1
DAY14      CALL MovePiece move.mv, move.mvTo
DAY09      you = you 'to' move.mvTo
         END
         CALL ComputerMoves
       END
DAY09  SAY prompt || clrScr

       EXIT

       /**********************************************************/
       /* Initialize variables.                                    */
       /**********************************************************/
DAY14  Initialization:
         you = ''
         computer = ''
DAY13    AnsEsc   = '1B'x || '['
         clrScr   = AnsEsc'2J'
         white    = AnsEsc'30;47m'
         black    = AnsEsc'37;40m'
         red      = AnsEsc'30;41m'
         prompt   = AnsEsc'37;44m'
         msgClr   = AnsEsc'37;44m'
DAY12    board.   = ''
         row = 0; col = 33
         yourMove = prompt || AnsEsc'1;1H' || 'Your move:' || AnsEsc'2;1H'
         color = red
DAY11    DO ltr = C2D('A') TO C2D('H')  /* do each row, 'A' to 'H' */
           row = row + 3
```

```
DAY08     IF col = 33 THEN /* live board columns alternate */
            DO
            col = 39
            num = 2
            END
DAY08     ELSE
            DO
            col = 33
            num = 1
            END
DAY09     letter = D2C(ltr)  /* get current board row letter */
          edge = letter ¦¦ 0 /* block moving off the board */
DAY12     board.edge = '-'
DAY09     edge = letter ¦¦ 9 /* block moving off the board */
DAY12     board.edge = '-'
          wrkCol = col       /* set up work column */
DAY08     IF letter = 'D' ¦ letter = 'E' THEN
            DO
            color = white    /* reset color in preparation for 'F' to 'H' */
DAY11       DO i = num FOR 4 by 2 /* empty board rows in center */
DAY09         k = letter ¦¦ i
DAY12         board.k.loc = AnsEsc ¦¦ row';'wrkCol'H'
              wrkCol = wrkCol + 12
            END
DAY11       ITERATE
            END
DAY11     DO i = num FOR 4 BY 2 /* board rows with pieces */
DAY09       k = letter ¦¦ i
DAY12       board.k = color ¦¦ '  '
            board.k.loc = AnsEsc ¦¦ row';'wrkCol'H'
            wrkCol = wrkCol + 12
          END
        END
DAY11   DO i = 0 TO 9        /* block moving off the board */
          k = 'I'i
DAY12     board.k = '-'
        END
DAY14   RETURN

      /*******************************************************/
      /* Draw the board and pieces in their current locations. */
      /*******************************************************/
      DrawBoard:
        topLine = '   '
DAY11   DO i = 1 TO 8
DAY09     topLine = topLine ¦¦ Center(i, 6)
        END
DAY09   SAY prompt ¦¦ clrScr ¦¦ Right(topLine, 78)
        cursor = ''
DAY09   whiteSquare = white ¦¦ Copies(' ', 6)
        blackSquare = black ¦¦ Copies(' ', 6)
        line.0 = Copies(whiteSquare ¦¦ blackSquare, 4)
        line.1 = Copies(blackSquare ¦¦ whiteSquare, 4)
        lead = Copies(' ', 78 - 50) /* spaces for left side of screen */
        brd = ''
        whichLine = 0
```

continues

Listing WR2.1. continued

```
DAY11   DO i = C2D('A') TO C2D('H') /* do each board row */
DAY09     letter = D2C(i)     /* get current board row letter */
DAY11     DO j = 1 TO 8       /* build up one row of the board */
DAY09       k = letter ¦¦ j   /* board row + board column */
DAY12       brd = brd ¦¦ board.k.loc ¦¦ board.k
          END
DAY08     IF letter = 'H' THEN /* keep from scrolling screen */
DAY13       cursor = AnsEsc'1;1H'
          SAY prompt ¦¦ lead ¦¦ '  'line.whichLine
          SAY prompt ¦¦ lead ¦¦ letter' 'line.whichLine
          SAY prompt ¦¦ lead ¦¦ '  'line.whichLine ¦¦ cursor
DAY08     whichLine = ¬ whichLine /* switch from 1 to 0 to 1 to ... */
        END
DAY09   SAY brd ¦¦ AnsEsc'1;1H' ¦¦ prompt
DAY14   RETURN

      /*********************************************************/
      /* Prompt the user for their next move.                  */
      /*********************************************************/
      PromptUser:
DAY13   SAY msgClr ¦¦ AnsEsc'8;1H' ¦¦ 'Your pieces are white.'
        SAY; SAY 'Use a letter/number'
        SAY 'combination to specify'
        SAY 'your move, like this:'
        SAY '  F3 to E4'
DAY08   IF you >< '' THEN     /* show any prior move */
          DO
DAY13     SAY; SAY 'You:'; SAY ' 'you
          SAY 'Computer'actionVerb':'; SAY ' 'computer
          END

DAY12   isOkay. = 0
DAY09   valid.1 = XRange('A', 'H')
        valid.2 = XRange('1', '8')

DAY11   DO UNTIL errorMsg = ''
DAY12     isOkay. = 0
          SAY yourMove ¦¦ Copies(' ', 15) ¦¦ AnsEsc'1;1H'
          PULL moves
DAY13     IF Abbrev('QUIT', moves, 1) THEN
DAY14       RETURN 1
DAY12     move. = ''; move.0 = 0
DAY11     DO i = 1            /* loop through entered moves */
DAY09       PARSE VAR moves move.i to! moves
DAY08       IF Length(move.i) >< 2 , /* validate the move */
DAY09       ¦ Pos(Left(move.i, 1), valid.1) = 0 ,
            ¦ Pos(Right(move.i, 1), valid.2) = 0 THEN
DAY11         LEAVE
DAY12       move.0 = move.0 + 1
            isOkay.i = 1
          END
          errorMsg = ''
          mv = move.1
```

```
DAY08      IF ¬ isOkay.1 ¦ move.0 = 1 ,
           ¦ Left(board.mv, Length(white)) >< white THEN
DAY09        errorMsg = AnsEsc'23;2H' ¦¦ "Can't move from" move.1
DAY08      ELSE
DAY11        DO i = 2 TO move.0 /* check all move-to locations */
               mv = move.i
DAY08          IF ¬ isOkay.i ¦ board.mv >< '' ,
               ¦ board.mv.loc = '' THEN
                 DO
DAY09            errorMsg = errorMsg ¦¦ AnsEsc'24;2H' ¦¦ ,
                        "Can't move to" move.i
DAY11            LEAVE i
                 END
DAY11        END i
DAY08      IF errorMsg >< '' THEN /* complain about a bad move */
             DO
DAY13        CALL Beep 232, 125
             SAY msgClr ¦¦ AnsEsc'24;2H' ¦¦ errorMsg
             END
         END
DAY14    RETURN 0

       /*********************************************************/
       /* Make the user's requested move. Checks for a jump and */
       /* removes the piece if it is a jump.                    */
       /*********************************************************/
DAY14  MovePiece: PROCEDURE EXPOSE board.
DAY14    fromLoc = Arg(1)
         toLoc = Arg(2)
DAY09    fromLtr = Left(fromLoc, 1)
         fromNum = Right(fromLoc, 1)
         toLtr = Left(toLoc, 1)
         toNum = Right(toLoc, 1)
DAY12    board.toLoc = board.fromLoc
DAY09    ltrDif = C2D(toLtr) - C2D(fromLtr)
DAY08    IF Abs(ltrDif) >< 1 THEN /* jumping? */
           DO
DAY09      jumpLoc = D2C(C2D(fromLtr) + ltrDif / 2)
           jumpLoc = jumpLoc ¦¦ ((toNum + fromNum) / 2)
DAY12      board.jumpLoc = '' /* wipe out the piece */
           END
         board.fromLoc = ''   /* remove piece from old location */
DAY14    RETURN

       /*********************************************************/
       /* Determine the next move for black.                    */
       /* The following algorithm implements a rather           */
       /* conservative approach to playing checkers. The        */
       /* algorithm is in 3 basic pieces:                       */
       /* 1. Look for any white pieces to jump.                 */
       /* 2. Try to keep any black pieces from being jumped.    */
       /* 3. Find a legal move that has a low likelihood of     */
       /*    having a black piece taken.                        */
       /*********************************************************/
       ComputerMoves:
         /* Look for any jump possibilities */
```

continues

Listing WR2.1. continued

```
DAY09  blk = red ¦¦ '  '
       wht = white ¦¦ '  '
       jumpedOne = 0
       computer = ''
       doMove = ''
       direction = ''
       actionVerb = ''
DAY11  DO i = C2D('A') TO C2D('G') /* look through all board rows */
         DO j = 1 TO 8              /* and all board columns */
DAY09      k = D2C(i) ¦¦ j
DAY08      IF board.k >< blk THEN  /* black piece on this square? */
DAY11        ITERATE
           /* black has a piece at location k */
DAY11      DO FOREVER
             doMove = ''
DAY09        d1l1 = D2C(i + 1) ¦¦ (j - 1) /* down 1, left 1 */
             d1r1 = D2C(i + 1) ¦¦ (j + 1) /* down 1, right 1 */
             d2l2 = D2C(i + 2) ¦¦ (j - 2) /* down 2, left 2 */
             d2r2 = D2C(i + 2) ¦¦ (j + 2) /* down 2, right 2 */
             /* check for white on left diagonal */
DAY08        IF board.d1l1 = white THEN
               DO
               /* can we jump it? */
DAY08          IF board.d2l2 = '' THEN /* yes! */
                 DO
                 doMove = d2l2
                 jump = d1l1
                 direction = -2
                 END
               END
             /* check for white on right diagonal */
DAY08        IF board.d1r1 = white & doMove = '' THEN
               DO
               /* can we jump it? */
               IF board.d2r2 = '' THEN /* yes! */
                 DO
                 doMove = d2r2
                 jump = d1r1
                 direction = 2
                 END
               END
DAY08        SELECT
               /* doing a jump */
DAY08          WHEN doMove >< '' THEN
                 DO
                 IF computer = '' THEN
                   computer = k
                 /* move our piece */
DAY12            board.doMove = board.k
DAY09            computer = computer 'to' doMove
                 board.k = ''
                 /* remove the white piece */
DAY12            board.jump = ''
                 k = doMove
```

```
DAY09           i = C2D(Left(k, 1))
DAY08           IF i >= C2D('G') THEN
DAY14             RETURN
                j = j + direction
                jumpedOne = 1
                END
              /* if we jumped one, we're done */
DAY08         WHEN jumpedOne THEN
                DO
                actionVerb = ' jumps'
DAY14           RETURN
                END
              /* no action for this piece */
DAY08         OTHERWISE
DAY11           LEAVE
            END
          END
DAY11   END j
      END i

      /* Guard against being jumped */
DAY11 DO i = C2D('A') TO C2D('H') WHILE doMove = ''
        DO j = 1 TO 8
DAY09     k = D2C(i) || j
DAY08     IF board.k >< blk THEN
DAY11       ITERATE
          /* black has a piece at location k */
DAY09     d1l1 = D2C(i + 1) || (j - 1) /* down 1, left 1 */
          d1r1 = D2C(i + 1) || (j + 1) /* down 1, right 1 */
DAY08     SELECT
            WHEN board.d1l1 = wht & board.u1r1 = '' ,
            & board.d1r1 = '' THEN
              doMove = d1r1
            WHEN board.d1r1 = wht & board.u1l1 = '' ,
            & board.d1l1 = '' THEN
              doMove = d1l1
DAY08       OTHERWISE
DAY11         ITERATE
          END
          actionVerb = ' moves'
DAY09     computer = k 'to' doMove
DAY12     board.doMove = board.k
          board.k = ''
        END
      END

      /* Look for a safe move */
DAY11 DO i = C2D('A') TO C2D('H') WHILE doMove = ''
        DO j = 1 TO 8
DAY09     k = D2C(i) || j
DAY08     IF board.k >< blk THEN
DAY11       ITERATE
          /* black has a piece at location k */
DAY09     d2   = D2C(i + 2) || j       /* down 2 */
          d2l2 = D2C(i + 2) || (j - 2) /* down 2, left 2 */
```

continues

Listing WR2.1. continued

```
      318:       d2r2 = D2C(i + 2) || (j + 2) /* down 2, right 2 */
      319:       d1l1 = D2C(i + 1) || (j - 1) /* down 1, left 1 */
      320:       d1r1 = D2C(i + 1) || (j + 1) /* down 1, right 1 */
      321:       l2   = D2C(i)     || (j - 2) /* left 2 */
      322:       r2   = D2C(i)     || (j + 2) /* right 2 */
DAY08 323:       SELECT
      324:         WHEN board.d2 >< wht & board.d2l2 >< wht ,
      325:         & board.d1l1 = '' THEN
      326:           doMove = d1l1
      327:         WHEN board.d2 >< wht & board.d2r2 >< wht ,
      328:         & board.d1r1 = '' THEN
      329:           doMove = d1r1
      330:         WHEN board.d2 = wht & board.l2 >< '' ,
      331:         & board.d1l1 = '' THEN
      332:           doMove = d1l1
      333:         WHEN board.d2 = wht & board.r2 >< '' ,
      334:         & board.d1r1 = '' THEN
      335:           doMove = d1r1
DAY08 336:         OTHERWISE
DAY11 337:           ITERATE
      338:       END
      339:       actionVerb = ' moves'
DAY09 340:       computer = k 'to' doMove
DAY12 341:       board.doMove = board.k
      342:       board.k = ''
DAY11 343:       LEAVE i
      344:     END j
      345:   END i
DAY14 346:   RETURN
```

As you learn more about programming, your programs tend to grow in length. A large part of this program is dedicated to validating user input and to managing and formatting the display.

This program plays checkers against a human opponent. It creates the checkerboard and the checkers using ANSI command strings. The current state of the game is tracked using a two-dimensional array. Several procedures help to simplify the programming task.

The `Initialization` procedure in lines 28 to 81 sets up various values that are used throughout the rest of the program. The procedure assigns several of the ANSI commands to variables (lines 31 to 37) so that the commands can be used by name. The compound variable `board.` contains the entire checkerboard. The checkerboard is created by the loop in lines 42 to 76. Each square of the checkerboard is designated by a letter-number combination in which the rows use a letter and the columns use a number. Thus the upper-left square is `A1`, and the lower-right square is `H8`. These letter-number values are used as the tail for `board.`. The pieces are stored in `board.` as an ANSI

color command and two spaces. The edges of the board (the area outside the visible squares) are marked with a value so that the program doesn't inadvertently move pieces off the board.

The `DrawBoard` procedure in lines 86 to 114 displays the checkerboard and the checkers. Rows are marked with letters and columns are marked with numbers.

The `PromptUser` procedure in lines 119 to 173 prompts the user for the next move. Instructions are displayed, and if this move is not the first, the prior moves for both the user and the computer are displayed (lines 120 to 129). The remainder of the procedure is dedicated to ensuring that the user input is valid. If the user enters `QUIT`, `PromptUser` returns 1; for all other cases, `PromptUser` returns 0. This setup allows the code at line 11 to check if the user entered a move or if the user wants to exit the program.

In lines 179 to 195, a single move is performed for the user by `MovePiece`. The procedure uses two arguments: the location the piece is moving from and the location the piece is moving to. If the move is greater than one row (line 188), the procedure assumes a piece is being jumped, and it removes the piece from the jumped square.

The checkers playing intelligence for the computer's side of the game is contained in the procedure `ComputerMoves` (lines 207 to 346). The move is calculated using an approach that is mostly brute force. The computer makes three attempts at moving a piece:

1. Try to find a white piece to jump. If a white piece can be jumped, perform the jump and look for possible multiple jumps. If any jumps were performed, return. If no white pieces can be jumped, proceed to step 2 (lines 217 to 281).
2. Look for any black pieces in danger of being jumped. If a black piece is in danger of being jumped, try to move it out of harm's way. If a piece is moved, return. If no pieces are in danger or they cannot be saved, go to step 3 (lines 284 to 307).
3. Look for a legal move that has a low chance of getting jumped (lines 310 to 346).

Each of these three steps starts by looking for any black pieces on the board. If there is no black piece on the current square, the code loops. Once a black piece is found, squares relative to that piece are checked to determine whether a jump or move can be performed.

The entire program is driven by the loop in lines 9 to 20. The loop draws the board by calling `DrawBoard` and then gets the user's next move by calling `PromptUser`. If `PromptUser` returns a `1`, then the loop is exited. Otherwise, each of the user's moves, which was stored in compound variable `move.`, is passed to `MovePiece`. Finally, `ComputerMoves` is called to get the computer's response, and the program loops for the next round of the game.

As written, this program has a few weaknesses. Here are some areas that you might want to try improving in the program:

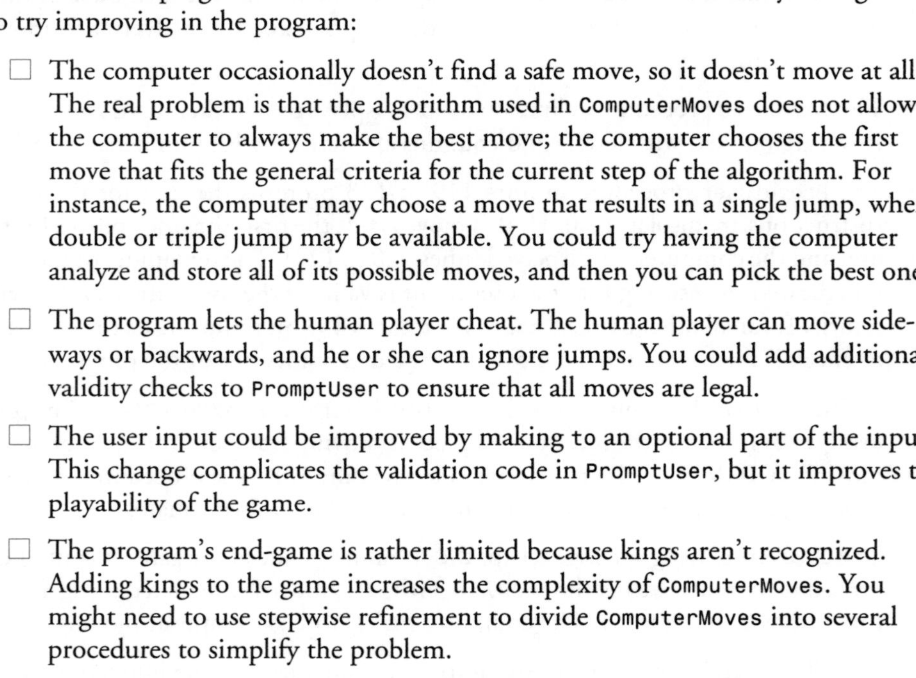

- The computer occasionally doesn't find a safe move, so it doesn't move at all. The real problem is that the algorithm used in `ComputerMoves` does not allow the computer to always make the best move; the computer chooses the first move that fits the general criteria for the current step of the algorithm. For instance, the computer may choose a move that results in a single jump, when a double or triple jump may be available. You could try having the computer analyze and store all of its possible moves, and then you can pick the best one.
- The program lets the human player cheat. The human player can move sideways or backwards, and he or she can ignore jumps. You could add additional validity checks to `PromptUser` to ensure that all moves are legal.
- The user input could be improved by making `to` an optional part of the input. This change complicates the validation code in `PromptUser`, but it improves the playability of the game.
- The program's end-game is rather limited because kings aren't recognized. Adding kings to the game increases the complexity of `ComputerMoves`. You might need to use stepwise refinement to divide `ComputerMoves` into several procedures to simplify the problem.

This program uses almost everything you've learned in your first two weeks of teaching yourself REXX. You can now write a wide variety of programs using REXX. Week 3 expands on what you've learned so far and adds several new concepts.

WEEK 3 AT A GLANCE

15

16

17

18

19

20

21

You have now finished your second week of learning how to program in REXX. At this point, you should feel comfortable with REXX, having touched on most areas of the language.

Where You're Going...

In the week that follows, you cover what we call "Getting the Most of REXX." In the following days, you take many of the topics from the first and second weeks and explore what they can do for you. You also learn to use REXX to take advantage of OS/2.

This third week wraps up your learning of REXX in 21 days; you should know the language by the time you finish this final week. You will spend much of your time learning to interact with the operating system. For instance, you spend a day (Day 15) learning about file input and output and another day (Day 21) finding out about interprocess communications.

Week 3 at a Glance

This week, you also learn about Workplace Shell objects and how to use the tools that OS/2 provides to make it easier to extend OS/2 applications. You learn to manipulate OS/2's extended attributes and .INI files. You also use REXX to manage your Workplace Shell desktop, including creating folders and shadows, changing backgrounds and colors, and controlling program and data objects.

File Input/Output

WEEK 3

So far, you have spent two weeks creating programs that produce an immediate result. However, most applications use existing data or create information that will be reused. That information is usually kept in files on your hard disk. Today you learn the following:

- How to read and write lines in a file
- How to read and write characters in a file
- How to open, close, and query the existence of files
- How to work with information not on disk

Introducing Input/Output Streams

REXX views all input and output information as a series of characters called a *stream*. A REXX program can manipulate most streams as either individual characters or as lines.

A stream can have any one of several possible sources or destinations. You're already familiar with the most common source and destination—standard input (also called *stdin*) and standard output (also called *stdout*). The standard input stream is normally connected to the keyboard; the standard output stream is normally connected to the screen. Both streams can be redirected from the command line. All REXX input functions default to using the stdin stream; all output functions default to using the stdout stream.

A stream can be a file, a serial interface, a printer, or some other device. Files and data objects are *persistent streams*; most devices are *transient streams*. Some operations that are valid with persistent streams cannot be used with transient streams. For instance, you can reread data from a persistent stream, but data can be read only once from a transient stream.

Persistent streams fully support the concept of a read/write location. The location changes as data is read from or written to the stream. You can also explicitly change the location. Transient streams don't support a read/write position because the data on the stream is dynamic.

As an analogy, this book is like a persistent stream. Your current read position is this paragraph, and you can skip forward or backward in the book to change that current read position. A live concert is like a transient stream. You can listen to the concert only in the order that it is played; once a composition is played, you cannot back up in time to listen to it again, nor can you scan ahead to listen to a composition that hasn't been played yet.

A program must open a stream to use it. When the program is done using the stream, it should close it. REXX's input and output functions open streams automatically. REXX closes any open streams when a program exits. An automatically opened stream, other than stdin, stdout, and stderr, is opened for both read and write access, and it cannot be opened by another process until the stream is closed. You can also explicitly open a stream for read-only or write-only access, and you can explicitly close a stream.

The following sections introduce the REXX built-in functions that you use to read and write streams.

Reading and Writing Lines

Text files in OS/2 consist of lines of information, separated by two special characters: a carriage return and a line feed. The REXX functions that read and write lines of text automatically handle these line-end characters, so you need to be concerned only with the data on the line.

Figure 15.1 shows how REXX views a stream of characters that make up three lines. The musical note and box are the character representations of the carriage return and line feed characters.

```
This is a test.♪◘This is only a test.♪◘Testing...♪◘
```

Figure 15.1. *The format of a text stream in OS/2.*

The REXX built-in function `LineIn` reads lines from a file. REXX keeps track of the current read position in the file; the first call to `LineIn` reads the first line in the file, and each subsequent call reads each line in the file in sequence. The syntax for `LineIn` is as follows:

```
value = LineIn([streamname] [, [line] [, count]])
```

`LineIn` reads a line of text from *`streamname`*, beginning at *`line`*. If you omit *`streamname`*, `LineIn` reads from standard input (the keyboard, unless input is redirected). If you omit *`line`*, then the next line is returned, beginning with the first line in the file; the only valid value for *`line`* is `1`. The value *`count`* must be `1` or `0`.

The `LineIn` function can open or close a stream, move the read/write pointer to the beginning of a stream, and read a line from the stream. Table 15.1 shows various forms of the `LineIn` call and the effect each call has on a stream.

Table 15.1. The effect of using various forms of `LineIn`.

Function Call	Effect of the Call
`LineIn()`	Returns a line of text from standard input
`LineIn(name)`	Opens `name` and returns the first line of text from the stream. Additional calls of this type read each line in sequence from the stream.
`LineIn(name, 1, 0)`	Opens `name` and moves the read/write pointer to the beginning of the stream; does not read any data from the stream

The `Lines` function determines whether any lines remain to read from a stream. Here's the syntax:

```
rc = Lines([streamname])
```

`Lines` returns `1` if there is data between the current read/write position and the end of stream; it returns `0` if there is no data left to read.

Listing 15.1 uses a combination of `Lines` and `LineIn` to read from CONFIG.SYS and display any lines containing `BASEDEV`.

Listing 15.1. Reading lines from a file.

```
/* list1501.cmd */

filename = 'C:\config.sys'

DO WHILE Lines(filename)
  line = LineIn(filename)
  IF Pos('BASEDEV', line) >< 0 THEN
    SAY line
END

EXIT
```

```
[D:\]list1501
BASEDEV=PRINT01.SYS
BASEDEV=IBM1FLPY.ADD
BASEDEV=AHA174X.ADD
BASEDEV=OS2DASD.DMD
BASEDEV=OS2SCSI.DMD
BASEDEV=OS2ASPI.DMD
BASEDEV=SBCD2.ADD /P:220
```

In the program in listing 15.1, each line from CONFIG.SYS is read, and lines that contain the text `BASEDEV` are displayed. Lines are read until the `Lines` function returns `0`. To make this program work correctly, you should change the drive letter on the third line of the program to match the location of your OS/2 CONFIG.SYS.

The `LineOut` function writes lines to a file. `LineOut` automatically opens the stream if it hasn't been opened yet and by default appends lines to the end of the file. Here's the syntax for `LineOut`:

```
rc = LineOut([streamname] [, [string] [, line])
```

`LineOut` writes *`string`* to *`streamname`* at *`line`*. If you don't supply *`string`* and *`line`*, `LineOut` closes the file. *`Line`* can only be `1`; if *`line`* is not supplied, string is written at the current read/write position for the stream. When `LineOut` opens a stream, its default action is to set the read/write position to the end of the stream.

The following example uses `LineOut` and `LineIn` to copy a text file, one line at a time:

```
DO WHILE Lines(inputFile)
  CALL LineOut outputFile, LineIn(inputFile)
END
```

The `LineOut` function can open or close a stream, move the read/write pointer to the beginning of a stream, and append or overwrite lines in the stream. Table 15.2 shows various forms of the `LineOut` call and the effect each call has on a stream.

Table 15.2. The effect of using various forms of `LineOut`.

Function Call	Effect of the Call
`LineOut( , text)`	Writes `text` to the standard output
`LineOut(name, text)`	Opens `name` and appends `text` to the end of the stream
`LineOut(name, text, 1)`	Opens `name` and `writes` text to the beginning of the stream
`LineOut(name)`	Closes stream `name`
`LineOut(name, , 1)`	Opens `name` and moves the read/write pointer to the beginning of the stream but does not write anything to the stream

The program in listing 15.2 reads CONFIG.SYS and writes each line to CONFIG.NEW. If the line is recognized as a list of paths, then the program checks each directory in the list and removes any directories that are not found.

Type **Listing 15.2. Cleaning path variables in CONFIG.SYS.**

```
/* list1502.cmd */

CALL SetLocal
config = 'C:\config.sys'
newcfg = 'C:\config.new'

IF Lines(newcfg) > 0 THEN
  DO
  CALL LineOut(newcfg) /* close the file */
  '@del' newcfg '> NUL'
  END

DO WHILE Lines(config) >< 0
  line = LineIn(config)
  line = Strip(line, 'B')
  SELECT
    WHEN Left(line, 9) = 'SET PATH=' THEN
      DO
      SAY 'Cleaning PATH...'
      PARSE VAR line . '=' thePath
      line = 'SET PATH=' || CleanPath(thePath)
      END
    WHEN Left(line, 8) = 'LIBPATH=' THEN
      DO
      SAY 'Cleaning LIBPATH...'
      PARSE VAR line . '=' thePath
      line = 'LIBPATH=' || CleanPath(thePath)
      END
    WHEN Left(line, 10) = 'SET DPATH=' THEN
      DO
      SAY 'Cleaning DPATH...'
      PARSE VAR line . '=' thePath
      line = 'SET DPATH=' || CleanPath(thePath)
      END
    OTHERWISE
      NOP
  END
  CALL LineOut newcfg, line
END

SAY 'All changes written to' newcfg
CALL EndLocal
EXIT

CleanPath: PROCEDURE
  thePath = Arg(1)
  newPath = ''
  IF Left(thePath, 1) = ';' THEN
    thePath = SubStr(thePath, 2)
```

```
DO WHILE thePath >< ''
  PARSE VAR thePath aDir ';' thePath
  SELECT
    WHEN aDir = '' THEN /* handle double semicolons */
      ITERATE
    WHEN aDir = '.' THEN
      newPath = '.;' || newPath
    WHEN Directory(aDir) >< aDir THEN
      SAY '  Removing "' || aDir || '" (dir not found)'
    OTHERWISE
      newPath = newPath || aDir || ';'
  END
END
RETURN newPath
```

```
[D:\]list1502
Cleaning LIBPATH...
Cleaning PATH...
  Removing "C:\NotHere" (dir not found)
Cleaning DPATH...
  Removing "L:\NLS" (dir not found)
  Removing "P:\NLS" (dir not found)
All changes written to C:\config.new
```

The program in listing 15.2 reads each line from CONFIG.SYS, checks and cleans the line if it defines the `PATH`, `LIBPATH`, or `DPATH`, and writes the line to CONFIG.NEW. The variables are cleaned by checking each directory in the list. The `Directory` function tries to change to each directory in the list; if `Directory` fails, then the directory is removed from the list. To make the program work correctly, you should ensure that the drive on lines four and five in the program matches the location of OS/2 on your system.

Reading and Writing Characters

At times, you don't want to write (or read) a line. You may need to process a file that consists of binary data, or you may want to write text to the screen without the cursor moving to the beginning of the next line.

The `CharIn` function reads one or more characters from an input stream. If the stream is not open, `CharIn` automatically opens the stream. Here's the syntax:

```
value = CharIn([streamname] [, [start] [, length]])
```

The `CharIn` function can open or close a stream, move the read/write position to a different point in a stream, and read one or more characters from the stream. Table 15.3 shows various forms of the `CharIn` call and the effect each call has on a stream.

Table 15.3. The effect of using various forms of `CharIn`.

Function Call	Effect of the Call
`CharIn()`	Reads one character from the standard input. (Execution stops until the user presses the Enter key, unless standard input is redirected.)
`CharIn(, , 3)`	Reads three characters from the standard input
`CharIn(name)`	Opens `name` and reads one character from the beginning of the stream
`CharIn(name, , 5)`	Opens `name` and reads five characters from the beginning of the stream
`CharIn(name, 1, 0)`	Moves the read/write pointer to the beginning of the stream without reading any data

The `Chars` function returns the number of characters remaining in the input stream. The syntax for `Chars` is as follows:

```
count = Chars([streamname])
```

`Chars` returns the number of characters following the current read/write position in *`streamname`*.

The program in listing 15.3 demonstrates how you can use `Chars` and `CharIn` to create a hexadecimal dump of any file. Notice how the `Translate` function inserts spaces in the hexadecimal string.

Listing 15.3. Using `CharIn` to read a binary file.

```
/* list1503.cmd */

PARSE ARG file
IF file = '' THEN
  SIGNAL Usage

toDots = XRange('7F'x, '1F'x) /* non-printing chars */
spaced = ''
packed = ''
letterA = C2D('A') /* decimal value for 'A' */
DO i = 0 TO 31 BY 2
  theseTwo = D2C(letterA + i) || D2C(letterA + i + 1)
  spaced = spaced theseTwo
```

```
  packed = packed || theseTwo
END

loc = 0
lines = 0
DO WHILE Chars(file) > 0
  data = CharIn(file, , 16) /* get 16 bytes */
  xdata = C2X(data)         /* convert to hex */
  data = Translate(data, Copies('.', 256), toDots)
  xdata = Translate(spaced, xdata, packed)
  CALL LineOut , D2X(loc, 4)':' xdata'  'data
  lines = lines + 1
  IF lines = 23 THEN /* display output in pages */
    DO
    SAY '--More--'
    PULL .
    lines = 0
    END
  loc = loc + 16
END

EXIT

Usage:
  SAY 'Usage:'
  SAY '  list1503 filename'
  EXIT
```

```
[D:\]list1503 C:\OS2\ANSI.EXE
0000:  4D 5A 13 00 0B 00 00 00 04 00 00 00 FF FF 00 00  MZ..............
0010:  B8 00 00 00 00 00 00 00 40 00 00 00 00 00 00 00  ........@.......
0020:  00 00 00 00 00 00 00 00 00 00 00 00 00 00 00 00  ................
0030:  00 00 00 00 00 00 00 00 00 00 00 00 80 00 00 00  ................
0040:  0E 1F BA 0E 00 B4 09 CD 21 B8 01 4C CD 21 54 68  ........!..L.!Th
0050:  69 73 20 70 72 6F 67 72 61 6D 20 63 61 6E 6E 6F  is program canno
0060:  74 20 62 65 20 72 75 6E 20 69 6E 20 44 4F 53 20  t be run in DOS 
0070:  6D 6F 64 65 2E 0D 0D 0A 24 00 00 00 00 00 00 00  mode....$.......
0080:  4E 45 05 0A 86 00 02 00 2B CF 7D 68 02 02 02 00  NE......+.}h....
0090:  00 14 00 14 F0 00 01 00 00 00 02 00 02 00 05 00  ................
00A0:  0C 00 40 00 50 00 50 00 58 00 62 00 08 01 00 00  ..@.P.P.X.b.....
00B0:  00 00 09 00 00 00 01 00 00 00 00 00 00 00 00 00  ................
00C0:  01 00 30 0F 70 0D 30 0F 09 00 13 02 01 0C 00 07  ..0.p.0.........
00D0:  04 41 4E 53 49 00 00 00 01 00 0A 00 13 00 1C 00  .ANSI...........
00E0:  20 00 00 08 44 4F 53 43 41 4C 4C 53 08 56 49 4F   ...DOSCALLS.VIO
00F0:  43 41 4C 4C 53 08 4B 42 44 43 41 4C 4C 53 03 4E  CALLS.KBDCALLS.N
0100:  4C 53 03 4D 53 47 00 00 08 41 4E 53 49 2E 45 58  LS.MSG...ANSI.EX
0110:  45 00 00 00 00 00 00 00 00 00 00 00 00 00 00 00  E...............
0120:  00 00 00 00 00 00 00 00 00 00 00 00 00 00 00 00  ................
0130:  00 00 00 00 00 00 00 00 00 00 00 00 00 00 00 00  ................
0140:  00 00 00 00 00 00 00 00 00 00 00 00 00 00 00 00  ................
0150:  00 00 00 00 00 00 00 00 00 00 00 00 00 00 00 00  ................
0160:  00 00 00 00 00 00 00 00 00 00 00 00 00 00 00 00  ................
--More--
```

Analysis The program in listing 15.3 displays a hexadecimal dump of a file. The file is read in 16-character blocks, each block of characters is converted to a hexadecimal string, and `Translate` inserts spaces in the string. `Translate` also converts nonprinting characters to periods in the data read from the file. An offset in the file, the hexadecimal string, and the converted characters from the file are concatenated and displayed as one line.

Because the technique used to insert spaces in the hexadecimal string may not be obvious, the following steps should help clarify the process:

1. The `spaced` and `packed` strings are created for use with `Translate`. The first characters in `spaced` look like this:

   ```
   AB CD EF GH IJ KL MN OP
   ```

   The first characters in `packed` look like this:

   ```
   ABCDEFGHIJKLMNOP
   ```

   Notice how the same characters appear in both strings.

2. Sixteen bytes of input data are converted to hexadecimal and stored in `xdata`, which results in 32 bytes in the hexadecimal string.

3. The `Translate` function is called, using `spaced` as the string to translate, `xdata` as the output table, and `packed` as the input table. If `xdata` is `987654`, then a (somewhat truncated) call to `Translate` would look like the following:

   ```
   xdata = Translate('AB CD EF', '987654', 'ABCDEF')
   ```

   `Translate` translates the `A` in `spaced` to `9`, based on the input table `packed` (from `A`) and the output table `xdata` (to `9`). Following the same pattern, `B` in `spaced` is translated to `8`, `C` to `7`, `D` to `6`, and so on. The resulting string is `98 76 54`.

The `CharOut` function writes one or more characters to a stream. If the stream is not open, `CharOut` opens it. The syntax for `CharOut` is as follows:

```
rc = CharOut([streamname] [, [string] [, start]])
```

`CharOut` writes *`string`* to *`streamname`* beginning at read/write position *`start`*.

The `CharOut` function can open or close a stream, move the read/write position to a different point in a stream, and write one or more characters to the stream. Table 15.4 shows various forms of the `CharOut` call and the effect each call has on a stream.

Table 15.4. The effect of using various forms of `CharOut`.

Function Call	Effect of the Call
`CharOut( , text)`	Writes `text` to the standard output
`CharOut(name, text)`	Opens `name` and appends `text` to the end of the stream
`CharOut(name, text, 8)`	Opens `name` and writes `text` beginning at the eighth character position in the stream. The function fails if the stream has fewer than eight characters.
`CharOut(name, , 34)`	Moves the read/write pointer to the 34th character position in the stream. No data is written. The function fails if the stream has fewer than 34 characters.

The program in listing 15.6 performs a safe copy of a file. The program checks to ensure that it is not overwriting a file of the same name as the output file. The `CharIn` and `CharOut` functions are used so that both binary and text files can be copied (a binary file is not organized as lines, so `LineIn` and `LineOut` would fail to process the file correctly).

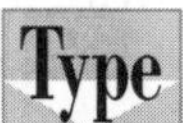

Listing 15.4. Copying a file using `CharIn` and `CharOut`.

```
/* list1504.cmd */

PARSE ARG copyFrom copyTo
IF copyFrom = '' ¦ copyTo = '' THEN
  DO
  SAY 'Usage:'
  SAY '  list1504 from-filename to-filename'
  EXIT
  END

insize = Chars(copyFrom)
IF insize = 0 THEN
  DO
  SAY copyFrom 'has no length or was not found'
  EXIT
  END

outsize = Chars(copyTo)
IF outsize >< 0 THEN
  DO
  SAY 'File "' ¦¦ copyTo ¦¦ '" exists.'
```

continues

Listing 15.4. continued

```
    DO UNTIL Abbrev('YES', ans, 1)
      CALL CharOut , 'Do you want to copy over it (Y/N)? '
      PULL ans
      IF Abbrev('NO', ans, 1) THEN
        DO
        SAY 'Copy not performed.'
        EXIT
        END
    END
    CALL CharOut(copyTo) /* close the file */
    'del' copyTo '> NUL'
    END

  buffer = CharIn(copyFrom, 1, insize)
  CALL CharOut copyTo, buffer

  EXIT
```

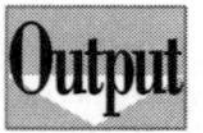

```
[D:\]list1504 list1504.cmd testing.cmd

[D:\]list1504 list1504.cmd testing.cmd
File "testing.cmd" exists.
Do you want to copy over it (Y/N)? y
```

In the program in listing 15.4, the contents of an input file are copied to an output file. If the output file exists, the user is prompted before the file is overwritten. Notice how `CharOut` displays the prompt so that the user input is to the right of the prompt.

The *Stream* Function

Sometimes it's necessary to do more than just read or write a stream. You may need to open a stream for read-only, move the read/write pointer in a persistent stream, or determine whether a file exists.

The `Stream` function opens, closes, and gets information about a stream. The syntax for `Stream` is as follows:

```
result = Stream(filename [, operation [, command]] )
```

The *`operation`* is either `Command`, `Description`, or `State` (or the characters `C`, `D`, or `S`). When *`operation`* is `Command`, the third parameter, *`command`*, must be one of the values shown in table 15.5.

Table 15.5. Commands for `Stream` operation `Command`.

Command	Description
`OPEN`	Opens the stream for both reading and writing
`OPEN READ`	Opens the stream for reading only
`OPEN WRITE`	Opens the stream for writing only. Reading the stream produces an empty string.
`CLOSE`	Closes the stream
`SEEK` [= | < | + | -] *`offset`*	Moves a persistent stream's read/write pointer to *`offset`*. The effects of the optional characters are as follows: = indicates offset is the distance from the beginning of the stream (default); < moves to *`offset`* from the end of the stream; + moves *`offset`* forward; and - moves *`offset`* backward.
`QUERY EXISTS`	If the stream exists, returns the fully qualified path and filename; otherwise returns an empty string
`QUERY SIZE`	Returns the size of the stream in bytes
`QUERY DATETIME`	Returns the date and time that the stream was last changed

When *`operation`* is `State`, `Stream` returns one of the values shown in table 15.6.

Table 15.6. Values returned by the `State` operation of the `Stream` function.

Returned Value	Meaning
`ERROR`	An erroneous operation was performed on the stream.
`NOTREADY`	An input or output operation will raise the `NotReady` condition. (See "Trapping Input and Output Errors" later in this lesson.)
`READY`	Input and output operations may be performed.
`UNKNOWN`	The stream is in an unknown state. Usually, this value indicates that the stream is not open or does not exist.

The `Description` operation returns the same values as `State`, except the returned value is followed by a colon and any additional information available. For instance, if a stream is at the end of the file, the value returned is `NOTREADY:EOF`.

Accessing Other Devices

Streams can be devices rather than files. Almost all devices are transient streams. Table 15.7 lists some of the more common device names.

Table 15.7. Valid device names.

Device Name	Description
`COM1:`, `COM2:`	Communication ports
`CON:`	Display screen input and output
`KBD:`	Keyboard input
`LPT1:`, `LPT2:`	Printer devices
`PRN:`	Default printer output
`STDERR:`	Standard error output
`STDIN:`	Standard input
`STDOUT:`	Standard output
`QUEUE:`	REXX external data queue (covered on Day 21)

You read and write devices the same way you read and write other streams.

The program in listing 15.5 uses a communication port to call the Automatic Computer Time Service (ACTS) and get the current date and time. (ACTS is maintained by the National Institute of Standards.)

Type **Listing 15.5. Setting the system date and time from ACTS.**

```
/* list1505.cmd */

zone  = -420   /* minutes adjustment for MST */
phone = '1 303-494-4774'
port  = 'COM1' /* modem's COM port (may be COM2, COM3, ...) */

days. = 31     /* days per month */
```

```
days.2  = 28
days.4  = 30
days.6  = 30
days.9  = 30
days.11 = 30

CALL Stream port, 'C', 'OPEN'
'@mode' port || ':1200,E,7,1 > NUL' /* set the modem parameters */

CALL LineOut port, 'ATDT' || phone  /* dial the number */

started = Time('E')
inStr = ''
errMsg = ''
DO UNTIL Pos('CONNECT', inStr) >< 0 /* wait for connection */
  inStr = LineIn(port)
  SELECT
    WHEN Pos('NO CARRIER', inStr) >< 0 THEN
      errMsg = 'No carrier.'
    WHEN Time('E') - started > 45 THEN  /* give up after 45 seconds */
      errMsg = 'Time out.'
    OTHERWISE
      NOP
  END
  IF errMsg >< '' THEN
    DO
    CALL Hangup
    SAY errMsg
    EXIT
    END
END

inStr = ''
DO UNTIL Pos('UTC', inStr) >< 0
  inStr = inStr || CharIn(port)
  IF Time('E') - started > 45 THEN
    DO
    CALL Hangup
    SAY 'Time out.'
    EXIT
    END
END

CALL Hangup
/* Expected string looks like (after misc. startup chars.): */
/* 49528 94-06-25 14:45:53 50 1 -.2 045.0 UTC */
PARSE VALUE Right(inStr, 41) WITH . yr '-' mnth '-' day ,
    hh ':' mm ':' ss daylightSavings .

minutes = 60 * hh + mm  /* Adjust from Greenwich Mean Time */
minutes = minutes + zone
IF minutes < 0 THEN
  DO
  minutes = 24 * 60 + minutes
  day = day - 1
```

continues

Listing 15.5. continued

```
    IF day = 0 THEN
      DO
      mnth = mnth - 1
      IF mnth = 0 THEN
        DO
        yr = yr - 1
        mnth = 12
        END
      IF yr // 4 = 0 THEN /* leap year? */
        days.2 = 29
      day = days.mnth
      END
    END
  hh = minutes % 60
  mm = Right(minutes // 60, 2, '0')
  '@date' mnth'-'day'-'yr  /* change system date ... */
  '@time' hh':'mm':'ss     /* ... and time. */
  SAY 'New date and time is:' Date() Time()

  EXIT

  Hangup: PROCEDURE EXPOSE port
    CALL LineOut port, ''
    CALL LineOut port, ''
    CALL LineOut port, 'ATH'  /* Standard modem hangup command */
    CALL Stream port, 'C', 'CLOSE'
    RETURN
```

```
[D:\]list1505
New date and time is: 25 June 1994 12:23:18
```

The program in listing 15.5 uses your modem to call the ACTS and update your computer's date and time settings. Although the program is fairly long, it's actually a rather simple program. The ACTS returns the current Greenwich Meridian Time (GMT) as a string. Because the string contains more information than is needed, the `PARSE` instruction extracts only the information that is needed. About a third of the program is concerned with adjusting the date and time to the current time zone. The steps for handling the communications are as follows:

1. The communications port is opened using `Stream`.
2. The OS/2 `MODE` command is executed to set the communications parameters for the port.
3. The modem is sent a dialing command concatenated to the phone number.

4. The program waits in a loop for 45 seconds for the `CONNECT` message from the modem. A `NO CARRIER` message from the modem causes the program to exit (it could attempt redialing the number instead).
5. The program enters a second loop and collects the date and time string from ACTS. This string ends with the characters `UTC`. After these characters are received, the loop exits. If `UTC` isn't received within 45 seconds, the program exits.
6. The modem is sent a hang-up command, and the communications port is closed.

The time and date are then adjusted to the current time zone. The user must set the `zone` variable to the number of minutes' difference between the user's time zone and GMT. The ACTS time is converted to the number of minutes since midnight, and the adjustment is applied. If the adjustment crosses a day, month, or year, the date is altered accordingly. Finally, the time is converted back to hours, minutes, and seconds, and the OS/2 `DATE` and `TIME` commands set the system date and time.

Note: At worst, the time set by this program should be no more than a second behind the actual ACTS time. Any time lost is caused by the processing between the point that the date and time string is received from ACTS and the `DATE` and `TIME` commands are executed.

Techniques for Working with Streams

This section introduces a few useful techniques for working with streams. These techniques include trapping errors, writing filter programs, and sending data to a printer.

Trapping Input and Output Errors

The stream input and output functions can raise the `NotReady` condition for a variety of errors. If your program isn't trapping the `NotReady` condition, your program continues running without interruption. If the `NotReady` condition is trapped by a `SIGNAL ON`, REXX immediately transfers control to the code following the `NotReady` label.

The most common reason that the NotReady condition is raised is an attempt to read past the end of a file. The following example uses the NotReady condition to break out of a file-copying loop when the end of a file is reached:

```
SIGNAL ON NotReady
DO FOREVER
  CALL LineOut outFile, LineIn(inFile)
END
NotReady:
```

You can use the NotReady condition with Stream and Condition to determine the reason the condition was raised. When Condition is called with the Description option, it returns the name of the stream that raised the condition. You can get further information about the current state of the stream by calling Stream with its Description option.

The program in listing 15.6 demonstrates how the NotReady condition can move exception testing code out of the main program. The program tests for a bad filename only when REXX raises the NotReady condition.

Listing 15.6. Using the NotReady condition to trap file errors.

```
/* list1506.cmd */

SIGNAL ON NotReady
PARSE ARG filename

DO WHILE Lines(filename)
  SAY LineIn(filename)
END

SAY '>>> end of file <<<'
EXIT

NotReady:
  nm = Condition('D')
  PARSE VALUE Stream(nm, 'D') WITH state ':' info
  SELECT
    WHEN info = 'EOF' THEN
      NOP
    WHEN state = 'UNKNOWN' THEN
      SAY 'File "' || nm || '" not found.'
    OTHERWISE
      SAY 'Error accessing file "' || nm || '"'
  END
  EXIT
```

```
[D:\]list1506 list1301.cmd
/* list1301.cmd */

DO FOREVER
  SAY "First name:"
  PARSE PULL firstName
  SELECT
  WHEN firstName = '?' THEN
    SAY "The applicant's first, or given, name."
  WHEN firstName = '' THEN
    SAY "The first name is required information."
  OTHERWISE
    LEAVE
  END
END

EXIT
>>> end of file <<<

[D:\]list1506 N:\WrongDrive.Txt
File "N:\WrongDrive.Txt" not found.
```

The program in listing 15.6 captures the `NotReady` condition. When the `NotReady` condition is raised, the name of the stream is captured using the `Condition` function. The `Stream` function gets information about the current state of the stream. Messages then are printed based on the stream's state.

Creating Filters

A filter is a special kind of program that reads standard input, manipulates the data read, and writes the result to standard output. The OS/2 SORT and MORE programs are examples of filters.

You can either explicitly use `STDIN:` and `STDOUT:`, or you can allow the input and output functions to default to the standard streams by not specifying any stream name.

Listing 15.7 shows how to write a filter; this particular filter removes duplicate lines from its input. This type of program is usually only used with sorted data.

Listing 15.7. Reading standard input and writing standard output.

```
/* list1507.cmd */

PARSE ARG infile outfile
IF outfile = '' THEN
  outfile = 'STDOUT'
IF infile = '' THEN
  infile = 'STDIN'
```

continues

Listing 15.7. continued

```
this = 0
DO WHILE Lines(infile)
  line.this = LineIn(infile)
  last = \ this  /* switch between 1 and 0 */
  IF line.this >< line.last THEN
    CALL LineOut outfile, line.this
  this = last
END

EXIT
```

```
[D:\]type list1507.dat
oranges
apples
peaches
celery
oranges
carrots
celery
mangoes

[D:\]sort < list1507.dat ¦ list1507
apples
carrots
celery
mangoes
oranges
peaches
```

In the program in listing 15.7, each line of input is read and compared to the last line of input read. If the lines are not equal, then the current line is written. The current and last lines are stored in a compound variable whose tail is either `0` or `1`. The not operator flips the value of the tail (`this`) so that the location where the current line is stored oscillates between the two positions. Assuming that the input is sorted, the resulting output contains only unique values.

Printing

Writing data to a printer requires some special consideration. For most dot-matrix printers and many laser printers, you can use `LineOut` to write directly to the printer device with good results. However, to produce a nicely formatted printout or to print anything on a PostScript printer, you need to send some special codes to the printer.

Most printers use special codes to perform a form feed, write bold text, or use a different font. Each type of printer is different, so you need to read your printer manual if you want to make the printer do anything other than the simplest printing actions.

15

One of the most common printer control codes is the form feed. The form feed character makes the printer move the paper to the top of the next page. For most printers, you can use the form feed character, which is an ASCII 12 (`D2C(12)` or `'0C'x`). If you use `CharOut` to send this character, the printer moves to the top of the next page without feeding additional blank lines.

Text sent to a PostScript printer requires quite a bit of processing because you must embed the text you want to print in a special PostScript program (PostScript itself is a programming language). If you send only the text to the printer, nothing prints. The program in listing 15.8 shows how to print a text file on a PostScript printer.

Type

Listing 15.8. Sending text to a PostScript printer.

```
/* list1508.cmd */

PARSE ARG filename printer
IF printer = '' THEN
  printer = 'PRN:'
IF filename = '' THEN
  DO
  SAY 'Usage:'
  SAY '  list1508 filename [printer-port]'
  EXIT
  END

pointsPerInch = 72
margins       = Trunc(pointsPerInch * 0.5)
pageLength    = 11 * pointsPerInch /* 8.5 x 11 inch paper */
linesPerPage = 66
lineHeight    = (pageLength - margins * 2) / linesPerPage
lineHeight    = Trunc(lineHeight)

CALL LineOut printer, '% Generated by list1508.cmd'
CALL LineOut printer, '/fnt /Courier findfont' lineHeight ,
    'scalefont def'
CALL LineOut printer, 'fnt setfont gsave'

lineLoc = pageLength - margins
DO i = 1 WHILE Lines(filename)
  IF i > linesPerPage THEN
    DO
    CALL LineOut printer, 'showpage grestore gsave'
    i = 1
    lineLoc = pageLength - margins
    END
  text = LineIn(filename)
  IF text >< '' THEN
    DO
    ix = Verify(text, '\()', 'M')
    DO WHILE ix >< 0
      text = Insert('\', text, ix - 1)
```

continues

Listing 15.8. continued

```
        ix = Verify(text, '\()', 'M', ix + 2)
      END
      CALL LineOut printer, margins lineLoc 'moveto (' || ,
          text || ') show'
      END
    lineLoc = lineLoc - lineHeight
  END

  CALL LineOut printer, 'showpage grestore'
  CALL CharOut printer, D2C(4)  /* ^D (end of job) */
  CALL Stream printer, 'C', 'Close'

  EXIT
```

```
[D:\]list1508 autoexec.bat CON:
% Generated by list1508.cmd
/fnt /Courier findfont 10 scalefont def
fnt setfont gsave
36 756 moveto (@ECHO OFF) show
36 746 moveto (ECHO.) show
36 736 moveto (PROMPT $p$g) show
36 726 moveto (PATH C:\\OS2;C:\\OS2\\MDOS;C:\\OS2\\MDOS\\WINOS2;C:\\;) show
36 716 moveto (LOADHIGH APPEND C:\\OS2;C:\\OS2\\SYSTEM) show
36 706 moveto (SET BLASTER=A220 I5 D1 H7 P300 T6) show
36 696 moveto (SET SOUND=D:\\SB16) show
36 676 moveto (rem %SOUND%\\SBCONFIG.EXE /S) show
36 666 moveto (SET TMP=C:\\) show
36 656 moveto (SET TEMP=C:\\OS2\\MDOS\\WINOS2\\TEMP) show
showpage grestore
```

◆

The program in listing 15.8 reads a file one line of text at a time, modifies the text so that it will print correctly, embeds the text in a PostScript program, and writes the text to the printer device. The output shown here is the PostScript program that is sent to the printer. The destination was forced to `CON:` so that the output could be captured; you normally send the PostScript output to a printer port. Following is how this program works:

- All measurements for the printer are in points. There are 72 points per inch.
- Locations are measured from the bottom-left corner of the page.
- The parentheses and the backslash have special meaning to PostScript. To remove the special meaning so that the characters are printed as part of the text, the characters must be *quoted*. PostScript uses a backslash to quote individual characters, so the program must scan the text and insert backslashes where necessary. Notice how the `Verify` function scans for any one of the three characters.

Summary

This lesson introduced the concept of streams. You learned how to read and write data in files and how to manipulate streams going to and from other devices.

The lesson showed you how to use the `Stream` function to control a stream and get information about the current state of a stream. You also learned how to trap the `NotReady` condition and use `Stream` to determine why the `NotReady` condition was raised.

The lesson covered the line-oriented and character-oriented input and output functions. The `LineIn`, `LineOut`, and `Lines` functions process text files that are made up of lines. The `CharIn`, `CharOut`, and `Chars` functions can read and write one or more characters from a text or binary file.

Q&A

Q How is the `STDERR` stream used?

A The `STDERR` stream is another standard output stream that also goes to the display by default. If you want a program to display a message to the user and standard output is redirected, then you can use `STDERR` in the program so that the message appears on the user's screen. Writing error messages to `STDERR` also allows the user to redirect errors to a separate file from any other output.

Q What is the difference between using the `PULL` and `SAY` instructions and using the `LineIn` and `LineOut` functions?

A The `PULL` and `SAY` instructions use only the standard input and standard output streams. You should use them in most situations in which you want to communicate with a user. If you don't want the user to redirect the input and output of your program, you can use `LineIn` and `LineOut` with the `KBD:` or `CON:` devices.

Workshop

The Workshop provides quiz questions to help strengthen your understanding of the material covered and exercises to provide you with experience in using what you've learned.

Quiz

1. What is a stream?
2. How are persistent streams different from transient streams?
3. What are the differences between reading/writing lines and reading/writing characters?
4. What information does the `Chars` function return?
5. Why would you want to open a stream for read-only access?
6. What is a filter?
7. Why should you close a stream when you're done with it?
8. How can you trap error conditions created when reading and writing streams?

Exercises

1. Design and write a filter program that performs the same functions as the OS/2 MORE program. The program should read standard input and write lines of text to standard output. The program should pause every 24 lines, display the message `-- More --`, and wait for the user to press Enter before displaying the next 24 lines. (MORE uses the current screen size, which may not be 24 lines. Your program won't have the capability to determine the current screen size.)
2. The following program contains errors. Find the errors and fix the program.

```
/* Ex15-2.cmd */
PARSE ARG filename
DO i = 1 UNTIL Lines(filename)
  SAY Right(i, 4) || ':' LineIn(filename, 1)
END
EXIT
```

3. Design and write a program that computes total pay earned for employees and that writes the result to a file. You should use an input file to supply the employee number, hourly wage, and hours worked. Here's an example input file:

```
4176 12.55 45.25
5011  8.25 40
9055 16.80 31.5
```

Don't worry about calculating overtime or withholding taxes. The program should also track the total amount owed all employees and display the final total when it's done processing the input file.

4. Modify the program in exercise 3 so that it includes the employees' names in the output file. A second input file that contains employee numbers and names should be read to determine the names of the employees. Here's an example of an employee name file:

```
4176 Walt Jackson
5011 Dick Kreuger
9055 Evelyn Hitch
```

Introducing RexxUtil Functions

WEEK 3

The RexxUtil functions provide REXX access to the OS/2 desktop, and they replace many of the OS/2 commands with much more powerful functions. This lesson introduces you to using RexxUtil and other external libraries. Today you learn the following:

- What the RexxUtil library is
- How to access external libraries
- How to use the RexxUtil function `SysGetKey` to process individual keystrokes
- How to use the RexxUtil functions `SysCurPos` and `SysCurState` to position and hide the cursor
- How to use the `INTERPRET` instruction to process a string as a REXX instruction
- How to create menus and input dialogs

RexxUtil and Other External Libraries

A *library* is a collection of functions that is available for use by more than one program. Just like a public library provides access to books, a library lets many programs share the same functions. Libraries that are accessible by REXX are always in the form of a *dynamic link library*, or DLL. A DLL is a reusable resource in OS/2—many programs can share the functions in a single DLL. An *external library* is a library that supplies functions that aren't a standard part of the REXX language.

The RexxUtil library is a DLL that is supplied with OS/2. It is an external library that is designed to extend the functionality of REXX in the OS/2 environment.

All external libraries are written in a programming language other than REXX, usually C or C++. An external library must be specially written to be used with REXX.

Registering External Functions

Before you can use an external function in a REXX program, you need to register the function with REXX. Registering a function adds that function to REXX until the next time OS/2 is shut down. REXX provides the built-in function `RxFuncAdd`, which registers external functions. The syntax for `RxFuncAdd` is as follows:

```
rc = RxFuncAdd(functionName, module, entryName)
```

The `functionName` is the name of the function to register. The `module` is the name of the DLL that contains the function. The `entryName` is the entry point within the function—in almost all cases, `entryName` is identical to `functionName`. In the few cases that they may be different, the documentation that came with the library should clearly state that `entryName` is different from `functionName`. The return code `rc` is either `0` or `1`. If `RxFuncAdd` cannot register the function, it returns `0`; otherwise, it returns `1`. Most programmers call `RxFuncAdd` as a procedure and ignore the return code. If `RxFuncAdd` fails, the program generates an error the first time an external function is called.

Many external libraries supply a function that, when called, registers all the other functions in the library. It's only necessary to register the one function and then call it to register all the functions in the library. You need to read the documentation for any external library to find out if such a function is supplied. If the library doesn't supply such a function, you need to use `RxFuncAdd` to register each function individually.

The RexxUtil library supplies the function `SysLoadFuncs` to register all the RexxUtil functions. You must register `SysLoadFuncs` and then call it to make all the RexxUtil functions available. Here's the actual code, with `RxFuncAdd` called as a procedure:

```
CALL RxFuncAdd 'SysLoadFuncs', 'RexxUtil', 'SysLoadFuncs'
CALL SysLoadFuncs
```

`RxFuncAdd` is a built-in REXX function that returns `0` if it successfully added the external function. If `RxFuncAdd` fails to register the function, it returns a code indicating the error.

The built-in function `RxFuncQuery` is useful for finding out whether an external function is registered. `RxFuncQuery` returns `0` if the external function is registered, or it returns `1` if the function is not registered. Notice that `RxFuncQuery` returns false if the function is registered. This response is probably the opposite of what you might expect.

The following example is a procedure that shows how you can combine these functions to load RexxUtil when necessary. You can include this procedure in a program and call it to load the library:

```
LoadRexxUtil: PROCEDURE
  IF RxFuncQuery('SysLoadFuncs') THEN
    DO
    IF RxFuncAdd('SysLoadFuncs', 'RexxUtil', 'SysLoadFuncs') THEN
      DO
      SAY "Error: Couldn't load RexxUtil library."
      RETURN 1
      END
    CALL SysLoadFuncs
    END
  RETURN 0
```

This procedure is actually a function; it returns `1` when it cannot load RexxUtil, and it returns `0` when it's successful. Also, this procedure takes a rather conservative approach.

If RexxUtil is already registered, `LoadRexxUtil` simply returns. If `RxFuncAdd` fails, an error message appears. You use `LoadRexxUtil` in your program as follows:

```
IF LoadRexxUtil() THEN
  EXIT
```

Here you can see why `LoadRexxUtil` returns `0` (false) when it is successful. If the function used `1` to indicate success, you would have to test for `¬ LoadRexxUtil()` instead.

A Simple Menu

Many applications need menus that enable the user to choose from a list of possible actions. You can set up menus in several different ways. The simplest style of menu to program is one that asks the user to enter a number. For example, the menu might look like this:

```
 1 Run your word processor
 2 Run your spreadsheet
 3 Quit for the day

Enter your selection:
```

The user selects from this type of menu by entering the number preceding the menu item. Although this type of menu is easy for you to program, it's not very friendly for the user. A menu of this type always contains two focal points: the user must look at the menu and at the entry prompt. Typing the wrong number is also easy.

The style of menu that you develop in this lesson is one that uses a reverse video "cursor bar." The user highlights a menu item by using the arrow keys and selects an item by pressing Enter. To implement this style of menu, you need RexxUtil functions. The following sections introduce the functions and demonstrate how each function works on its own. Then you put them together to implement the menu.

Processing Individual Keys

REXX does not supply any built-in function to process individual keystrokes. Also, the built-in input methods require the user to press Enter following any input. Both of these problems are solved by the RexxUtil function `SysGetKey`.

The `SysGetKey` function returns a code after an individual keystroke; the code indicates what key the user pressed. Here's the syntax for `SysGetKey`:

```
key = SysGetKey([option])
```

The *key* is the key that was pressed. The *option* is either ECHO or NOECHO. The default is ECHO, which means that the typed character appears on the screen. If you use the NOECHO option, typed characters do not appear on the screen.

You can use SysGetKey to capture almost all the keys that can be pressed on the keyboard, including the function keys, the cursor (or arrow) keys, and keys that are used in combination with the Alt and Ctrl keys. Some of these special keys create two-byte values, called *extended key codes*. These two-byte key codes always begin with either a hexadecimal 00 (for example, '00'x) or a hexadecimal E0 (for example, 'E0'x). SysGetKey must be called twice to retrieve both bytes of an extended key code.

OS/2 reserves some keys for its own use; these keys cannot be captured. For instance, Alt+Ctrl+Del reboots the system, and Ctrl+Esc displays the Window List window.

Refer to Appendix E for a listing of all values that can be returned by SysGetKey. The short program in listing 16.1 is useful for testing key codes on different machines. Some keyboards have additional keys, or, in rare cases, they may send different codes for some key combinations. This program enables you to determine what key codes are being sent.

Type

Listing 16.1. Getting codes for keys.

```
/* list1601.cmd */
IF LoadRexxUtil() THEN
  EXIT

printable = XRange(' ', '~')
SAY 'Press keys to see keycodes. Press Q to exit.'

DO UNTIL key = 'Q'
  key = SysGetKey('NOECHO')
  SELECT
  WHEN key = '00'x ¦ key = 'E0'x THEN
    DO
    char = '-extended-'
    key = key ¦¦ SysGetKey('NOECHO')
    END
  WHEN Pos(key, printable) >< 0 THEN
    char = '>'key'<'
  OTHERWISE
    char = '-unprintable-'
  END
  SAY Right(C2X(key), 4) char
END

EXIT

/* Load the RexxUtil library */
LoadRexxUtil: PROCEDURE
  IF RxFuncQuery('SysLoadFuncs') THEN
```

continues

Listing 16.1. continued

```
      DO
      IF RxFuncAdd('SysLoadFuncs', 'RexxUtil', 'SysLoadFuncs') THEN
        DO
        SAY "Error: Couldn't load RexxUtil library."
        RETURN 1
        END
      CALL SysLoadFuncs
      END
    RETURN 0
```

```
[D:\]list1601
Press keys to see keycodes. Press Q to exit.
  08 -unprintable-
  09 -unprintable-
  41 >A<
  42 >B<
  43 >C<
  44 >D<
  61 >a<
  62 >b<
  63 >c<
  64 >d<
E047 -extended-
E04F -extended-
  11 -unprintable-
003B -extended-
003C -extended-
003D -extended-
  71 >q<
  51 >Q<
```

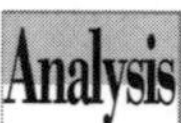

The program in listing 16.1 begins by registering the RexxUtil functions. A range of printable values is created using the `XRange` function. This range determines whether the current key press is a value that can be displayed. The central function of the program is in the loop; the program iterates until the user enters a capital *Q* (that is, Shift+Q). `SysGetKey` is called and the key is tested to determine whether it is an extended key. If it is an extended key, `SysGetKey` is called again to get the second byte. If `key` isn't an extended key, it is tested to see whether the value is printable. The `SAY` instruction displays the hexadecimal value of `key` and the character if it is printable, or text describing the type of key if the character isn't printable.

Positioning and Hiding the Cursor

Controlling the position of the cursor allows a program to place data on the screen at any location. The RexxUtil function `SysCurPos` enables you to both get the current cursor position and set a new cursor position. Here's the syntax:

```
pos = SysCurPos([row, col])
```

The *pos* is a string that contains both the row and column of the cursor when `SysCurPos` was called. The form of *pos* is `'row col'` (for example, `'5 27'`). The easiest way to retrieve the row and column from the returned string is to use the `PARSE` instruction:

```
PARSE VALUE SysCurPos() WITH row col
SAY 'Cursor is at' row',' col
```

The upper-left corner of the screen is row zero, column zero. Because these values are zero-based, you must be careful when you calculate screen positions. The last row on a 25-line screen is row 24; the last column on an 80-column screen is column 79.

16

Having the cursor blinking on-screen is sometimes distracting. Because the menu has its own style of cursor, a blinking underline somewhere else on the screen may confuse the user. The function `SysCurState` hides the cursor. Because there are only two states for the cursor, visible or hidden, the syntax is quite simple:

```
CALL SysCurState state
```

The single parameter *`state`* is either `ON` or `OFF`. When `SysCurState` is called with `ON`, the cursor is visible; when it's called with `OFF`, the cursor is invisible, or hidden.

Creating the Menu

You need to learn only a couple more things before you can create the menu. The first step for displaying the menu is to clear the screen. You can use two different methods to clear the screen. One method is to use an ANSI command string (see the lesson for Day 13); the other method is to use the RexxUtil function `SysCls`. `SysCls` is extremely simple:

```
CALL SysCls
```

Although `SysCls` is fast and simple to use, the disadvantage to `SysCls` is that it only clears the screen to black. If you want a color background, you have to use the ANSI command string method.

When the user selects a menu item, the program should perform some action. You can design the menu function, for example, to return a number that represents the selected menu item. The number is then checked in a `SELECT` instruction, and the action for the corresponding menu item is performed.

Instead of having the program return a number here, you embed the action in the compound variable that contains the menu. Thus, the menu function directly executes the action that accompanies the selected menu item. The only problem is that the code is a string that has been assigned to a variable. To execute the code, you need to use the `INTERPRET` instruction:

```
INTERPRET expression
```

The *expression* is evaluated, and then REXX executes the result as REXX code. `INTERPRET` allows a program to store code in a variable and then execute the code later. One interesting use of `INTERPRET` is to process user input as REXX code; the short program in listing 16.2 does exactly that.

Listing 16.2. Using `INTERPRET` interactively.

```
/* list1602.cmd */
SIGNAL ON Syntax

Top:
DO FOREVER
  SAY
  SAY 'Enter a REXX instruction' Copies('*', 22) 'EXIT to quit'
  PARSE PULL instruction
  INTERPRET instruction
END

EXIT

Syntax:
  SAY '>>> Syntax error:' ErrorText(rc) '<<<'
  SIGNAL Top
```

```
[D:\]list1602

Enter a REXX instruction ********************** EXIT to quit
SAY Hello, world!
>>> Syntax error: Unexpected "," or ")" <<<

Enter a REXX instruction ********************** EXIT to quit
SAY Hello world!
HELLO WORLD!

Enter a REXX instruction ********************** EXIT to quit
DO i = 1 TO 5; SAY 'i =' i; END
i = 1
i = 2
i = 3
i = 4
i = 5

Enter a REXX instruction ********************** EXIT to quit
exit
```

The program in listing 16.2 loops, requesting and accepting input. Whatever is input is executed as a REXX instruction using `INTERPRET`. Syntax errors are trapped using the `SIGNAL ON` instruction. When a syntax error occurs, the error is displayed, and the program branches back to start the loop again. The only way to exit the loop is for the user to enter either an `EXIT` or a `RETURN` instruction.

The REXXTRY program supplied with OS/2 is designed to perform the same function as the program in listing 16.2. REXXTRY is designed to be portable (that is, to run in environments other than OS/2) and is much more bulletproof than your program here. It can also accept an instruction as a command-line argument, like this:

REXXTRY *instruction*

You now have all the tools necessary to understand the menu program. The layout, text, and actions for the menu are stored in a single compound variable to simplify accessing the necessary data. Most of the real action takes place in a single procedure. The program implementing the menu is in listing 16.3.

Type **Listing 16.3. Displaying and processing a menu.**

```
/* list1603.cmd */
IF LoadRexxUtil() THEN
  EXIT

CALL CharOut 'CON:', '1B'x || '[37;40m'
CALL SysCls
CALL CharOut 'CON:', Center('Simple Menu', 80)

menu.0 = 3
menu.1.row = 5; menu.1.col = 34
menu.1.txt = 'First line'
menu.1.act = 'CALL Line1'

menu.2.row = 6; menu.2.col = 34
menu.2.txt = 'Second line'
menu.2.act = 'CALL Line2'

menu.3.row = 7; menu.3.col = 34
menu.3.txt = 'Exit'
menu.3.act = 'RETURN'

CALL DoMenu

CALL SysCurState 'ON'
'cls'
EXIT

/* Procedure for menu line 1 */
Line1: PROCEDURE
  CALL SysCurPos 24, 1
  text = Left('First line of menu selected', 60) /* overwrite old messages */
  CALL CharOut 'CON:', text
  RETURN

/* Procedure for menu line 2 */
Line2: PROCEDURE
  CALL SysCurPos 24, 1
```

continues

Listing 16.3. continued

```
    text = Left('Second line of menu selected', 60)
    CALL CharOut 'CON:', text
    RETURN

  /*********************************************************/
  /* Display and process the menu.                          */
  /*********************************************************/
  DoMenu: PROCEDURE EXPOSE menu.
    colorNormal = '1B'x || '[37;40m'
    colorReverse = '1B'x || '[30;47m'
    keyEnter = '0D'x
    keyUp = '48'x
    keyDown = '50'x
    keyPrefix1 = '00'x
    keyPrefix2 = 'E0'x

    CALL SysCurState 'OFF'
    CALL CharOut 'CON:', colorNormal
    DO i = 1 TO menu.0 /* display the menu */
      CALL SysCurPos menu.i.row, menu.i.col
      CALL CharOut 'CON:', menu.i.txt
    END
    i = 1 /* selection bar starts on the first item */
    DO FOREVER
      CALL SysCurPos menu.i.row, menu.i.col
      CALL CharOut 'CON:', colorReverse || menu.i.txt
      CALL CharOut 'CON:', colorNormal
      key = SysGetKey('NOECHO')
      next = i
      SELECT
        WHEN key == keyEnter THEN
          INTERPRET menu.i.act
        WHEN key == keyPrefix1 | key == keyPrefix2 THEN
          DO
          key = SysGetKey('NOECHO')
          SELECT
            WHEN key == keyUp THEN
              IF i > 1 THEN
                next = i - 1
            WHEN key == keyDown THEN
              IF i < menu.0 THEN
                next = i + 1
            OTHERWISE
              NOP;
          END
          END
        OTHERWISE
          NOP;
      END
      IF next >< i THEN
        DO
        CALL SysCurPos menu.i.row, menu.i.col
        CALL CharOut 'CON:', menu.i.txt
        i = next
```

```
    END
  END
  RETURN

/* Load the RexxUtil library */
LoadRexxUtil: PROCEDURE
  IF RxFuncQuery('SysLoadFuncs') THEN
    DO
    IF RxFuncAdd('SysLoadFuncs', 'RexxUtil', 'SysLoadFuncs') THEN
      DO
      SAY "Error: Couldn't load RexxUtil library."
      RETURN 1
      END
    CALL SysLoadFuncs
    END
  RETURN 0
```

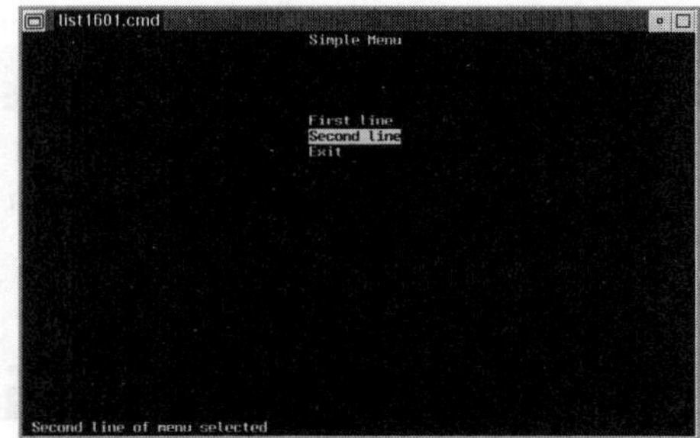

Figure 16.1. *A menu created by listing 16.3.*

In listing 16.3, the program begins by clearing the screen and then centering the heading `Simple Menu` on the screen. The compound variable `menu.` is set up with three menu items. Each item entry has the on-screen row and column that the item is displayed (`menu.x.row` and `menu.x.col`), the text of the item (`menu.x.txt`), and the action to execute when the item is selected (`menu.x.act`). The `DoMenu` procedure is called to display and process the menu. The two procedures, `Line1` and `Line2`, are called as actions from the menu. Their only function is to display a line of text indicating that they were called. The `DoMenu` procedure starts with several assignments that assign meaningful names to several strings. The cursor is hidden and the screen color is set to white on black. The menu is displayed by moving the cursor to the menu item's row and column using `SysCurPos` and then displaying the item's text using `CharOut`.

The `DO FOREVER` loop is the heart of the menu processor. The current menu item, tracked using the variable `i`, is highlighted using reverse video (black on white), and then `SysGetKey` is called. The value returned from `SysGetKey` is checked using strict comparison because the program must compare for an exact match. The current value of `i` is saved in `next`, and then the `SELECT` instruction processes the key as follows:

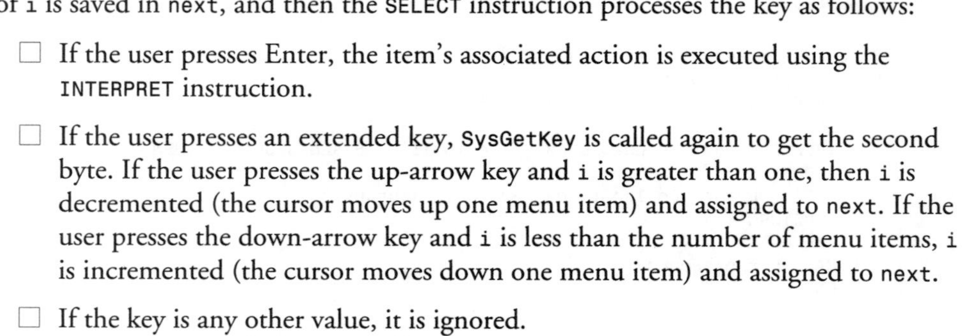

- If the user presses Enter, the item's associated action is executed using the `INTERPRET` instruction.
- If the user presses an extended key, `SysGetKey` is called again to get the second byte. If the user presses the up-arrow key and `i` is greater than one, then `i` is decremented (the cursor moves up one menu item) and assigned to `next`. If the user presses the down-arrow key and `i` is less than the number of menu items, `i` is incremented (the cursor moves down one menu item) and assigned to `next`.
- If the key is any other value, it is ignored.

Finally, if `next` is different from `i`, then the current menu item is changing. The highlight is removed from the old item, and `next` is assigned to `i`.

You can use the program in listing 16.3 as the core code for several different types of menus. If you use the line draw characters to create a box around the menu, you can build a simple pop-up menu. With a little more work, you can create a menu bar with pull-down submenus.

Creating a User Input Dialog

You can use the concepts used to create and process a menu as a base for creating formatted data input screens. The input screens work somewhat like the input dialogs that OS/2 PM programs use.

An input dialog needs more information for each item than a menu does. You can put the information in a compound variable so that all the data for each item is kept together.

An input dialog requires a great deal of cursor positioning. `SysCurPos` is used once, and sometimes twice, with every keystroke. The input from `SysGetKey` must be filtered to determine if a keystroke is data that needs to be added to the field or if it requires an action such as deleting a character or moving to the next field.

Listing 16.4 shows how a program can create a simple input dialog. Tab moves from field to field, Backspace deletes characters in the field, and Enter signals the program that the user has finished entering data. You can attach actions to the fields so that data can be verified as the user enters it, or the action can manipulate the data in some other way before it's added to the field. The action is executed for each character added to the field. The `INTERPRET` instruction is again used to execute the actions.

> **Note:** Beginning with this listing, the `LoadRexxUtil` function is not included in the listing code. You should insert `LoadRexxUtil` at the end of the program whenever you see it called in the first line. If you are using HPFS, you can put the function in a file named LOADREXXUTIL.CMD, instead.

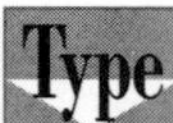

Listing 16.4. Displaying and processing an input dialog.

```
/* list1604.cmd */
IF LoadRexxUtil() THEN
  EXIT

panel. = ''
panel.0 = 6

panel.1.row = 5; panel.1.col = 15
panel.1.prompt = 'First name:'
panel.1.data = ''
panel.1.maxLeng = 15
panel.1.act = 'IF curCol = 15 THEN key = Translate(key)'

panel.2.row = 5; panel.2.col = 45
panel.2.prompt = 'Last name:'
panel.2.data = ''
panel.2.maxLeng = 20

panel.3.row = 6; panel.3.col = 15
panel.3.prompt = 'Address:'
panel.3.data = ''
panel.3.maxLeng = 30

panel.4.row = 7; panel.4.col = 15
panel.4.prompt = 'City:'
panel.4.data = ''
panel.4.maxLeng = 20

panel.5.row = 7; panel.5.col = 45
panel.5.prompt = 'State:'
panel.5.data = ''
panel.5.maxLeng = 2
panel.5.act = 'key = Translate(key)'

panel.6.row = 7; panel.6.col = 54
panel.6.prompt = 'Zip:'
panel.6.data = ''
panel.6.maxLeng = 5
panel.6.act = 'IF Datatype(key) >< 'NUM' THEN key = ""'

CALL DoPanel

CALL SysCls
```

continues

Listing 16.4. continued

```
EXIT

/* Display and process a panel */
DoPanel: PROCEDURE EXPOSE panel.
  CALL CharOut 'CON:', '1B'x || '[37;40m'
  CALL SysCls
  kTab     = '09'x
  kBackTab = '0F'x
  kPrefix1 = '00'x
  kPrefix2 = 'E0'x
  kEnter   = '0D'x
  kBkSpace = '08'x
  printable = XRange(' ', '~')

  DO i = 1 TO panel.0 /* display the prompts */
    prmptCol = panel.i.col - Length(panel.i.prompt) - 1
    CALL SysCurPos panel.i.row, prmptCol
    CALL CharOut 'CON:', panel.i.prompt panel.i.data
  END

  i = 1
  DO FOREVER
    curCol = panel.i.col + Length(panel.i.data)
    CALL SysCurPos panel.i.row, curCol
    key = SysGetKey('NOECHO')
    SELECT
      WHEN key == kPrefix1 | key == kPrefix2 THEN
        DO
        key = SysGetKey('NOECHO')
        SELECT
          WHEN key == kBackTab THEN
            IF i > 1 THEN
              i = i - 1
            ELSE
              i = panel.0
          OTHERWISE
            NOP
        END
        END
      WHEN key == kTab THEN
        IF i < panel.0 THEN
          i = i + 1
        ELSE
          i = 1
      WHEN key == kBkSpace THEN
        IF curCol >< panel.i.col THEN
          DO
          CALL SysCurPos panel.i.row, curCol - 1
          CALL CharOut 'CON:', ' '
          newLen = Length(panel.i.data) - 1
          panel.i.data = Left(panel.i.data, newLen)
          END
      WHEN key = kEnter THEN
```

```
      RETURN
    WHEN Pos(key, printable) >< 0 THEN
      DO
      IF Length(panel.i.data) >= panel.i.maxLeng THEN
        DO
        IF i < panel.0 THEN
          i = i + 1
        ELSE
          i = 1
        END
      ELSE
        DO
        INTERPRET panel.i.act
        CALL CharOut 'CON:', key
        panel.i.data = panel.i.data || key
        END
      END
    OTHERWISE
      NOP
  END
END
RETURN
```

```
First name: Sherlock          Last name: Holmes
   Address: 151 B Baker Street
      City: London                State: CT  Zip: 24162
```

In the program in listing 16.4, the data necessary to create an input dialog is stored in the compound variable `panel.`. Each entry in `panel.` contains the row and column of the left end of the entry field, the text for the prompt, the data, the maximum length of the field, and an action. The action is optional, which is why `panel.` is initialized to an empty string.

The `DoPanel` procedure uses `panel.` to implement the dialog. `DoPanel` sets the ANSI color to white on black, and then it clears the screen. The first loop displays the prompts and the fields. The prompt is displayed right-justified one space before the start of the field. The `DO FOREVER` loop manages the cursor positioning and data input for the dialog. The current column is calculated so that the cursor is at the end of the data for the field. `SysGetKey` is called to get the next keystroke. The keystroke is then processed as follows:

- If the key is an extended key, the second byte is input and the key is tested to see whether it is BackTab. If it isn't BackTab, no action is taken. For BackTab, `i` is decremented if it is greater than one; otherwise, `i` is set to the total number of fields. This has the effect of moving to the prior field, or to the last field if the cursor is currently in the first field.

- If the user presses Tab and if `i` is less than the total number of fields, `i` is incremented; otherwise, `i` is set to one. This has the effect of moving to the next field, or to the first field if the cursor is currently in the last field.

- If the user presses Backspace and if the cursor isn't at the beginning of the field, the last character in the field is deleted. The deletion is done on-screen by moving the cursor back one column and writing a space to the screen. The data is shortened by one byte using `Left` with a length one byte shorter than the current data length.
- If the user presses Enter, `DoPanel` returns.
- If the key is a printable character and if the data length is less than the maximum field length, the character is appended to the field. If the data length is greater than or equal to the maximum field length, the character is ignored and the program moves to the next field. When a character is appended to a field, the action is performed first. The action may alter the character or even remove it by setting `key` to an empty string. The character is then written to the current cursor position and is concatenated to the data for the field.

For all other cases, the key is ignored. Once the key has been processed, the program loops and the new current column is calculated.

You can greatly extend the program in listing 16.4. First, it might be nice if the cursor keys allowed the user to move the cursor into a field so that he or she could edit the data. There should be some way to exit without saving data. You might also add other types of fields, such as check boxes or lists.

Summary

This lesson introduced you to external function libraries in general and the RexxUtil library in particular. You learned how to register external functions using `RxFuncAdd` and how to use `RxFuncQuery` to determine whether a function is already registered.

The lesson showed you how to use `SysGetKey` to get individual keystrokes. You learned how to use `SysGetKey` to get extended key codes, and you also learned that `SysGetKey` can get key codes without displaying its input.

The lesson discussed using `SysCurPos` to get the current cursor position and how to change the position of the cursor. You can make the cursor visible or hidden by using the `SysCurState` function. You also learned that you can quickly clear the screen using the `SysCls` function.

REXX code can be stored in a variable and executed later using the `INTERPRET` instruction. You saw how to use `INTERPRET` to create a program that enables you to try REXX instructions without writing a program.

Finally, the lesson showed you how to use RexxUtil functions to implement a menu and an input dialog.

Q&A

Q What kinds of libraries are available for REXX?

A A fairly wide selection of libraries is available for REXX. Most libraries are shareware ("try before you buy"). Available libraries implement functions such as text-based dialogs, SQL database access, dBASE file access, communications, networking, PM dialog boxes, and OS/2 system functions such as threads, named pipes, and semaphores. Also included are libraries with visual programming environments (see Appendix B) that can turn REXX into a full-fledged PM and Workplace Shell programming language.

Q Does registering several libraries make REXX run slower?

A There's practically no difference in speed when you register several libraries. Some libraries, such as RexxUtil, offer functions that replace commands and are considerably faster than the command. The speed gained by using the function can easily make up for any speed lost in registering it.

Q Some of the RexxUtil functions do the same thing as some ANSI commands. Which should I use?

A The choice isn't very clear cut. The RexxUtil functions are faster and require less setup, but they don't support any color control. The ANSI commands offer color control, but they require ANSI to be enabled. Cursor positioning is simpler and faster using `SysCurPos` rather than the ANSI cursor positioning commands. If you need color, you should use a mix of RexxUtil functions and ANSI commands. Even if you're not using color, you should use the ANSI command to set the color to white on black so that the screen is in a known state. Some users use color in their command windows, and your program may produce strange-looking output if you don't set the color first.

Workshop

The Workshop provides quiz questions to help strengthen your understanding of the material covered and exercises to provide you with experience in using what you've learned.

Quiz

1. What is a DLL?
2. Why do you need to register an external function?
3. How is `SysGetKey` different from `CharIn`?
4. What does the `SysCurPos` function do?
5. What does the `INTERPRET` instruction do?
6. What is the effect of the instruction `CALL SysCurState 'OFF'`?
7. What does the `RxFuncQuery` function do?
8. What is the effect of calling the RexxUtil function `SysLoadFuncs`?
9. What is an extended key code?
10. How is `SysCls` different from the ANSI clear screen command?

Exercises

1. Using the panel code from listing 16.4, design and implement some method of delineating the fields. You should try to devise some method that clearly shows the user the length of the field.
2. Design and implement a tic-tac-toe program. The program should allow two humans to play against each other. Your design should include the following:
   a. Accept entries only in positions that are not already occupied by an X or an O.
   b. Ensure that each player takes his or her turn. Don't accept two X's or two O's in a row.
   c. The first player should always be X.
   d. Recognize both win and draw conditions.
   e. At the end of a game, prompt the players to see whether they want to play again.
3. Using the menu code in listing 16.3 as a base, design and implement a program that can load the menu text and actions from a file. The program should display the menu beginning on the third line of the screen, with the menu items displayed vertically. The program should always add `Quit` or `Exit` as the last menu item. Get the name of the menu file from the command line. Each line of the file should have the following format:

```
"menu-item-text" action-code
```

More RexxUtil Functions

WEEK 3

Yesterday you learned the basics of using the RexxUtil library. This lesson introduces several more RexxUtil functions. These functions can give your programs the capability of processing lists of files, getting information about drives, storing and retrieving additional information concerning files, and working with .INI files. Today you learn the following:

- How to get a list of drives and how to get information on drives
- How to get a directory listing and how to create and remove directories
- How to search files for text
- How to delete files
- What extended attributes are and how to retrieve and modify the extended attributes for a file
- How to retrieve and modify entries in .INI files

Drives, Directories, and Files

As your REXX programs work more in conjunction with the operating system, your programs will need to find out about and manage the drives, directories, and files on the user's system. RexxUtil supplies several functions that can help you do so.

Getting Information About Drives

An installation program needs to check the diskette label to ensure that the right disk is in drive A:. A backup program needs to check the free space on a target drive. A network program may need to find out what drives are attached. RexxUtil includes two functions that can quickly retrieve the information that each of these programs needs.

The `SysDriveMap` function returns a list of drives. The list can be tailored to determine what drives are in use, what drives are free, or what drives are local or on the network. Here's the syntax for `SysDriveMap`:

```
map = SysDriveMap([drive] [, opt])
```

The *`map`* is a single string containing the list of drives. Each drive is listed as a letter followed by a colon, with a single space between each drive, like this:

```
C: D: E:
```

The *drive* is the first drive letter with which the map should begin. The *opt* determines what types of drives are included in *map*. Table 17.1 lists the options and how they affect the result.

Table 17.1. Valid options for the `SysDriveMap` function.

Option	Drives Returned
`DETACHED`	Only detached network resources
`FREE`	Drives that are not in use (that is, drive letters that are not currently attached to a resource)
`LOCAL`	Only local drives (that is, not network drives)
`REMOTE`	Only remote drives
`USED`	All local and remote drives that are accessible; the default

17

If you want a list of all the drives that are attached to a system, you can call `SysDriveMap` without using any parameters:

```
drives = SysDriveMap()
```

You can use `PARSE VAR` or the built-in `Word` function to retrieve each drive from the string.

The `SysDriveInfo` function gets information about a single drive. Here's the syntax:

```
info = SysDriveInfo(drive)
```

`SysDriveInfo` returns a single string containing the drive letter, free space, total space, and volume label for *drive*. For example, on our system, `SysDriveInfo('C:')` may return the following string:

```
C:  65722368      104841216    OS2
```

If you use `PARSE` to separate the values in the string returned by `SysDriveInfo`, remember that volume labels can contain spaces. Because there are several spaces between the used space and the volume label in the string, `PARSE` leaves leading spaces on the volume label. If the volume label never contained spaces, you can add a trailing period to force `PARSE` to remove the leading spaces. Instead, you need to use an extra step to remove the spaces. The following example separates the values and ensures that the volume label has no leading or trailing spaces:

```
PARSE VALUE SysDriveInfo('C:') WITH drive free used label
label = Strip(label, 'B')
```

The program in listing 17.1 displays the free and total space for all the local drives on a system.

Listing 17.1. Getting free and total space for all local drives.

```
/* list1701.cmd */
IF LoadRexxUtil() THEN
  EXIT

drives = SysDriveMap( , 'Local')

DO WHILE drives >< ''
  PARSE VAR drives drive drives
  info = SysDriveInfo(drive)
  IF info >< '' THEN
    DO
    PARSE VAR info driveNm freeBytes totalBytes volLabel
    volLabel = Strip(volLabel, 'B')
    freeK = freeBytes % 1024
    totalK = totalBytes % 1024
    SAY
    SAY 'Volume in drive' driveNm 'is' volLabel'.'
    SAY ' 'freeK 'K bytes free;' totalK 'K bytes total.'
    END
END

EXIT
```

```
[D:\]list1701

Volume in drive C: is OS2.
 64190 K bytes free; 102384 K bytes total.

Volume in drive D: is OS2 DATA.
 492621 K bytes free; 923632 K bytes total.

Volume in drive E: is HOBBES_1192.
 0 K bytes free; 541730 K bytes total.

Volume in drive G: is DCF2 VDU G.
 90976 K bytes free; 512000 K bytes total.
```

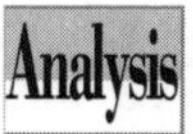

In the program in listing 17.1, `SysDriveMap` is called to get a list of all local drives. The program loops over the list of drives, calling `SysDriveInfo` for each drive. The returned information is parsed, and the free and total values are calculated as kilobytes. The information is then displayed.

Making and Removing Directories

You can use the OS/2 commands `mkdir` and `rmdir` to make and remove directories. However, these commands may display messages and can cause problems with carefully formatted screens. The RexxUtil functions `SysMkDir` and `SysRmDir` supply the same functionality as the OS/2 commands without displaying messages. The RexxUtil functions are also slightly faster than their OS/2 counterparts.

You use `SysMkDir` to create a new directory. The syntax is as follows:

```
rc = SysMkDir(dirspec)
```

The *dirspec* is any valid directory specification. If the directory is created, `SysMkDir` returns `0`; otherwise, it returns a value indicating an error (see table 17.2). Here's an example:

```
IF SysMkDir("D:\MyWork") = 0 THEN
  CALL Directory "D:\MyWork"
```

You use `SysRmDir` to remove an existing directory. The syntax is as follows:

```
rc = SysRmDir(dirspec)
```

The *dirspec* is any valid directory specification for an existing directory. `SysRmDir` returns `0` if the directory was removed; otherwise, it returns a value indicating an error (see table 17.2).

Table 17.2. Error codes returned by `SysMkDir` and `SysRmDir`.

Error Code	Meaning
0	Directory created/removed successfully
2	File not found
3	Path not found
5	Access denied
16	Current directory (`SysRmDir` only)
26	Not a DOS disk
87	Invalid parameter
108	Drive locked
206	Filename exceeds range

17

Getting Directory Listings

The SysFileTree function returns a listing in a compound variable that contains all the files that match a file specification. You pass a quoted stem name to the function, and it fills in array values for that stem. You can optionally control the types of files returned and change the attributes for the files.

Because SysFileTree has so many options, the syntax is more complex than any of the RexxUtil functions that you've seen so far:

```
rc = SysFileTree(filespec, stem [,[options] [, [targ-attr] [, new-attr]]])
```

The *filespec* is a specification of the file and directory names to search for. The *filespec* may contain wildcard characters (* and ?). The *stem* receives the result of the search. SysFileTree sets *stem.0* to the number of matching files and directories found, and *stem.1*, *stem.2*, *stem.3*, and so on, contain the entries for each matching item. The *options* change the result returned by SysFileTree and are any valid combination of the option characters shown in table 17.3.

Table 17.3. Valid options for SysFileTree.

Option	Effect on Result
B	Both files and directories are returned. This option is the default.
D	Only directories are returned.
F	Only files are returned.
O	Only file and directory names are returned. Without this option, date, time, size, and attributes are included in the returned values.
S	The current directory and all of its subdirectories are included in the search.
T	Date and time are formatted as YY/MM/DD/HH/MM.

The *targ-attr* is a *target attribute mask* for file specification matches. You use the *targ-attr* to search for files having specific attributes such as hidden, archive, or system. The mask is a string that has the order ADHRS, which stands for the *attributes archive, directory, hidden, read-only, and system*. Each position in the mask indicates how the corresponding attribute affects the search.

The characters used in the mask are * (attribute doesn't affect the search), + (attribute must be set), and - (attribute must not be set). The default mask is *****. Table 17.4 shows some example attribute masks and explains their effects on the search.

Table 17.4. Some example attribute masks and their effects.

Mask	Effect on the Search
+****	Finds all files with the archive attribute set
-++--	Finds only hidden directories
**+++	Finds all files with the hidden, read-only, and system attributes set

17

The *new-attr* is also an attribute mask. You use it to set or clear the attributes of each matching file. Including *new-attr* has the same effect as using the OS/2 `attrib` command.

This is the first time you've encountered a function that returns a value in a compound variable. You must put the *stem* in quotation marks when it's passed to `SysFileTree` because you want to pass the name of the variable instead of the value of the variable. The following example produces a directory listing for the C:\OS2 directory:

```
CALL SysFileTree 'C:\OS2\*.*', 'files.'
DO i = 1 TO files.0
  SAY files.i
END
```

Notice that `SysFileTree` set the value of `files.0` to the number of values returned in `files.`. Each of the matching entries is stored in `files.`, one per array element. Here are a few lines of output from the preceding example:

```
6/06/94   9:26a          0  A-H--  C:\OS2\EPM.!!!
6/06/94   9:26a       1972  A--R-  C:\OS2\EPM.INI
4/22/93   5:20p       1634  ----  C:\OS2\EXTDSKDD.SYS
4/29/93   9:20p     105399  ----  C:\OS2\FDISK.COM
4/29/93   9:24p      73267  ----  C:\OS2\FDISKPM.EXE
4/29/93   9:46p      30665  ----  C:\OS2\FIND.EXE
4/29/93   9:49p      66832  ----  C:\OS2\FORMAT.COM
```

Notice that the output contains some differences from the output you normally get from the OS/2 `dir` command. All the filenames are fully qualified (they include the drive and directory). The file attributes are included in the listing, and hidden files are included by default. If you want only a list of filenames without the date, time, size, and attributes, you must use the `O` option. The filenames are always fully qualified.

One of the options of `SysFileTree` is the `S` option, which tells `SysFileTree` to search subdirectories. This option makes it possible to implement quickly a utility that can search an entire drive for a file (see listing 17.2).

Listing 17.2. Using `SysFileTree` to search for files on a drive.

```
/* list1702.cmd */
IF LoadRexxUtil() THEN
  EXIT

PARSE ARG fileSpec
IF fileSpec = '' THEN
  fileSpec = '*.*'

CALL SysFileTree fileSpec, 'files.', 'FSO'

DO i = 1 TO files.0
  SAY files.i
END

EXIT
```

```
[D:\]list1702 C:\config.*
C:\config.sys
C:\OS2\INSTALL\CONFIG.SAV
C:\OS2\INSTALL\CONFIG.SYS
```

The `SysFileTree` function in listing 17.2 searches for any files matching a file specification the user enters on the command line. The options `FSO` tell `SysFileTree` to search for files in the current directory and all subdirectories and to return only the names of matching files. The results of the search are displayed.

Searching for Text in Files

A common task for programs (and users) is looking for information that is hidden away in a file. The RexxUtil function `SysFileSearch` provides an easy way to search a file for all occurrences of a string.

`SysFileSearch` returns from a file all lines that match a search string. The lines are returned in a compound variable. The search can optionally be case sensitive, and line numbers can optionally be added to the beginning of each matching line. The syntax is fairly simple:

```
rc = SysFileSearch(needle, haystack, stem [, option])
```

The *rc* is `0` when `SysFileSearch` succeeds (even if it doesn't find anything), `2` if it runs out of memory, and `3` if it can't open the file. The *needle* is the string to search for. *Haystack* is the file to search; *haystack* must be a single filename and cannot contain any wildcard characters. The *stem* is a stem name that is assigned the result of the search. `SysFileSearch` sets *stem.0* to the number of matching lines; *stem.1*, *stem.2*, *stem.3*, and so on, contain the matching lines from the files. *Option* is `C` if the search should be case sensitive, and/or `N` if line numbers should be included with each matching line.

The OS/2 `find` command is limited to searching a single file. You can use `SysFileSearch` in combination with `SysFileTree` to search for the same text in more than one file (see listing 17.3). With the addition of `SysDriveMap`, a utility can search all drives and directories.

17

Type **Listing 17.3. Searching for text in more than one file.**

```
/* list1703.cmd */
IF LoadRexxUtil() THEN
  EXIT

PARSE ARG '"' search '"' fileSpec
IF search = '' ¦ fileSpec = '' THEN
  DO
  SAY 'Usage:'
  SAY '  list1703 "search-string" file-spec'
  EXIT
  END

fileSpec = Strip(fileSpec, 'B')
CALL SysFileTree fileSpec, 'files.', 'FSO'
DO i = 1 TO files.0
  IF SysFileSearch(search, files.i, 'lines.') = 0 ,
  & lines.0 > 0 THEN
    DO
    SAY files.i':'
    DO j = 1 TO lines.0
      SAY '  'lines.j
    END
    SAY
    END
END

EXIT
```

```
[D:\]list1703 "CDROM" C:\config.*
C:\config.sys:
  DEVICE=C:\OS2\OS2CDROM.DMD /Q
  DEVICE=C:\OS2\MDOS\VCDROM.SYS

C:\OS2\INSTALL\CONFIG.SYS:
  DEVICE=C:\OS2\MDOS\VCDROM.SYS
```

In the program in listing 17.3, you use SysFileTree and SysFileSearch together to search for text in all the files in a directory and its subdirectories. SysFileTree is called first to get the list of files. Then, for each file, SysFileSearch is called to find any matching text. If the file contains any matching text, the filename is displayed, followed by the matching lines.

Deleting Files

You can use the function SysFileDelete to delete a file. The syntax for SysFileDelete is as follows:

```
rc = SysFileDelete(file)
```

The *rc* is 0 when SysFileDelete successfully deletes *file*, and a nonzero value when *file* cannot be deleted. The return code is the only indication of an error; unlike OS/2's delete command, SysFileDelete does not display any error messages. SysFileDelete does not support wildcards; *file* must be a single filename.

You can combine the SysFileDelete function with SysFileTree to delete several files. The program can prompt the user for each file and delete only the files the user approves (see listing 17.4). You can extend this technique to include subdirectories and even multiple drives.

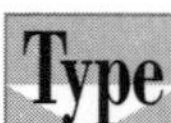

Listing 17.4. Deleting files with verification.

```
/* list1704.cmd */
IF LoadRexxUtil() THEN
  EXIT

PARSE ARG fileSpec
IF fileSpec = '' THEN
  fileSpec = '*.*'

CALL SysFileTree fileSpec, 'files.', 'FO'

msg. = 'unknown error code'
msg.0 = 'File deleted successfully.'
msg.2 = 'Error: file not found.'
msg.3 = 'Error: path not found.'
msg.5 = 'Error: access denied.'
msg.26 = 'Error: not a DOS disk.'
msg.32 = 'Error: sharing violation.'
msg.36 = 'Error: sharing buffer exceeded.'
msg.87 = 'Error: invalid parameter.'
msg.206 = 'Error: filename exceeds range.'

DO i = 1 TO files.0
  ok = 0
  DO UNTIL ok
```

```
    CALL CharOut 'CON:', 'Delete' files.i' (Y/N/Q)? '
    PULL ans
    SELECT
      WHEN Abbrev('YES', ans, 1) THEN
        DO
        ok = 1
        retcd = SysFileDelete(files.i)
        SAY '   'msg.retcd
        END
      WHEN Abbrev('NO', ans, 1) THEN
        ok = 1
      WHEN Abbrev('QUIT', ans, 1) THEN
        EXIT
      OTHERWISE
        NOP;
    END
  END
END

EXIT
```

```
[D:\Work]list1704 *.bak
Delete D:\work\AARON.bak (Y/N/Q)? y
  File deleted successfully.
Delete D:\work\CONFIG.bak (Y/N/Q)? n
Delete D:\work\members.bak (Y/N/Q)? y
  File deleted successfully.
```

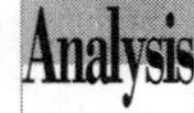

The program in listing 17.4 gets a listing of all files matching a file specification and queries the user to determine whether each file should be deleted. The compound variable `msg.` contains all the errors that `SysFileDelete` is known to return. When you use a compound variable, a message is displayed about the status of the deletion. The special variable `rc` cannot be used here because `rc` is only set for system commands. The listing of files is created by `SysFileTree`. Each filename is displayed in the prompt, and the user's response controls whether the file is deleted or ignored, or the program is exited. An invalid response causes the same prompt to be displayed again.

Extended Attributes

An *extended attribute*, or *EA*, is information that is associated with a file but not contained in the file itself. Some of the common uses of extended attributes are as follows:

- Describing the contents of the file
- Setting the icon for the file
- Describing the type of the file

- Associating a file with an application
- Keeping notes or historical information about the file

OS/2 stores extended attributes differently on disk depending on whether the drive is formatted as HPFS or FAT. Accessing extended attributes in other programming languages is often considered an advanced topic; using the RexxUtil functions, however, reading and writing a file's extended attributes are almost as easy as reading and writing the file itself.

To read an extended attribute, you use the `SysGetEA` function. The function gets a single EA for a file. The syntax is as follows:

```
rc = SysGetEA(file-name, ea-name, variable)
```

The *`file-name`* is the name of the file to which the EA is attached. The *`ea-name`* is the name of the extended attribute; the name can be one of the standard extended attributes (see table 17.5) or an application-specific EA. The *`ea-name`* is case sensitive, so `type` is not equivalent to `TYPE`. The *`variable`* is the name of a variable into which `SysGetEA` stores the extended attribute. `SysGetEA` returns `0` if it is successful, or a nonzero result if it fails. A nonzero result usually means that *`file-name`* isn't valid, or the file is inaccessible.

OS/2 defines a set of standard extended attributes. The standard EA names all begin with a period and are all uppercase. Table 17.5 lists the standard extended attributes.

Table 17.5. Standard extended attributes.

Standard EA	Description
`.ASSOCTABLE`	Associates data files with the applications that use or create the data files
`.CODEPAGE`	Indicates that the codepage for the file differs from the codepage for the application (or the system default)
`.COMMENTS`	Contains any notes about the file
`.HISTORY`	Contains a record of the changes made to the file
`.ICON`	Specifies the icon for the file
`.KEYPHRASES`	Associates phrases or words with the file that can be searched by an application
`.LONGNAME`	Stores the long name of a file when that file is stored on a file system that doesn't support long names (that is, FAT)

Standard EA	Description
`.SUBJECT`	Contains a summary of the contents or purpose of the file
`.TYPE`	Indicates the data type of the file
`.VERSION`	Records the level or version of the file

The value stored in an EA contains more than just a text string. All extended attributes have a data type indicator, a length, and the information itself. Both the type and length are stored as binary information, so you need to do some manipulation to display these values:

```
IF SysGetEA(fileName, '.SUBJECT', 'subject') = 0 ,
& subject >< '' THEN
  DO
  PARSE VAR subject eat 3 leng 5 text
  SAY '.SUBJECT'
  SAY C2X(Reverse(eat)) C2D(Reverse(leng))
  SAY text
  END
```

In this example, `SysGetEA` retrieves a file's subject. The data is parsed to get each of the fields in the EA. The EA type is the first two bytes, the length is the next two bytes, and the remainder of the EA is the text of the subject. The bytes of both the type and the length are stored in reverse order, so the `Reverse` function reorders the bytes correctly. The type is converted to hexadecimal, and the length is converted to decimal. Here's a sample of the output from this code:

```
.SUBJECT
FFFD 11
A test file
```

The EA types are predefined, so your code needs to compare only the value of EA type to determine what kind of data is stored in the extended attribute. The EA data types are listed in table 17.6.

17

Table 17.6. Extended attribute data type indicators.

Data Type	Value	Description
`EAT_ASN1`	`'FFDD'x`	ASN.1 field data
`EAT_ASCII`	`'FFFD'x`	ASCII text
`EAT_BINARY`	`'FFFE'x`	Binary data
`EAT_BITMAP`	`'FFFB'x`	Bitmap data

continues

Table 17.6. continued

Data Type	Value	Description
EAT_EA	'FFEE'x	The name of another extended attribute associated with this EA, but stored elsewhere
EAT_ICON	'FFF9'x	Icon data
EAT_METAFILE	'FFFA'x	Metafile data
EAT_MVMT	'FFDF'x	Multi-Value Multi-Type data
EAT_MVST	'FFDE'x	Multi-Value Single-Type data

The standard extended attributes may have different types depending on how much or what kind of data has been stored in the EA. The .TYPE EA is a good example. If only one type is associated with a file, then .TYPE is usually an EAT_ASCII value. If more than one type is associated with a file, then .TYPE is an EAT_MVMT value, and each of the nested types is an EAT_ASCII value. The layout for this multi-type value is

```
EAT_MVMT codepage count
  EAT_ASCII length type-text
  EAT_ASCII length type-text
```

Except for the *type-text*, all the elements are two-byte binary values, stored in byte-reversed order. *Count* is the number of items. *Codepage* is zero if the items are stored using a different codepage from the default; for almost all REXX applications, you can ignore *codepage*. *Length* is the length of *type-text* in bytes.

The other kind of multiple value type, EAT_MVST, contains only a single type:

```
EAT_MVST codepage count EAT_ASCII
  text
  text
```

You use this EA type to store the standard extended attributes .COMMENTS and .KEYPHRASES.

The following example displays a .TYPE EA. The EA type is tested to determine whether .TYPE contains one or several types.

```
IF SysGetEA(commandLine, '.TYPE', 'type') = 0 THEN
  DO
  PARSE VAR type eat 3 5 leng 7 type
  SAY '.TYPE'
  eat = Reverse(eat)
  leng = C2D(Reverse(leng))
  SELECT
    WHEN eat == 'FFFD'x THEN /* EAT_ASCII */
      SAY type
```

```
    WHEN eat == 'FFDF'x THEN /* EAT_MVMT */
      DO leng
        PARSE VAR type eat 3 size 5
        eat = Reverse(eat)
        size = C2D(Reverse(size))
        PARSE VAR type 5 text +(size) type
        SAY text
      END
    OTHERWISE
      SAY 'Unrecognized EA type' C2X(eat)
  END
  END
```

If you had to write this much code to display each of the standard extended attributes, you would probably decide that it's not worth the trouble. Luckily, it's possible to create a generic routine that can parse all the standard EA types. Once you have written the basic procedure, you can display almost any extended attribute. Listing 17.5 implements the heart of this generic routine.

Note: You can check the EA values for a file by looking in the Settings notebook for that file. The `.SUBJECT`, `.COMMENTS`, `.KEYPHRASES`, and `.HISTORY` EAs are all accessible from the File tab in the Settings notebook.

Type **Listing 17.5. Displaying the extended attributes for a file.**

```
/* list1705.cmd */
IF LoadRexxUtil() THEN
  EXIT

PARSE ARG commandLine
IF commandLine = '' THEN
  DO
  SAY 'File name was expected.'
  EXIT
  END
/* extended attribute types */
eat. = ''
eat.ascii    = 'FFFD'x
eat.asn1     = 'FFDD'x
eat.binary   = 'FFFE'x
eat.bitmap   = 'FFFB'x
eat.ea       = 'FFEE'x
eat.icon     = 'FFF9'x
eat.metafile = 'FFFA'x
eat.mvmt     = 'FFDF'x
eat.mvst     = 'FFDE'x

/* standard EA's */
eaNames.0 = 7
```

continues

Listing 17.5. continued

```
eaNames.1 = '.SUBJECT'
eaNames.2 = '.COMMENTS'
eaNames.3 = '.TYPE'
eaNames.4 = '.LONGNAME'
eaNames.5 = '.HISTORY'
eaNames.6 = '.KEYPHRASES'
eaNames.7 = '.VERSION'

DO j = 1 TO eaNames.0
  IF GetAndFormatEA(commandLine, eaNames.j) THEN
    DO
    SAY eaNames.j':'
    DO i = 1 TO ea.0
      SAY '   'ea.i.type':' ea.i.data
    END
    END
END

EXIT

/* Get an EA and parse it. */
GetAndFormatEA: PROCEDURE EXPOSE eat. ea.
  fileName = Arg(1)
  eaName = Arg(2)
  ea.0 = 0
  IF SysGetEA(fileName, eaName, stuff) = 0 ,
  & stuff >< '' THEN
    DO
    CALL FormatEA stuff, 1
    RETURN 1
    END
  RETURN 0

/* Recursive function to parse EAs. */
FormatEA: PROCEDURE EXPOSE eat. ea.
  stuff = Arg(1)
  count = Arg(2)
  PARSE VAR stuff eat 3 .
  eat = Reverse(eat)
  SELECT
    WHEN eat == eat.ascii THEN
      DO
      ea.0 = count
      PARSE VAR stuff 3 leng 5
      leng = C2D(Reverse(leng))
      PARSE VAR stuff 5 ea.count.data +(leng) stuff
      ea.count.type = 'ASCII'
      END
    WHEN eat == eat.icon THEN
      DO
      ea.0 = count
      PARSE VAR stuff 3 leng 5
      leng = C2D(Reverse(leng))
      PARSE VAR stuff 5 ea.count.data +(leng) stuff
```

```
    ea.count.type = 'ICON'
    END
  WHEN eat == eat.mvmt THEN
    DO
    PARSE VAR stuff 5 leng 7 stuff
    leng = C2D(Reverse(leng))
    DO i = 0 TO (leng - 1)
      stuff = FormatEA(stuff, count + i)
    END
    END
  WHEN eat == eat.mvst THEN
    DO
    PARSE VAR stuff 5 leng 7 stuff
    leng = C2D(Reverse(leng))
    DO i = 0 TO (leng - 1)
      stuff = FormatEA(stuff, count + i)
      stuff = Reverse(eat.ascii) || stuff
    END
    END
  OTHERWISE
    ea.0 = count
    ea.count.type = '???'
    ea.count.data = 'Unknown EA type' C2X(eat)
END
RETURN stuff
```

```
[D:\Download]list1705 cdr2.zip
.SUBJECT:
  ASCII: Computer Darkroom II v2.00
.COMMENTS:
  ASCII:          FILTER COLOR BLACK WHITE

  COMPUTER DARKROOM II v2.00\-Reduce the cost of
  photographic printing. Make one test print only. COMPUTER
  DARKROOM will calculate the new exposure time for changes
  in f-stop, magnification, paper type, contrast grade or
  filters, exposure factor, and color correcting filters.
  Black & white negatives, color negatives, and color
  slides. Easy to use interface, mouse support, creates a
  database, large database of paper types. Not yet reviewed.

.HISTORY:
  ASCII: PBSAPP DL 11/30/93
.KEYPHRASES:
  ASCII: DARKROOM
  ASCII: COMPUTER
  ASCII: PHOTOGRAPHY
  ASCII: CALCULATION
  ASCII: PAPER
  ASCII: CONTRAST
```

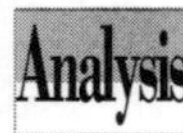

In the program in listing 17.5, you set up two compound variables. One contains the EA types, and the other contains several of the standard extended attributes. The program calls `GetAndFormatEA` for each standard extended attribute and displays any EA information that is returned. `GetAndFormatEA` gets the EA from the file and then calls `FormatEA` to parse the EA information. `FormatEA` parses the EA type from the beginning of the string and then acts based on the type. If the EA type is a simple type (such as `EAT_ASCII`), then the EA is parsed and stored in the `ea.` compound variable. If the type is a multiple type, the count is parsed, and then `FormatEA` recurses for each EA contained in the multiple type.

Now that you know how to retrieve extended attributes, creating and storing the standard EAs are fairly straightforward processes. The RexxUtil function that stores extended attributes is `SysPutEA`. Here's the syntax:

```
rc = SysPutEA(file-name, ea-name, ea-data)
```

The *`file-name`* is the file to which the EA is attached. The *`ea-name`* is either one of the standard extended attributes or an application-specific EA. The *`ea-data`* is the actual extended attribute that is to be stored.

You must build the entire EA so that it is in the same form that is used when you retrieve an EA. You therefore must concatenate the EA type and the length at the beginning of the string. These values must be two bytes long, binary, and byte reversed. Here's an example of how you can create a length value in the correct format:

```
len = Reverse(Right(D2C(5), 2, '00'x))
```

The value `5` is converted to a character (the binary value `5`). The result is right justified in a two-byte long string that is padded on the left with binary zeros (`'00'x`). The resulting value is byte reversed.

The program in listing 17.6 optionally adds a subject to a file. The current subject is displayed first so that the user can decide whether the subject needs to be changed. You can also use this program as a basis to create programs that can set other extended attributes.

Listing 17.6. Setting the `.SUBJECT` extended attribute.

```
/* list1706.cmd */
IF LoadRexxUtil() THEN
  EXIT

PARSE ARG fileName
IF fileName = '' THEN
  DO
  SAY 'File name was expected.'
  EXIT
  END
```

```
/* extended attribute types */
eat. = ''
eat.ascii    = 'FFFD'x
eat.asn1     = 'FFDD'x
eat.binary   = 'FFFE'x
eat.bitmap   = 'FFFB'x
eat.ea       = 'FFEE'x
eat.icon     = 'FFF9'x
eat.metafile = 'FFFA'x
eat.mvmt     = 'FFDF'x
eat.mvst     = 'FFDE'x

IF SysGetEA(fileName, '.SUBJECT', 'subject') = 0 ,
& subject >< '' THEN
  DO
  PARSE VAR subject 3 leng 5
  leng = C2D(Reverse(leng))
  PARSE VAR subject 5 curSubject +(leng)
  IF curSubject >< '' THEN
    SAY 'Subject is currently:' curSubject
  END

CALL CharOut 'CON:', 'New subject for file: '
PARSE PULL newSubject

IF newSubject >< '' THEN
  DO
  leng = Right(D2C(Length(newSubject)), 2, '00'x)
  subj = Reverse(eat.ascii) ¦¦ Reverse(leng) ¦¦ newSubject
  CALL SysPutEA fileName, '.SUBJECT', subj
  END

EXIT
```

```
[D:\Download]list1706 fmreset.txt
Subject is currently: Sound card
New subject for file: How to reset the sound card
```

The program in listing 17.6 displays the current subject for a file and optionally sets the subject for the file. `SysGetEA` retrieves the current subject. The subject is displayed; if the file doesn't contain a subject, nothing is displayed. The user is then prompted for a new subject for the file. If the user doesn't enter anything, the program simply exits. Otherwise, an `EAT_ASCII` type EA is created by concatenating the data type, the length, and the subject text. Finally, `SysPutEA` is called to store the new subject.

Accessing and Modifying .INI Files

OS/2 .INI files store application- and system-specific information. Data such as window locations, fonts, and colors is stored in the .INI files. OS/2 has two primary .INI files:

the user .INI file named OS2.INI and the system .INI file named OS2SYS.INI. Most of the information used to create your OS/2 desktop is stored in these two .INI files.

Information is stored in a binary format in the .INI files. The information is segregated by application, and each application's data is stored under one or more keys.

You can use the `SysIni` function to list, modify, and delete the information contained in .INI files. The syntax you use to retrieve a value for a single application/key combination is as follows:

```
value = SysIni([inifile], app, key)
```

The *`inifile`* is either a fully qualified filename, `USER` for the OS2.INI file, `SYSTEM` for the OS2SYS.INI file, or `BOTH` for both of the OS/2 .INI files. The *`app`* is the application name in the .INI file. The *`key`* is a key name for *`app`*. The *`value`* returned is whatever is stored in the .INI file for that application and key.

To get the value for application `PM_INFO`, key `Version`, you use the following call:

```
ver = SysInfo('BOTH', 'PM_INFO', 'Version')
```

To get the names of all the keys defined for an application, you replace the key name with `ALL:` and pass a stem name to the function. Here's the syntax:

```
success = SysIni([inifile], app, 'ALL:', stem)
```

In this syntax, *`success`* is either an empty string or `ERROR:`. `SysIni` sets *`stem.0`* to the number of key names, and *`stem.1`*, *`stem.2`*, *`stem.3`*, and so on, contain the key names.

To retrieve all the application names defined in an .INI file, you use `ALL:` in place of the application name and pass a stem name to the function:

```
success = SysIni([inifile], 'ALL:', stem)
```

The following example gets all the application names from OS2.INI and then gets all the keys for the first application:

```
CALL SysIni 'USER', 'ALL:', 'apps.'
CALL SysIni 'USER', apps.1, 'ALL:', 'keys.'
```

You can use the `SysIni` function to remove information from an .INI file. When you're dealing with the OS/2 .INI files, removing information can be a dangerous operation. Back up your .INI files first and then use the `SysIni` delete option with care. The syntax is as follows:

```
success = SysIni([inifile], app, key, 'DELETE:')
success = SysIni([inifile], app, 'DELETE:')
```

If SysIni succeeds, *success* is an empty string; otherwise, *success* contains ERROR:.

To set the value associated with a specific application and key, you use the following form of SysIni:

```
success = SysIni([inifile], app, key, value)
```

The program in listing 17.7 displays information contained in the user and system .INI files. Depending on what is entered on the command line, the program either lists all applications defined, all keys for an application, or the value for an application/key combination.

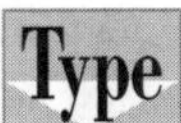

Listing 17.7. Listing values from the user and system .INI files.

```
/* list1707.cmd */
IF LoadRexxUtil() THEN
  EXIT

PARSE ARG app key
SELECT
  WHEN app = '' THEN
    success = SysIni('BOTH', 'ALL:', 'iniData.')
  WHEN key = '' THEN
    success = SysIni('BOTH', app, 'ALL:', 'iniData.')
  OTHERWISE
    iniData.1 = SysIni('BOTH', app, key)
    iniData.0 = 1
    success = ''
END

IF success = 'ERROR:' THEN
  SAY "Couldn't get value(s) from INI files."
ELSE
  DO i = 1 TO iniData.0
    SAY iniData.i
  END

EXIT
```

```
[D:\]list1707 PM_Fonts
SYSMONO
COURIER
HELV
TIMES
MARKSYM.OFM
HELV.OFM
HELVB.OFM
HELVBI.OFM
HELVI.OFM
COUR.OFM
COURB.OFM
```

```
COURBI.OFM
SYMB.OFM
TNR.OFM
TNRB.OFM
TNRBI.OFM
TNRI.OFM
ARCHI___.OFM
COURI.OFM
ONDI.OFM
SANCB.OFM
SANC.OFM
SANCI.OFM
COMI.OFM

[D:\]list1707 PM_Fonts COMI.OFM
D:\FONTS\COMI.OFM
```

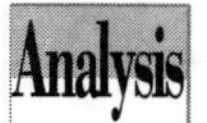

The program in listing 17.7 displays values from the OS/2 .INI file based on command-line input. The `SELECT` instruction determines which form of `SysIni` is used. If no arguments are entered on the command line (`app = ''`), the program displays all the applications. The program assumes a single command-line argument (`key = ''`) is an application name and retrieves all the key names for that application. When two arguments are present (`OTHERWISE`), they are used as the application and key names, and the value for that specific application and key is displayed. The `IF` instruction ensures that the `SysIni` call succeeded, and it displays whatever values were retrieved from the .INI file.

Summary

This rather long lesson introduced several more functions from the RexxUtil library. You learned how to use `SysDriveMap` and `SysDriveInfo` to get information about the drives on a system. You learned how to use `SysFileTree` to search for files and how to use `SysFileSearch` to search for text within files. You also learned how to create and remove directories using `SysMkDir` and `SysRmDir` and how to delete files using `SysFileDelete`.

The lesson introduced extended attributes and the two RexxUtil functions, `SysGetEA` and `SysPutEA`, needed to retrieve and set extended attributes. You learned about the standard extended attributes and the EA types.

Finally, you saw how to use the `SysIni` function to get, modify, and delete information stored in .INI files. You also learned how data is stored in an .INI file.

Q&A

Q Why do the EA type and length have to be byte swapped?

A You have to byte swap the EA type and length because of a peculiarity of the Intel hardware. When binary integers occupy two or more bytes, they can be stored in two possible ways. If you have the two-byte value '1234'x (which is decimal 4,660), then the two bytes are '12'x and '34'x. One way to store these bytes is with the big end of the number stored at the lowest memory address (see the lesson for Day 3), so the value in memory looks like '1234'x. The other way to store these bytes is with the little end of the number stored at the lowest memory address, so the value in memory looks like '3412'x. These storage methods, called *big-endian* and *little-endian*, are enforced by the computer processor chip.

Q How much information should my program keep in the OS/2 .INI files?

A If your program needs to save configuration information, it's best if you do not store it in the OS/2 .INI files. If the user reinstalls OS/2 or if the OS/2 .INI files are re-created, then your application's information will be lost. Also, many users don't like to have their OS/2 .INI files filled up with data from applications. You should create an application-specific .INI file in your program's home directory and use that .INI file to save configuration information. Store only the location of your application-specific .INI file in the OS2.INI file. If you keep information in an OS/2 .INI file, you should also give the user an option to remove (uninstall) that information.

Workshop

The Workshop provides quiz questions to help strengthen your understanding of the material covered and exercises to provide you with experience in using what you've learned.

Quiz

1. What does the following clause do?

```
CALL SysFileTree '*.*', 'files.', 'S'
```

2. What function do you use to delete files?
3. What is an extended attribute?

4. Name five standard extended attributes.
5. How is data stored in an .INI file?
6. What function call do you use to find out what LAN drives are attached to a system?
7. What does the following clause do?

```
CALL SysFileSearch 'SET', 'c:\config.sys', 'lines.'
```

8. Why should you use `SysMkDir` and `SysRmDir` instead of the OS/2 commands?

Exercises

1. Design and write a program that deletes a directory and all the files and subdirectories under that directory. Be sure to have a backup before you start testing the program!
2. Design and write a program that displays all the files in a directory that have a string in the `.KEYPHRASES` EA that matches a command-line parameter. The user should enter a file specification and the key phrase on the command line.
3. The following program contains errors. Test, debug, and fix the program.

```
/* Ex17-3.cmd */
IF LoadRexxUtil() THEN
  EXIT

PARSE ARG cmdLine
IF cmdLine = '' THEN
  DO
  SAY 'Usage:'
  SAY '  DelXcpt filespec [filespec ...]'
  SAY
  SAY 'Deletes files in current directory except for those'
  SAY 'matching one of the filespec parameters given on'
  SAY 'the command line.'
  EXIT
  END
```

```
specs. = ''
DO i = 1 WHILE cmdLine >< ''
  PARSE VAR cmdLine specs.i cmdLine
END
specs.0 = i

keepers = ''
DO i = 1 TO specs.0
  CALL SysFileTree specs.i, 'files.', 'FO', '**--'
  DO j = 1 TO files.0
    keepers = keepers ¦¦ files.j ¦¦ '00'x
  END
END

errors.0   = 'Deleted'
errors.2   = 'File not found'
errors.3   = 'Path not found'
errors.5   = 'Access denied'
errors.26  = 'Not a DOS disk'
errors.32  = 'Sharing violation'
errors.36  = 'Sharing buffer exceeded'
errors.87  = 'Invalid parameter'
errors.206 = 'Filename exceeds range'

CALL SysFileTree '*.*', 'files.', 'FO', '**--', '**+**'
DO i = 1 TO files.0
  IF Pos(files.i ¦¦ '00'x, keepers) = 0 THEN
    DO
    rc = SysDelete(files.i)
    SAY errors.rc':' files.i
    END
END

EXIT
```

Creating Workplace Shell Objects

WEEK 3

One of REXX's unique benefits is its capability to work intimately with OS/2's Workplace Shell. The Workplace Shell (or WPS) is an object-oriented user interface that defines the OS/2 desktop. The RexxUtil library contains functions that create, modify, and delete WPS objects. Today you learn the following:

- The terminology and concepts needed for working with WPS objects
- How to create folders
- How to create color palettes and font palettes
- How to create shadows
- How to create program objects

Types of WPS Objects

This lesson isn't meant to be a thorough introduction to object-oriented programming; you need only a general understanding to use REXX with the WPS efficiently. However, you should know some of the terminology so that you can get a better grasp of what is really happening when you perform some action with an object. The special terms used throughout this lesson are defined in table 18.1.

Table 18.1. Definitions of object-oriented terms.

Term	Definition
object	A way of associating data with actions (or *methods*)
class	A definition of a generic object. A class is used to manufacture objects that have a common behavior and layout.
instance	An actual, specific object. Instances are manufactured by classes.
method	A unit that defines part of the behavior of an object. Methods are usually implemented as functions.

You are probably already familiar with these concepts (if not their names) from your use of the Workplace Shell. The WPS defines several classes; an individual program object, folder, or printer icon on your desktop is an instance of one of these classes. Each class has a default set of behaviors and data. When an object is created, many classes enable you to modify some of the data and behaviors; you can use the class to produce objects that are customized in some way. For instance, a program object is customized to set the program name, the starting directory, and the type of session in which the program runs.

You can get a list of all the classes that are defined by the Workplace Shell by calling the RexxUtil function `SysQueryClassList`. Here's the syntax:

```
rc = SysQueryClassList(stem)
```

The *stem* is a stem name that `SysQueryClassList` uses to return the list of classes. The number of classes is stored in *stem.0*; *stem.1*, *stem.2*, and so on, contain the class name and module (or DLL) name that implements the class. The return code *rc* is always `0`.

Listing 18.1 shows how to use `SysQueryClassList` in a program to display all the WPS classes.

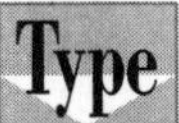

Listing 18.1. Listing all defined Workplace Shell classes.

```
/* list1801.cmd */
IF LoadRexxUtil() THEN
   EXIT

CALL SysQueryClassList('classes.')
DO i = 1 TO classes.0
  IF i // 24 = 0 THEN
    DO
    CALL CharOut , '--more--'
    CALL SysGetKey 'NOECHO'
    SAY
    END
  SAY classes.i
END

EXIT
```

```
[D:\]list1801
Mindex MINXOBJ
WPTouch TCP
WPPrinter WPPRINT
WPSpool WPPRINT
PDView WPSPL
WPRPrinter WPPRINT
WPFdr WPNLS
WPIme WPNLS
WPA_mnem WPNLS
WPObject PMWP
WPSystem WPCONFIG
WPFileSystem PMWP
WPDataFile PMWP
WPProgramFile PMWP
WPFolder PMWP
WPDrives PMWP
WPShredder PMWP
WPDisk PMWP
WPNetwork PMWP
WPAbstract PMWP
```

```
WPProgram PMWP
WPMouse WPCONFIG
WPKeyboard WPCONFIG
--more--
```

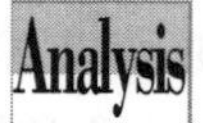

In the program in listing 18.1, `SysQueryClassList` is called to get a list of all defined WPS classes. Because the list of classes can be quite long, the listing is displayed one page (24 lines) at a time. The output displayed here is just one page of several pages of output produced by the program.

The output from listing 18.1 shows that many classes are defined for the Workplace Shell. Out of that long list of classes, you really need to work with only a few in REXX. The classes that you may find most useful are listed in table 18.2.

Table 18.2. Some useful Workplace Shell classes.

WPS Class	Description
`WPColorPalette`	The color palette object class
`WPFolder`	The folder object class. A folder holds other objects.
`WPFontPalette`	The font palette object class
`WPProgram`	The program object class. This object is different from a program file.
`WPSchemePalette`	The scheme palette object class
`WPShadow`	The shadow object class

Now that you know what classes are defined, look at how to use them to create new instances of desktop objects. You can use the function `SysCreateObject` to create almost any of the types of objects that you see on the desktop. When you want to create an object, you need to know what class to use, what title you want the object to have, where the object should be located (that is, on the desktop or within a specific folder), any special setup parameters, and what should be done if the object already exists. This information is a lot to pass in a single function call, and the `SysCreateObject` syntax reflects that:

```
rc = SysCreateObject(class-name, title, location, [, [setup-string]
    [, opt]])
```

`SysCreateObject` returns `1` if it successfully creates the object, and it returns `0` if it fails to create the object. The *`class-name`* is the class of the object being created, such as `WPFolder` or `WPColorPalette`. The *`title`* is the text that will be displayed as the title of the object.

The *location* is the folder that the instance of the object should be put in. You can specify *location* as a fully qualified directory name, such as C:\Desktop\OS!2 System, or as an *object ID*. An object ID is a unique name for an object that remains with the object even if the object is moved to a different folder. The object ID allows your program to find the object, no matter where on the desktop the object is stored. Object IDs always start with a less-than sign (<) and end with a greater-than sign (>). The object ID for the desktop is <WP_DESKTOP>. Most of the objects installed by OS/2 are assigned object IDs (see Appendix D).

The *opt* tells SysCreateObject what to do when the object already exists in *location*. The *opt* can be ReplaceIfExists, UpdateIfExists, or FailIfExists. You can use the first character of the option instead of spelling it out, so R, U, and F are also valid.

The *setup-string* is a collection of settings made up of *key-name=value* pairs that change the behavior of the object. Each pair is separated by a semicolon. If a *key-name* accepts multiple values, each *value* is separated by a comma. A settings string that uses more than one key and has multiple values for a key looks like this:

```
"key1=value;key2=value,value,value;"
```

To have a literal comma or semicolon as part of a *value*, you use ^, and ^;.

Each class defines key names that control certain aspects of the class. However, some key names are common across almost all WPS classes. Table 18.3 lists some of the common settings that you can use when you create a Workplace Shell object.

Table 18.3. Common settings for Workplace Shell objects.

Key Name	Value	Description
CCVIEW	DEFAULT	The system concurrent view setting is used.
	YES	A new view of the object is created every time it is opened.
	NO	Any open views of the object resurface when the object is opened.
HELPLIBRARY	*file-name*	Sets the help library to *file-name*
HELPPANEL	*id*	Sets the object's default help panel to *id*
HIDEBUTTON	YES	Object has a hide button.
	NO	Object has a minimize button.

continues

Table 18.3. continued

Key Name	Value	Description
`ICONFILE`	*`file-name`*	Sets the object's icon to *`file-name`*
`ICONPOS`	*`x,y`*	Sets the object's initial icon position within its folder
`ICONRESOURCE`	*`id,dll`*	Sets the object's icon to *`id`* within *`dll`* (a dynamic link library)
`MINWIN`	`HIDE`	Object is hidden when minimized.
	`VIEWER`	Object is put in the Minimized Window Viewer when minimized.
	`DESKTOP`	Object is put on the desktop when minimized.
`NOCOPY`	`YES`	Cannot copy the object
	`NO`	Can copy the object
`NODELETE`	`YES`	Cannot delete the object
	`NO`	Can delete the object
`NODRAG`	`YES`	Cannot drag the object
	`NO`	Can drag the object
`NODROP`	`YES`	Cannot drop on the object
	`NO`	Can drop on the object
`NOLINK`	`YES`	Cannot create a shadow of the object
	`NO`	Can create a shadow of the object
`NOMOVE`	`YES`	Cannot move the object
	`NO`	Can move the object
`NOPRINT`	`YES`	Cannot print the object
	`NO`	Can print the object
`NORENAME`	`YES`	Cannot rename the object
	`NO`	Can rename the object

Key Name	Value	Description
NOSHADOW	YES	Cannot create a shadow of the object
	NO	Can create a shadow of the object
NOTVISIBLE	YES	The object is not visible.
	NO	The object is visible.
OBJECTID	<*name*>	Sets the object's identity. *Name* must be unique for the current desktop.
OPEN	SETTINGS	Opens the settings view when the object is created
	DEFAULT	Opens the default view when the object is created
SETTINGS	YES	Can modify object settings
	NO	Cannot modify object settings
TEMPLATE	YES	Turns the object into a template
	NO	Clears the template setting
TITLE	*title*	Sets the title of the object

The best way to learn how to use `SysCreateObject` is actually to see it in action. In the following section, you use `SysCreateObject` to create instances of a couple of the simpler WPS classes.

Creating Font Palettes and Color Palettes

A simple application of `SysCreateObject` is to create additional instances of the Font Palette and the Color Palette. When OS/2 is installed, it creates one instance of each of these objects in the System Setup folder.

The Font Palette is simple to create. You call `SysCreateObject` with the `WPFontPalette` class, give the object a title, and set the location of the object. You don't need to use any settings. The program in listing 18.2 demonstrates how you create a new instance of the Font Palette.

Listing 18.2. Creating a new Font Palette.

```
/* list1802.cmd */
IF LoadRexxUtil() THEN
  EXIT

rc = SysCreateObject('WPFontPalette',,
      'New Fonts', '<WP_DESKTOP>',, 'ReplaceIfExists')

IF rc = 0 THEN
  SAY 'Could not create New Fonts.'

EXIT
```

```
[D:\]list1802
```

The output from running `list1802` is shown in figure 18.1.

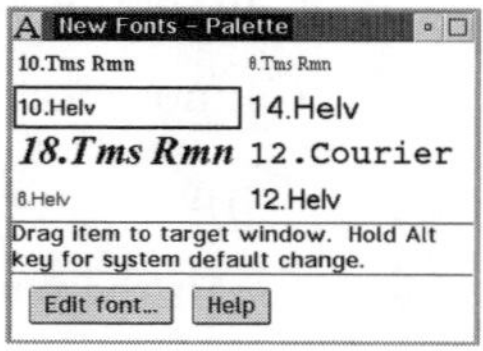

Figure 18.1. *The output from running the program in listing 18.2.*

In the program in listing 18.2, a new instance of the `Font Palette` is created by calling `SysCreateObject`. The object has the class of `WPFontPalette` and is given the title `New Fonts`. It's located on the desktop by using the object ID of the desktop, `<WP_DESKTOP>`. If the object exists, it is replaced.

The `WPColorPalette` class adds one key name of its own. You use the key name `COLORS` to set the colors in the palette. The palette defaults to 30 "color buckets," which can each be set. If you don't supply a `COLORS` setting, a default set of colors is used; look at the Color Palette in the System Setup folder to see the default colors. You set each color by using a hexadecimal string that encodes the red, green, and blue values. The values can be `00` to `FF` (0 to 255 decimal). The color value must begin with the characters `0x`, and the colors are encoded as `RRGGBB`, where `RR` is red, `GG` is green, and `BB` is blue. Here are some example color values:

```
0xFF0000  /* pure red */
0xFFFFFF  /* bright white */
0xA0A0A0  /* gray */
0xFFFF00  /* bright yellow */
```

The program in listing 18.3 creates three color palettes, one each for red, green, and blue. The intensity for each color is varied from the darkest shade to the brightest shade across 30 steps.

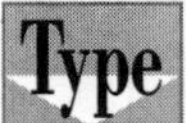

Listing 18.3. Creating red, green, and blue color palettes.

```
/* list1803.cmd */
IF LoadRexxUtil() THEN
  EXIT

red = 'COLORS=0x000000'
blue = 'COLORS=0x000000'
green = 'COLORS=0x000000'

step = 255 % 30
DO color = (step * 3) TO 255 BY step
  val = D2X(color, 2)
  red = red ¦¦ ',0x' ¦¦ val ¦¦ '0000'
  green = green ¦¦ ',0x00' ¦¦ val ¦¦ '00'
  blue = blue ¦¦ ',0x0000' ¦¦ val
END

rc = SysCreateObject('WPColorPalette',,
      'Red Shades',,
      '<WP_DESKTOP>',,
      'OBJECTID=<TYR_REDS>;' ¦¦ red';',,
      'ReplaceIfExists')
IF rc = 0 THEN
  SAY 'Could not create Red Shades.'

rc = SysCreateObject('WPColorPalette',,
      'Blue Shades',,
      '<WP_DESKTOP>',,
      'OBJECTID=<TYR_BLUES>;' ¦¦ blue';',,
      'ReplaceIfExists')
IF rc = 0 THEN
  SAY 'Could not create Blue Shades.'

rc = SysCreateObject('WPColorPalette',,
      'Green Shades',,
      '<WP_DESKTOP>',,
      'OBJECTID=<TYR_GREENS>;' ¦¦ green';',,
      'ReplaceIfExists')
IF rc = 0 THEN
  SAY 'Could not create Green Shades.'

EXIT
```

```
[D:\]list1803
```

The output from running `list1803` is shown in figure 18.2.

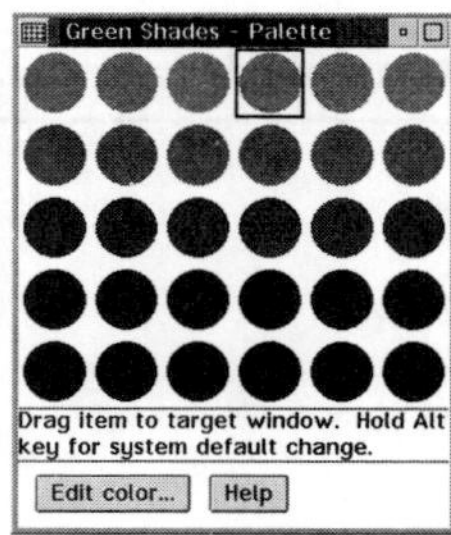

Figure 18.2. *The output from running the program in listing 18.3.*

The program in listing 18.3 creates three new instances of the Color Palette. Each instance is given a different title, object ID, and settings. All three objects are created on the desktop. If an object already exists, it is replaced. Each object is given a unique object ID.

The color settings are created by the first loop. The shades are generated by calculating a color value that is stepped to generate 30 shades. The color is converted to a two-byte hexadecimal value and inserted in the color encoding string at different positions to produce the three different colors.

Creating Folders

A folder is an object that is a *container*. In other words, folders are used to hold other objects, including other folders.

You can open folders in any of several different views (see fig. 18.2). The three basic views are the icon view, the tree view, and the details view. Each of these views can have different styles. For instance, any of the three views can use either regular-size icons or mini-icons.

Folders have several additional settings beyond the common settings listed in table 18.3. The additional settings are shown in table 18.4.

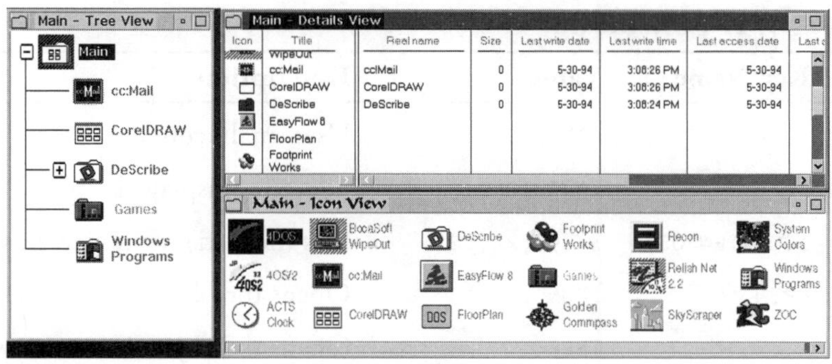

Figure 18.3. *The same folder displayed in tree view, details view, and flowed icon view.*

Table 18.4. Valid settings for folder objects.

Key Name	Value	Description
BACKGROUND	*file-name*	Sets the folder background to *file-name*. The *file-name* must be in the \OS2\BITMAP directory on the boot drive.
DETAILSFONT	*font-size.name*	Sets the font and the font size for details view
DETAILSVIEW	*s1*[,*s2*,...]	Sets the styles for details view
	NORMAL	Uses normal-size icons
	MINI	Uses small icons
	INVISIBLE	No icons displayed
ICONFOlistingsNT		*font-size.name* Sets the font and the font size for icon view
ICNVIEW	*s1*[,*s2*,...]	Sets the styles for icon view
	FLOWED	Sets the icon view to flowed
	NONFLOWED	Sets the icon view to non-flowed
	NONGRID	Sets the icon view to non-grid
	NORMAL	Uses normal-size icons

continues

18

Table 18.4. continued

Key Name	Value	Description
	MINI	Uses small icons
	INVISIBLE	No icons displayed
ICONVIEWPOS	*x1,y1,x2,y2*	Sets the initial icon view position
OPEN	ICON	Opens the object in icon view
	TREE	Opens the object in tree view
	DETAILS	Opens the object in details view
TREEFONT	*font-size.name*	Sets the font and the font size for tree view
TREEVIEW	*s1*[,*s2*,...]	Sets the styles for tree view
	NORMAL	Uses normal-size icons
	MINI	Uses small icons
	INVISIBLE	No icons displayed
	LINES	Draws lines for the tree
	NOLINES	No lines used for the tree
WORKAREA	YES	Makes the folder a work area
	NO	The folder is not a work area.

The program in listing 18.4 demonstrates how to use several of these settings.

Listing 18.4. Creating and opening a folder in one of three views.

```
/* list1804.cmd */
IF LoadRexxUtil() THEN
  EXIT

PARSE ARG cmdLine
IF Left(cmdLine, 1) = '"' THEN
  PARSE VAR cmdLine '"' folder.name '"' folder.type .
ELSE
  PARSE VAR cmdLine folder.name folder.type .
folder.type = Translate(folder.type)

IF folder.name = '' THEN
  DO
```

```
  SAY 'Usage:'
  SAY '  list1804 folder-name [folder-view]'
  SAY
  SAY '  folder-name is the title for the new folder'
  SAY '  folder-view is DETAILS, TREE, or FLOWED'
  EXIT
  END

folder.objId = Translate(folder.name, '__', '^ ')
folder.name  = Translate(folder.name, '0A'x, '^')

SELECT
  WHEN Abbrev('DETAILS', folder.type, 1) THEN
    view = 'OPEN=DETAILS;'
  WHEN Abbrev('TREE', folder.type, 1) THEN
    view = 'OPEN=TREE;'
  WHEN Abbrev('FLOWED', folder.type, 1) THEN
    view = 'ICONVIEW=FLOWED,NORMAL;ICONFONT=8.Helv;OPEN=ICON'
  OTHERWISE
    view = ''
END

rc = SysCreateObject('WPFolder',,
       folder.name,,
       '<WP_DESKTOP>',,
       'OBJECTID=<'folder.objId'>;' || view,,
       'ReplaceIfExists')

EXIT
```

[D:\]**list1804 "Test^One" F**

[D:\]**list1804 "Second^Test^List 18.4" D**

[D:\]**list1804 "Test Three" Tree**

The results from executing these three commands are shown in figure 18.4.

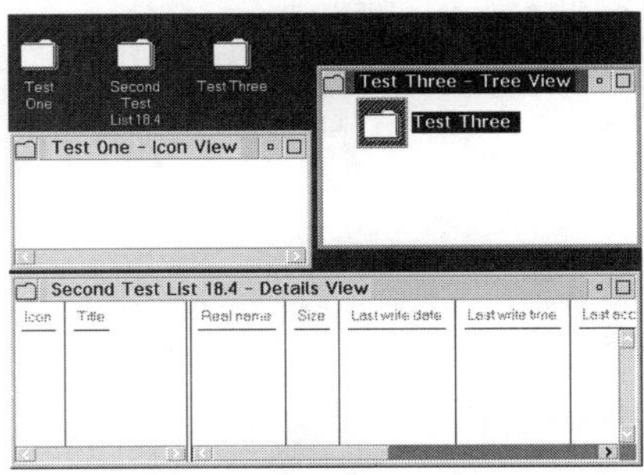

Figure 18.4. *The output from running the program in listing 18.4.*

The program in listing 18.4 gets a folder name and a view from the command line. The folder's object ID is created by replacing some characters in the string with underscores. The folder's title is created by translating any ^ characters in the folder name to line feeds ('0A'x), which has the effect of making the title occupy more than one line when the folder is displayed as an icon. The settings for the object are based on the desired view. Finally, SysCreateObject is called to create an instance of the WPFolder class on the desktop using the title, object ID, and settings created earlier in the program.

Creating Shadows

A *shadow object* creates a link, or reference, to another object. Most changes to the shadow object directly affect the original object and vice versa. Only the Delete, Copy, and Move actions affect the shadow without affecting the original. Using shadow objects, you can access the same object from several different locations in the Workplace Shell.

You create a shadow by using the WPShadow class with SysCreateObject. The WPShadow class adds one new key name, SHADOWID. The SHADOWID is either a filename or the object ID of the object that is to be shadowed.

You can create the shadow with a different title from the original, and the shadow can have its own object ID. Listing 18.5 demonstrates how you can create a folder containing several shadowed files.

Listing 18.5. Creating a folder containing shadowed files.

```
/* list1805.cmd */
IF LoadRexxUtil() THEN
  EXIT

PARSE ARG '"' folder.name '"' cmdLine
IF folder.name = '' | cmdLine = '' THEN
  DO
  SAY 'Usage:'
  SAY '  list1805 "folder" filespec [filespec ...]'
  EXIT
  END

specs.0 = 0
specs. = ''
DO i = 1 WHILE cmdLine >< ''
  specs.0 = i
  PARSE VAR cmdLine specs.i cmdLine
END

folder.objId = Translate(folder.name, '__', '^ ')
folder.title  = Translate(folder.name, '0A'x, '^')
```

```
rc = SysCreateObject('WPFolder', folder.title,,
     '<WP_DESKTOP>',,
     'OBJECTID=<' || folder.objId || '>;' ||,
     'ICONVIEW=FLOWED,NORMAL;ICONFONT=8.Helv;',,
     'ReplaceIfExists')

IF rc = 0 THEN
  DO
  SAY 'Could not create' folder.name
  EXIT
  END

DO i = 1 TO specs.0
  CALL SysFileTree specs.i, 'files.', 'FO' /* find the files */
  DO j = 1 TO files.0
    title = FileSpec('Name', files.j)
    rc = SysCreateObject('WPShadow', title,,
         '<'folder.objId'>',,
         'SHADOWID=' || files.j || ';',,
         'ReplaceIfExists')
    IF rc = 0 THEN
      SAY 'Could not create shadow of' files.j
  END
END

EXIT
```

18

[D:\]list1805 "Listing 18.5" C:\OS2\BOOK*.inf D:\Book*.inf

The output from running this command is shown in figure 18.5.

Figure 18.5. *The output from running the program in listing 18.5.*

The program in listing 18.5 creates a folder on the desktop. The folder is then populated with shadows of any files matching the file specifications given on the command line. You created the folder the same way you did in listing 18.4. The shadows are created using the `WPShadow` class, with the location set to the folder's object ID. The title of the shadow is set to the name of the file.

Creating Program Objects

A program object points at an executable program, and it enables you to run the program by double-clicking on the object. The program object can control the type of session that is used to start the program, and it can create a customized environment for the program.

You create program objects using the `WPProgram` class. The additional key names defined by `WPProgram` are listed in table 18.5.

Table 18.5. Valid settings for program objects.

Key Name	Value	Description
`ASSOCFILTER`	*`file-filter`*	Sets the filename filter for files associated with this program to *`file-filter`*. Additional filters are separated by commas.
`ASSOCTYPE`	*`type-name`*	Sets the type of files (same as `.TYPE` EA) associated with this program to *`type-name`*. Several type names can be listed, separated by commas.
`EXENAME`	*`file-name`*	Makes the object reference the executable program named *`file-name`*
`MAXIMIZED`	`YES`	The program is opened with its window maximized.
`MINIMIZED`	`YES`	The program is opened with its window minimized.
`NOAUTOCLOSE`	`YES`	The window remains open on program termination.
	`NO`	The window is closed on program termination.
`PARAMETERS`	parameters	Sets the program parameters list
`PROGTYPE`	`ENH`	Win-OS/2 enhanced mode full-screen session

Key Name	Value	Description
	ENHSEAMLESSVDM	Win-OS/2 window-enhanced mode separate session
	ENHSEAMLESSCOMMON	Win-OS/2 window-enhanced mode common session
	FULLSCREEN	OS/2 full-screen session
	PM	OS/2 Presentation Manager session
	SEPARATEWIN	Win-OS/2 windowed-separate session
	STD	Win-OS/2 standard mode full-screen session
	STDSEAMLESSVDM	Win-OS/2 windowed-standard mode separate session
	STDENHSEAMLESSCOMM	Win-OS/2 windowed-standard mode common session
	VDM	DOS full-screen session
	WIN	Win-OS/2 full-screen session
	WINDOWABLEVIO	OS/2 windowed session
	WINDOWEDVDM	DOS windowed session
	WINDOWEDWIN	Win-OS/2 windowed session
SET	*variable=value*	Sets an environment *variable* to *value*; for DOS and Win-OS/2, specifies DOS settings
STARTUPDIR	pathname	Sets the working directory

If your REXX program is creating program objects for several programs, you can safely ignore the PROGTYPE key name. The WPS automatically determines the type of the program and uses sensible defaults for that program type.

In listing 18.6, you learn how to create a folder that contains program objects for all the executable files in a directory.

Type

Listing 18.6. Populating a folder with program objects.

```
/* list1806.cmd */
IF LoadRexxUtil() THEN
  EXIT

PARSE ARG folder.name
IF folder.name = '' THEN
  DO
  SAY 'Usage:'
  SAY '   list1806 folder-name'
  EXIT
  END

pwd = Directory()
execs.0 = 4
execs.1.spec = pwd || '\*.exe'
execs.1._title = ''
execs.2.spec = pwd || '\*.cmd'
execs.2._title = '0A'x || '(CMD file)'
execs.3.spec = pwd || '\*.com'
execs.3._title = ''
execs.4.spec = pwd || '\*.bat'
execs.4._title = '0A'x || '(BAT file)'

folder.objId = Translate(folder.name, '__', '^ ')
folder.title  = Translate(folder.name, '0A'x, '^')

rc = SysCreateObject('WPFolder', folder.title,,
     '<WP_DESKTOP>',,
     'OBJECTID=<' || folder.objId || '>;' ||,
     'ICONVIEW=FLOWED,NORMAL;ICONFONT=8.Helv;',,
     'ReplaceIfExists')

IF rc = 0 THEN
  DO
  SAY 'Could not create' folder.name
  EXIT
  END

DO i = 1 TO execs.0
  CALL SysFileTree execs.i.spec, 'files.', 'FO'
  DO j = 1 TO files.0
    title = Reverse(FileSpec('Name', files.j))
    PARSE VAR title 5 title  /* remove the file extension */
    title = Reverse(title) || execs.i._title
    rc = SysCreateObject('WPProgram', title,,
        '<'folder.objId'>',,
        'EXENAME=' || files.j || ';' ||,
        'STARTUPDIR=' || pwd || ';',,
        'ReplaceIfExists')
    IF rc = 0 THEN
      SAY 'Could not create program object for' files.j
  END
END

EXIT
```

```
[C:\OS2\APPS]list1806 OS/2 Apps
```

The output from running this command is shown in figure 18.6.

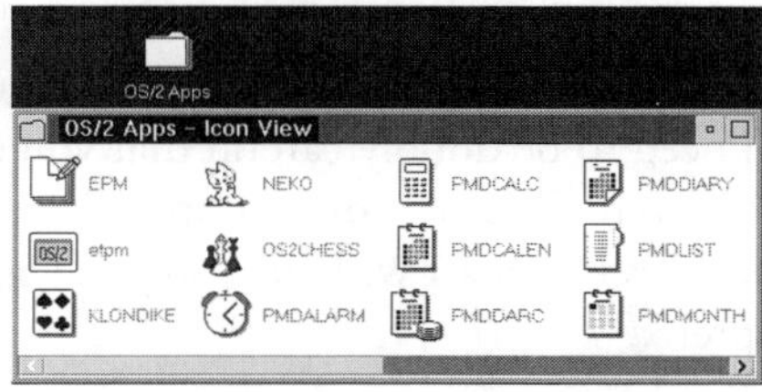

Figure 18.6. *The output from running the program in listing 18.6.*

In the program in listing 18.6, you created a folder on the desktop. The program then searches the current directory for any executable files. A program object is created for each file found, using the `WPProgram` class and setting the location to the folder. The title for the program object is created by stripping the directory name and the extension and concatenating any optional title text. The `STARTUPDIR` is set to the current directory (`pwd`), and the `EXENAME` is set to the fully qualified name of the executable file. As the program is currently written, you need to put it on the path and run it from within the directory containing the program files that you want to put in a folder. An excellent enhancement to this program would be to allow the directory name to be entered as a command-line argument, too.

18

Summary

This lesson introduced you to using REXX to create Workplace Shell objects. You learned some basic object-oriented concepts used by the WPS. Objects are instances of classes; a class defines the data and behavior of a generic object. You learned how to list all the classes that are defined by the Workplace Shell using `SysQueryClassList`. You can use the RexxUtil function `SysCreateObject` to create almost any type of WPS object.

You learned how to use settings to change the behavior of an object. You also learned how to set the title and location of an object.

The lesson showed you how to use `SysCreateObject` to create font palettes, color palettes, folders, shadows, and program objects. You now know that folders are containers that can hold other objects, shadows are references to any other type of object, and a program object points to an executable file.

Q&A

Q What happens when an object ID is not unique?

A `SysCreateObject` should return `0` (that is, failure), but an error in the current versions of the Workplace Shell allows a duplicate object ID to be created. Therefore, you need to be doubly careful that you create unique object IDs. We usually use a prefix that uses our company's initials (`TGC_`). The Workplace Shell uses object IDs that start with `WP_`, so you should avoid creating object IDs with that prefix.

Q I deleted my Productivity folder. Can I use REXX to get it back?

A Rebuilding one of the standard OS/2 folders is easy, although for a folder with as many files as Productivity it can be a little tedious. First, you need to find the file \OS2\INI.RC on your boot drive. Load this file in your editor and search for the line containing the text `Productivity`. You should find a line that begins with the following:

```
"PM_InstallObject" "Productivity;WPFolder;<WP_OS2SYS>"
```

Notice that the lines following this line are indented. These lines list all the objects that go in the Productivity folder. If you look carefully at each of these lines, you'll notice that they contain all the parameters needed by `SysCreateObject` to re-create each object. You need to copy these lines from the INI.RC file and save them in a work file (such as WORK.TXT). Then you can read and parse WORK.TXT and call `SysCreateObject` for each line. You need to translate the `?` in the settings to your OS/2 boot drive. Here's the heart of the program to parse the lines and create the objects:

```
DO WHILE Lines('work.txt')
  opt = 'FAIL'
  PARSE VALUE LineIn('work.txt') WITH '"' . '" "' title ';' ,
      class ';' location '"' '"' settings '"'
  IF Pos(';', location) >< 0 THEN
    PARSE VAR location location ';' opt
  settings = Translate(settings, 'C', '?')
  rc = SysCreateObject(class, title, location,,
      settings, opt)
END
```

Workshop

The Workshop provides quiz questions to help strengthen your understanding of the material covered and exercises to provide you with experience in using what you've learned.

Quiz

1. What is the difference between a class and an object?
2. What is the relationship between an object ID and an object's location?
3. What is a container?
4. What are the three basic views available to folders?
5. What makes a shadow different from other objects?
6. What is an object ID?
7. Using Appendix D, find out what the object ID is for:
   a. The desktop.
   b. The OS/2 System folder.
   c. The Information folder.
   d. The `REXX Information` object.

Exercises

1. Design and write a program that creates a shadow of the `REXX Information` object on the desktop.
2. Design and write a program that creates a folder containing shadows of all the icon (`*.ico`) files on your hard disk.
3. Modify the program in listing 18.4 to use the WAVE.BMP bitmap as the folder background, and a 12-point Helv font when it creates a folder using the flowed icon view.

Manipulating Workplace Shell Objects

WEEK 3

Now that you know how to create Workplace Shell objects, the next step is to learn how to manipulate those objects. Today you learn the following:

- How to delete WPS objects
- How to find the desktop, folders, and object IDs
- How to open an object to any supported view
- How to change an object's settings
- How to set an object's icon and how to set a folder's background

Deleting an Object

Workplace Shell objects are easy to delete if you know the object ID or fully qualified filename for the object. The RexxUtil function `SysDestroyObject` needs only one parameter:

```
rc = SysDestroyObject(object)
```

If `SysDestroyObject` is successful, it returns `1`; otherwise, it returns `0`. The *`object`* is completely removed from the desktop. If the object being destroyed is a folder, the contents of the folder are also removed from the desktop.

Enumerating WPS Objects

REXX does not contain a function that gets a list of the Workplace Shell objects. If you need to find a specific object, get a list of folders on the desktop, or find what folder an object is stored in, you must do some detective work. The following sections help you get started in doing some of that detective work.

Finding Folders and the Desktop

Because folders always represent directories, getting a list of folders is easy if you know the name of the directory containing the desktop. You might assume that the desktop is always contained in the C:\DESKTOP directory, but this assumption may prove to be wrong. If the system is upgraded from an earlier version of OS/2 or the desktop has been rebuilt, the desktop may have a different directory name.

The desktop itself is a folder that has the work area attribute set. Information about active work area folders is stored in the system .INI file under the `FolderWorkareaRunningObjects`

application. The keys for this .INI application are the directories that define any work area folders. The first key is usually the current desktop, but you must test the directory to be certain.

Note: Most non-desktop work area folders are saved as directories below the desktop's directory. However, the folder for *any* directory on any drive can have the work area attribute set.

By itself, this method of finding the desktop directory doesn't work on all systems under all conditions. If the user has modified the desktop location and not yet rebooted, it's possible that the new desktop doesn't appear in the .INI file. The only way that you can be absolutely certain that you have found the desktop's directory is to create a folder on the desktop and then search for a directory having the folder's name. Your new folder's directory will be a directory below the desktop.

The program in listing 19.1 finds the desktop directory by testing the work area directories listed in the system .INI file. It creates an invisible folder first so that it can double-check that it has found the desktop. If none of the work area directories produce the current desktop, the program searches all local drives for the invisible folder. For most OS/2 systems, the extra checking is a belt-and-suspenders operation, but it is the only way that you can always be certain that you can find the desktop.

19

After the program locates the desktop, you can determine what folders are defined by getting a list of the directories below the desktop directory. Each directory represents a folder on the desktop. The folder's title is stored in the directory's `.LONGNAME` extended attribute.

Listing 19.1. Finding the Workplace Shell's desktop directory.

```
/* list1901.cmd */
IF LoadRexxUtil() THEN EXIT

CALL SysIni 'SYSTEM', 'FolderWorkareaRunningObjects',,
  'ALL:', 'workarea.'
desktopDir.0 = 0
/* Narrow the possibilities */
DO i = 1 TO workarea.0
  classinfo = ''
  IF SysGetEA(workarea.i, '.CLASSINFO', 'classinfo') = 0 ,
  & Pos('WPDesktop', classinfo) >< 0 THEN
    DO
    desktopDir.0 = desktopDir.0 + 1
```

continues

Listing 19.1. continued

```
    k = desktopDir.0
    desktopDir.k = workarea.i
    END
END
/* Create an invisible folder and then search for it */
folderName = 'XYZ98_XY'  /* unlikely folder name */
rc = SysCreateObject('WPFolder', folderName,,
    '<WP_DESKTOP>',,
    'NOTVISIBLE=YES;OBJECTID=<'folderName'>;', 'R')

theDesktop = ''
curDir = Directory()
DO i = 1 TO desktopDir.0
  thisOne = desktopDir.i || '\' || folderName
  IF Directory(thisOne) = thisOne THEN
    DO
    theDesktop = desktopDir.i
    CALL Directory theDesktop  /* get out of temp dir */
    LEAVE
    END
END

CALL Directory curDir

/* If not found using the quick method, use the slow one */
IF theDesktop = '' THEN
  DO
  drives = SysDriveMap(, 'LOCAL')
  DO WHILE drives >< ''
    PARSE VAR drives thisDrive drives
    CALL SysFileTree thisDrive'\'folderName, 'dirs.', 'DOS'
    IF dirs.0 >< 0 THEN
      DO
      tail = '\' || folderName
      PARSE VAR dirs.1 theDesktop (tail) .
      LEAVE
      END
  END
  END

SAY 'The desktop is in directory' theDesktop

rc = SysDestroyObject('<'folderName'>')

EXIT
```

```
[D:\]list1901
The desktop is in directory C:\DESKTOP
```

Analysis

The program in listing 19.1 uses two separate phases to search for the desktop's directory. First, it searches each of the directories listed in the system .INI file's `FolderWorkareaRunningObjects` application. If it fails to find the desktop, it then searches all directories on all the local drives. The first step uses the `.CLASSINFO` extended attribute to narrow the search quickly to only directories with the `WPDesktop` class. The WPS uses the `.CLASSINFO` EA to maintain persistent information about an object. The program verifies the desktop directory by creating an invisible folder and then searching each potential desktop directory for that folder. The folder is destroyed after the search is complete.

Getting a List of Object IDs

All the object IDs that the Workplace Shell knows about are stored in the user .INI file. The keys stored under the `PM_Workplace:Location` application are the defined object IDs.

You can get a list of all object IDs by calling the RexxUtil `SysIni` function:

```
CALL SysIni 'USER', 'PM_Workplace:Location', 'ALL:',,
    'objid.'
```

The object IDs are stored in the compound variable `objid.`.

The value stored for each object ID is the binary *handle* of the object. A handle is a numeric value that is created by the system to uniquely identify the object. The object's handle is used as a key under other application entries in the user .INI file. The handle value is used as either a 16-bit value (two bytes) or a 32-bit value (four bytes). When handles are used as keys, they are converted to hexadecimal characters; when handles are stored as values, they *usually* appear as binary.

If you're using a handle to look for a specific piece of information, you need to check the contents of the .INI files to see how the handle is stored. The program in listing 17.7 should help you determine what kind of handle is used in the .INI files. After you know which size of handle you need to use, you can set up a compound variable that uses the handle as the tail so that you can quickly look up information associated with that handle.

The program shown in listing 19.2 uses this approach to display the objects contained in two folders. The `PM_Abstract:FldrContent` application in the user .INI file contains handles for all objects in a folder that do not have a representation on disk (they are children of the `WPAbstract` class). The keys for this application are the hexadecimal representation of each folder's 16-bit handle.

Listing 19.2. Getting a list of objects within a folder.

```
/* list1902.cmd */
IF LoadRexxUtil() THEN EXIT

CALL SysIni 'USER', 'PM_Workplace:Location', 'ALL:',,
    'objid.'

objects. = 'not defined'
DO i = 1 TO objid.0
  handle = SysIni('USER', 'PM_Workplace:Location', objid.i)
  handle = C2X(Reverse(Left(handle, 2)))
  handle = Strip(handle, 'L', '0')
  id = objid.i
  objects.id = handle
  objects.handle = id
END

ids.0 = 2
ids.1 = '<WP_DESKTOP>'
ids.2 = '<WP_INFO>'

DO i = 1 TO ids.0
  id = ids.i
  handle = objects.id
  SAY Left(id, 30) handle
  stuff = SysIni('USER', 'PM_Abstract:FldrContent', handle)
  DO WHILE stuff >< ''
    PARSE VAR stuff handle 3 5 stuff
    handle = C2X(Reverse(Left(handle, 2)))
    handle = Strip(handle, 'L', '0')
    SAY '  'Left(objects.handle, 30) handle
  END
END

EXIT
```

```
[D:\]list1902
<WP_DESKTOP>                    1C3D
  <WP_SHRED>                      11DC
  <TGC_ToEsther>                  C16B
  <TGC_CeleComm>                  E3D5
  <DCF/2 Shutdown>                E295
  <TGC_Mesa>                      4F7F
  <TGC_Drives_Shadow>             915E
  <TGC_InBox_Shadow>              ACD5
  <TGC_Fastback_Shadow>           7D22
  <Binar_Skyscraper>              87E6
  not defined                     7E4
  not defined                     169B
  not defined                     449B
  not defined                     6ACE
```

```
<WP_INFO>                    65B9
  <WP_GLOSS>                   4925
  <WP_CMDREF>                  2BF9
  <WP_REXREF>                  54E8
  <WP_RDME>                    71F9
  <WP_STHR>                    3E66
  <WP_MINDEX>                  6769
   not defined                  5D6B
   not defined                  81AE
```

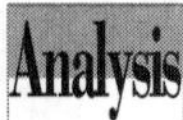

The program in listing 19.2 begins by getting a list of object IDs from the user .INI file. Each object ID is then used to get the handle for the ID, and an associative memory is created in the compound variable `objects.`. Using the object ID as a tail gets the handle; using the handle as a tail gets the object ID. The `objects.` variable is then used to display the object IDs and handles for objects in two folders. Any objects without object IDs are displayed as `not defined`.

Once you know how to follow the chain of handles in the .INI files, you can retrieve a great deal of useful information. Most of the object data is stored as binary data interspersed with character strings. Because the character strings contain most of the information that is of interest, you can use `Translate` and `PARSE` to remove the binary "noise."

Listing 19.3 produces a list of the titles of all objects contained in a folder. It uses code from the preceding two listings as procedures. Folder titles come from the directory's `.LONGNAME` EA, and other object titles come from the data stored in the user .INI file for that object.

Note: Because of the size and complexity of listing 19.3, it includes line numbers.

Listing 19.3. Getting a list of all objects in a folder.

```
/* list1903.cmd */
IF LoadRexxUtil() THEN EXIT

CALL GetObjectIDs
desktopDir = GetDesktopDir()

ids.0 = 2
ids.1 = '<WP_OS2SYS>' /* OS/2 System folder  */
ids.2 = '<WP_CONFIG>' /* System Setup folder */

folderDir = ''
```

continues

Listing 19.3. continued

```
dirTitles. = ''
DO i = 1 TO ids.0
  id = ids.i
  handle = objects.id
  SAY Left(id, 25) GetFolderTitleFromID(id, desktopDir)
  stuff = SysIni('USER', 'PM_Abstract:FldrContent', handle)
  DO WHILE stuff >< '' /* do each handle */
    PARSE VAR stuff handle 3 5 stuff
    handle = Strip(C2X(Reverse(Left(handle, 2))), 'L', '0')
    val = SysIni('USER', 'PM_Abstract:Objects', handle)
    IF val = 'ERROR:' THEN ITERATE
    val = Translate(val, '^', '0A'x) /* multi-line title to one line */
    val = Translate(val, Copies('00'x, 256),,
        XRange('7F'x, '1F'x)) /* unprintable chars become '00'x */
    val = Translate(Translate(val, 'FF'x, ' '), ' ', '00'x)
    IF objects.handle >< '' THEN
      objID = Left(objects.handle, 25)
    ELSE
      objID = Left(handle, 25)
    /* pull the title out of the data */
    PARSE VAR val 'WPAbstract' objTitle 'WPObject'
    objTitle = Strip(Translate(objTitle, ' ', 'FF'x))
    objTitle = Strip(Left(objTitle, Length(objTitle) - 1))
    SAY '  'objID objTitle
  END
  CALL GetSubDirFolderTitles folderDir
  aFolder = Left('(folder)', 25)
  DO j = 1 TO dirTitles.0
    SAY '  'aFolder Translate(dirTitles.j, '^', '0A'x)
  END
END
EXIT

/* Get all known object IDs */
GetObjectIDs: PROCEDURE EXPOSE objects.
  CALL SysIni 'USER', 'PM_Workplace:Location', 'ALL:',,
      'objid.'
  objects. = ''
  DO i = 1 TO objid.0
    handle = SysIni('USER', 'PM_Workplace:Location',,
        objid.i)
    handle = Strip(C2X(Reverse(Left(handle, 2))), 'L', '0')
    id = objid.i
    objects.id = handle
    objects.handle = id
  END
  RETURN

/* Get the title of a folder from the ID */
GetFolderTitleFromID: PROCEDURE EXPOSE folderDir
  folderID = Arg(1); desktopDir = Arg(2)
  title = ''
  IF folderID = '<WP_DESKTOP>' THEN
```

```
    folderDir = desktopDir
  ELSE
    DO
    CALL SysFileTree desktopDir'\*', 'dirs.', 'DOS' /* get dirs only */
    DO i = 1 TO dirs.0
      CALL SysGetEA dirs.i, '.CLASSINFO', 'info'
      IF Pos(folderID, info) >< 0 THEN
        DO
        folderDir = dirs.i
        LEAVE
        END
    END
    END
  CALL SysGetEA folderDir, '.LONGNAME', 'title'
  PARSE VAR title 5 title
  RETURN title

/* Get the titles for immediate subdirectories */
GetSubDirFolderTitles: PROCEDURE EXPOSE dirTitles.
  parent = Arg(1)
  CALL SysFileTree parent'\*', 'dirs.', 'DO'
  dirTitles.0 = dirs.0
  DO i = 1 TO dirs.0
    CALL SysGetEA dirs.i, '.LONGNAME', 'title'
    PARSE VAR title 5 dirTitles.i
  END
  RETURN

/* Get the desktop directory */
GetDesktopDir: PROCEDURE
  CALL SysIni 'SYSTEM', 'FolderWorkareaRunningObjects',,
    'ALL:', 'desktopDir.'
  /* Create an invisible folder and then search for it */
  folderName = 'XYZ98_XY'
  rc = SysCreateObject('WPFolder', folderName,,
     '<WP_DESKTOP>',,
     'NOTVISIBLE=YES;OBJECTID=<'folderName'>;', 'R')
  theDesktop = ''
  curDir = Directory()
  DO i = 1 TO desktopDir.0
    thisOne = desktopDir.i || '\' || folderName
    IF Directory(thisOne) = thisOne THEN
      DO
      theDesktop = desktopDir.i
      CALL Directory theDesktop
      LEAVE
      END
  END
  CALL Directory curDir
  /* If not found using the quick method, use the slow one */
  IF theDesktop = '' THEN
    DO
    drives = SysDriveMap(, 'LOCAL')
    DO WHILE drives >< ''
      PARSE VAR drives thisDrive drives
```

19

continues

Listing 19.3. continued

```
120:      CALL SysFileTree thisDrive'\'folderName, 'dirs.', 'DOS'
121:      IF dirs.0 >< 0 THEN
122:        DO
123:        tail = '\' || folderName
124:        PARSE VAR dirs.1 theDesktop (tail) .
125:        LEAVE
126:        END
127:    END
128:    END
129:  CALL SysDestroyObject '<'folderName'>'
130:  RETURN theDesktop
```

```
[D:\]list1903
<WP_OS2SYS>                 OS/2 System
  (folder)                    Command Prompts
  (folder)                    Drives
  (folder)                    Games
  (folder)                    Minimized^Window Viewer
  (folder)                    Productivity
  (folder)                    Startup
  (folder)                    System Setup
  (folder)                    Templates
<WP_CONFIG>                 System Setup
  <WP_CLOCK>                  System Clock
  <WP_KEYB>                   Keyboard
  <WP_INST>                   Selective Install
  <WP_MOUSE>                  Mouse
  <WP_DDINST>                 Device Driver Install
  <WP_WINCFG>                 WIN-OS/2 Setup
  <WP_MIGAPP>                 Migrate Applications
  <WP_SYSTEM>                 System
  <WP_CNTRY>                  Country
  <WP_FNTPAL>                 Font Palette
  <WP_CLRPAL>                 Color Palette
  <WP_SCHPAL>                 Scheme Palette
  <WP_SPOOL>                  Spooler
  <WP_SOUND>                  Sound
```

The program in listing 19.3 begins by getting a list of object IDs (line 4) and the desktop directory (line 5). The loop on lines 13 through 42 displays the contents of a folder. The steps for displaying the folder contents are as follows:

1. The folder's object ID and title are displayed (line 16). The call to `GetFolderTitleFromID` gets the folder's title from the directory's `.LONGNAME` EA. As a side effect, this procedure also sets the `folderDir` variable to the folder's fully qualified directory name.

2. `SysIni` is called to get the handles for the `WPAbstract` class objects in the folder from the user .INI file (line 17).
3. Each handle is parsed, and the handle gets information about that object from the user .INI file (lines 19 to 21). On lines 23 to 26, the data is filtered through `Translate` several times to remove any unprintable characters. Line feeds are translated to `^` so that multiline titles can be printed on a single line. Spaces are translated to `'FF'x` so that `PARSE` doesn't break up titles containing spaces. Unprintable characters are translated to spaces so that `PARSE` can separate printable values from binary data.
4. If the object has an object ID, the ID is displayed; otherwise, the handle is displayed (lines 27 to 30).
5. In lines 32 to 34, the title is extracted by parsing the data from step 3. We observed that the title always appears between the strings `WPAbstract` and `WPObject`, so we used these two values as delimiters in the `PARSE`. Spaces are stripped from the title, and the trailing character is deleted (an excess character always appears in the string).
6. The object ID and title are displayed (line 35).
7. Lines 37 to 41 get the folder titles for the directories immediately below `folderDir`. The titles are stored by `GetSubDirFolderTitles` in the `dirTitles.` compound variable. Each title is displayed by the loop in lines 39 to 41.

19

The `GetFolderTitleFromID` procedure (lines 61 to 80) searches for a folder with a matching object ID and returns the title for that folder. The `.CLASSINFO` EA for a desktop directory contains the object ID, so `Pos` quickly determines whether the object ID matches. When the matching object ID is discovered, the string stored in the `.LONGNAME` EA is returned.

The `GetSubDirFolderTitles` procedure (lines 83 to 91) gets a list of directories immediately below the directory name passed to the procedure. The `dirTitles.` compound variable is set to the value of the `.LONGNAME` EA for each directory found.

Open on Command

A REXX program can open an object in any view that the object supports. To open an object, you must have the object ID or a fully qualified pathname. Once you have that information, you open the object by setting its key name `OPEN` to the view you want.

You can use the RexxUtil function SysSetObjectData to change the object's settings. (This section discusses using the function only for opening an object. The next section covers using SysSetObjectData for changing other settings.) The syntax for this function is as follows:

```
rc = SysSetObjectData(object, settings)
```

Using SysSetObjectData with a setting string of OPEN=DEFAULT has the same effect as double-clicking the left mouse button on the object. When it is a program object, the program starts; when it is a folder, the folder opens to the default view; when it is a file, the associated program runs with the file as a parameter.

You also can open an object using a specified view. For instance, if you use OPEN=SETTINGS, then the settings notebook is opened for the object. You can open other views as long as the requested view is valid for the object's class.

The program in listing 19.4 shows how to open an object in any view you want. The user indicates the object and, optionally, the view on the command line.

Listing 19.4. Opening an object using different views.

```
/* list1904.cmd */
IF LoadRexxUtil() THEN
  EXIT

PARSE ARG cmdLine
IF Left(cmdLine, 1) = '"' THEN
  PARSE VAR cmdLine '"' obj '"' option .
ELSE
  PARSE VAR cmdLine obj option .

IF obj = '' THEN
  SIGNAL Usage

option = Translate(option)

SELECT
  WHEN option = '' ¦ Abbrev('DEFAULT', option, 3) THEN /* DEF is shortest */
    settings = 'DEFAULT'
  WHEN Abbrev('TREE', option, 1) THEN
    settings = 'TREE'
  WHEN Abbrev('ICON', option, 1) THEN
    settings = 'ICON'
  WHEN Abbrev('DETAILS', option, 3) THEN             /* DET is shortest */
    settings = 'DETAILS'
  WHEN Abbrev('SETTINGS', option, 1) THEN
    settings = 'SETTINGS'
  OTHERWISE
    SAY 'The option "'option'" is not recognized.'
    SAY 'Assuming DEFAULT.'
```

```
    settings = 'DEFAULT'
END

settings = 'OPEN=' ¦¦ settings ¦¦ ';'

rc = SysSetObjectData(obj, settings)
IF rc = 0 THEN
  SAY 'Could not open' obj

EXIT

Usage:
  SAY 'Usage:'
  SAY '   list1901 "object-ID" [option]'
  SAY
  SAY '   Option is one of:'
  SAY '     DEFAULT, TREE, ICON, DETAILS, or SETTINGS'
  EXIT
```

Output

```
[D:\]list1904 "<TGC_Main>" TREE

[D:\]list1904 "<TGC_Main>" ICON

[D:\]list1904 "<TGC_Main>" SET

[D:\]list1904 "<TGC_Main>" DETAIL
```

The output from running these commands is shown in figure 19.1.

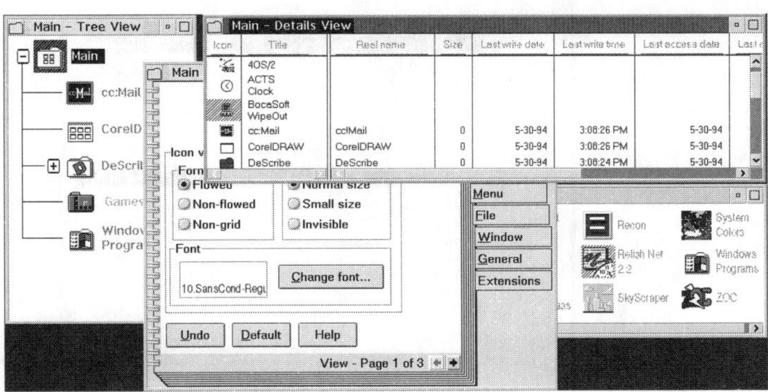

Figure 19.1. *The output from running the program in listing 19.4.*

In the program in listing 19.4, the command line is parsed to get the object ID or pathname, and the option. A view is chosen based on the value of `option`. `SysSetObjectData` is then called to open the object using the selected view.

19

Updating Settings

When you're changing the object, you can use any of the settings that you use when creating an object. The `SysSetObjectData` function can quickly alter the settings for one or more objects.

The program in listing 19.5 changes the settings for the details view of the Productivity folder.

Listing 19.5. Changing the settings of the Productivity folder.

```
/* list1905.cmd */
IF LoadRexxUtil() THEN
  EXIT

settings = 'DETAILSFONT=14.Tms Rmn Italic;' ¦¦,
           'DETAILSVIEW=STANDARD;'

rc = SysSetObjectData('<WP_TOOLS>', settings)

EXIT
```

The details view of the Productivity folder before running the program in listing 19.5 appears in figure 19.2.

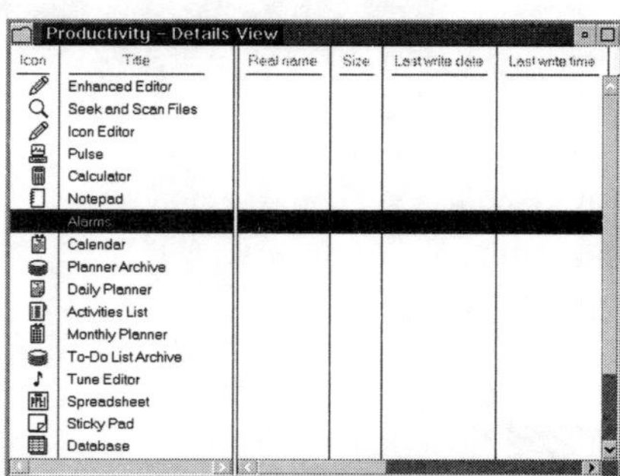

Figure 19.2. *The details view of the folder before running the program in listing 19.5.*

```
[D:\]list1905
```

The result of running this command is shown in figure 19.3.

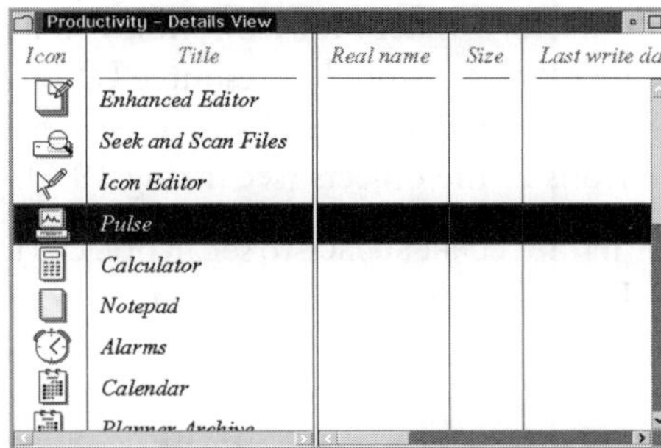

Figure 19.3. *The result of running the program in listing 19.5.*

The program in listing 19.5 changes the settings for the details view of the Productivity folder. The font is changed to 14 point Times Roman Italic. The icon size is changed to standard size.

Icons and Backgrounds

You also can use the `SysSetObjectData` function to change icons and backgrounds. The key name for setting a folder background is `BACKGROUND`. If you want to change the background for a folder, you need to make sure that the bitmap is in the \OS2\BITMAPS directory or that you supply the fully qualified filename. OS/2 refers to the bitmap file whenever it needs to paint a folder's background. If you delete or move the bitmap file, the folder loses its background.

You can keep icon files anywhere. To set an object's icon using an icon file, use the key name `ICONFILE`. The icon is copied to either the `.ICON` EA for the object or into an .INI file. If you change several icons on your desktop, you may find that your .INI files grow considerably. Each icon is at least 888 bytes long.

You can also use the RexxUtil function `SysSetIcon` to set the icon for a file. The syntax for `SysSetIcon` is as follows:

```
rc = SysSetIcon(file-name, icon-file-name)
```

`SysSetIcon` returns `1` if the icon is set, and it returns `0` if it fails. Notice that `SysSetIcon` only affects files, so you cannot use it to set the icon for a program object, the shredder, or any other object that doesn't have a disk representation.

If you search your OS/2 system for icon files, you'll only discover one or two. Most of the icons used by OS/2 are stored in resource DLLs. OS/2 doesn't provide an easy way to see what icons are stored in these DLLs. To see these icons, you need to create objects and assign the icons to the objects (see listing 19.6).

You use the key name `ICONRESOURCE` to set an object's icon from a DLL. You have to know what module (DLL) the icon is in and what the resource number of the icon is within that module.

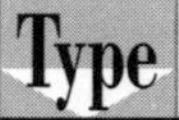

Listing 19.6. Creating a folder of OS/2 system icons.

```
/* list1906.cmd */
IF LoadRexxUtil() THEN EXIT

folderID = '<TYR_ICONS>'
rc = SysCreateObject('WPFolder',,
     'Teach Yourself REXX^Icon Folder',,
     '<WP_DESKTOP>', 'OBJECTID=' || folderID || ';',,
     'ReplaceIfExists')

IF rc = 0 THEN
  DO
  SAY 'Could not create the folder'
  EXIT
  END

class = 'WPAbstract'
icons. = 1
icons.0 = 3

icons.1 = 'PMWP'
icons.PMWP.0 = 73
DO i = 5 TO 12 /* no icons in 5 to 12, 14, 15, 21, or 23 */
  icons.PMWP.i = 0
END
icons.PMWP.14 = 0
icons.PMWP.15 = 0
icons.PMWP.21 = 0
icons.PMWP.23 = 0
DO i = 30 TO 55
  icons.PMWP.i = 0
END
icons.PMWP.32 = 1
icons.PMWP.33 = 1
icons.PMWP.44 = 1
icons.PMWP.46 = 1
icons.PMWP.48 = 1
icons.PMWP.52 = 1
icons.PMWP.53 = 1

icons.2 = 'WPCONFIG'
icons.WPCONFIG.0 = 16
```

```
icons.3 = 'WPPRTMRI'
icons.WPPRTMRI.0 = 23
icons.WPPRTMRI.1  = 0
icons.WPPRTMRI.2  = 0
icons.WPPRTMRI.17 = 0
icons.WPPRTMRI.18 = 0

DO i = 1 TO icons.0
  module = icons.i
  DO j = 1 TO icons.module.0
    IF icons.module.j THEN
      DO
      title = module Right(j,2)
      rc = SysCreateObject(class, title, folderID,,
           'ICONRESOURCE=' || j module || ';',,
           'ReplaceIfExists')
      END
  END
END

EXIT
```

```
[D:\]list1906
```

The output from running this command is shown in figure 19.4.

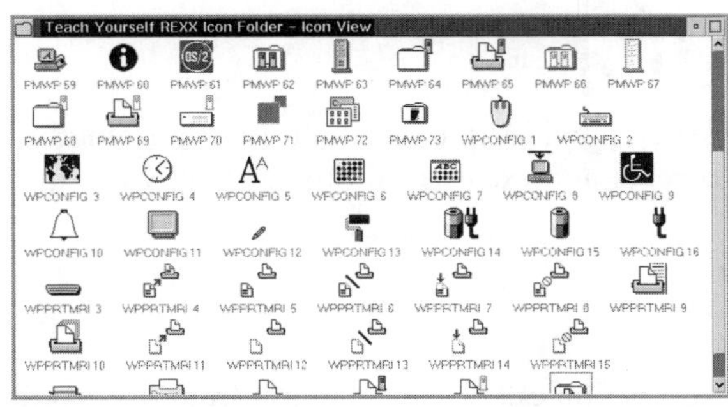

Figure 19.4. *The output from running the program in listing 19.6.*

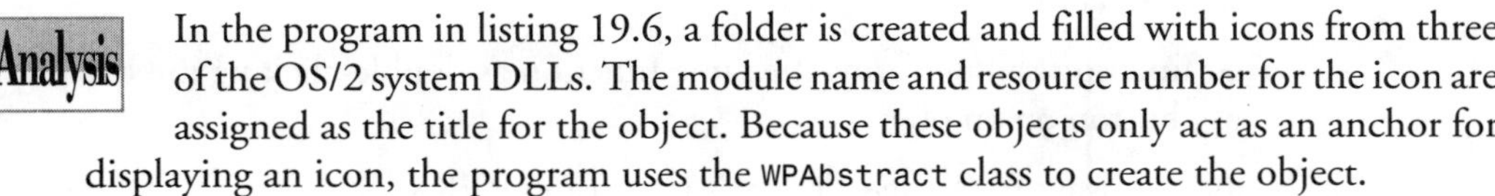

In the program in listing 19.6, a folder is created and filled with icons from three of the OS/2 system DLLs. The module name and resource number for the icon are assigned as the title for the object. Because these objects only act as an anchor for displaying an icon, the program uses the `WPAbstract` class to create the object.

19

Summary

This lesson discussed some methods for finding the desktop's directory and for determining what objects are contained in a folder. You also learned a few methods for getting other information about objects from the .INI files and the extended attributes.

The lesson showed you how to use `SysSetObjectData` to change an object's settings and to open an object. You can open any supported view by setting the `OPEN` key name to the view you want. You also learned how you can change other object settings, such as icon, background, font, and so on.

Q&A

Q Is there any way to determine quickly whether an object ID is for a folder?

A If you examine the 32-bit handles stored for each object ID in the user .INI application `PM_Workplace:Location`, you'll discover that the first hexadecimal digit is either `1`, `2`, or `3`. You can use this digit to determine the general object type quickly. The digit is always `3` for folders.

Workshop

The Workshop provides quiz questions to help strengthen your understanding of the material covered and exercises to provide you with experience in using what you've learned.

Quiz

1. What function call deletes an object from the desktop?
2. Where does OS/2 store all object IDs?
3. What is a handle?
4. What function call performs the same function as double-clicking the left mouse button on an object?
5. Name two ways to change a folder's icon using REXX.

Exercises

1. Design and write a program that can randomly select a bitmap from the \OS2\BITMAPS directory and then set the background of the OS/2 System folder to that bitmap.

2. Design and write a program that can set the font for the icon view of all folders on the desktop.

Extending OS/2 Applications

WEEK 3

Because REXX is a standard part of OS/2 and because it is fairly easy to integrate REXX into an application program, many application programs now use REXX as a macro language. Today you learn the following:

- Pitfalls to avoid when using REXX as a macro language
- How to write REXX macros for the Enhanced Editor
- How to use REXX with other applications

REXX as a Macro Language

All the REXX programs that you have written so far are started by the OS/2 command interpreter. The commands that your REXX programs execute are all OS/2 commands. These programs execute in a text-only environment.

You can design OS/2 applications to support REXX in a way that allows REXX to act as a macro language for the application. The application support for REXX can range from minimal (only command-line arguments are supported) to giving REXX macros full access to application data and functions.

Most OS/2 applications run in a graphical environment called the *Presentation Manager*, or *PM*. A REXX program (or macro) that runs as part of a graphical application's environment has some limitations:

- Standard input and output are not available. You cannot use `SAY` or `PULL` to communicate with the user.
- Output from the `TRACE` instruction and error messages from REXX are lost.
- You cannot use any RexxUtil functions that access the keyboard or screen.

Testing and debugging a REXX macro in a PM application represents a special challenge. Because the error messages don't show up, the only indication that your macro is failing is that the macro does not do what you expect. You can save yourself a lot of time by trapping syntax errors using `SIGNAL ON Syntax` and then displaying the error yourself.

When a REXX program or macro is running under PM, you can use the RexxUtil function `RxMessageBox` to display a message. The message is displayed as a standard message dialog box with your choice of buttons (such as OK, Cancel, or Enter). `RxMessageBox` can *only* be run in a PM environment. Here's the syntax for `RxMessageBox`:

```
rc = RxMessageBox(text , [title] , [button] , [icon])
```

The *`text`* is the message that you want displayed. You can make the text appear on two or more lines in the message box by inserting linefeed characters (`'0A'x`) between each

line. The `title` is the title of the message box; the default title is `Error`. The `button` is the style of button to use in the message box; table 20.1 lists the valid options for `button`. The `icon` is the style of icon that should appear in the message box. Table 20.2 lists the valid options for `icon`.

Table 20.1. Valid button styles for `RxMessageBox`.

Button Style	Buttons Displayed
ABORTRETRYIGNORE	An Abort button, a Retry button, and an Ignore button
CANCEL	A single Cancel button
ENTER	A single Enter button
ENTERCANCEL	An Enter button and a Cancel button
OK	A single OK button; the default
OKCANCEL	An OK button and a Cancel button
RETRYCANCEL	A Retry button and a Cancel button
YESNO	A Yes button and a No button
YESNOCANCEL	A Yes button, a No button, and a Cancel button

Table 20.2. Valid icon styles for `RxMessageBox`.

Icon Style	Icon Displayed
ASTERISK	Asterisk icon
ERROR	Error icon
EXCLAMATION	Exclamation icon
HAND	Hand icon
INFORMATION	Information icon
NONE	No icon is displayed; this is the default.
QUERY	Query icon
QUESTION	Question icon
WARNING	Warning icon

RxMessageBox returns a value indicating which button the user selected (see table 20.3). For displaying errors, the message box usually has one button, so you don't need to check the returned value.

Table 20.3. Values returned by RxMessageBox.

Returned Value	Button Selected
1	OK button
2	Cancel button
3	Abort button
4	Retry button
5	Ignore button
6	Yes button
7	No button
8	Enter button

The following example shows how you can use RxMessageBox to display a syntax error:

```
Syntax:
  LF = '0A'x
  PARSE SOURCE . . progName
  msg = 'File:' FileSpec('Name', progName) ¦¦ LF
  msg = msg ¦¦ 'Line' sigl':' SourceLine(sigl) ¦¦ LF
  msg = msg ¦¦ ErrorText(rc)
  CALL RxMessageBox msg, 'Syntax Error', 'OK', 'ERROR'
  RETURN 3
```

Notice how linefeed characters are embedded in the text so that the text displays on three lines; see figure 20.1.

When you are debugging a REXX macro, you can use RxMessageBox to display the values of variables and "I am here" messages. If you need to track a lot of data, then clicking OK in response to each message can become tedious. An alternative to using RxMessageBox is to write information to a log file using the LineOut or CharOut functions.

Figure 20.1. *A REXX syntax error displayed by* `RxMessageBox`*.*

DO | **DON'T**

DON'T use `SAY`, `PULL`, or `SysGetKey` to communicate with the user when your REXX macro is run by a PM application.

DO use `RxMessageBox` to display messages in PM.

Extending the Enhanced Editor

The Enhanced Editor provides REXX with access to almost all EPM's data and functionality. From a REXX macro, you can open and close files, modify the menus, define actions for keys and the mouse, execute EPM commands, and insert, delete, and replace text.

If you select Quick Reference from the Enhanced Editor's Help menu, you discover a short section on writing EPM macros in REXX. This documentation represents the entirety of publicly available information on writing EPM REXX macros. It barely represents the tip of the iceberg for what a REXX program can do from within the Enhanced Editor. The following sections provide you with those important details.

Introducing EPM REXX Macros

In this section, you learn the details of how to enhance EPM. Besides giving you the ability to make EPM work your way, the lessons you learn here will help you understand how other OS/2 applications use REXX, too.

An EPM REXX macro is named using an .ERX file extension. You run REXX macros using the `RX` command at EPM's command line (press Ctrl+I from within the editor to see the command-line dialog). To run a REXX macro named `FIXIT.ERX`, you enter the following at EPM's command line:

```
RX FIXIT
```

Note: In this section, we assume that you have some familiarity with using the Enhanced Editor. If you need a quick introduction, refer to Appendix G.

Any EPM commands that you can enter at the EPM command line can also be run from a REXX macro. EPM commands are run the same way any command is executed from REXX. For instance, the following code moves the cursor to the top of the current file and locates the first line containing `SAY`:

```
'top'
'l /SAY/'
```

Note that the current command processor for an EPM macro is EPM, not the OS/2 command processor. All these commands are sent to, and processed by, the Enhanced Editor.

The REXX special variable `rc` is set to the return code from the last EPM command. Successful commands in EPM always return zero. In the preceding example, the program could test to see whether the locate command found `SAY` by testing like this:

```
IF rc = 0 THEN
```

You can insert lines of text into a file loaded in EPM using the `EtkInsertText` function. Here's the syntax for the function:

```
CALL EtkInsertText text [, line [, file-ID]]
```

The `EtkInsertText` function inserts *`text`* on a line of its own at the line number *`line`* in the file represented by *`file-ID`*. If *`file-ID`* isn't given, the current file is used. If *`line`* isn't given, the current line is used. The following example inserts a comment on line one of the current file:

```
CALL EtkInsertText "/* a new comment */", 1
```

The *file-ID* is a number that EPM uses internally as a handle for a file. A file keeps the same file ID as long as it's loaded, even if the filename is changed. You can get the file ID for the current file by calling the `EtkQueryFileID` function:

```
file-ID = EtkQueryFileID()
```

After you have the file ID for the current file, you can switch to a different file and use the file ID to access the first file. You can use the file ID to make a file the active file by using the `activateFileID` EPM command. This command enables you to quickly make a different file the current file:

```
userFile = EtkQueryFileID()
'e work1.txt' /* create a new file -- becomes the current file */
workFile = EtkQueryFileID()
'activateFileID' userFile /* switch back to original file */
```

You use the `EtkDeleteText` function to delete a line of text. The function defaults to deleting the current line of text in the current file. You can tell it to delete a different line of text or to delete a line of text in a file that isn't the current file. The syntax for `EtkDeleteText` is as follows:

```
CALL EtkDeleteText [line [, file-ID]]
```

You use the `EtkReplaceText` function to replace a line of text. Replacing a line of text is equivalent to using `EtkDeleteText` and `EtkInsertText` with the same line number. `EtkReplaceText` defaults to replacing the current line of text in the current file. You can tell the function to replace a specific line of text or to replace a line of text in a file that isn't the current file. Here's the syntax:

```
CALL EtkReplaceText text [, line [, file-ID]]
```

The Enhanced Editor maintains a set of variables for each file. These variables keep track of information that is specific to each file, such as the filename, the current line and column, the number of modifications, the number of lines in the file, and so on. You can get and set the value of many of the variables from a REXX program.

To get the value, you use the special `extract` command. This command is only available from an EPM REXX macro and cannot be entered at EPM's command line. The `extract` command retrieves the value of the EPM variable and stores the value in a REXX compound variable that has a stem with the same name as the EPM variable. For instance, to find out what line the cursor is on in the current file, you can use the following:

```
'extract /line'
```

The number of values returned is stored in `line.0` (in this case, one value is returned). The current line number is stored in `line.1`. `Extract` can retrieve several values in one invocation. The following example gets the current line of text, the current line number, and the total lines in the file:

```
'extract /getline/line/last'
```

The `extract` command only retrieves values for the current file. To retrieve values for a different file, you must switch to that file. The variable names that `extract` can access are listed in table 20.4.

You can use the `EtkSetFileField` function to set the value of an EPM variable. The function can either set variables in the current file, or a specific file ID can be given. Here's the syntax:

```
CALL EtkSetFileField field-name, value [, file-ID]
```

The *`field-name`* is the EPM variable to set (see table 20.4). The *`value`* is the new value to store in that variable. The following example sets the filename of the current file to MYFILE.TXT:

```
CALL EtkSetFileField 'filename', 'myfile.txt'
```

Table 20.4. EPM internal variables that can be extracted and set.

Variable	Description
`autosave`	The number of changes before autosaving (`0` turns `autosave` off)
`col`	The cursor column position relative to the beginning of the line. Valid values are `1` to `255`.
`cursorx`	The cursor column position relative to the window
`cursory`	The cursor row position relative to the window
`dragcolor`	The color of the highlighted mouse drag area
`dragstyle`	The type of mark for a mouse drag. Valid values are `0` (don't show drag), `1` (block mark), `2` (line mark), and `3` (char mark).
`eaarea`	A pointer to EPM's extended attributes area
`filename`	The fully qualified name of the current file
`font`	The default font number

Variable	Description
`fontheight`	The font height in pixels
`fontwidth`	The font width in pixels
`getline`	The contents of the current line
`getmark`	The extents for the current mark. If a mark exists, five values are returned: beginning line, ending line, left column, right column, and file ID for the file containing the mark.
`getmarktype`	The type of the mark; an empty string if no mark is active. Mark types are `LINE`, `CHAR`, `BLOCK`, `CHARG`, and `BLOCKG`.
`last`	The total number of lines in the file
`line`	The current cursor line number relative to the beginning of the file. The valid range is `0` to `last`.
`lockhandle`	Indicates if the file is locked against access by other users. A value of `1` means the file is locked; `0` means the file is not locked.
`markcolor`	The color for marked text
`modify`	The number of modifications made to the file
`mousex`	The current mouse X coordinate
`mousey`	The current mouse Y coordinate
`textcolor`	The text color
`userstring`	A user-definable value
`version`	The version of the Enhanced Editor
`visible`	Indicates if the file is currently visible
`windowheight`	Number of lines visible in the window
`windowwidth`	Number of columns visible in the window
`windowx`	The window's X coordinate (always `0` in current EPM versions)
`windowy`	The window's Y coordinate (always `0` in current EPM versions)

Writing an EPM REXX Macro

The EPM REXX macro in listing 20.1 combines several functions and commands to generate skeleton code automatically for a REXX program. The macro optionally takes the programmer's name as a command-line argument.

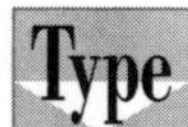

Listing 20.1. An EPM macro that creates a REXX program skeleton.

```
/* list2001.erx */
SIGNAL ON Syntax

PARSE ARG author

'extract /filename'
filename.1 = FileSpec('N', filename.1)

text. = ''
text.0 = 20

text.1  = '/*' || Copies('*', 70) || '*/'
text.2  = '/*' Left(filename.1, 68) '*/'
text.3  = '/*' Left('Created:' date(), 68) '*/'
text.4  = '/*' Left(' Author:' author, 68) '*/'
text.5  = text.1
text.6  = 'SIGNAL ON Syntax'
text.7  = 'SIGNAL ON Halt'
text.10 = 'EXIT'
text.12 = 'Syntax:'
text.13 = '  SAY SourceLine(sigl)'
text.14 = '  SAY "Syntax error on line" sigl || ":"'
text.15 = '  SAY ErrorText(rc)'
text.16 = '  Trace ?R; NOP; EXIT'
text.18 = 'Halt:'
text.19 = '  SAY "Ctrl+Break pressed. Exiting..."'
text.20 = '  EXIT'

DO i = 1 TO text.0
  CALL EtkInsertText text.i
END
CALL EtkDeleteText
CALL EtkSetFileField 'line', 9

RETURN 0

Syntax:
  err = rc
  'e ".Macro Error" /C'
  CALL EtkSetFileField 'autosave', 0
  CALL EtkSetFileField 'filename', '.Macro Error'
  PARSE SOURCE . . program
  CALL EtkInsertText 'Syntax error in' program
  CALL EtkInsertText '  'sigl':' SourceLine(sigl)
  CALL EtkInsertText '  Syntax error ('err'):' ErrorText(err)
  CALL EtkSetFileField 'modify', 0
  RETURN 1
```

Output

You execute the macro in listing 20.1 by opening a new file in EPM, opening the command dialog by pressing Ctrl+I, and entering the command **`rx list2001`**. You can optionally enter your name as a parameter to the command. Figure 20.2 shows how to run the macro from listing 20.1.

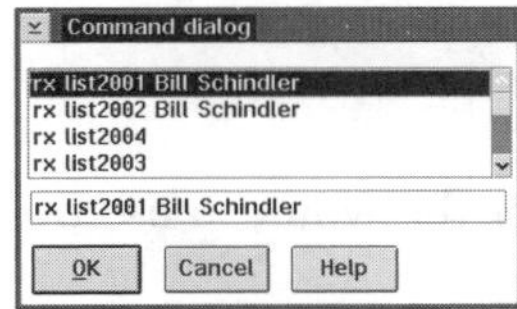

Figure 20.2. *Running the macro in listing 20.1.*

The results of running the macro are shown in figure 20.3.

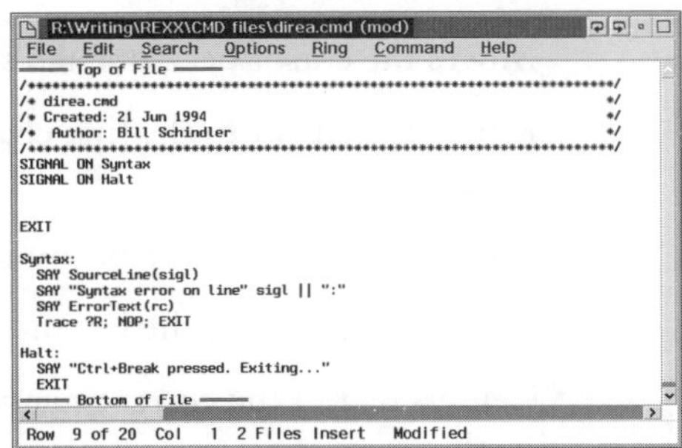

Figure 20.3. *The results of running the macro in listing 20.1.*

20

Analysis

Most of the macro in listing 20.1 is involved in setting up the `text.` compound variable. The filename for the current file is extracted and the path portion is removed using `FileSpec`. Once `text.` is initialized, the loop executes `EtkInsertText` to insert all the lines from `text.` into the current file. When the loop finishes, the extra blank line at the end of the file (EPM creates a new file with one blank line) is deleted. Finally, the cursor is moved to line nine by setting EPM's line variable.

If a syntax error is encountered, the macro creates a new file within EPM. Error information is formatted and written into the file. The file is given an odd name, and the modify variable is set to zero so that EPM doesn't prompt the user to save this file. Notice that `rc` must be saved in another variable because executing the EPM `edit` command changes the value of `rc`.

Processing and Defining Keys

An EPM REXX macro can execute keys by calling the `EtkProcessEditKey` function. The keys that you execute with `EtkProcessEditKey` are referenced by function name rather than the keyboard key name that function is assigned to. The syntax for `EtkProcessEditKey` is as follows:

```
CALL EtkProcessEditKey key
```

Table 20.5 lists the key names that you can use with `EtkProcessEditKey`.

Table 20.5. Key names that can be used with `EtkProcessEditKey`.

Key Name	Action
`ADJUST_BLOCK`	Overlays a marked block at the cursor. The source is replaced with spaces.
`BACKTAB`	Moves the cursor back one tab stop
`BACKTAB_WORD`	Moves the cursor to the first character of the previous word
`BEGIN_LINE`	Moves the cursor to the beginning of the line
`BOTTOM`	Moves the cursor to the last line of the file
`CENTER`	Centers text in the current margins or in the current mark
`COPY_MARK`	Copies marked text to the current cursor position
`DELETE_CHAR`	Deletes the character at the current cursor position
`DELETE_LINE`	Deletes the current line
`DELETE_MARK`	Deletes any marked text
`ERASE_END_LINE`	Deletes text from the cursor to the end of the current line
`INSERT_TOGGLE`	Toggles between the insert and replace modes
`JOIN`	Joins the next line with the current line
`MARK_BLOCK`	Starts or changes a block mark
`MARK_BLOCKG`	Starts or changes a block mark. The mark is to the left of the cursor.

Key Name	Action
MARK_CHAR	Starts or changes a character mark
MARK_CHARG	Starts or changes a character mark. The mark is to the left of the cursor.
MARK_LINE	Starts or changes a line mark
MARK_LINEG	Starts or changes a line mark (same as MARK_LINE)
MOVE_MARK	Moves marked text to the current cursor position
NEXT_FILE	Makes the next file in the edit ring the current file
OVERLAY_BLOCK	Overlays a marked block at the cursor
PREVFILE	Makes the previous file in the edit ring the current file
REFLOW	Reformats marked text using the current margins
REFRESH	Updates any portions of the EPM window that need to be updated
REPEAT_FIND	Repeats the last search command
RUBOUT	Performs a destructive backspace (that is, deletes the character to the left of the cursor, and moves the cursor left one column)
SHIFT_LEFT	Shifts marked text one position left
SHIFT_RIGHT	Shifts marked text one position right
SPLIT	Splits the current line at the cursor position
TAB_WORD	Moves the cursor to the first character of the next word
TOP	Moves the cursor to the first line of the file
UNDO	Restores the current line after modification
UNMARK	Removes any marks

You use the EPM command dokey when you do need to execute a key by its keyboard name. The key names used with dokey usually match the names on the keyboard keycaps. The Shift, Alt, and Ctrl keys use the single letters S, A, and C, respectively. Thus, Ctrl+F1 is C+F1 when used with dokey.

You can define new actions for keys using the EPM `buildaccel` command. The keys are called *accelerators* because they provide a shortcut for accessing an application's functionality. Accelerators are kept in named tables that can be extended and activated. Using the `buildaccel` command, you can create a new accelerator table or extend an existing one. Here's the syntax:

```
buildaccel table flags key index command
```

The *`table`* is the name of the accelerator table; you can use `*` to select the currently active accelerator table. The *`flags`* indicates the type of key and the shift keys that are combined with the key. The *`key`* is the key that is being added to the table. The *`index`* is a unique number for each accelerator key; safe values for *`index`* are usually in the `1000` to `9000` range. The *`command`* is the command that is executed when the key is pressed.

The `activateaccel` command makes an accelerator table active. Here's the syntax for `activateaccel`:

```
activateaccel [table]
```

If *`table`* isn't supplied, `activateaccel` uses the current table. If `buildaccel` has updated the current table, the new accelerator keys don't become active until after `activateaccel` is used.

The EPM REXX macro in listing 20.2 shows how to set up and activate an accelerator table. You should be aware of a few design issues before you begin examining this macro. The macro not only defines an accelerator table, but it also makes itself the command that is executed for each of the keys. Each accelerator calls the macro using a different command-line argument. The macro then distinguishes the key presses by examining the command-line argument.

The reason behind all this fiddling with command-line parameters is that the macro is actually not running most of the time. Once the accelerator table is set up, the macro exits. When the user presses one of the defined keys, the macro is executed with a command-line argument indicating what key was pressed. The macro performs the associated function and exits. Because the macro is invoked for certain keystrokes, it must perform its work quickly; otherwise, the macro interferes with the user's typing.

Listing 20.2. Defining and using accelerators with EPM.

```
/* list2002.cmd */
PARSE UPPER ARG cmd

SELECT
  WHEN cmd = '' THEN
    DO
    CALL CreateAccel
```

```
    'sayerror REXX keys active' /* display message on EPM's status line */
    END
  WHEN cmd = 'ENTER' THEN
    DO
    CALL EtkProcessEditKey 'SPLIT'
    firstLoc = FormatIt(0) - 1
    '+1'
    'extract /getline'
    getline.1 = Strip(getline.1, 'B')
    IF firstLoc > 0 THEN
      CALL EtkReplaceText Copies(' ', firstLoc) ¦¦ getline.1
    ELSE
      CALL EtkReplaceText getline.1
    CALL EtkSetFileField 'col', firstLoc + 1
    CALL FormatIt 0
    END
  WHEN cmd = 'SPACE' THEN
    CALL FormatIt 1
  WHEN cmd = 'FORMAT' THEN
    CALL FormatIt 0
  WHEN cmd = 'STOP' THEN
    DO
    'activateaccel defaccel'
    'sayerror REXX keys inactive'
    END
  OTHERWISE
    'sayerror Unrecognized key command:' cmd
END

RETURN 0

/* Format line */
FormatIt: PROCEDURE
  spaceOver = Arg(1)
  'extract /getline/col/fontheight/fontwidth'
  font = 'System VIO.HH' ¦¦ fontheight.1 ¦¦,
      'WW' ¦¦ fontwidth.1 ¦¦ '.2.0.1'
  endCol = col.1
  IF spaceOver THEN
    DO
    getline.1 = Insert(' ', getline.1, endCol - 1)
    endCol = endCol + 1
    END
  CALL EtkReplaceText getline.1
  CALL InitKeywords
  ln = Translate(getline.1)
  DO i = 1 TO Words(ln)
    wrd = Word(ln, i)
    IF kw.wrd THEN
      DO
      start = WordIndex(ln, i)
      stop = start + Length(wrd)
      CALL EtkSetFileField 'col', start
      CALL EtkProcessEditKey 'MARK_CHARG'
      CALL EtkSetFileField 'col', stop
      CALL EtkProcessEditKey 'MARK_CHARG'
```

continues

Listing 20.2. continued

```
        'processFontRequest' font
        CALL EtkProcessEditKey 'UNMARK'
        END
    END
    CALL EtkSetFileField 'col', endCol
    loc = WordIndex(getline.1, 1)
    RETURN loc

/* Initialize the keywords */
InitKeywords: PROCEDURE EXPOSE kw.
    kw. = 0           ; kw.ARG       = 1; kw.CALL      = 1;
    kw.DO         = 1; kw.ELSE      = 1; kw.END       = 1;
    kw.EXIT       = 1; kw.EXPOSE    = 1; kw.IF        = 1;
    kw.NOP        = 1; kw.ON        = 1; kw.OTHERWISE = 1;
    kw.PARSE      = 1; kw.PROCEDURE = 1; kw.RETURN    = 1;
    kw.SAY        = 1; kw.SELECT    = 1; kw.SIGNAL    = 1;
    kw.SOURCE     = 1; kw.TO        = 1; kw.THEN      = 1;
    kw.UNTIL      = 1; kw.UPPER     = 1; kw.VAR       = 1;
    kw.VALUE      = 1; kw.WHEN      = 1; kw.WHILE     = 1;
    RETURN

/* Create the accelerator keys */
CreateAccel: PROCEDURE
    CALL VirtKeys

    PARSE SOURCE . . macroName
    macroName = FileSpec('Name', macroName)

    'buildaccel rxx' AF_VIRTUALKEY ,
                VK_NEWLINE 9400 'rx' macroName 'ENTER'
    'buildaccel rxx' AF_VIRTUALKEY ,
                VK_SPACE   9401 'rx' macroName 'SPACE'
    'buildaccel rxx' (AF_VIRTUALKEY + AF_SHIFT) ,
                VK_F12     9402 'rx' macroName 'STOP'
    'buildaccel rxx' (AF_CHAR + AF_ALT) ,
                C2D('X')   9403 'rx' macroName 'FORMAT'
    'buildaccel rxx' (AF_CHAR + AF_ALT) ,
                C2D('x')   9403 'rx' macroName 'FORMAT'
    'buildaccel *'   (AF_VIRTUALKEY + AF_ALT) ,
                VK_F12     9403 'rx' macroName
    'activateaccel'
    'activateaccel rxx'
    RETURN

/* Give the virtual key codes names */
VirtKeys:
    AF_CHAR        =  1; AF_VIRTUALKEY =  2;
    AF_SCANCODE    =  4; AF_SHIFT      =  8;
    AF_CONTROL     = 16; AF_ALT        = 32;
    AF_LONEKEY     = 64;

    VK_BREAK     =  4; VK_BACKSPACE =  5; VK_TAB       =  6;
    VK_BACKTAB   =  7; VK_NEWLINE   =  8; VK_SHIFT     =  9;
    VK_CTRL      = 10; VK_ALT       = 11; VK_ALTGRAF   = 12;
    VK_PAUSE     = 13; VK_CAPSLOCK  = 14; VK_ESC       = 15;
    VK_SPACE     = 16; VK_PAGEUP    = 17; VK_PAGEDOWN  = 18;
```

```
VK_END       = 19; VK_HOME      = 20; VK_LEFT      = 21;
VK_UP        = 22; VK_RIGHT     = 23; VK_DOWN      = 24;
VK_PRINTSCRN = 25; VK_INSERT    = 26; VK_DELETE    = 27;
VK_SCRLLOCK  = 28; VK_NUMLOCK   = 29; VK_ENTER     = 30
VK_SYSRQ     = 31;

VK_F1   = 32; VK_F2   = 33; VK_F3   = 34; VK_F4   = 35;
VK_F5   = 36; VK_F6   = 37; VK_F7   = 38; VK_F8   = 39;
VK_F9   = 40; VK_F10  = 41; VK_F11  = 42; VK_F12  = 43;
RETURN
```

You start the macro in listing 20.2 within EPM by pressing Ctrl+I and entering **`rx list2002`**. As you enter REXX code in a file, the macro automatically underlines REXX keywords whenever you press the Spacebar or Enter. Figure 20.4 shows how a program looks when you enter it with this macro running.

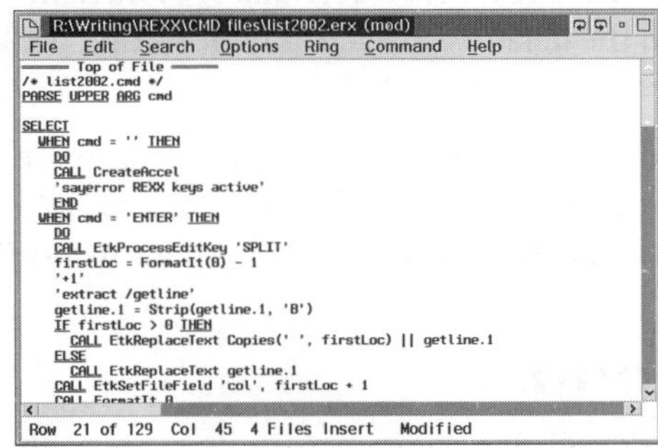

Figure 20.4. *The effect of entering code while the macro in listing 20.2 is running.*

The macro in listing 20.2 begins by getting the command-line argument and then testing it for one of the possible command strings:

- No parameter: The accelerator is created and activated.
- `ENTER`: The current line is split at the cursor position. The new line is shifted right so that it is indented to the same level as the original line. Keywords on both lines are underlined. Unlike underlines in a word processor, EPM stores these attributes in the file's EAs. Your program will still run because REXX never sees the underlines.
- `SPACE`: A space is inserted at the current cursor position and the keywords on the current line are underlined. Both actions are performed by the `FormatIt` procedure.

- `FORMAT`: The keywords on the current line are underlined with no other action taken.
- `STOP`: The accelerator is deactivated by activating the default accelerator.

The `FormatIt` procedure accepts one parameter that indicates whether a space should be inserted at the current cursor position. The font string is set up using the default font size with an underline attribute. The current line is replaced so that any old formatting information is removed. Each word from the line is then tested to determine whether it is a keyword. When a keyword is found, the word is marked and the `processFontRequest` command is executed to underline the word.

The `InitKeywords` procedure initializes the compound variable `kw.` so that `FormatIt` can quickly determine whether a word is a keyword.

The `CreateAccel` procedure builds an accelerator table named `rxx`. One additional key (Alt+F12) is added to the default accelerator table so that the keys can be turned on and off easily. Both tables are then activated.

The `VirtKeys` procedure gives names to the values that represent the virtual keys. Even though only a few virtual keys are used by this macro, all the virtual keys have been defined so that you can reuse this procedure in other macros.

Creating Menus

The Enhanced Editor's pull-down menus are fully configurable. You can add new menus to the menu bar, and you can add and delete menu items. To help clarify what the parts of the menu are called, see figure 20.5.

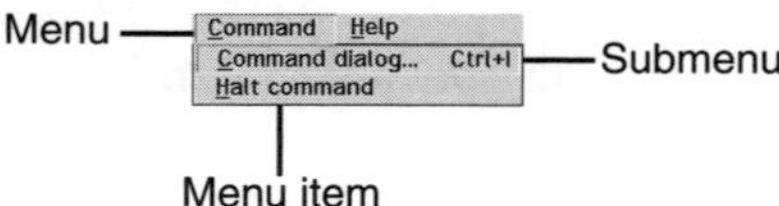

Figure 20.5. *The parts of a menu.*

You can use the `buildsubmenu` and `buildmenuitem` commands to create new menus and menu items. The menu has a name, and each submenu and menu item have a unique number that identifies that item. Each item for a menu refers to the menu name and number so that EPM knows on which menu the item belongs. Here's the syntax for both commands:

```
buildsubmenu menu-name submenu-ID menu-text attrib help [command]
buildmenuitem menu-name submenu-ID menu-ID menu-text attrib help command
```

The `menu-name` is the name of the menu bar; the normal EPM menu bar is `default`. The `submenu-ID` is a unique number for the submenu (that is, a single menu on the menu bar). The `menu-ID` is a unique number for a menu item. The `menu-text` is the actual text that appears on the menu. The `help` refers to a help panel number in a help file; `help` is usually set to `0`. The `attrib` is a number that sets an attribute for the menu item, such as gray, checked, or separator. The `command` is any valid EPM command.

The `deletemenu` command removes individual menu items or entire menus from EPM's menu bar. The syntax for `deletemenu` is as follows:

```
deletemenu menu-name submenu-ID menu-ID item-only
```

The `menu-name` and `submenu-ID` must match the name and menu ID of an existing menu. You can delete an entire menu by setting `menu-ID` to `0`; otherwise, you should set `menu-ID` to the `menu-ID` used when `buildmenuitem` created the menu item.

The EPM REXX macro in listing 20.3 creates a `REXX` menu on the menu bar and defines menu items that execute the other macros defined in this lesson.

Listing 20.3. Adding a menu to the Enhanced Editor.

```
/* list2003.erx */
PARSE UPPER ARG cmd

spc = 'FF'x     /* A 'hard' space */
hlp = '01'x     /* To delimit prompt text */
IF cmd = 'OFF' THEN
  DO
  'deleteMenu default 1990 0 0'
  'buildMenuItem default 1 1910' spc '4 0'
  'buildMenuItem default 1 1999 Add'spc'REXX'spc'menu 0 0',
      'rx list2003 RESET'hlp'Add REXX menu to menu bar'
  END
ELSE
  DO
  'buildSubmenu default 1990 REXX 0 0'
  'buildMenuItem default 1990 1991 ~Skeleton 0 0' ,
        /* Note tilde (~) precedes hot key */
      'rx list2001'hlp'Insert REXX skeleton code in file'
  'buildMenuItem default 1990 1992 Formatter'spc'o~n  0 0',
      'rx list2002'hlp'Turn formatting keys on'
  'buildMenuItem default 1990 1994 Formatter'spc'o~ff 0 0',
      'rx list2002 STOP'hlp'Turn formatting keys off'
  'buildMenuItem default 1990 1911' spc '4 0'  /*Insert separator bar */
  'buildMenuItem default 1990 1995 Remove'spc'~menu   0 0',
      'rx list2003 OFF'hlp'Remove the REXX menu'
```

continues

20

Listing 20.3. continued

```
    IF cmd = 'RESET' THEN
      DO
      'deleteMenu default 1 1910 1'
      'deleteMenu default 1 1999 1'
      END
    END
'showmenu default'      /* make the changes visible */

RETURN 0
```

You start the macro in listing 20.3 within EPM by pressing Ctrl+I and entering **`rx list2003`**. The macro creates the menu shown in figure 20.6.

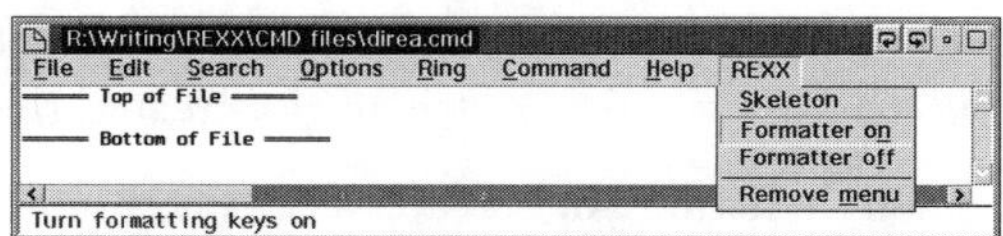

Figure 20.6. *The menu created by the macro in listing 20.3.*

The macro in listing 20.3 is designed to allow the menu to be created and removed. If the command-line argument is `OFF`, the REXX menu is removed and a menu item is added to the Command menu to allow the menu to be turned back on. If the command-line argument is not `OFF`, the REXX menu is created, with several menu items. If the argument is `RESET`, then the menu item added to the Command menu is deleted. All changes are displayed by invoking the `showmenu` command.

Following are some tips that should help you understand some of the subtleties of creating a menu like the one created in listing 20.3:

- A status message is displayed in EPM's message area for each menu option. The message is added to `buildMenuItem` by preceding the message with a binary one (`'01'x`) and concatenating the result to the command.
- The parameters to `buildMenuItem` are separated by spaces. To have spaces within a menu name, you can use the alternate space character (`'FF'x`).
- An *`attrib`* of `4` creates a separator line in the menu. An alternate space character is used as a placeholder for the *`menu-text`*.

Using the Mouse

You can use the mouse to perform several different actions within most OS/2 applications. The default actions usually include marking, copying, and moving text. Any mouse attached to an OS/2 system has at least two buttons, and you can use the mouse buttons in combination with the Ctrl, Alt, and Shift keys on the keyboard.

EPM lets you attach any command to a mouse event such as clicking, dragging, or double-clicking. You use the `register_mouse` command to attach a command to a mouse event:

```
register_mouse global button action shifts command
```

The value of *`global`* is either `0` (the registered action is effective only for the current file) or `1` (the registered action is global). The *`button`* indicates the mouse button and is either `1`, `2`, or `3`. The *`action`* is one of the values shown in table 20.6. The *`shifts`* indicates the shift keys and can be the sum of any combination of `0` (none), `1` (Shift), `2` (Ctrl), and `4` (Alt). The *`command`* is the EPM command to execute for the mouse event. If *`command`* is blank, the mouse event is not active.

Table 20.6. Action names used with `register_mouse`.

Action Name	Description
`CLICK`	A single press and release of a mouse button
`SECONDCLK`	A mouse button is double-clicked.
`BEGINDRAG`	A mouse button is pressed and the mouse is moved.
`ENDDRAG`	The mouse button is released after a drag.
`CANCELDRAG`	The drag is canceled (by pressing Esc).

When *`action`* is `ENDDRAG` or `CANCELDRAG`, the *`button`* and *`shifts`* values are not used. The command for `BEGINDRAG` should register handlers for `ENDDRAG` and `CANCELDRAG`.

Caution: An error in the Enhanced Editor version 5.51 causes registration of an `ENDDRAG` or `CANCELDRAG` mouse handler to fail. The registration error keeps REXX macros from creating mouse drag handlers.

In the following example, when the user clicks mouse button 1 (usually the left mouse button) while pressing the Ctrl key, EPM's scroll bars are toggled on or off:

```
'register_mouse 1 1 CLICK 2 setscrolls'
```

The EPM REXX macro in listing 20.4 registers commands for three different mouse events. One of the commands uses the macro in listing 20.2 to underline REXX keywords in the current line. The other commands remove any formatting and add a comment containing today's date.

Listing 20.4. Creating a mouse handler for the Enhanced Editor.

```
/* list2004.erx */
PARSE UPPER ARG cmd

SELECT
  WHEN cmd = '' THEN  /* Register mouse actions */
    DO
    'register_mouse 1 1 CLICK  4 rx list2004 FORMAT'
    'register_mouse 1 2 CLICK  4 rx list2004 UNFORMAT'
    'register_mouse 1 1 CLICK  6 rx list2004 COMMENT'
    END
  WHEN cmd = 'FORMAT' THEN
    DO
    'MH_GotoPosition'    /* Move cursor to click point */
    'rx list2002 FORMAT'
    END
  WHEN cmd = 'UNFORMAT' THEN
    DO
    'MH_GotoPosition'
    'extract /getline'
    CALL EtkReplaceText getline.1
    END
  WHEN cmd = 'COMMENT' THEN
    DO
    'MH_GotoPosition'
    'extract /getline'
    IF Length(getline.1) < 60 THEN
      DO
      ln = Left(getline.1, 60)
      cmt = '/*' Left(Date('U'), 10) '*/'
      ln = ln ¦¦ cmt
      CALL EtkReplaceText ln
      END
    ELSE
      CALL Beep 226, 100
    END
  OTHERWISE
    NOP
END

RETURN 0
```

You start the macro in listing 20.4 within EPM by pressing Ctrl+I and entering **`rx list2004`**. Figure 20.7 shows the effect of using the defined mouse events on several lines of a REXX program.

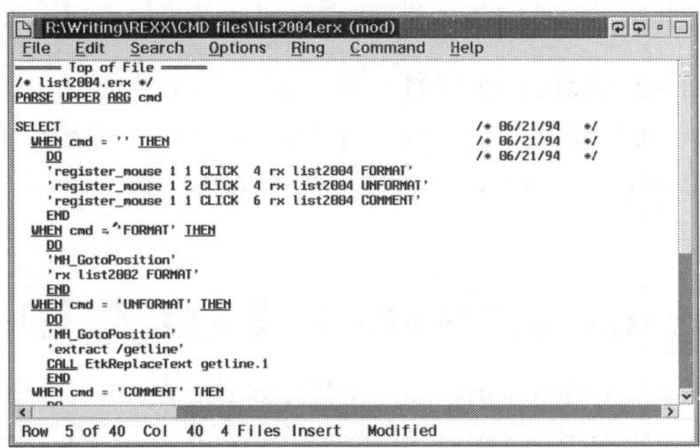

Figure 20.7. *The effect of using the mouse handler defined in listing 20.4.*

The macro in listing 20.4 is started with a command-line argument that indicates the action to be performed. These actions are as follows:

- No parameter: Three mouse handlers are registered. The mouse events used are Alt+left-click (mouse button 1), Alt+right-click (mouse button 2), and Alt+Ctrl+left-click (mouse button 1). (Note that if you have swapped your mouse buttons, these definitions will be reversed.)
- `FORMAT`: The `MH_GotoPosition` command moves the cursor to the current mouse position. The code formatting macro in listing 20.2 is executed with the `FORMAT` argument, which underlines any REXX keywords on the line.
- `UNFORMAT`: The `MH_GotoPosition` command moves the cursor to the current mouse position. The line is extracted and then replaced in order to remove any formatting.
- `COMMENT`: The `MH_GotoPosition` command moves the cursor to the current mouse position. The line is extracted, and if it has fewer than 60 characters, a comment containing the current date is appended to the right end of the line. The line is then replaced. If the line is 60 characters or longer, the macro beeps.

20

Creating a Profile

The Enhanced Editor supports running an EPM REXX macro named `PROFILE.ERX` automatically as part of the editor's startup. You can use this macro to change settings, register mouse handlers, create accelerator tables, and modify the menus.

To use the profile, you create a `PROFILE.ERX` and then turn on EPM's profile support by entering **`profile on`** at EPM's command prompt. Then, from the Options menu, select Save options to make the profile setting permanent.

Other Applications That Use REXX

A growing number of applications use REXX as their macro language or give you access to REXX from the application's own macro language. Here's a sample of what's currently available:

- LiveWire, a shareware text mode communications application
- DeScribe 4.1 for OS/2
- Lotus Ami Pro for OS/2
- Simmware's RexxWare, a Novell Netware NLM application that provides network management utilities

The following sections give you a broad overview of how the first three of these packages incorporate REXX.

LiveWire

LiveWire provides several additional functions for REXX to help you work with the telephone system. For instance, LiveWire has its own functions for hanging up the phone, dialing, and exiting. LiveWire includes two special commands, `GetLW` and `SetLW`, which get and set LiveWire attributes (configurable settings). These attributes include cursor location, screen color, phone book entries, timeout values, terminal emulations, capture, and log.

LiveWire's REXX macros are named using a .CMD extension. LiveWire registers itself as a subcommand handler for REXX programs that are run inside LiveWire. LiveWire passes on any commands that are not valid functions to the OS/2 command interpreter. Standard REXX output, tracing output, and error output are written to LiveWire's terminal screen. In addition, LiveWire redirects the output from the REXX instruction `SAY` to the terminal screen.

DeScribe 4.1

The DeScribe 4.1 word processor provides an extremely simple REXX interface. To call a REXX macro, you need to write a DeScribe macro that uses the statement `RunREXXFile` to execute the REXX macro. You can pass arguments to the REXX macro, and the REXX macro can return a value to the DeScribe macro by using the `RETURN` instruction.

Currently, DeScribe doesn't provide any support beyond calling a REXX macro in the same manner that REXX calls an external function. Although this support is limited, your REXX macros can still perform quite a bit of data manipulation.

AmiPro

Lotus AmiPro for OS/2 provides several ways to integrate REXX programs:

- You can run a REXX program directly from Ami Pro by choosing Macros from the Tools menu and then choosing Play REXX file.
- You can call REXX programs from Ami Pro macros.
- You can use REXX commands in Ami Pro macro files.
- You can use Ami Pro macro functions in REXX programs.
- You can exchange parameters between Ami Pro macros and REXX programs.

If you create an Ami Pro macro to start a REXX program, you use `RexxCmd` to start the program and pass any optional arguments. The REXX program retrieves those arguments using the `ARG` instruction. If the REXX program includes a `RETURN` instruction, the return value is available in the Ami Pro macro as the return value of `RexxCmd`.

To execute a single REXX statement from an Ami Pro macro, you use `RexxFunction`. `RexxFunction` takes a REXX statement string as the parameter. If the REXX file includes a `RETURN` instruction, the return value is available in the Ami Pro macro as the return value of `RexxFunction`.

REXX programs executed from Ami Pro use the .CMD extension.

To communicate with the user from a REXX program invoked from Ami Pro, you write an Ami Pro macro that displays a dialog box. The REXX program gets the value of the button that dismissed the dialog box. If you want to display a message box or simply get an answer to a question, you can also use the Ami Pro functions `Message` and `Query`.

Ami Pro intercepts the REXX instructions `SAY` and `PULL`, and it translates them to `Message` or `Query` functions. Ami Pro saves the prompt and displays it in the query box. However, in REXX you normally prompt for a response with `SAY` and immediately get the response with PULL so that the message you pass to SAY does not display until the next SAY or PULL function.

Summary

This lesson introduced you to using REXX as a macro language for OS/2 applications. You learned how to write EPM REXX macros and how to extend the Enhanced Editor by creating accelerator keys, menus, and mouse actions. The lesson also gave you an overview of how other OS/2 applications use REXX.

Q&A

Q What other information is available for programming EPM?

A Two documents are available: *The EPM Editor Technical Reference Manual* and *The EPM User's Guide*. The Enhanced Editor also has its own internal macro language called *E*. You can download online versions of the documentation plus the editor toolkit, sample code, sample EPM REXX macros, and the E compiler from CompuServe and several BBSs.

Workshop

The Workshop provides quiz questions to help strengthen your understanding of the material covered and exercises to provide you with experience in using what you've learned.

Quiz

1. What does the `RxMessageBox` function do?
2. What file extension is used for an EPM REXX macro?
3. What function do you use in an EPM REXX macro to replace a line of text?
4. What is the `extract` command used for in an EPM REXX macro?
5. What commands do you use to define accelerator keys in EPM?
6. What does the `register_mouse` command do?

Exercises

1. Look in the manuals and the help files for any OS/2 applications that you own. List any applications that have REXX support.
2. Design and write an EPM REXX macro that uppercases the word the mouse pointer is on when the user presses Ctrl+left-click.
3. Modify listing 20.2 so that it doesn't underline keywords within one-line comments. Ensure that it works correctly for lines that contain both code and comments.

Interprocess Communications

WEEK 3

OS/2 is designed to run more than one program at the same time. Until now, the lessons in this book have acted as though each one of those programs operated independently, and obviously many programs do so quite well. However, one of the advantages to a multitasking operating system is that programs can communicate with each other. Today you learn how you can use REXX to do so. Today you learn the following:

- ☐ What a semaphore is and how to use a file as a semaphore
- ☐ How to communicate with other programs using named pipes
- ☐ How to use REXX's queues to communicate between two REXX programs

Files as Semaphores

When two programs need to use the same resource, such as a keyboard, a printer, a serial port, or a file, the programs must have some way to determine when it's okay to use the resource and when the resource is in use by the other program.

A *semaphore* is used to signal the beginning and end of an operation, and to prevent more than one process from accessing the same resource at the same time. OS/2 has several types of semaphores built in, but these semaphores are not accessible from REXX unless you use a third-party library.

An alternative way of creating a semaphore is to use a file. You need to predetermine the location and name of the file so that both programs look in the same place. The file doesn't need to have anything in it—your program needs to test only for the presence (or absence) of the file. To test for the file, your program must loop, testing for the file each time. Following is the first way you might program this loop:

```
flag = 0
DO UNTIL flag
  flag = (Stream(semFile, 'C', 'Query Exists') = '')
END
```

This example is called a *polling loop*. In a single tasking system, a polling loop doesn't create any problems because nothing else is happening on the machine. A polling loop in a multitasking system, however, creates a great deal of unnecessary overhead by executing thousands of times per second. The program doesn't need to check for the file more than once per second; often it doesn't need to check more than once every five seconds, or even once a minute.

The RexxUtil function `SysSleep` suspends your program for a given number of seconds. The only parameter that `SysSleep` requires is a number indicating how many seconds you want your program to go to sleep. Here's the polling loop rewritten to test for the file once every two seconds:

```
DO WHILE Stream(semFile, 'C', 'Query Exists') >< ''
  CALL SysSleep 2
END
```

When you design a program that needs to perform polling, give careful thought to the frequency at which it needs to poll. For example, you don't need to check for new electronic mail every second. Every five minutes will probably do. Taking more of the computer's CPU power than necessary gives your application the reputation of being a hog; on the other hand, not polling often enough makes the application seem unresponsive.

DO | **DON'T**

DO think carefully about the polling requirements of your programs.

DO use `SysSleep` to control CPU usage.

DON'T assume that your application owns the system or is the most important one running.

The program in listing 21.1 starts the program in listing 21.2 and then polls a semaphore file. Listing 21.2 collects data and stores it in a file that listing 21.1 then displays. The file is a unique resource that both programs want to use, so the semaphore controls access to the file.

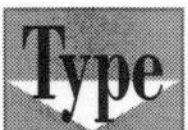

Listing 21.1. Polling a semaphore file.

```
/* list2101.cmd */
IF LoadRexxUtil() THEN EXIT

semfile = 'D:\tyr.sem'
resfile = 'D:\c_dupes.txt'

'@detach list2102.cmd' /* start a separate process */

DO UNTIL Stream(semFile, 'C', 'Query Exists') = ''
  CALL SysSleep 5
END

SAY 'Duplicate files on drive C:'
SAY
DO WHILE Lines(resfile)
  line = LineIn(resfile)
  SAY line
END
CALL LineOut resfile /* close the file */
'@del' resfile '> NUL'

EXIT
```

Listing 21.2. Creating and deleting a semaphore file.

```
/* list2102.cmd */
IF LoadRexxUtil() THEN EXIT

semfile = 'D:\tyr.sem'
wrkfile1 = 'D:\work.1'
wrkfile2 = 'D:\work.2'
resfile = 'D:\c_dupes.txt'

CALL Stream semfile, 'C', 'OPEN WRITE'
CALL Stream semfile, 'C', 'CLOSE' /* create semaphore as an empty file */

CALL SysFileTree 'C:\*', 'files.', 'FOS'
DO i = 1 TO files.0
  CALL LineOut wrkfile1, FileSpec('N', files.i) '¦' files.i
END
CALL LineOut wrkfile1
'@sort <' wrkfile1 '>' wrkfile2 /* sort on file name */
'@del' wrkfile1 '> NUL'

this = 0
line. = ''
didFirst = 0
DO WHILE Lines(wrkfile2)
  PARSE VALUE LineIn(wrkfile2) WITH line.this.file ,
      ' ¦ ' line.this.fullPath
  last = \ this
  IF line.this.file = line.last.file THEN
    DO
    IF \ didFirst THEN
      DO
      CALL LineOut resfile, line.this.file
      CALL LineOut resfile, '  'line.last.fullPath
      END
    CALL LineOut resfile, '  'line.this.fullPath
    didFirst = 1
    END
  ELSE
    didFirst = 0
  this = last
END
CALL LineOut wrkfile2
'@del' wrkfile2 '> NUL'

CALL LineOut resfile /* close the file */
'@del' semfile '> NUL'  /* delete the semaphore */
EXIT
```

```
[D:\]list2101
The process ID is 296
Duplicate files on drive C:

CONFIG.SYS
  C:\CONFIG.SYS
```

```
  C:\OS2\INSTALL\CONFIG.SYS
OS2.INI
  C:\OS2\INSTALL\OS2.INI
  C:\OS2\OS2.INI
OS2SYS.INI
  C:\OS2\INSTALL\OS2SYS.INI
  C:\OS2\OS2SYS.INI
pscript.drv
  C:\OS2\DLL\PSCRIPT\pscript.drv
  C:\OS2\MDOS\WINOS2\SYSTEM\pscript.drv
pscript.hlp
  C:\OS2\DLL\PSCRIPT\pscript.hlp
  C:\OS2\MDOS\WINOS2\SYSTEM\pscript.hlp
```

The program in listing 21.2 creates a semaphore file and then creates a file that holds a list of duplicate filenames on drive C. The program in listing 21.1 starts the program in listing 21.2 as a detached process and then waits for the semaphore file to be deleted. When the semaphore file is deleted, listing 21.1 opens the results file and prints the information collected by listing 21.2. If your system doesn't have a drive D, you will, of course, need to edit the program so that it uses a valid drive on your system.

The following notes highlight some intricacies involved in using semaphores:

- The OS/2 `DETACH` command requires two or three seconds to execute but returns to the caller almost immediately. If the program in listing 21.1 used a `DO WHILE` to check for the semaphore file, it would incorrectly determine that the semaphore was cleared on the first test (while `DETACH` is still loading listing 21.2). The `DO UNTIL` forces the `SysSleep` to execute before the semaphore is checked. You may need to change the wait time if you find that listing 21.1 starts reading the results file too soon. Immediately after the `DETACH` command, you might also put a loop that waits for the semaphore file to appear.
- The `DETACH` command always generates a process ID message.
- The program in listing 21.2 must close the results file before exiting. If the file isn't closed, then listing 21.1 cannot access the file because OS/2 sees the file as being in use.

Named Pipes

An application may need to allow many other programs to communicate with it. The application doesn't know what other applications are trying to send it data. If the application needs to allow *any* program to send it data—OS/2, DOS, or Windows—then the best facility to use is a *named pipe*.

You use a named pipe for communications between two unrelated processes. The processes can be on the same machine, or they can be on different computers connected in a network. Any program that knows the name of a named pipe can open and use that named pipe. A named pipe has a special name that looks like a filename; all named pipes have a name such as `\PIPE\pipename`, where *pipename* is the name of the pipe.

REXX can't create a named pipe (unless you have a third-party library that supports named pipes); the only way that REXX has access to a named pipe is if another program has created it. Therefore, you use named pipes primarily to communicate with applications that provide the feature as a conduit between what you want to do and the service that the other application provides.

The first step is for a program, called a *server*, to create and connect to the named pipe. Although REXX has no standard functions to create a named pipe, several third-party libraries do offer this function. The second step is for another program, called a *client*, to open the named pipe. The client and server can then exchange data through the pipe.

Several OS/2 applications define a named pipe so that any program can send requests to that application. One example is BocaSoft's System Sounds. This program defines a pipe named `\PIPE\BS_SSND`. When you send a number to this pipe, System Sounds plays a corresponding sound file (defined by the user). The following loop plays all the defined sounds:

```
DO index = 1 TO 49
  CALL CharOut , Right(index, 3)
  CALL Stream '\pipe\bs_ssnd', 'C', 'OPEN WRITE'
  CALL LineOut '\pipe\bs_ssnd', index
  CALL Stream '\pipe\bs_ssnd', 'C', 'CLOSE'
  CALL SysSleep 2
  IF index // 20 = 0 THEN /* display 20 numbers to a line */
    SAY
END
```

Notice that the pipe is opened and closed once each time around the loop. If the pipe isn't closed each time, System Sounds plays only the first sound and ignores any further indexes sent to it. Because the `LineOut` function automatically opens a file, the first `Stream` call isn't strictly necessary, but it is included for completeness. `SysSleep` gives System Sounds enough time to play the sound.

The RexxUtil function `SysWaitNamedPipe` allows a REXX program to wait on a busy named pipe. If you check the return code from `Stream` when you open a named pipe, you may get a return code of `231`. This return code indicates that the named pipe is busy. You can tell `SysWaitNamedPipe` to either wait for a number of milliseconds or wait until the pipe isn't busy. Here's the syntax:

```
result = SysWaitNamedPipe(pipename [, timeout])
```

A `timeout` of `-1` sets an indefinite wait (that is, it waits until the pipe isn't busy); other `timeout` values indicate a number of milliseconds to wait for the pipe.

Queues

A *queue* is an ordered list of data that can be accessed from either end. REXX provides several instructions and built-in functions to create, delete, and access queues. Data can be accessed either in *last in, first out* sequence (called *LIFO*) or *first in, first out* sequence (called *FIFO*).

REXX defines a queue named `SESSION`, which is available only on a per process basis. This means that two REXX programs run from two different OS/2 sessions (that is, OS/2 command prompts) have a different queue named `SESSION`. You can create additional queues, called *private queues*, that are accessible to any process running on the system. The `SESSION` queue makes it easy for programs run one after another at a single command prompt to communicate with each other. A private queue is necessary if two programs running at the same time need to communicate or if you need multiple queues.

Note: OS/2 provides another type of queue that follows different rules from the REXX queues. If you need to create or access an OS/2 system queue, you need to acquire a third-party library that provides support for OS/2 queues.

The OS/2 program RXQUEUE is a filter that puts data from another program on a REXX queue. You use RXQUEUE either at the command line or as a command from within a REXX program. By default, the `SESSION` queue is used, but you can specify a private queue. The following example puts the output from the `PSTAT` command on the `SESSION` queue:

```
[D:\]pstat ¦ rxqueue
```

Once the data is on the queue, a REXX program can retrieve it by using the `PULL` instruction. You're already familiar with the `PULL` instruction as a way to get data from the standard input. When data has been placed on the `SESSION` queue, `PULL` gets its input from the queue instead of standard input.

The RXQUEUE program can put data on the queue in either LIFO or FIFO order by using the `/LIFO` or `/FIFO` command-line flags. If neither command flag is specified, then FIFO order is used. For instance, if you want the last line output by the `dir` command to be the first line in the queue, you use the following:

```
[D:\]dir ¦ rxqueue /LIFO
```

You can also clear the queue by using the /CLEAR command-line flag. This flag removes all the data in the queue without deleting the queue itself.

In a REXX program, you can put data on a queue using the PUSH and QUEUE instructions. The PUSH instruction adds lines to the queue in LIFO order (the last line put on the queue by PUSH is the first line retrieved by PULL). The QUEUE instruction adds lines to the queue in FIFO order.

Refer to the program in listing 21.3 to help you understand the difference between PUSH and QUEUE. Notice that PUSH puts lines at the front of the queue, and QUEUE puts lines at the back of the queue.

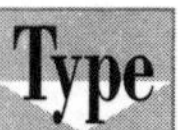

Listing 21.3. Using QUEUE and PUSH.

```
/* list2103.cmd */

PUSH 'first push'
QUEUE 'first queue'
PUSH 'second push'
QUEUE 'second queue'

DO 4
  PULL var
  SAY var
END

EXIT
```

```
[D:\]list2103
SECOND PUSH
FIRST PUSH
FIRST QUEUE
SECOND QUEUE
```

In the program in listing 21.3, four lines are alternately pushed and queued. The lines are then pulled from the queue and displayed. Notice that the pushed lines come off the queue in reverse order from the order they were put on the queue.

You can also read and write lines in a queue using the LineIn and LineOut functions. In place of a regular filename, you use QUEUE:. The LineIn function guarantees that your program is reading data from the queue, whereas the PULL instruction resorts to standard input if the queue is empty.

The Queued function returns the number of lines that are currently on the queue. You can use Queued for queues like you use Lines and Chars for files. For instance, the following example loops, reads, and displays all lines from a queue:

```
DO WHILE Queued() >< 0
  PULL line
  SAY line
END
```

The RxQueue function can create and delete private queues. A private queue can be accessed by any program on the system that knows the name of the queue. RxQueue is also used to set the current queue that is being used in a REXX program and to get the name of the current queue.

Private queues exist until you either specifically delete the queue or you shut down the system. You create a private queue by using the Create option with the RxQueue function. For example, you create a queue named mystuff like this:

```
qName = RxQueue('Create', 'mystuff')
```

If mystuff already exists, then REXX generates a name and creates a queue by that name. It's usually a good idea to compare the returned queue name to the intended queue name. If the returned name is different from the intended one, then your program is trying to create a queue that already exists.

After you create the queue, you need to make it the active queue in your program to use it. You use the Set option to activate the queue and get the name of the previously active queue:

```
oldQ = RxQueue('Set', qName)
```

Now the PULL, PUSH, and QUEUE instructions all act on the private queue instead of SESSION. You can reset the queue back to the session queue by either specifying the Set option with either SESSION or oldQ (that is, the return value from the original RxQueue Set call) as the queue name.

You can retrieve the name of the current queue by using the Get option. Unless you've set the queue to a private queue, the following example should display SESSION:

```
SAY RxQueue('Get')
```

When your program is finished using a private queue, you should delete the queue. The private queue remains in existence until you explicitly delete it (or shut down), so leaving the queue around when you no longer need it is a waste of system resources. You delete the queue by using the Delete option:

```
CALL RxQueue 'Delete', qName
```

Any program that knows the name of the queue can delete the queue.

Syntax

The *RxQueue* Function

```
queue = RxQueue("Create" [, queuename])
```

The `RxQueue "Create"` function creates a queue *queuename*, or if *queuename* is not supplied, a name is supplied by REXX. The returned value is the name of the new queue. If *queuename* already exists, REXX supplies a different name and creates a new queue. The queue created by `RxQueue` is available to all programs in the system.

```
rc = RxQueue("Delete", queuename)
```

The `RxQueue "Delete"` function deletes the queue *queuename*. When the queue is deleted, any data remaining in the queue is also deleted. The return codes are shown in table 21.1.

Table 21.1. Return codes for the `RxQueue "Delete"` option.

Return Code	Meaning
0	The queue was deleted.
5	The queue name is not valid.
9	The queue does not exist.
10	The queue is busy (another program is waiting on the queue).
12	A memory failure occurred.
1000	There is a possible error in OS2.INI.

```
queue = RxQueue("Get")
```

The `RxQueue "Get"` function returns the name of the queue that is currently in use.

```
queue = RxQueue("Set", queuename)
```

The `RxQueue "Set"` function changes the current queue to *queuename*. `RxQueue` returns the name of the previous queue.

Example 1

```
newQ = RxQueue('Create', 'testing')
```

Example 2

```
currentQ = RxQueue("Get")
```

Example 3

```
result = RxQueue("Delete", newQ)
```

Example 4

```
lastQ = RxQueue('Set', newQ)
```

The programs in listing 21.4 and listing 21.5 work together to create and display a directory listing. The program in listing 21.4 creates a queue and then runs listing 21.5 in a detached session.

Type **Listing 21.4. Creating a queue and getting data from another program.**

```
/* list2104.cmd */
IF LoadRexxUtil() THEN EXIT
SIGNAL ON Halt NAME OuttaHere
SIGNAL ON Syntax NAME OuttaHere

qNm = 'TYRQ0'
CALL RxQueue 'Create', qNm
CALL RxQueue 'Set', qNm

'detach list2105.cmd' qNm

CALL CharOut , 'Waiting...'
DO UNTIL Queued() >< 0
  CALL CharOut , '.'  /* let user know we're still alive */
  CALL SysSleep 1
END

SAY; SAY

DO WHILE Queued() >< 0
  fileName = LineIn('QUEUE:')
  SAY fileName
END

OuttaHere:

CALL RxQueue 'Delete', qNm
EXIT
```

Type **Listing 21.5. Putting data in a queue for another program's use.**

```
/* list2105.cmd */
IF LoadRexxUtil() THEN EXIT
SIGNAL ON NotReady
```

continues

Listing 21.5. continued

```
PARSE ARG qNm
CALL RxQueue 'Set', qNm

CALL SysFileTree 'C:\OS2\*.*', 'files.', 'FO'

DO i = 1 TO files.0
  CALL LineOut 'QUEUE:', files.i
END

EXIT

NotReady:
  SAY 'not ready'
  EXIT
```

```
[D:\]list2104
The process ID is 62
Waiting....

C:\OS2\AHA174X.ADD
C:\OS2\ANSI.EXE
C:\OS2\ATTRIB.EXE
C:\OS2\BACKUP.EXE
C:\OS2\BOOT.COM
C:\OS2\CACHE.EXE
C:\OS2\CDFS.IFS
C:\OS2\CHKDSK.COM
C:\OS2\CLIPOS2.EXE
C:\OS2\CLOCK01.SYS
C:\OS2\CMD.EXE
C:\OS2\COM.SYS
C:\OS2\COMP.COM
C:\OS2\CREATEDD.EXE
C:\OS2\DISKCOMP.COM
C:\OS2\DISKCOPY.COM
C:\OS2\DOS.SYS
C:\OS2\DOSCALLS.LIB
C:\OS2\E.EXE
C:\OS2\EAUTIL.EXE
```

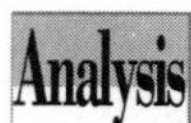

The program in listing 21.4 creates a private queue and then starts the program in listing 21.5 as a detached process. The name of the private queue is passed to the detached process as a command-line argument. The detached process gets a directory listing and writes each line to the private queue. Listing 21.4 waits for data to appear in the queue and displays a period on the screen about once per second while it's waiting. Once data appears in the queue, listing 21.4 removes lines from the queue and displays them. (Note that the output shown is only the first screen of data.)

You should be aware that there is a possible timing problem in listing 21.4. If data doesn't appear in the queue as fast as the program reads the data, the program may exit the loop

too soon. One way of solving this problem is to have the program in listing 21.5 write an end-of-data line when all the data is written to the queue. Then listing 21.4 can check for the end-of-data line to ensure that all data has been read from the queue.

Summary

This lesson discussed methods for communicating between two or more programs. You learned about three different methods: semaphores, named pipes, and queues. You also learned how to use a file as a semaphore, and you learned about the dangers of polling. The lesson showed you how to send data to a named pipe.

Finally, you saw how to use the REXX session queue and how to create and use private queues.

Q&A

Q I can send a message through a private queue instead of using a semaphore. Which way is best?

A If your programs are always run together on the same system, then a private queue is probably the best way to signal that a resource is free or in use. However, the queue works in this capacity when no more than two programs need to coordinate access to a resource. Reading the queue removes the message, so only one program can read the message. The semaphore is useful when more than two programs need to share a resource, or the programs may be running on different systems attached to a LAN (local area network).

Workshop

The Workshop provides quiz questions to help strengthen your understanding of the material covered and exercises to provide you with experience in using what you've learned.

Quiz

1. What is a semaphore?
2. What is a named pipe?
3. What is a queue?

4. How is the SESSION queue different from a private queue?
5. Why is polling a problem on a multitasking system?
6. What caveats should you keep in mind when using semaphores?
7. What are the roles of a named pipe client and server?
8. What do you use the RxQueue function for?
9. What is the difference between the PUSH and QUEUE instructions?
10. How do you create a named pipe using REXX?

Exercises

1. Rewrite listings 21.1 and 21.2 so that they produce a list of duplicate filenames for all local drives. Because of data limitations in the OS/2 SORT program, you need to sort the list within your REXX program. (**Note:** One possible way of storing all the filenames before sorting is to use a queue.)
2. Because this is the last exercise of the book, you determine its real content. Think about what programs might make using your computer easier, more fun, or more efficient. Select a program that interests you, design it, and write it. The best way to improve your programming skills is to *use* them. After you write a few of your own programs, you'll discover that you can easily remember and use all the things you learned in this book.

WEEK

IN REVIEW

3

The Week in Review— Week 3

You have completed your third and final week of learning how to program in REXX. You started the week by learning how to use streams to read and write files and devices. You then learned how to use external function libraries and how to use the RexxUtil DLL in particular. You saw how RexxUtil functions are used to get directory listings, get and set extended attributes, access .INI files, and control keyboard and screen input and output. You learned how to create and manipulate Workplace Shell objects. At the end of the week, you learned how to use REXX to extend OS/2 applications and perform interprocess communications. The following program pulls together many of these topics.

Note: The numbers to the left of the line numbers indicate the lesson (that is, DAY15 indicates the lesson for Day 15) that first explains the material represented by that line of code. If you don't understand the line of code or it seems confusing, refer to the indicated lesson.

Listing WR3.1. Week 3 review listing.

```
/* DirEA.cmd
 * List a directory, showing .SUBJECT and .COMMENTS EAs for each
 * file. Also shows .KEYPHRASES and displays in short or long
 * formats.
 *
 * Use the command "dirEA /?" to see usage instructions.
 *
 * Author:  Bill Schindler
 *
 * --------------------------- History -------------------------
 * 12-Jan-1994  wfs  Created.
 *
 * 05-Feb-1994  wfs  Check for directory in file spec argument
 *                   Add option for showing .COMMENTS EA
 *                   Add usage subroutine
 *
 * 02-Jun-1994  wfs  ==Version 1.10 begins==
 *                   Fixed problem displaying multi-value
 *                   comments.
 *                   Added routines and fixed code in
 *                   preparation for displaying additional EA
 *                   values.
 *                   Did some code clean up and simplified some
 *                   processing.
 *                   Add -K flag and display key words.
 *                   Changed long form to display subject,
 *                   comments, & keywords.
 *
 * 05-Jun-1994  wfs  Added simple filtering for files with a
 *                   specific key word.
 *
 * 09-Jun-1994  wfs  Fixed a problem with sizing the subject
 *                   string. The display routines were
 *                   truncating the subject about 10 characters
 *                   too early.
 *                   Allow multiple file specifications on the
 *                   command line.
 *                   Allow command line flags to appear anywhere
 *                   on the command line.
 * -------------------------------------------------------------
 */

DAY16 IF LoadRexxUtil() THEN
        EXIT
```

```

/*
 *Process any command line arguments
 */
PARSE ARG filespec

i = 0
doComments = 0
useLongForm = 0
doKeywords = 0
doSearch = 0
searchFor = ''
doSubdirs = ''
specs. = ''
specs.0 = 0

DO WHILE filespec >< ''
  PARSE VAR filespec wrk filespec
  IF Left(wrk, 1) = '/' ¦ Left(wrk, 1) = '-' THEN
    DO /* process command line switches */
    sep = Left(wrk, 1)          /* save the / or - */
    pgmArg = SubStr(wrk, 2)     /* strip leading / or - */
    pgmArg = Translate(pgmArg) /* uppercase the arg */

    SELECT
      /* show .COMMENTS */
      WHEN pgmArg = 'C' THEN
        doComments = 1
      /* do subdirectories */
      WHEN pgmArg = 'S' THEN
        doSubdirs = 'S' /* used with SysFileTree */
      /* long format */
      WHEN pgmArg = 'L' THEN
        useLongForm = 1
      /* show .KEYPHRASES */
      WHEN pgmArg = 'K' THEN
        DO
        doKeywords = 1
        doSearch = 1
        END
      /* search for matching .KEYPHRASES */
      WHEN Left(pgmArg, 2) = 'K:' THEN
        DO
        IF doKeywords THEN
          doSearch = 1 /* search and display */
        ELSE
          DO
          doSearch = -1 /* don't display keywords */
          doKeywords = 1
          END
        PARSE VAR pgmArg . ':' searchFor
        END
      /* show usage and exit */
      /* variations on /help are also allowed for users
       * that don't have a clue */
      WHEN pgmArg = '?' ¦ Abbrev('HELP', pgmArg, 1) THEN
```

Listing WR3.1. continued

DAY17

```
    DO
    CALL ShowUsage
    EXIT
    END
   /* oops... */
   OTHERWISE
    SAY
    SAY "Invalid command line argument '" ¦¦ sep ¦¦ ,
      pgmArg ¦¦ "'"
    EXIT
  END
  END
 ELSE /* not a switch, must be a file spec */
  DO
  i = i + 1 /* count file specs */
  specs.0 = i
  IF Left(wrk, 1) = '"' THEN
   PARSE VALUE wrk filespec WITH '"' wrk '"' filespec
  specs.i = wrk
  END
END

IF useLongForm THEN
 DO /* force comments and keywords for long form */
 doComments = 1
 doKeywords = 1
 END

IF specs.0 = 0 THEN
 DO /* no filespecs, so default to '*.*' */
 specs.0 = 1
 specs.1 = '*.*'
 END
ELSE /* check filespecs, and add '*.*' where needed */
 DO i = 1 TO specs.0
  /* Assumption alert! Can't tell files from dirs without
   * a trailing '\', so we assume it's a file if we don't
   * find a trailing '\'! */
  IF Right(specs.i, 1) = '\' THEN
   specs.i = specs.i ¦¦ '*.*'
 END

/*
 * Read the directory
 */
files. = ''
files.0 = 0
wrk. = ''
DO i = 1 TO specs.0
 CALL SysFileTree specs.i, 'wrk.', 'F' ¦¦ doSubdirs, '***-*'
                                                /* ASDHR */
 k = files.0 + 1 /* next available space in files. */
 files.0 = files.0 + wrk.0
 DO j = 1 TO wrk.0 /* collect files for each filespec */
  files.k = wrk.j
```

```
      k = k + 1
    END
  END

  IF files.0 > 1 THEN
    DO
DAY15    CALL CharOut , 'Total of' files.0 'files found for'
    delim = ''
    DO i = 1 TO specs.0
DAY15      CALL CharOut , delim "'"specs.i"'"
      delim = ','
    END
    SAY
    END
  SAY

DAY17  IF files.0 = 0 THEN /* no matching files? */
    DO
    SAY 'No files found for "'filespec'"'
    EXIT
    END

  /*
   * Collect and parse the EAs for each file found
   */
  longestFN = 4    /* longest filename(minimum) */
  longestType = 4  /* longest EA type(minimum)  */
  longestSubj = 7  /* longest subject(minimum)  */
  filename. = ''

  /* extended attribute types */
  eat. = ''
DAY17  eat.ascii    = 'FFFD'x
  eat.asn1     = 'FFDD'x
  eat.binary   = 'FFFE'x
  eat.bitmap   = 'FFFB'x
  eat.ea       = 'FFEE'x
  eat.icon     = 'FFF9'x
  eat.metafile = 'FFFA'x
  eat.mvmt     = 'FFDF'x
  eat.mvst     = 'FFDE'x

  CALL GetEAData /* collect EA stuff for all files */

  /*
   * Display the files and associated EAs
   */
  IF \ useLongForm THEN /* display the column headings */
    SAY ' 'Center('File', longestFN) '¦' ,
        Center('Subject', longestSubj)
  PARSE VALUE SysTextScreenSize() WITH rows cols

  lastSubdir = ''
  extraDirs = 0
  matching = 0

```

continues

Listing WR3.1. continued

```
DO i = 1 to files.0
  IF searchFor >< '' THEN /* key word search? */
    DO
    IF Pos(searchFor, files.i.keywords) = 0 THEN
      ITERATE /* skip files that don't match key word */
    matching = matching + 1
    IF doSearch = -1 THEN /* display keywords? */
      files.i.keywords = '' /* ...nope */
    END
  IF ¬ doComments THEN /* page the output? */
    CALL PageIt

  IF doSubdirs = 'S' THEN
    IF lastSubdir >< FileSpec('PATH', filename.i) THEN
      DO /* show new directory name whenever it changes */
      lastSubdir = FileSpec('PATH', filename.i)
      IF useLongForm THEN
        DO
        SAY
        extraDirs = extraDirs + 1
        IF \ doComments THEN /* page the output? */
          CALL PageIt
        END
      SAY 'Directory:  ' || FileSpec('DRIVE', filename.i) ||,
          lastSubdir
      extraDirs = extraDirs + 1
      IF \ doComments THEN /* page the output if no comments */
        CALL PageIt
      END
  /*
   * Build a single line with the file name and subject
   */
  IF useLongForm THEN
    DO /* long form puts subject on a separate line from file */
    SAY Left(files.i, 28) || '   ' ||,
        FileSpec('name', filename.i)
    IF files.i.subject >< '' THEN
      SAY '   Subject: ' || files.i.subject
    END
  ELSE /* not using long form */
    DO
    fn = Left(FileSpec('Name', filename.i), longestFN)
    subj = Left(files.i.subject, longestSubj)
    SAY ' ' || fn '|' subj
    END
  IF files.i.keywords >< '' THEN
    SAY '   Key words: ' || files.i.keywords
  IF files.i.comment >< '' THEN
    DO
    SAY; SAY files.i.comment; SAY
    END
END

/* Show how many files matched a key word */
IF searchFor >< '' THEN
```

```
  DO
  SAY; SAY matching 'files matched key word "'searchFor'".'
  END

EXIT

/* ---------------------------------------------------------------
 * G e t E A D a t a
 * Get and format EAs for each file. Command line switches
 * control which EAs are collected.
 */
GetEAData:
  DO i = 1 to files.0
    /*
     * Get .SUBJECT EA
     */
    PARSE VAR files.i 38 filename.i
    /* track longest filename for column width */
    longestFN = Max(longestFN,,
        Length(FileSpec('Name', filename.i)))
    IF GetAndFormatEA(filename.i, '.SUBJECT') THEN
      DO
      subjLen = ea.1.length
      subj = ea.1.data
      END
    ELSE
      subj = ''
    files.i.subject = subj
    longestSubj = Max(longestSubj, Length(subj))
    /*
     * Get .COMMENTS EA
     */
    IF doComments THEN
      DO
      cmt = ''
      IF GetAndFormatEA(filename.i, '.COMMENTS') THEN
        DO j = 1 TO ea.0
          IF Right(cmt, 1) = '0D'x THEN
            cmt = cmt ¦¦ '0A'x
          cmt = cmt'  'Strip(ea.j.data, 'L')
        END
        files.i.comment = cmt
      END
    /*
     * Get .KEYPHRASES EA
     */
    IF doKeywords THEN
      DO /* collect the key phrases */
      kw = ''
      IF GetAndFormatEA(filename.i, '.KEYPHRASES') THEN
        DO j = 1 TO ea.0
          kw = kw ea.j.data
        END
      files.i.keywords = Strip(kw, 'L')
      END
  END
```

continues

Listing WR3.1. continued

```
  /* track longest subject for column size */
  longestSubj = Min(longestSubj, 80 - (longestFN + 6))
  RETURN

/* -------------------------------------------------------------
 * G e t A n d F o r m a t E A
 * Function to get an EA and parse it. The EA is broken into its
 * components and stored in the ea. compound variable.
 */
GetAndFormatEA: PROCEDURE EXPOSE eat. ea.
  fileName = Arg(1) /* file to use */
  eaName = Arg(2)   /* which EA to get and format */
  ea.0 = 0
DAY17  IF SysGetEA(fileName, eaName, stuff) = 0 ,
  & stuff >< '' THEN
    DO /* format the EA */
    CALL FormatEA stuff, 1
    RETURN 1
    END
  RETURN 0

/* -------------------------------------------------------------
 * F o r m a t E A
 * Recursive function to parse EAs.
 */
FormatEA: PROCEDURE EXPOSE eat. ea.
  stuff = Arg(1) /* the stuff to parse */
  count = Arg(2) /* current count of EAs */
  PARSE VAR stuff eat 3 .
DAY17  eat = Reverse(eat) /* convert little-endian to big-endian */
  SELECT
    /* EAT_ASCII */
    WHEN eat == eat.ascii THEN
      DO
      ea.0 = count
      PARSE VAR stuff 3 leng 5   /* get the length */
      leng = C2D(Reverse(leng))  /* change endian */
      PARSE VAR stuff 5 ea.count.data +(leng) stuff
      ea.count.length = leng
      ea.count.type = 'ASCII'
      END
    /* EAT_MVMT */
    WHEN eat == eat.mvmt THEN
      DO
      PARSE VAR stuff 5 leng 7 stuff /* get the length */
      leng = C2D(Reverse(leng))      /* change endian */
      count = count - 1
      DO i = 1 TO leng  /* do each sub-type */
        stuff = FormatEA(stuff, count + i)
      END
      END
    /* EAT_MVST */
    WHEN eat == eat.mvst THEN
      DO
      PARSE VAR stuff 5 leng 7 stuff /* get the length */
```

```
      leng = C2D(Reverse(leng))       /* change endian */
      count = count - 1
      DO i = 1 TO leng
        stuff = FormatEA(stuff, count + i)
        stuff = Reverse(eat.ascii) || stuff
      END
      END
    /* Unrecognized EA type */
    OTHERWISE
      ea.0 = count
      ea.count.type = '???'
      ea.count.data = 'Unknown EA' C2X(eat)
      ea.count.length = 15
  END
  RETURN stuff

/* ------------------------------------------------------------------
 * P a g e I t
 */
PageIt:
  /*
   * Handle displaying more than one screen of data. Since we're
   * not calculating the length of a .COMMENTS EA, we don't
   * bother paging the output when the 'C' option is turned on.
   */
  IF ((i + extraDirs) // (rows - 1)) = 0 THEN DO
DAY15    CALL CharOut 'CON:', '-- more --'
DAY16    CALL SysGetKey 'NOECHO' /* toss whatever key is pressed */
    SAY  /* start on the next line */
    END
  RETURN

/* ------------------------------------------------------------------
 * S h o w U s a g e
 */
ShowUsage: PROCEDURE
  SAY
  SAY "Lists comments and subject EAs for one or more files"
  SAY "  dirEA Version 1.10."
  SAY
  SAY "  Usage:  dirEA [options] [filespec [filespec ...]]"
  SAY
  SAY "  Options:"
  SAY "    -?        Displays this usage screen"
  SAY "    -C        Display both subject and comments"
  SAY "    -L        Produce a long format listing"
  SAY "              (includes subject, key words, and comments)"
  SAY "    -S        Processes pathname and its subdirectories"
  SAY "    -K        Display key words"
  SAY "    -K:word   Only display files with matching key word"
  SAY
  SAY "  The filespec parameter defaults to '*.*'"
  RETURN

/* ------------------------------------------------------------------
 * L o a d R e x x U t i l
```

continues

Listing WR3.1. continued

```
     434:  */
     435: LoadRexxUtil: PROCEDURE
DAY16 436:    IF RxFuncQuery('SysLoadFuncs') THEN
     437:      DO
     438:      IF RxFuncAdd('SysLoadFuncs', 'RexxUtil', 'SysLoadFuncs')
     439:        THEN DO
     440:        SAY "Error: Couldn't load RexxUtil library."
     441:        RETURN 1
     442:        END
     443:      CALL SysLoadFuncs
     444:      END
     445:    RETURN 0
```

A 445-line program may seem extremely long to you, but if you have entered the code from the listings presented during this week, then you will find that you've already written about a third of this program. The procedures `LoadRexxUtil`, `GetAndFormatEA`, and `FormatEA` are similar to the procedures of the same names introduced on Days 16 and 17. This program is a real example of reusing code that was written for a different program.

DIREA displays a directory listing with subject, comments, and keyphrases for each file. The default display is in two columns, with the filename on the left and the subject on the right. The user can control what information is displayed and the format of the information by using command-line flags. The user can also enter more than one file specification on the command line to compare files in different directories or look at a narrowed selection of files.

The program is an actual utility program that was originally written for use on our network. Notice the large comment at the beginning of the program (lines 1 to 41). This comment has a short description of the program, tells who wrote it, and contains a history of all modifications. This information helps anyone reading the code see what the program does and how it evolved. The history also helps you determine whether a current error was caused by an earlier modification. As a program ages, most new errors are introduced by recent changes. The history helps you quickly locate recent changes that are more likely to be the cause of a new error.

On line 43, the `LoadRexxUtil` function is called to register functions from the RexxUtil library. `LoadRexxUtil` is identical to the function introduced on Day 16.

The entire command line is loaded into the single variable `filespec` (line 49). The program allows you to enter command-line arguments in any order, so the command line

cannot be processed by a single `PARSE` instruction. The loop on lines 61 to 121 parses the command-line arguments one at a time. The assignments on lines 51 to 59 initialize several program variables that are used throughout the rest of the program.

Note: DIREA started its life accepting a single file specification on the command line. The switches were introduced later. Because the command line was originally only a file specification, the variable was named `filespec`. As the program was modified, `filespec` ceased to name the actual use of the variable, but the variable name was never changed. An evolutionary change like this is common in many programs, and you need to be aware that variables sometimes take on new aspects as a program changes.

The loop in lines 61 to 121 parses the command-line arguments stored in `filespec`, one word at a time. If the current argument begins with a `-` or a `/`, the argument is processed as a command-line switch. Otherwise, the argument is treated as a file specification. Command-line switches are processed (lines 64 to 112) by removing the first character (the `-` or `/`) and then setting variables depending on the actual switch value. File specifications are processed by adding each specification to the compound variable `specs.`. If the specification is in double quotation marks, it is parsed again to get the entire specification. (HPFS file and directory names may contain spaces—the double quotation marks and a second parse are required to handle this problem.)

Each file specification is used to get a list of matching files (lines 149 to 158). The directory listing for the current file specification is added to the list of all matching files found. Hidden files are masked out of the directory search performed by `SysFileTree`.

If any matching files are found, a message showing the total number found is displayed (lines 160 to 169). If no files are found, the program displays a message and exits (lines 172 to 176).

The extended attributes are collected by the call to `GetEAData` on line 198. `GetEAData` gets each EA based on what command-line switches were set. It calls `GetAndFormatEA`, which in turn calls `FormatEA` in order to collect the requested EA data. (`GetAndFormatEA` and `FormatEA` were introduced on Day 17 and are documented in that lesson.) `GetEAData` loops through each file and adds any EA data to `files.` compound variable. The function also tracks the longest filename and the longest subject so that columns can be formatted correctly later in the program.

After the EA information is collected, the program displays a column heading (lines 203 to 205) and displays the information found within the loop on lines 212 to 263. If a keyword search is active (lines 213 to 220), the EA `.KEYPHRASES` is searched for a matching value. If a matching keyword isn't found, the program iterates, effectively skipping over the file.

If comments aren't being displayed, the `PageIt` procedure is called. The action is taken at several points in the loop as more lines are displayed. The `PageIt` procedure (lines 397 to 408) determines whether the screen is full and, if so, displays a prompt so that the output doesn't just scroll. The user can press any key to display the next screen of information.

If subdirectories are included in the file listing, the program displays the directory name each time the directory changes (lines 224 to 240).

The program then displays the filename, subject, and other EA information (lines 244 to 262). The output is formatted depending on the value of `useLongForm`. The default output is the filename and subject formatted as two columns. If `useLongForm` is true, then the file's date, time, size, and name are displayed on one line, and the extended attributes are displayed on lines below it. Each EA is displayed only if the file has a value for that particular EA.

Finally, if a keyword search was active (lines 266 to 269), the number of files that matched the keyword is displayed.

Like any program, DIREA isn't perfect. Here are a few of the known problems:

- The file specifications are not checked for uniqueness. If the user enters the same file specification twice, DIREA displays the same files twice.
- Having the output paged for all formats would be nice. To page the output when it contains comments, you need to parse each comment and determine how many lines the comment requires.
- The column headings are displayed when no files match a given keyword. To fix this problem, you need to change the point that matching files are selected so that the program knows if there are any matching files before the headings are displayed.

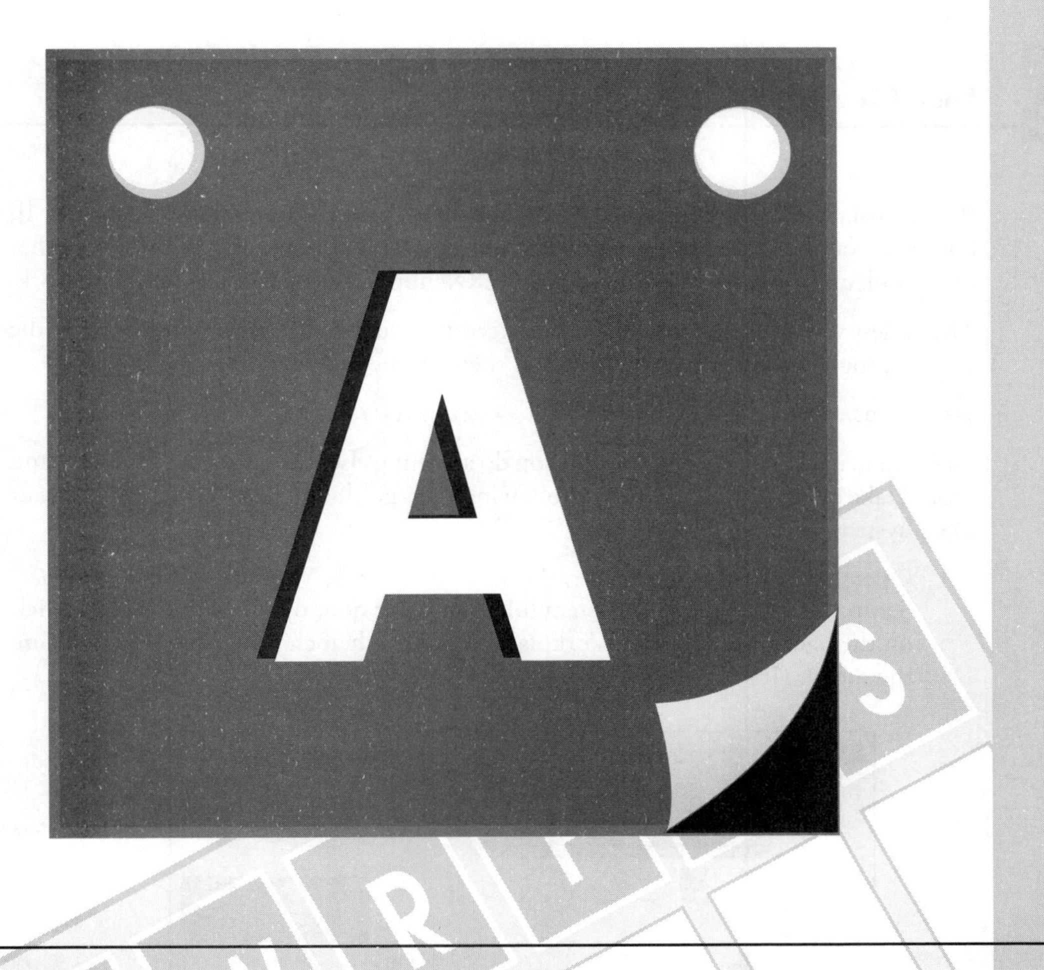

Installing REXX

Installing REXX

If you installed OS/2 with all the defaults, REXX was automatically installed. If, however, you did a selective install to try to cut down on the amount of disk space that OS/2 took up, you may have to install the REXX support files before you can get to work.

The easiest way to find out whether you need to install REXX is to type in one of the sample programs and try to run it. If you then get the following message:

```
SYS1801: OS/2 Procedures Language 2/REXX is not installed.
```

then you need to install REXX before you do anything else. Installing REXX is easy and should take only a few minutes. The following steps guide you in adding REXX to your OS/2 system:

1. Open the System Setup folder, shown in figure A.1. You can find the System Setup folder in the OS/2 System folder on your desktop. Or you can right-click on the background of the Workplace Shell and then choose System Setup from the menu. (It's the choice right under Shutdown.)

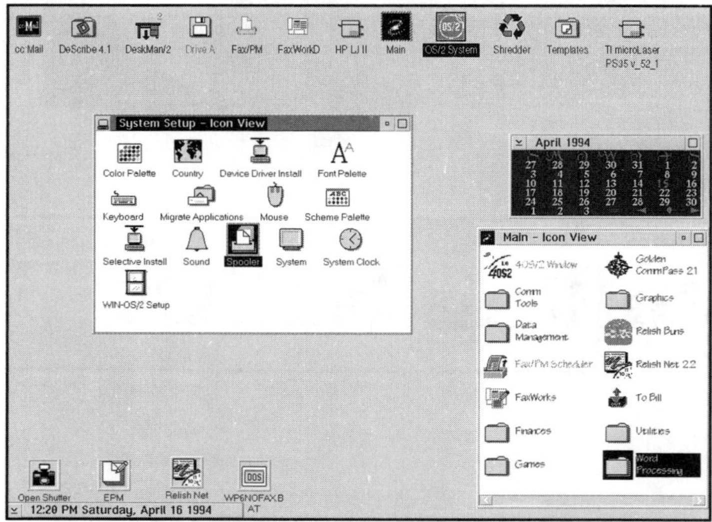

Figure A.1. *Choose Selective Install from the System Setup folder.*

2. Start the Selective Install program by double-clicking on its icon. As you can see from figure A.2, Selective Install lets you install just about any kind of option for your OS/2 system. The first screen is completely concerned with hardware, so you don't need to check any of the displays, printer drivers, and so on. Just click once on OK.

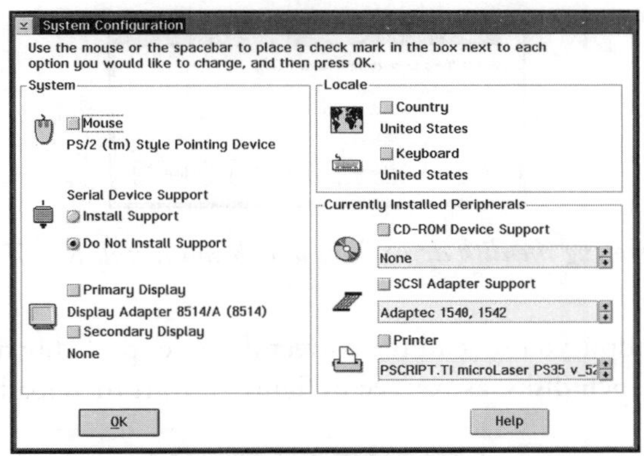

Figure A.2. *The Selective Installation Program.*

3. The second screen in Selective Install, shown in figure A.3, lists the software and software drivers that you can install. The only one to be concerned with here is REXX. Click once on the box next to REXX, and a check mark appears. Click on OK.

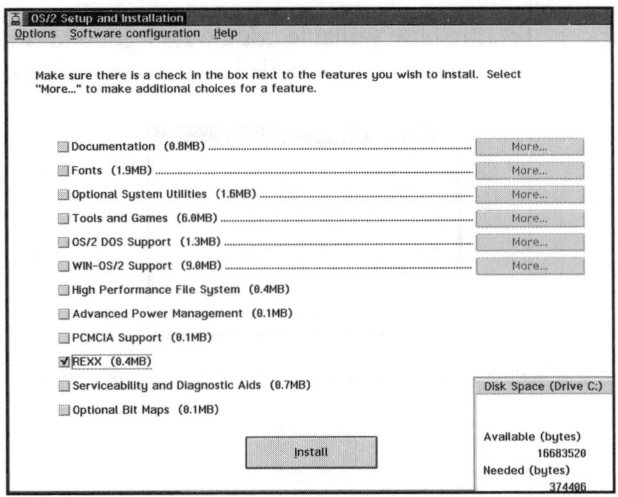

Figure A.3. *Choosing to install REXX support.*

4. OS/2 prompts you for the disk drive to use for the installation. This drive is probably your A: drive, as shown in figure A.4, but you can install REXX from a CD-ROM drive or another disk drive, if necessary.

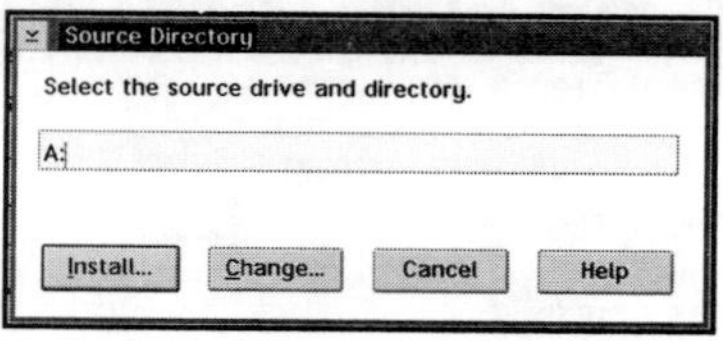

Figure A.4. *Choosing the disk drive from which you install REXX.*

5. OS/2 prompts you to load the correct diskette (probably diskette #9, if you're using 3.5-inch disks, as you see in figure A.5). It then loads the files.

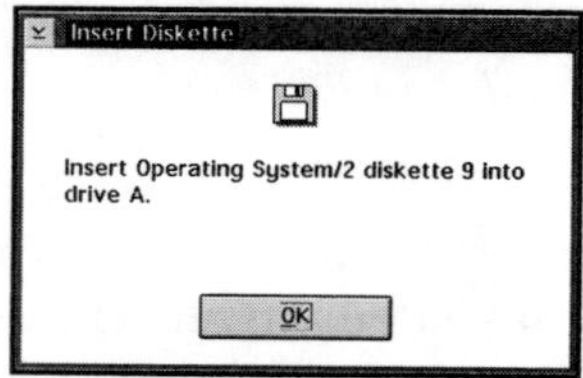

Figure A.5. *The REXX support files are on diskette #9.*

6. Although the files are now available, it's always a good idea to shut down and reboot your system after you've installed new system software (see fig. A.6).

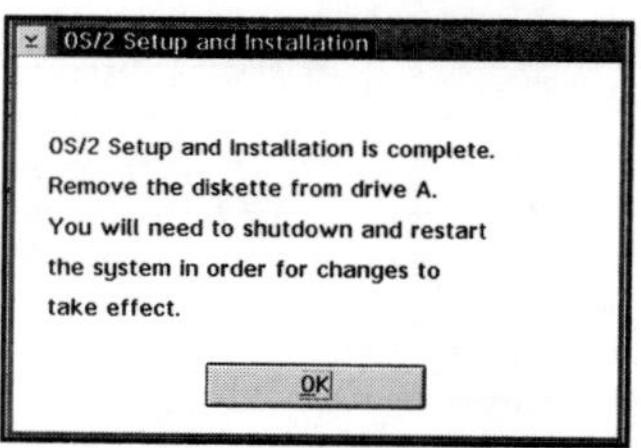

Figure A.6. *The changes take effect after you shut down and reboot.*

Visual REXX Tools

In this appendix, you examine three visual REXX tools to learn the different approaches to implementing visual programming with REXX.

This appendix is not intended to be a review of the products used. Because new versions of software are released regularly, far more often than book revisions, offering a product review wouldn't be useful. The purpose here is to explain what visual REXX programming is about.

Introducing Visual Programming

Visual programming tools simplify the job of programming, especially in a graphical environment. The visual REXX tools help you create OS/2 PM programs that use REXX as the underlying program language. Some of the benefits of using a visual REXX tool include the following:

- You don't have to know as much to get started. Memorizing a long list of procedure names isn't necessary, and the tool always gets the syntax right.
- Because the development process is rapid, you get near-immediate gratification.
- You can select REXX instructions from a menu or list box, so you can use the visual tool to help you learn REXX faster.
- Visual tools make it easier to create a graphic user interface for your programs. You use the tool to create windows and place graphical objects such as buttons, check boxes, and entry fields in those windows. You visually connect the objects through drag-and-drop programming.

Figure B.1 shows an example of a visual programming environment. The programming environment contains a visual design tool, an editor for writing and editing code, an interactive debugger, and other tools to aid in generating and testing the program.

In this appendix, we explore creating a simple application. We alternate among the three programming tools (VisPro/REXX, VXRexx, and GpfRexx) as we create a user group meeting check-in program.

How Visual Programming Works

The visual programming tools all follow a similar process. When you use the tool, your application starts as a window that is essentially a blank canvas. The tool provides a menu

and an icon bar that enable you to select the objects that you want to add to the window. Figure B.2 shows three visual REXX programming tools as they appear when you first create a new application.

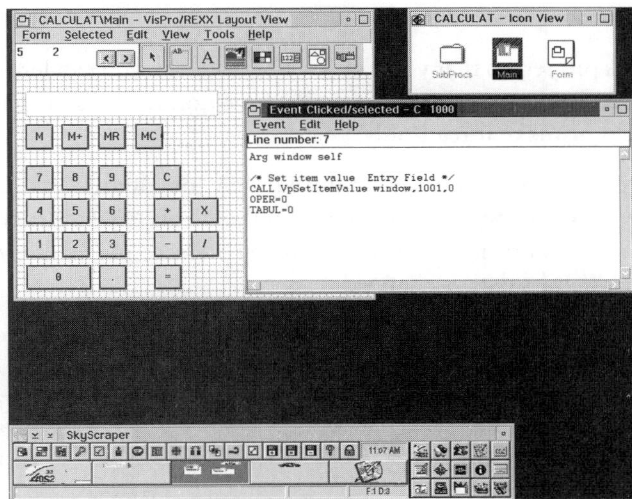

Figure B.1. *A visual programming environment (VisPro/REXX).*

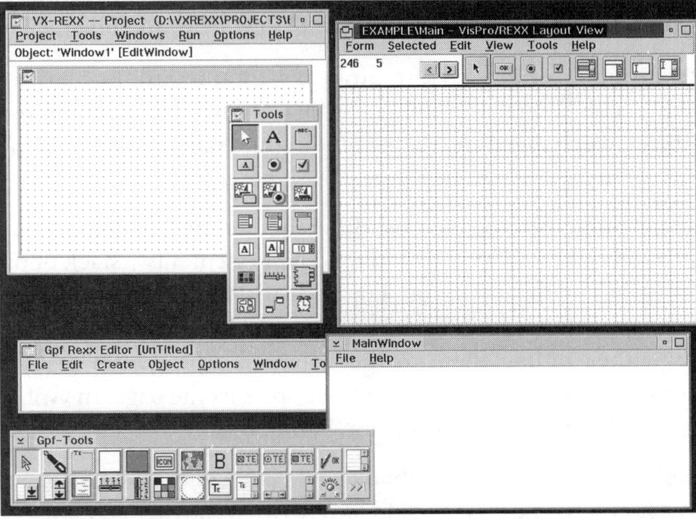

Figure B.2. *Creating a new application with (from top left) VXRexx, VisPro/REXX, and GpfRexx.*

The images that appear on the icon bars represent PM objects such as push buttons, text, radio buttons, and containers. You select an icon and then use the mouse to position the object in the application's window (the "blank canvas"). You can use the mouse to change the size and location of the object. You can also select several objects and center, align, or move them.

Each object has properties that you can set. For instance, you can left-align, right-align, or center the text in an entry field, you can set a maximum character length, and you can disable the field or make it read-only.

After you have all the objects placed in the window (or, alternatively, as you place them in the window), you can begin to write code for the events to which each object responds. For example, a push button can respond to being pressed, and an entry field might need to take action when its data is changed.

You can write the code for an event, or you can use drag-and-drop programming to let the visual programming tool do most of the work.

Visually Designing an Interface

In VXRexx and VisPro/REXX, you start writing a visual REXX program by dragging off a template and dropping it in the Projects folder. When you drop the template, it creates a new directory with any required initial files. The new project gets a default name (for example, Project:1). You set the new project's name by changing the object's name. For GpfRexx, you start a new project by selecting New from the File menu.

For our user group meeting check-in project, we wanted to use a notebook so that we could quickly access several windows of information. After positioning and sizing the notebook object, we changed and set the binding and tab properties for the notebook (see fig B.3).

The three visual programming tools use different methods for defining and attaching the pages of the notebook. An OS/2 PM notebook is essentially a stack of dialog boxes that are bound together by the notebook. For both VisPro/REXX and VXRexx, you define each page as a separate window. Once the pages are defined, you associate them with the notebook by either adding them to the notebook's properties or by creating a link between the notebook and the window that represents the page. In GpfRexx, you define each page by working directly on the notebook object.

After we finished laying out the notebook pages (see fig. B.4), we began writing the code for the events for each object. We could have written the event code as we added objects to the notebook, but because we already knew how we wanted each page designed, it was easier to do all the layout work at the beginning.

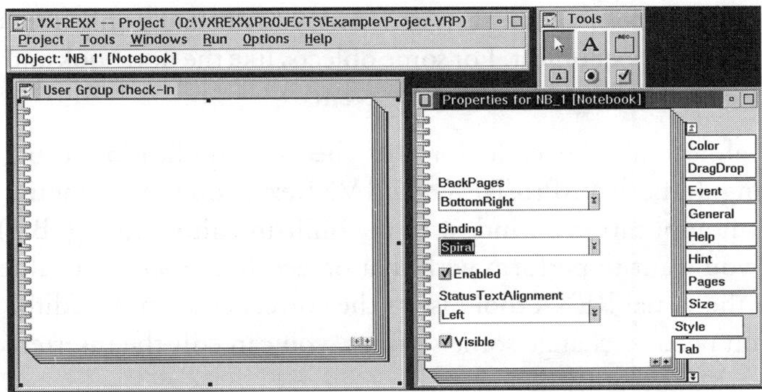

Figure B.3. *Setting properties for a notebook object (VXRexx).*

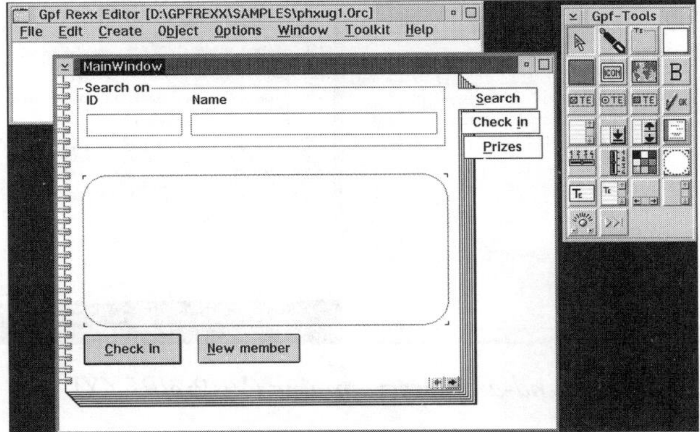

Figure B.4. *The final layout for the application (GpfRexx).*

Programming for Events

Each object has a set of events associated with it. Events result from actions performed on an object. For example, a push button has a *click* event, and an entry field has a *when changed* event. All events have a default action that usually does nothing.

You create a program by writing code for events. Whenever an event occurs, the code attached to that event is executed.

Up to this point, the work we've done in defining our meeting check-in application has not looked very much like REXX programming. So far, we have a user interface that's nice to look at, but it doesn't do anything interesting. Writing code for events makes the program *do* something.

Although some objects have long lists of events, you normally only need to define actions for one or two events per object. For some objects, like the notebook and descriptive text, we didn't need to define actions for any events.

We wrote almost all the code for the check-in application using drag-and-drop programming. In both VisPro/REXX and VXRexx, you use the mouse to drag from an object in your application's window to the built-in editor (see fig. B.5). You select the action that you want to perform with that object, like "Get item value" or "Give item focus," and the visual REXX tool inserts the correct code in the editor for that specific action. If you need to change some settings, you can edit the inserted code.

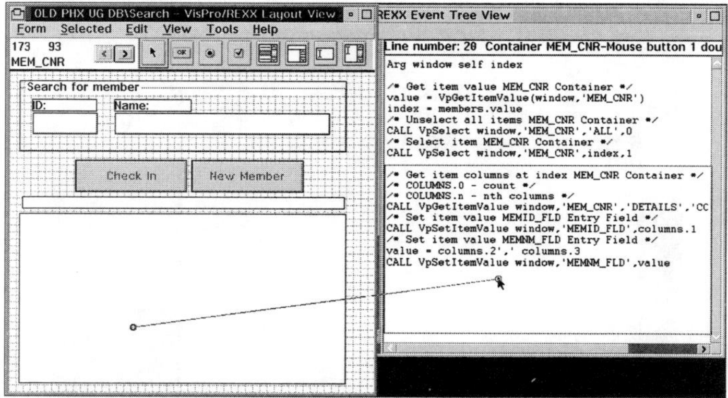

Figure B.5. *Using drag-and-drop programming (VisPro/REXX).*

GpfRexx uses a different approach to adding event code. You attach actions to events while you're viewing the listing of events for an object. You create actions from a separate window (see fig. B.6).

As you write events, it's a good idea to test each one to ensure that it works correctly. By the time we finished writing all the necessary action code, we had test run the program more than 50 times.

Testing and Debugging

Testing is an important activity for developing any program. All the visual REXX tools include a test mode that enables you to run your application and see how it works. When you find an error, you can quickly return to the tool to fix the problem. The test mode is also handy for trying out different ways of programming the same event—write the code one way, test it, then write the code the other way, and test it again.

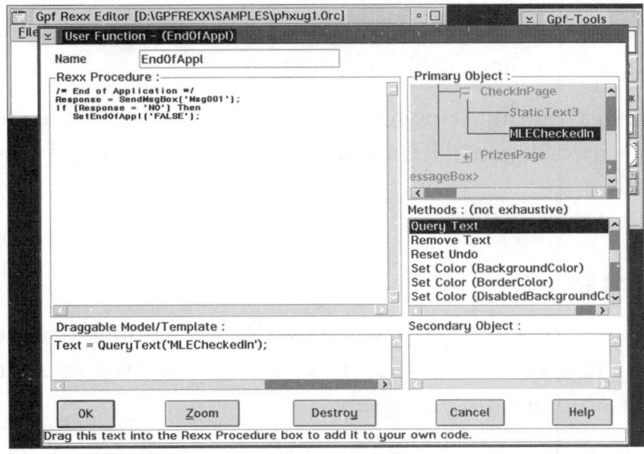

Figure B.6. *Creating action code in GpfRexx.*

One of the real benefits of using a visual REXX tool is that a source-level debugger is included (see fig. B.7). You can stop your program at any point, single-step through code, and examine variables.

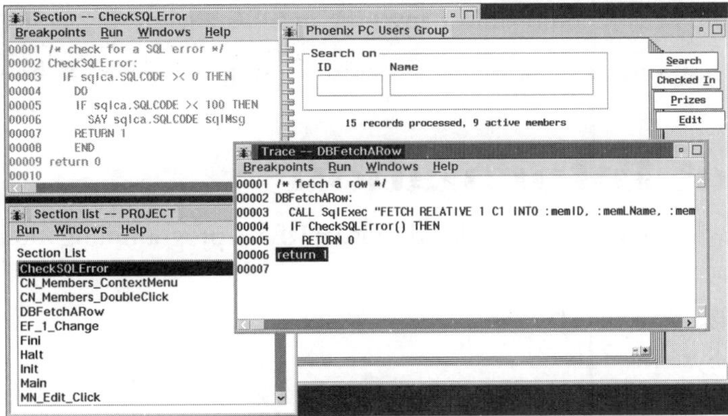

Figure B.7. *Using a source-level debugger to find an error (VXRexx).*

Generating the Application

The final step is to generate the application. All three tools can generate an executable file that has the REXX code embedded as data within it. You select a menu option to generate the program, and a few seconds later the process is finished. The user runs the program just like any other OS/2 PM program.

If you plan on distributing your final application, you'll need to include a DLL that contains all the special visual REXX functions. A different DLL is supplied by each vendor.

Limitations

There is no question that a program written in REXX is going to be slower than the same program written in C or C++. However, REXX may surprise you with how capable it is as an OS/2 PM programming language.

Some types of programs you shouldn't consider doing in REXX. Anything that does a lot of number crunching, such as statistical analysis or a large spreadsheet, is probably going to be painfully slow. Programs that need to use several graphics or perform a great deal of intensive processing, such as desktop publishing, also is a poor fit for visual REXX.

There are also limitations in accessing all the OS/2 PM functions. These limitations are caused by missing functions in the libraries supplied by the visual REXX vendors. Over time, the vendors will probably fill in most of the missing functions, and a visual REXX program will be able to do almost anything in OS/2 PM.

Many applications *do* work well when written using visual REXX, however.

Contact Information

The following companies provided the visual REXX programming tools that are shown in this appendix:

GpfRexx
Gpf Systems, Inc.
30 Falls Road
Moodus, CT 06469-0414
Phone: (203) 873-3300

VisPro/REXX
Hockware, Inc
P.O. Box 336
Cary, NC 27512-0336
Phone: (919) 380-0616

VXRexx
Watcom International Corporation
415 Phillip Street
Waterloo, Ontario, CANADA N2L 3X2
Phone: (519) 886-3700

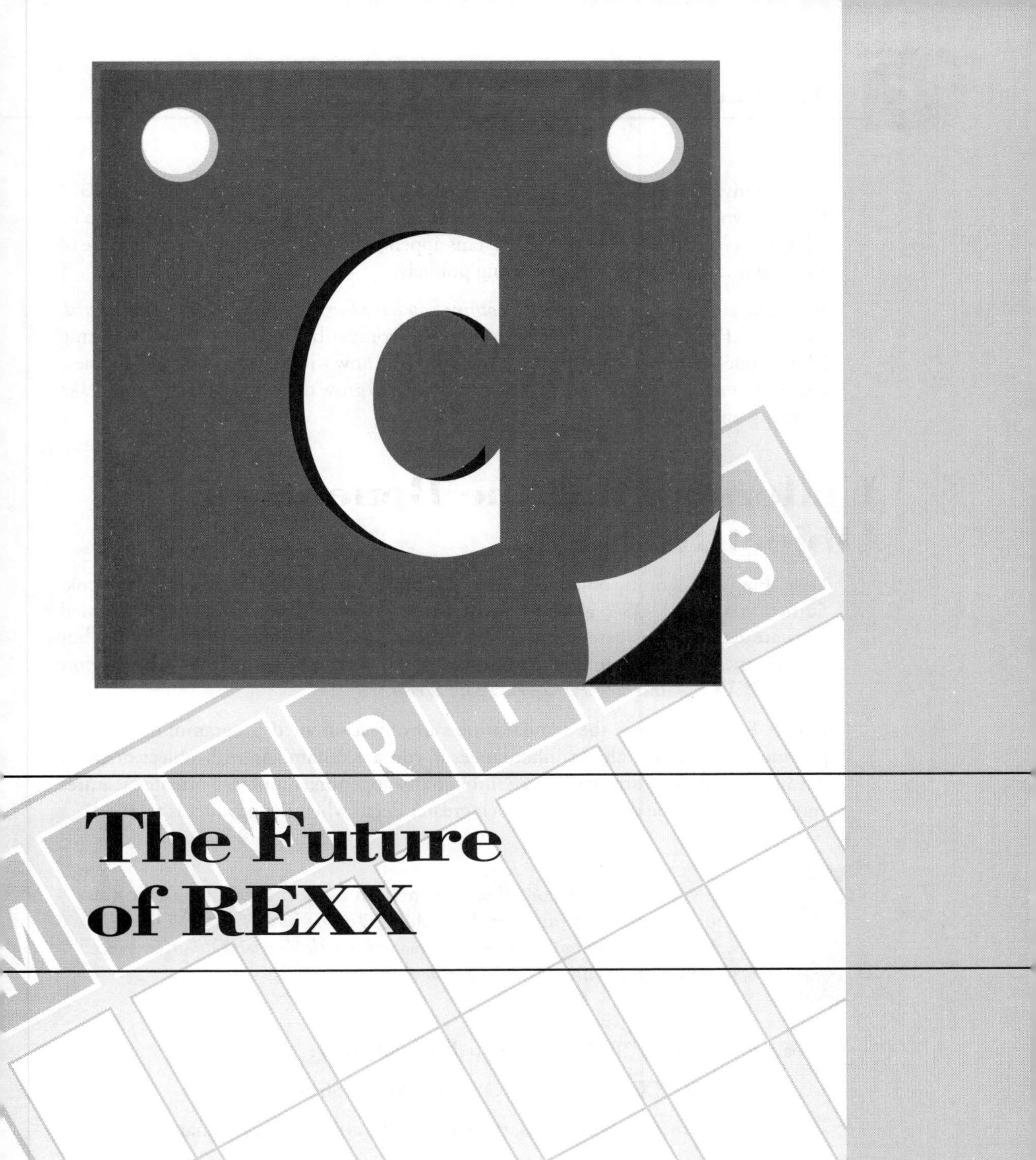

The Future of REXX

Just like any other software development tool, REXX is constantly being improved. IBM has been working on some significant enhancements to REXX which are expected to be released in late 1994 or in early 1995. This appendix gives a broad overview of some of the new features that IBM is discussing publicly.

It's important to keep in mind that *nothing you have learned in this book will be wasted.* The new REXX, called *Object REXX*, is upwardly compatible and will work with existing REXX code. In other words, the programs you write now will continue to work. The new enhancements add functionality and are intended to grow the language; they won't take anything away.

Understanding the Benefits of Object REXX

Describing and defining object-oriented programming is outside the scope of this book. Suffice to say that OS/2 is based on an object-oriented design, and object-oriented software design is considered the way of the future. (This might sound like a cop-out, but to cover the topic adequately, this appendix would have to be named *Teach Yourself the Object REXX Enhancements in a Few More Weeks.*)

Object REXX does use the standard tools of object-oriented programming, such as polymorphism and multiple inheritance. If you are unfamiliar with object-oriented terminology, don't worry as you read through this appendix; the object-oriented features and their use will be described in much greater detail when the product is released.

Note: If you want to explore object orientation in more detail, take a look at these books, available from Sams Publishing: *Teach Yourself Object-Oriented Programming with Visual C++ in 21 Days* and *Teach Yourself Object-Oriented Programming with Turbo C++ in 21 Days.*

In particular, Object REXX promises to do the following:

- ☐ Simplify REXX's access to the OS/2 Workplace Shell
- ☐ Provide structured data tools, such as records, arrays, and dictionaries
- ☐ Make it easier to write concurrent, multithreaded applications
- ☐ Provide better development tools

Object REXX is expected to appear first on OS/2 and Windows; other platforms are under consideration.

At this time, IBM is providing detailed information about some of the features and remaining quiet about others.

Simplifying WPS Access

Object REXX will give wider access to OS/2's system DLLs. Programmers won't need to create special DLLs for REXX. Instead, you will be able to access OS/2's DLLs through language statements instead of using complex function calls.

It will be easier to create graphical applications using REXX, without added extensions or third-party packages. The third-party packages, like those discussed in Appendix B, will continue to work, of course. However, Object REXX will add several features to the language in this area.

For instance, your REXX programs will be able to send messages to WPS objects. The operator that REXX will use to control this capability is called the *twiddle*; the character used is the tilde (~). All message sends will return a result.

Operations that incorporate message sends have three elements: a target name, a method name, and optional arguments, like this:

```
target~msgname(arguments)
```

For instance, the following statement will open the Information folder using a requested view with the style you want — for instance, the Settings View:

```
info~wpOpen(0,0,0)
```

You can write object methods in REXX or in another language. (See Day 18 for a discussion of methods.) They will provide full access to object variables, and they can access other methods for both the object and the superclass objects.

A period (.) at the beginning of a variable name refers to a *class object*. They are defined by the environment rather than by your program. To create a new folder, you type the following:

```
.wpfolder~new
```

Notice that `.wpfolder` refers to the same WPS class, `WPFolder`, that is used to create a folder using the RexxUtil function `SysCreateObject`.

Other object-oriented additions to the language include the following:

- The `METHOD` instruction for variable access
- The `USE` instruction for argument assignment
- The `REPLY` instruction for concurrent operations

As a result, REXX will gain better multitasking capabilities. You will be able to generate and subclass SOM (System Object Model) objects and embed OLE clients in your REXX programs.

The plans for Object REXX include enhanced debugging tools, a WYSIWYG (What You See Is What You Get) development tool, and class browsing tools for locating objects. IBM has not yet discussed these tools in fine detail.

Object REXX promises great things and points toward a future in which REXX may be the only programming language you need to know. Watch the computer industry publications for more up-to-date information.

Standard Workplace Shell Objects

The object IDs for all of the standard OS/2 objects are created when you install OS/2. The list of object IDs in table D.1 was created from OS/2 2.1. Newer versions of OS/2 may define new object IDs. See listing D.1 for a simple REXX program that generates a list of object IDs from your current OS/2 installation.

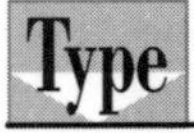

Listing D.1. A REXX program to list the standard object IDs.

```
/* GetClass.cmd */

IF RxFuncQuery(SysLoadFuncs) THEN
  DO
    CALL RxFuncAdd 'SysLoadFuncs', 'RexxUtil', 'SysLoadFuncs'
    CALL SysLoadFuncs
  END

SIGNAL ON NotReady
PARSE ARG rcFile outFile
IF rcFile = '' THEN
  rcFile = "C:\OS2\INI.RC"
IF outFile = '' THEN
  outFile = 'STDOUT:'
TAB = '09'x

DO FOREVER
  line = LineIn(rcFile)
  IF Word(line, 1) = '"PM_InstallObject"' THEN
    DO
    PARSE VAR line '"' . '"' '"' objName ';' class ';' .,
          'OBJECTID=' objId '>' .
    IF class = 'WPShadow' | objId = '' THEN
      ITERATE
    CALL LineOut outFile, objName || TAB || class || TAB || objId || '>'
    END
END

NotReady:
  EXIT
```

See table D.1 for an example of the output from this program. The table was sorted after the program generated it, so your results will be in a different order.

The program reads the INI.RC file looking for lines that start with `"PM_InstallObject"`. When a matching line is found, it is parsed for the object name, the object class, and the object ID. Objects without IDs, or of class `WPShadow` are skipped. A line containing the object name, object class, and object ID is written to the output file. Tabs are inserted between the fields so that the file can be easily formatted in a word processor.

Table D.1. Object classes and IDs for standard OS/2 objects.

Object Name	Object Class	Object ID
	WPPower	<WP_POWER>
	WPWinConfig	<WP_WINCFG>
Activities List	WPProgram	<WP_DLIST>
Alarms	WPProgram	<WP_DALARM>
Calculator	WPProgram	<WP_DCALC>
Calendar	WPProgram	<WP_DCALEM>
Cat and Mouse	WPProgram	<WP_NEKO>
Clipboard Viewer	WPProgram	<WP_CLIPV>
Color Palette	WPColorPalette	<WP_CLRPAL>
Command Prompts	WPFolder	<WP_PROMPTS>
Command Reference	WPProgram	<WP_CMDREF>
Country	WPCountry	<WP_CNTRY>
Daily Planner	WPProgram	<WP_DDIARY>
Database	WPProgram	<WP_DBASE>
Desktop	WPDesktop	<WP_DESKTOP>
Device Driver Install	WPProgram	<WP_DDINST>
DOS Full Screen	WPProgram	<WP_DOSFS>
DOS from Drive A:	WPProgram	<WP_DOS_DRV_A>
DOS Window	WPProgram	<WP_DOSWIN>
Drives	WPDrives	<WP_DRIVES>
Dual Boot	WPProgram	<WP_DBOOT>
Enhanced Editor	WPProgram	<WP_EPM>
Font Palette	WPFontPalette	<WP_FNTPAL>
Games	WPFolder	<WP_GAMES>
Glossary	Mindex	<WP_GLOSS>

continues

Table D.1. continued

Object Name	Object Class	Object ID
Icon Editor	WPProgram	<WP_ICON>
Information	WPFolder	<WP_INFO>
Jigsaw	WPProgram	<WP_JIGSAW>
Keyboard	WPKeyboard	<WP_KEYB>
Master Help Index	Mindex	<WP_MINDEX>
Migrate Applications	WPProgram	<WP_MIGAPP>
Minimized^Window Viewer	WPMinWinViewer	<WP_VIEWER>
Monthly Planner	WPProgram	<WP_DMNTH>
Mouse	WPMouse	<WP_MOUSE>
Network	WPNetwork	<WP_NETWORK>
Notepad	WPProgram	<WP_DNOTE>
Nowhere	WPFolder	<WP_NOWHERE>
OS/2 Chess	WPProgram	<WP_CHESS>
OS/2 Full Screen	WPProgram	<WP_OS2FS>
OS/2 System	WPFolder	<WP_OS2SYS>
OS/2 System Editor	WPProgram	<WP_SYSED>
OS/2 Window	WPProgram	<WP_OS2WIN>
Picture Viewer	WPProgram	<WP_PICV>
Planner Archive	WPProgram	<WP_DDARC>
PM Chart	WPProgram	<WP_CHART>
PM Terminal	WPProgram	<WP_TERM>
Printer	PDView	<WP_PDVIEW>
Productivity	WPFolder	<WP_TOOLS>
Pulse	WPProgram	<WP_PULSE>
REXX Information	WPProgram	<WP_REXREF>

Object Name	Object Class	Object ID
ReadMe	WPShadow	<WP_RDME>
Reversi	WPProgram	<WP_RVRSI>
Scheme Palette	WPSchemePalette	<WP_SCHPAL>
Scramble	WPProgram	<WP_SCRBL>
Seek and Scan Files	WPProgram	<WP_SEEK>
Selective Install	WPProgram	<WP_INST>
Shredder	WPShredder	<WP_SHRED>
Solitaire - Klondike	WPProgram	<WP_KLDK>
Sound	WPSound	<WP_SOUND>
Spooler	WPSpool	<WP_SPOOL>
Spreadsheet	WPProgram	<WP_SPREAD>
Start Here	WPProgram	<WP_STHR>
Startup	WPStartup	<WP_START>
Sticky Pad	WPProgram	<WP_STICKY>
System	WPSystem	<WP_SYSTEM>
System Clock	WPClock	<WP_CLOCK>
System Setup	WPFolder	<WP_CONFIG>
Templates	WPTemplates	<WP_TEMPS>
To-Do List	WPProgram	<WP_TODO>
To-Do List Archive	WPProgram	<WP_DTARC>
Touch	WPTouch	<WP_TOUCH>
Tune Editor	WPProgram	<WP_TUNE>
Tutorial	WPProgram	<WP_TUTOR>
View	WPProgram	<WP_VIEWINF>
WIN-OS/2 Full Screen	WPProgram	<WP_WINFS>

Multimedia became a standard part of OS/2 with the release of version 2.1. Because multimedia is installed separately from the base OS/2 system, the object IDs don't appear in the default setup. Table D.2 shows the object IDs for the standard multimedia installation.

Table D.2. Object classes and IDs for multimedia objects.

Object Name	Object Class	Object ID
Multi^media	WPFolder	<MMPM2_FOLDER>
Multimedia^Setup	WPProgram	<MMPM2_SETUP>
Multimedia Data^Converter	WPProgram	<MMPM2_MMCONVERTER>
Multimedia^With REXX	WPProgram	<MCIREXX_INF>
Multimedia^Install	WPProgram	<MMPM2_MINSTALL>

Table D.3 shows the object IDs for some of the common OS/2 applications.

Table D.3. Object classes and IDs for common applications.

Object Name	Object Class	Object ID
Relish Net^32-Bit	WPProgram	<Relish Net 32-Bit>
BocaSoft^System^Sounds	WPProgram	<SYSTEM_SOUNDS>
DeScribe	WPFolder	<DeScribe 4.0 Folder>
DeScribe 4.0^32-Bit	WPProgram	<DeScribe 4.0 Exe>

Table D.4 shows object IDs added to the Workplace Shell by Lotus cc:Mail.

Table D.4. Object classes and IDs for Lotus cc:Mail.

Object Name	Object Class	Object ID
cc:Mail	ccFolder	<CCMAILFOLDER>
Find	ccMsgLst	<CCFIND>
Directory	ccMsgLst	<CCDIRECTORY>
Private Mailing Lists	ccMsgLst	<CCPRVMLISTS>
Mailing Lists	ccMsgLst	<CCPUBMLISTS>
Bulletin Board List	ccMsgLst	<CCBBSLIST>
Folder List	ccMsgLst	<CCFOLDERLIST>
New Message	Outbox	<CCMSGTEMPLATE>
Archive.cca	ccFile	<CCARCHIVE>
Inbox	ccMsgLst	<CCINBOX>

The object IDs for the IBM C Set++ compiler are shown in table D.5.

Table D.5. Object classes and IDs for IBM C Set++.

Object Name	Object Class	Object ID
IBM C/C++^Tools 2.0	WPFolder	<IBMCPPFOLDER>
IBM C/C++ Tools^2.0 Window	WPProgram	<CSETENV.CMD>
IBM C/C++ Tools^ReadMe	WPProgram	<README.INF>
PM Debugger	WPProgram	<IPMD.EXE>
Execution Analyzer	WPProgram	<PROFIT.EXE>
C++ Browser	WPProgram	<BRS.EXE>

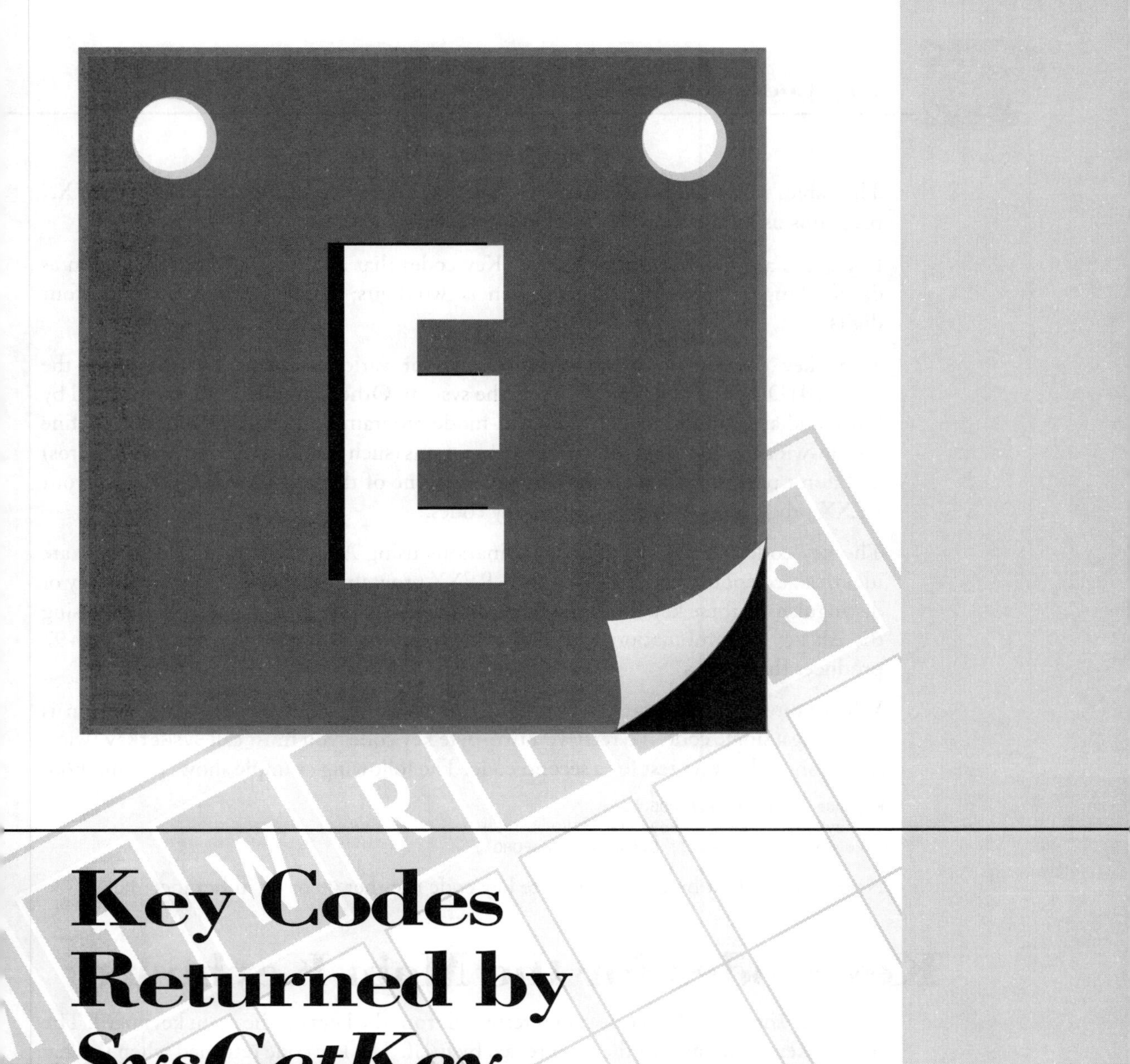

Key Codes Returned by *SysGetKey*

The tables in this appendix list all of the key codes that can be accessed by REXX programs using the RexxUtil function `SysGetKey`.

Key codes are shown in hexadecimal. Key codes that are not accessible are shown as dashes. Single-byte key codes are shown as two digits; double-byte key codes are four digits.

Some key combinations are not accessible for various reasons. For instance, the Alt+Ctrl+Delete combination reboots the system. Other combinations are reserved by OS/2 and are not accessible by any text-mode programs. Some OS/2 programs define system-wide functions for some key combinations (such as screen capture or key macros) and don't pass those key combinations on. If one of these programs is running, your REXX program cannot detect those key codes.

The key codes returned by key combinations using Alt, Alt+Ctrl, and Alt+Shift are identical, except for Alt+Ctrl+Delete. A REXX program using `SysGetKey` has no way of distinguishing these key combinations. Also, you can enter any character code by using the Alt key in combination with digits on the numeric keypad (for instance, Alt+97 produces the letter `a`).

When you use the `SysGetKey` function, you should not assume that the function is returning a single code. To retrieve a two-byte key code, you must call `SysGetKey` twice, so you should always test for a second code. The following example shows one method:

```
keyCode = SysGetKey('NOECHO')
IF keyCode = '00'x | keyCode = 'E0'x THEN
  keyCode = keyCode || SysGetKey('NOECHO')
```

Note that the first byte of a two-byte key code is either `00` or `E0` in hexadecimal.

Key Codes for the Main Keyboard

Table E.1 shows the key code values returned from the keys on the main keyboard. The normal key is the value of the key pressed by itself. The key code returned when the key is pressed in combination with each of the shift keys (Shift, Alt, and Ctrl) is also shown.

Table E.1. Key codes for the main keyboard.

Key Name	Normal	Shift	Alt	Ctrl	Alt+ Ctrl	Alt+ Shift	Ctrl+ Shift
Backspace	08	08	000E	7F	000E	000E	7F
Enter	0D	0D	001C	0A	001C	001C	0A

Key Name	Normal	Shift	Alt	Ctrl	Alt+ Ctrl	Alt+ Shift	Ctrl+ Shift
Escape	1B	1B	--	--	--	--	--
Spacebar	20	20	20	20	20	20	20
Tab	09	000F	--	0094	--	--	0094
0	30	29	0081	--	0081	0081	--
1	31	21	0078	--	0078	0078	--
2	32	40	0079	0003	0079	0079	0003
3	33	23	007A	--	007A	007A	--
4	34	24	007B	--	007B	007B	--
5	35	25	007C	--	007C	007C	--
6	36	5E	007D	1E	007D	007D	1E
7	37	26	007E	--	007E	007E	--
8	38	2A	007F	--	007F	007F	--
9	39	28	0080	--	0080	0080	--
A	61	41	001E	01	001E	001E	01
B	62	42	0030	02	0030	0030	02
C	63	43	002E	--	002E	002E	--
D	64	44	0020	04	0020	0020	04
E	65	45	0012	05	0012	0012	05
F	66	46	0021	06	0021	0021	06
G	67	47	0022	07	0022	0022	07
H	68	48	0023	08	0023	0023	08
I	69	49	0017	09	0017	0017	09
J	6A	4A	0024	0A	0024	0024	0A
K	6B	4B	0025	0B	0025	0025	0B
L	6C	4C	0026	0C	0026	0026	0C

continues

Table E.1. continued

Key Name	Normal	Shift	Alt	Ctrl	Alt+ Ctrl	Alt+ Shift	Ctrl+ Shift
M	6D	4D	0032	0D	0032	0032	0D
N	6E	4E	0031	0E	0031	0031	0E
O	6F	4F	0018	0F	0018	0018	0F
P	70	50	0019	--	0019	0019	--
Q	71	51	0010	11	0010	0010	11
R	72	52	0013	12	0013	0013	12
S	73	53	001F	--	001F	001F	--
T	74	54	0014	14	0014	0014	14
U	75	55	0016	15	0016	0016	15
V	76	56	002F	16	002F	002F	16
W	77	57	0011	17	0011	0011	17
X	78	58	002D	18	002D	002D	18
Y	79	59	0015	19	0015	0015	19
Z	7A	5A	002C	1A	002C	002C	1A
’	27	22	0028	--	0028	0028	--
,	2C	3C	0033	--	0033	0033	--
-	2D	5F	0082	1F	0082	0082	1F
.	2E	3E	0034	--	0034	0034	--
/	2F	3F	0035	--	0035	0035	--
;	3B	3A	0027	--	0027	0027	--
=	3D	2B	0083	--	0083	0083	--
[	5B	7B	001A	1B	001A	001A	1B
\	5C	7C	002B	1C	002B	002B	1C
]	5D	7D	001B	1D	001B	001B	1D
‘	60	7E	0029	--	0029	0029	--

Key Codes for the Function Keys

All function key combinations return a two-byte key code beginning with 00 (see table E.2).

Table E.2. Key codes for the function keys.

Key Name	Normal	Shift	Alt	Ctrl	Alt+ Ctrl	Alt+ Shift	Ctrl+ Shift
F1	003B	0054	0068	005E	0068	0068	005E
F2	003C	0055	0069	005F	0069	0069	005F
F3	003D	0056	006A	0060	006A	006A	0060
F4	003E	0057	006B	0061	006B	006B	0061
F5	003F	0058	006C	0062	006C	006C	0062
F6	0040	0059	006D	0063	006D	006D	0063
F7	0041	005A	006E	0064	006E	006E	0064
F8	0042	005B	006F	0065	006F	006F	0065
F9	0043	005C	0070	0066	0070	0070	0066
F10	0044	005D	0071	0067	0071	0071	0067
F11	0085	0087	008B	0089	008B	008B	0089
F12	0086	0088	008C	008A	008C	008C	008A

Key Codes for the Cursor Pad

The cursor pad is the set of cursor-movement keys that are separate from the numeric keypad. The keys on the cursor keypad are almost always a darker color than the letter keys or the numeric keypad. The arrow keys are typically laid out in the form of an inverted "T" with the Page Down, Page Up, Home, End, Insert, and Delete keys grouped above the arrow keys.

The cursor-movement keys are the only keys on the keyboard that return a first-byte value of E0. Table E.3 shows the values returned by the cursor pad keys.

Table E.3. Key codes for the cursor pad.

Key Name	Normal	Shift	Alt	Ctrl	Alt+ Ctrl	Alt+ Shift	Ctrl+ Shift
Down Arrow	E050	E050	00A0	E091	00A0	00A0	E091
Left Arrow	E04B	E04B	009B	E073	009B	009B	E073
Right Arrow	E04D	E04D	009D	E074	009D	009D	E074
Up Arrow	E048	E048	0098	E08D	0098	0098	E08D
Delete	E053	E053	00A3	E093	--	00A3	E093
End	E04F	E04F	009F	E075	009F	009F	E075
Home	E047	E047	0097	E077	0097	0097	E077
Insert	E052	E052	00A2	E092	00A2	00A2	E092
Page Down	E051	E051	00A1	E076	00A1	00A1	E076
Page Up	E049	E049	0099	E084	0099	0099	E084

Key Codes for the Numeric Keypad

The numeric keypad has an extra shift state that is controlled by the NumLk key. When the NumLk state is on (that is, the NumLk light on the keyboard is on), the keypad number keys are active. When the NumLk state is off, the keypad cursor-control keys are active.

Table E.4 shows the values returned with both the NumLk key on and off.

Table E.4. Keypad key codes.

Key Name	Normal	Shift	Alt	Ctrl	Alt+ Ctrl	Alt+ Shift	Ctrl+ Shift
Down Arrow	0050	32	02	0091	02	02	0091
Left Arrow	004B	34	04	0073	04	04	0073
Right Arrow	004D	36	06	0074	06	06	0074

Key Name	Normal	Shift	Alt	Ctrl	Alt+ Ctrl	Alt+ Shift	Ctrl+ Shift
Up Arrow	0048	38	08	008D	08	08	008D
Delete	0052	30	- -	0092	- -	- -	0092
End	004F	31	01	0075	01	01	0075
Enter	0D	0D	00A6	0A	00A6	00A6	0A
Home	0047	37	07	0077	07	07	0077
Insert	0052	30	- -	0092	- -	- -	0092
Page Down	0051	33	03	0076	03	03	0076
Page Up	0049	39	09	0084	09	09	0084
0	30	0052	- -	0092	- -	- -	0092
1	31	004F	01	0075	01	01	0075
2	32	0050	02	0091	02	02	0091
3	33	0051	03	0076	03	03	0076
4	34	004B	04	0073	04	04	0073
5	35	004C	05	008F	05	05	008F
5 (NumLk off)	004C	35	05	008F	05	05	008F
6	36	004D	06	0074	06	06	0074
7	37	0047	07	0077	07	07	0077
8	38	0048	08	008D	08	08	008D
9	39	0049	09	0084	09	09	0084
*	2A	2A	0037	0096	0037	0037	0096
+	2B	2B	004E	0090	004E	004E	0090
-	2D	2D	004A	008E	004A	004A	008E
/	2F	2F	00A4	0095	00A4	00A4	0095
=	3D	3D	0083	- -	0083	0083	- -

Answers

This appendix lists the answers for the quizzes and the exercise sections at the end of each lesson. For the exercises, there is usually more than one correct solution; the answer presented is only one of many possible answers. (Determining which one is the *best* answer is a skill that you will develop over time.) In some cases, additional information is provided to help you solve the exercise.

Answers for Day 1, "Getting Started"

Quiz

1. Ease of use; rich selection of built-in functions; it's free, included with OS/2; and you can use it to customize and extend OS/2 easily.
2. Design, code, test and debug.
3. Stepwise refinement is the process of solving big problems by breaking them into several smaller, manageable pieces.
4. Type **`help REX0000`**, where 0000 is the error number.
5. CMD.

Exercises

1. It prints out the program.
2. The program randomly selects a number between 1 and 10. The user attempts to guess the number, and the program indicates whether the number was high, low, or correct.
3. ```
   REX0006: Error 6 running D:\Ex1-3.cmd, line 2:
   Unmatched "/*" or quote
   ```

   Type **`help rex0006`**.

```
REX0006: ***Unmatched "/*" or quote***

EXPLANATION: A comment or literal string was started but never finished.
             This may be detected at the end of the program (or the end
             of data in an INTERPRET instruction) for comments, or at
             the end of a line for strings.
```
```

Answers for Day 2, “REXX Ground Rules”

Quiz

1. A comment with the `/*` in the first two positions of line one.
2. An instruction tells REXX to do something. A command is anything that is not a REXX instruction or label. Commands are passed to the invoking environment, whereas instructions are processed by REXX.
3. By writing text enclosed in `/*` and `*/`.
4. You add comments to clarify confusing code and to document what each part of a program does. Comments help anyone reading the program understand what the program does and how it works.
5. `EXIT` tells REXX the program has ended.
6. Code is hard to read and hard to change. It can hide errors. It hides the format of the program.
7. Yes.
8. A group of instructions with a label at the beginning and a `RETURN` instruction at the end. The procedure is called from elsewhere in the program.
9. A function returns a value; a procedure does not return a value.

Exercises

1. `/**/`
2. You can put everything on a single line, but we prefer to have each part of the comment on separate lines like this:

```
/* Ex2-2.cmd
 * Author:  Bill Schindler
 * Created: July 7, 1994
 */
```

3. `/* Backup config.sys */`
   comment

```
'copy config.sys \backup'
```
command
```
IF rc >< 0 THEN /* Error in copying? */
```
an instruction followed by a comment
```
  SAY "Couldn't copy config.sys — rc =" rc
```
instruction
```
EXIT
```
instruction

4. The program displays a file with line numbers added on the left side of each line. If you run the program by entering ex2-4 ex2-4.cmd, it produces the following output:

```
 1: /* Ex2-4.cmd */
 2:
 3: ARG filename                  /* Get the command line argument */
 4: IF filename = '' THEN         /* If no argument ... */
 5:   DO                          /* ... show proper usage and exit */
 6:   SAY 'Usage: number <file name>'
 7:   SIGNAL OuttaHere
 8:   END
 9:
10: SIGNAL ON NotReady            /* So the following loop ends */
11:
12: lineNum = 1
13: DO FOREVER                    /* Read the file, add line numbers */
14:   SAY Right(lineNum, 3, ' ')':' LineIn(filename)
15:   lineNum = lineNum + 1
16: END
17:
18: NotReady:
19:   IF lineNum = 1 THEN
20:     SAY 'Could not open "' ¦¦ filename ¦¦ '"'
21:
22: OuttaHere:
23:   EXIT
```

Line 1 has a comment; lines 3, 4, 5, 10, and 13 end with comments. Lines 3, 4, 5, 6, 7, 8, 10, 12, 13, 14, 15, 16, 19, 20, 22, and 23 are instructions. Lines 18 and 22 are labels. Line 14 contains two function calls.

5. The program prompts for a first and last name, and then it displays the full name centered in a box, like this:

```
*****************************************************************
*                        Esther Schindler                       *
*****************************************************************
```

Answers for Day 3, "Variables and Constants"

Quiz

1. An integer is a whole number, without decimal points. Floating point numbers have fractional parts (that is, a decimal point). Exponential numbers are expressed as a power of 10.
2. Use quotation marks twice when the same kind of quotation mark is used within a string and delimiting the string. If the quotation mark is different from the delimiting quotation marks, use only one mark.
3. The value of an uninitialized variable is its name in capital letters.
4. A variable is a container for other values.
5. Constants are values that don't change. The contents of a variable can change.
6. `NUM` or `CHAR`.
7. Alphabetic and numeric characters, plus `!`, _, and `?`.
8. You can use any characters within a string, as long as the string is enclosed in quotation marks.
9. Assignment copies a value into a variable.

Exercises

1. a. valid
   b. valid
   c. not valid (begins with `@`)
   d. valid
   e. valid
   f. not valid (contains `&`)
   g. valid
   h. valid (but `then` is also an instruction)
   i. not valid (contains -)
   j. valid
   k. not valid (begins with digits)

2. Your answer will obviously depend on the city you live in:

   ```
   city = "Cave Creek"
   ```

3. You can do this one of two ways:

   ```
   myString = '"I''ve got a bad feeling about this," said Han'
   ```

   or

   ```
   myString = """I've got a bad feeling about this,"" said Han"
   ```

4. `Datatype(testValue)`

5. `Datatype(lastName, 'U')`

6. a. valid
   b. valid
   c. valid
   d. valid
   e. not valid
   f. not valid

7. a. valid
   b. not valid (mixed quotation marks)
   c. not valid (same quotation mark type embedded in string)
   d. valid
   e. valid

Answers for Day 4, "Instructions, Expressions, and Operators"

Quiz

1. A clause is a complete instruction, including any necessary information and options.
2. Separate each clause with a semicolon (;).
3. Put a comma at the end of the line. Another, but not recommended, method is to use a comment that extends from the end of one line to the beginning of the next.
4. Operators do something to the data in order to produce a result.
5. `CALL` executes the procedure and then returns to execute the next instruction after the `CALL`. `SIGNAL` goes to the label without any allowance for returning.
6. +, /, -, *, **.
7. Spaghetti code is code that jumps from one place to another in the program. It is used to refer to programs that aren't organized in logical units.
8. A symbol immediately followed by a colon.
9. Expressions are made up of strings, symbols, function calls, operators, and parentheses.

Exercises

1. Here's the rewritten program:

```
/* Ex4-1.cmd */
SAY 'This program adds two numbers'
SAY 'Enter the first number:'
PULL num1
SAY 'Enter the second number:'
PULL num2
/* Now we add the two numbers together */
answer = num1 + num2
SAY 'The sum of' num1 'plus' num2 'is' answer
EXIT
```

2. Here's the rewritten program:

```
/* Ex4-2.cmd */
SAY 'Enter a number:'
PULL number
SAY "You entered" number
EXIT
```

3. a. valid
   b. not valid (spaces between the symbol and the colon)
   c. not valid (quotation marks)
   d. valid
   e. not valid (comment)
   f. valid

4. The following program only has the errors fixed. If you reformatted the code so that each clause is on a line by itself, then give yourself extra credit!

```
/* Ex4-4.cmd */
SAY "This is a test"; SAY "This is only a test"
SAY "Now starting the test"; 'dir',
'*.cmd'
EXIT
```

5. A comma is missing following the second SAY, and the GetName label should be followed by a colon.

```
/* Ex4-5.cmd */
SAY "Please enter your full name:"
CALL GetName
SAY "There are",
    Length(name) "characters in your name."
EXIT
GetName:
  PULL name
  RETURN
```

Answers for Day 5, "Arithmetic"

Quiz

1. Operator precedence is the order in which operators in expressions are evaluated.
2. Spaces and comments are ignored.
3. The ** operator raises the value to an integer power.
4. Use // to get the remainder.
5. Unary operators have one operand; binary operators have two operands.
6. Left to right.
7. Division, remainder, subtraction, and power.
8. Addition and assignment.
9. The % operator performs division and produces only the integer part of the result.
10. You can use parentheses to change the order of evaluation.

Exercises

1. a. 23
   b. 40
   c. 4
   d. 16
   e. 34
   f. 2

2. Use parentheses to change the order of evaluation.

```
/* Ex5-2.cmd */
SAY "Enter a Fahrenheit temperature to convert:"
PULL fahrenheit
celsius = 5 / 9 * (fahrenheit - 32)
SAY fahrenheit "degrees Farenheit =" celsius "degrees Celsius"
EXIT
```

3. The variables count and total were not initialized before being used. The total is calculated incorrectly. The label Done is missing.

```
/* Ex5-3.cmd */
SAY "This program adds 5 numbers"

count = 5
total = 0
GetANumber:
IF count = 0 THEN
  SIGNAL Done
count = count - 1
SAY "Enter a number:"
PULL number
total = number + total
SIGNAL GetANumber

Done:
SAY "The sum is" total
EXIT
```

Answers for Day 6, "Executing System Commands"

Quiz

1. If a command is not enclosed in quotation marks, REXX may try to execute the command as a REXX instruction.
2. `Directory` can change to a different drive, as well as a directory. Also, `Directory` is slightly faster because it's a built-in function.
3. `SAY` can easily display blank lines. `SAY` doesn't require turning echo on or off. `ECHO` can have a problem about handling certain characters, whereas `SAY` does not have any problem.
4. The period throws away whatever the user typed before pressing Enter.
5. The `NUL` device is a "bit bucket." Whatever is sent to `NUL` is thrown away.

6. `SetLocal` saves the current drive, directory, and environment. `EndLocal` restores the drive, directory, and environment to the state when `SetLocal` was last called.
7. A return code is the computer's way of telling you what happens when you run a command.
8. The `rc` variable gets the return code from the last command executed.
9. Add a REXX comment at the beginning of the program. Change `ECHO` commands to `SAY` instructions. Put quotation marks around each command. Add an `EXIT` instruction to the end of the program. Make other changes as required (that is, use the `Directory` function, `PULL` instruction, and so on).
10. A return code of zero indicates the command was successful.

Exercises

1. Here's the rewritten program:

```
/* Ex6-1.cmd */
'@echo off'
SAY 'Put the diskette to be checked in Drive A:'
SAY 'Press Enter to continue.'
PULL .
'chkdsk A: /F'
EXIT
```

2. Here's the rewritten program:

```
/* Ex6-2.cmd */
'cls'
SAY 'Making a copy of the desktop EAs'
'eautil C:\Desktop C:\desktop.eas /S /R /P'
SAY 'All done!'
EXIT
```

3. `POLL` should be `PULL .`. The `FORMAT` command should be in quotation marks because the colon and slash characters have special meanings for REXX.

```
/* Ex6-3.cmd */
/* Format a diskette in drive A: */
SAY "Put the diskette to be formatted in Drive A:"
```

```
SAY "Press Enter when ready..."
PULL .
'format A: /ONCE'
EXIT rc
```

Answers for Day 7, "Basic Input/Output"

Quiz

1. The stdin is standard input, which is the keyboard unless stdin is redirected.
2. The stdout is standard output, which is the display unless stdout is redirected.
3. `Copies` repeats one or more characters a given number of times.
4. The `PARSE ARG` instruction reads parameters that the user typed at the command prompt without any change.
5. `PULL` uppercases input values; `PARSE PULL` reads the input without any change.
6. `SAY Center(string, 79)`
7. Use the `Format` function: `Format(number, , 2)`.
8. The `NUMERIC DIGITS` instruction controls the number of digits used in arithmetic operations. It also determines how large a number must be before exponential notation is used.
9. A short help message that describes the use of a utility or program.
10. A program should work the way the user expects it to work. A program should not surprise the user by being different.

Exercises

1. Quotation marks are added around the following results so that you can see any leading and trailing spaces.

   a. `' 12.10'`
   b. `' 9.95E+2'`
   c. `' 1'`
   d. `' 1.000E+003'`

2. a. arg1 = COGITO ERGO SUM
   b. arg1 = Cogito Ergo Sum
   c. arg1 = Cogito
      arg2 = Ergo Sum
   d. arg1 = COGITO
      arg2 = ERGO
      arg3 = SUM
   e. arg1 = Cogito
      arg2 = Ergo
      arg3 = Sum
      arg4 and arg5 get empty strings

3.
```
/* Ex7-3.cmd */
SAY 'Enter a line of text:'
PARSE PULL text
SAY text
EXIT
```

4.
```
/* Ex7-4.cmd */
PARSE ARG params
SAY params
EXIT
```

5.
```
/* Ex7-5.cmd */
SAY 'Use the Ex7-5 command to echo any command line parameters.'
SAY
SAY 'SYNTAX:  Ex7-5 [any text]
SAY
SAY 'Where:'
SAY '   [any text]  Is any text you want to have echoed.'
SAY
PARSE ARG params
SAY params
EXIT
```

6.
```
/* Ex7-6.cmd */
SAY 'Enter a line of text:'
PARSE PULL text
SAY Copies('-', 79)
SAY Center(text, 79)
SAY Copies('-', 79)
EXIT
```

7.
```
/* Ex7-7.cmd */
PARSE ARG dirname
'dir' dirname '/w'
EXIT
```

8.
```
/* Ex7-8.cmd */

SAY 'Enter three dollar amounts:'
PULL amount1 amount2 amount3
sum = amount1 + amount2 + amount3

SAY Format(amount1, 9, 2)
SAY Format(amount2, 9, 2)
SAY Format(amount3, 9, 2)
SAY Copies('=', 12)
SAY Format(sum, 9, 2)

EXIT
```

9. The `Format` function is required to set the decimal places, and the `NUMERIC DIGITS` instruction is required so that the result is not displayed using exponential notation.

```
/* Ex7-9.cmd */
NUMERIC DIGITS 12
val1 = 974532.39
val2 = 31000.25
val3 = 5.01
theResult = (val1 * val2) / val3
SAY 'The result is' Format(theResult,, 2)
EXIT
```

10. The `heightInInches` variable is misspelled. The parameters for the Format function do not allow for enough digits for centimeters. The best formatting in this case is to set only the decimal digits and let Format use the default formatting for the whole digits.

```
/* Ex7-10.cmd */
cmPerInch = 2.54
SAY "Give your height in inches:"
PULL heightInInches
heightInCm = heightInInches * cmPerInch
heightInMeters = heightInCm / 100
```

```
SAY 'You are' Format(heightInCm, , 2) 'centimeters'
SAY 'which is' Format(heightInMeters, , 2) 'meters.'
EXIT
```

Answers for Day 8, "Making Decisions"

Quiz

1. Program control clauses change the order of program execution.
2. The number `1` is true; the number `0` is false.
3. Relational operators create a condition by comparing two values.
4. An operator that allows more than one comparison operation to be performed in a single expression.
5. The `IF` instruction uses the result of a condition to alter the flow of a program.
6. a. `+` has higher precedence than `<`
   b. `\` has higher precedence than `**`
   c. `&` has higher precedence than `&&`
   d. `\>` has equal precedence to `><`
7. The `DO` and `END` instructions.
8. The `ELSE` instruction works with the `IF` instruction and is executed when the condition in the `IF` instruction is false.
9. The `SELECT` instruction is used to replace a series of `IF` ... `ELSE IF` instructions.
10. `OTHERWISE` is executed when all the `WHEN` conditions in a `SELECT` are false.

Exercises

1. a. `1` (true)
   b. `0` (false)
   c. `1` (true)
   d. `1` (true)
   e. `1` (true)
   f. `1` (true)

2. ```
SELECT
  WHEN song = "oldie" THEN
    SAY 'Woolie Bullie'
  WHEN song = "classical" THEN
    SAY 'Symphony No. 4 in D minor'
  WHEN song = "rock" THEN
    SAY 'One of These Days'
  WHEN song = "big band" THEN
    SAY 'In The Mood'
  OTHERWISE
    SAY 'Poisoning Pigeons in the Park'
END
```

3. ```
/* Ex8-3.cmd */
SAY 'Enter two numbers:'
PULL num1 num2
IF num1 > num2 THEN
  DO
  largest = num1
  smallest = num2
  END
ELSE
  DO
  largest = num2
  smallest = num1
  END
SAY 'The largest number is' largest
SAY 'The smallest number is' smallest
SAY 'The difference is' (largest - smallest)
EXIT
```

4. ```
/* Ex8-4.cmd */
ARG newDir
IF newDir = '/?' ¦ newDir = '-?' THEN
  DO
  SAY 'Use the DD command to change the current drive and'
  SAY 'directory or display the current ones.'
  SAY
  SAY 'SYNTAX: DD [drive:][directory]'
  SAY
```
```

```
    SAY 'Where:'
    SAY '  [drive:][directory] Specifies the drive and'
    SAY '                      directory you want to change to'
    EXIT
    END

  SAY
  SAY Directory(newDir)
  EXIT
```

5. The XCOPY command should be in quotation marks. The SAY instructions following IF should be enclosed between DO and END.

```
/* Ex8-5.cmd */
SAY 'Insert diskette for backup in Drive A:'
SAY 'Press Enter when ready.'
PULL .

'xcopy C:\OS2\*.ini A:\ > NUL'
IF rc >< 0 THEN
  DO
  SAY 'Error' rc 'encountered while copying files.'
  SAY 'Disk in Drive A: may be full.'
  END

EXIT
```

Answers for Day 9, "Manipulating Strings"

Quiz

1. The Length function.
2. WordLength determines the length of a single word in a string.
3. Use Translate or PARSE UPPER VAR.
4. Use C2D to get the decimal code of a character.

5. Abuttal is a string concatenation operation performed by putting two or more terms next to each other.
6. The `||` concatenates two strings without any intervening spaces. The space operator concatenates two strings with a single intervening space.
7. Strict comparison compares for an exact match, including leading and trailing spaces. Regular comparison ignores leading spaces and pads the shorter operand to the same length as the longer operand.
8. The `SubStr` function returns a piece of a string.
9. The `LastPos` function.
10. The template tells `PARSE` how the source string is to be parsed.

Exercises

1. a. `moonlight`
   b. `hopechest`
   c. `This time tomorrow`
   d. `This          time tomorrow`
2. a.
```
saveIt = /* THIS, IS A TEST! */
```
   b.
```
a = /*
b = This,
c = is a test! */
```
   c.
```
a = /*
b = !tset a si ,sihT */
```
   d.
```
a = /* This
 b = is
 c = a test! */
```
   e.
```
a = /
b = This, is a test
c = /
```
   f.
```
a = /* This,
b =  a test! */
```
   g.
```
a = This, is a test
b = * This, is a test!
```
3.
```
/* Ex9-3.cmd */
SAY Right("Bill Schindler", 79)
SAY Right("555 My Address", 79)
```

```
SAY Right("Phoenix, AZ 85123", 79)
EXIT
```

4.
```
/* Ex9-4.cmd */
SAY "Enter a date:"
PULL date
PARSE PULL month '-' day '-' year
EXIT
```

5.
```
/* Ex9-5.cmd */
SAY "Enter a decimal character code:"
PULL code
SAY code "is the character" D2C(code)
EXIT
```

6. The word `Program:` has the colon truncated. The right sides of the box aren't lined up.

```
/* Ex9-6.cmd
 * Create a skeletal REXX program.
 */

PARSE ARG pgmName '"' author '"' .

IF pgmName = '' & author = '' THEN
  DO
  SAY "Use Ex9-6 to create a REXX program skeleton."
  SAY
  SAY 'SYNTAX:  Ex9-6 programname "authorname"'
  EXIT
  END

progLine = Left('Program:', 11) || pgmName
authLine = Left('Author:', 11) || author
dateLine = Left('Created:', 11) || Date()

SAY '/* ' || D2C(218) || Copies(D2C(196), 70) || D2C(191)
SAY ' * ' || D2C(179) Left(progLine, 69) || D2C(179)
SAY ' * ' || D2C(179) Left(authLine, 69) || D2C(179)
SAY ' * ' || D2C(179) Left(dateLine, 69) || D2C(179)
SAY ' * ' || D2C(192) || Copies(D2C(196), 70) || D2C(217)
```

F

```
SAY ' */'
SAY
SAY
SAY 'EXIT'

EXIT
```

Answers for Day 10, "Testing and Debugging"

Quiz

1. The purpose of testing is to execute a program with the intention of finding errors.
2. The purpose of debugging is to diagnose and correct errors.
3. A good test case is one that has a good chance of finding a previously unknown defect.
4. `TRACE Results` traces all clauses before execution and displays final results of expression evaluation.
5. Use the prefix `?` with the `TRACE` instruction.
6. The `SIGNAL ON` instruction is used to trap error conditions.
7. `SIGNAL ON Error`
8. The variable `sigl` contains the line number of the clause that was executing when a condition was raised.
9. `SAY ErrorText(rc)`
10. The `SourceLine` function returns either the number of lines in the program or the text on a given line in the program.

Exercises

1. We use EPM, so the program was modified as follows:

```
/* Ex10-1.cmd */
SIGNAL ON Syntax
SAY "Enter your first and last name:"
PARSE PULL firstName lastName
fullName = lastName ¦ ',' firstName
SAY fullName
EXIT

Syntax:
  PARSE SOURCE . . pgmName
  errorMsg = "'messagebox" ErrorText(rc)"'"
  errorLine = "'" ¦¦ sigl ¦¦ "'"
  "EPM" pgmName errorLine errorMsg
  EXIT
```

2.
```
/* Ex10-2.cmd */
SIGNAL ON Halt
SAY "Enter some text:"
PARSE PULL text
SAY "You entered:" text
EXIT

Halt:
  SAY "User requested halt. Exiting."
  EXIT
```

3. The input should be converted to uppercase so that the comparison works correctly. The result from `Reverse` should be stored in `backwards`, not `forwards`.

```
/* Ex10-3.cmd */

SAY 'What is the potential palindrome?'
PARSE PULL palindrome
```

```
possible = Translate(palindrome)
forwards = Translate(Space(possible, 0))
backwards = Reverse(forwards)
backwards = Translate(backwards, ",'", "',")

IF forwards = backwards THEN
  SAY '"'palindrome'" is a palindrome'
ELSE
  SAY '"'palindrome'" is not a palindrome'

EXIT
```

Answers for Day 11, "Using Loops"

Quiz

1. A loop is a block of instructions that is executed more than once.
2. The condition for the do-while loop is tested at the beginning of each iteration of the loop. The condition for the do-until loop is tested at the end of each iteration of the loop.
3. Executes the code within the loop 15 times.
4. An infinite loop is a loop that can potentially execute forever.
5. `DO i = 3 TO 12`
6. ```
   DO i = 2 TO 20 BY 2
     SAY i
   END
   ```
7. An infinite loop.
8. The `ITERATE` instruction immediately begins the next iteration of the loop.
9. ```
   IF response = 'yes' THEN
     LEAVE
   ```
10. At the end of each loop iteration.
11. At the beginning of each loop iteration.

12. A variable that is used to control the execution of the loop.
13. REXX tests the variable after `END` to ensure that it is the control variable for the current loop.
14. `FOR` limits the number of loop iterations.

Exercises

1.
```
/* Ex11-1.cmd */
ast = "*********"
DO i = Length(ast) TO 1 BY -2
  SAY Center(Left(ast, i), Length(ast))
END
EXIT
```

Note: There are many possible ways of answering exercises 2 and 3. If your program works correctly, then your answer is right! (From this point on, many of the programming exercises are not answered.)

4. The variables `firstName` and `lastName` aren't initialized, so the first loop immediately exits without prompting for input. The same problem appears for `areacode`, `prefix`, and `number`. You can fix the error by using `UNTIL` with both loops, but think carefully about how to change the conditions so that the loop exits properly.

Answers for Day 12, "Compound Variables"

Quiz

1. Compound variables are a special kind of variable that can group together many different values.
2. The part of a compound variable name that precedes the first period is the stem (that is, a stem is a symbol followed by a period).

3. The tail is the part of the compound variable name that follows the first period.
4. To find a value in an array, you create a compound variable whose tails are the indices into the array. You can use another REXX variable to refer to a specific array item by using the value of the variable as an array index (that is, use the variable as a tail in a compound variable).
5. Structures are compound variables that are used to group together information that is related in some manner.
6. A derived variable name is one that uses the values of another variable to replace the simple variable in the tail.

Exercises

1.
```
/* Ex12-1.cmd */

SAY "Enter your birth date as mm dd yyyy:"
SAY "(like 11 17 1975)"
PULL month day year

dow = Zeller()

weekdays.0 = "Sunday"
weekdays.1 = "Monday"
weekdays.2 = "Tuesday"
weekdays.3 = "Wednesday"
weekdays.4 = "Thursday"
weekdays.5 = "Friday"
weekdays.6 = "Saturday"

SAY
SAY "You were born on a" weekdays.dow

EXIT

/* Zeller's Congruence
 * This function takes month, day, and year as input.
 * It returns a number that represents the day of the week
 * for the given date; 0 = Sunday ... 6 = Saturday.
 */
Zeller:
```

```
IF month > 2 THEN
  DO
  adjMonth = month - 2
  adjYear = year
  END
ELSE
  DO
  adjMonth = month + 10
  adjYear = year - 1
  END

century = adjYear % 100
yearInCentury = adjYear - 100 * century
dayOfWeek = ((13 * adjMonth - 1) % 5 + day + yearInCentury + ,
      yearInCentury % 4 + century % 4 - century - century + 77) ,
      // 7
RETURN dayOfWeek
```

Answers for Day 13, "Dealing with User Input"

Quiz

1. The user interface is any part of a program that interacts with the user.
2. Programs should beep when you really have to get the user's attention—if an error is encountered, for instance.
3. ANSI commands are a set of standardized codes that control cursor positioning, color, and other aspects of the display.
4. In defensive programming, you always act as though the unexpected is going to happen. Never assume user competence in your code, although you should always treat the user respectfully "in person" (that is, through the user interface).
5. Some reasons to check user input include typos, a bad phone connection creating line noise, misunderstood instructions in the user interface, a late night out drinking with friends (that is, the user is brain-dead).

6. `Abbrev` allows a program to recognize shortened forms of user input easily.
7. Use the `Datatype` function to verify the input: `Datatype(input, 'W')`.
8. An argument is information provided to a program by being included on the command line with the program name.

Answers for Day 14, "Using Subroutines"

Quiz

1. Functions are subroutines that return a value.
2. Functions return a value; procedures don't. A function call is followed by parentheses; a procedure is called using the `CALL` instruction.
3. By default, all program variables are visible throughout a program. Use `PROCEDURE` and `PROCEDURE EXPOSE` to limit visibility.
4. Use `ARG`, `PARSE ARG`, or the `Arg` function to access procedure arguments.
5. Recursion occurs when a subroutine calls itself.
6. REXX searches the current program first, then built-in functions, and then external function libraries.
7. A function can be named using any valid REXX symbol.
8. If you use stepwise refinement correctly, you break down the program into several logical pieces. Often, you can make each piece into a subroutine.
9. You cannot pass a compound variable as an argument. You must use `PROCEDURE EXPOSE` to make the variable accessible.

Exercises

2. The `EXIT` instruction is missing. The parameters for `Abbrev` are not in the correct order. `GetYesNoResponse` is called as a function, but it doesn't return a value.

Answers for Day 15, "File Input/Output"

Quiz

1. A stream is the flow of data that is interpreted as input or output.
2. Persistent streams can be read, repositioned, and read or written again. Transient streams do not support a read/write position because the stream is dynamic.
3. Reading or writing lines transfers a line of text to or from the stream. REXX automatically appends line-end characters when a line is written and strips the line-end characters when a line is read. Reading or writing characters transfers one or more characters to or from the stream. The data is read exactly as it exists in the stream and is written with no alterations.
4. `Chars` returns the number of characters following the current read/write position in a stream.
5. Other tasks may need to use the stream at the same time, and you're certain that you don't need to change the data.
6. A filter is a program that reads standard input, modifies the data in some manner, and writes the result to standard output.
7. You close a stream so that it can be accessed by other programs.
8. Use `SIGNAL ON NotReady`.

Exercises

2. The exit condition for the loop should be `WHILE Lines(filename)`. `LineIn` repeatedly reads the first line in the file.

Answers for Day 16, "Introducing RexxUtil Functions"

Quiz

1. A dynamic link library. Many programs can share functions stored in a DLL.
2. REXX doesn't know about the function until the function is registered.
3. `SysGetKey` doesn't wait for the user to press the Enter key, and `SysGetKey` can capture almost any key press. `SysGetKey` gets characters only from the keyboard. `CharIn` requires the user to press Enter, and it cannot capture special keys. `CharIn`, however, can read data from files or devices other than the keyboard.
4. `SysCurPos` returns the current position of the cursor on the screen and optionally repositions the cursor on the screen.
5. `INTERPRET` executes REXX code stored in a string.
6. Turns the cursor off (that is, makes the cursor invisible).
7. `RxFuncQuery` determines whether an external function is registered.
8. `SysLoadFuncs` registers all the functions in the RexxUtil library.
9. An extended key code is a two-byte code sent by a single key press.
10. `SysCls` is faster than the ANSI clear screen command. However, `SysCls` cannot clear the screen to a color, whereas the ANSI clear screen command can.

Answers for Day 17, "More RexxUtil Functions"

Quiz

1. Gets a list of all files in the current directory and all directories below the current directory.
2. `SysFileDelete`
3. An extended attribute is information that is associated with a file but not contained in the file itself.

4. .ASSOCTABLE, .CODEPAGE, .COMMENTS, .HISTORY, .ICON, .KEYPHRASES, .LONGNAME, .SUBJECT, .TYPE, .VERSION
5. Stored in a binary format as application, key, and data.
6. `map = SysDriveMap(, 'REMOTE')`
7. Searches the file C:\CONFIG.SYS for the string `SET` and puts matching lines in the compound variable `lines.`.
8. The `SysMkDir` and `SysRmDir` functions are faster and do not print any messages on the screen.

Exercises

3. The `specs.0` is set one too high. The program changes the file attributes unnecessarily. The `SysDelete` function should be `SysFileDelete`.

Answers for Day 18, "Creating Workplace Shell Objects"

Quiz

1. A class is a definition of a generic object. An instance is an actual, specific object.
2. The object's location can change without affecting the object ID.
3. A container is an object that can hold other objects.
4. Icon view, tree view, and details view.
5. A shadow is a link, or reference, to another object.
6. A unique name for an object. Object IDs always begin with a < and end with a >.
7. a. `<WP_DESKTOP>`
   b. `<WP_OS2SYS>`
   c. `<WP_INFO>`
   d. `<WP_REXREF>`

Answers for Day 19, "Manipulating Workplace Shell Objects"

Quiz

1. `SysDestroyObject`
2. Object IDs are stored in the user .INI file under the application `PM_Workplace:Location`.
3. A handle is a unique numeric value that identifies an object.
4. `SysSetObjectData(object, 'OPEN=DEFAULT')`
5. `SysSetIcon` or `SysSetObjectData`

Answers for Day 20, "Extending OS/2 Applications"

Quiz

1. `RxMessageBox` displays a message dialog in a graphical format (that is, under Presentation Manager).
2. REXX EPM macros use the .ERX extension.
3. `EtkReplaceText` is used in REXX macros to replace a line of text.
4. The `extract` command lets you get information about a file or the EPM session being edited in EPM.
5. Use the `buildaccel` command to define accelerator keys in EPM. The `activateaccel` command activates defined accelerator keys.
6. You use `register_mouse` to attach a command to a mouse event.

Answers for Day 21, "Interprocess Communications"

Quiz

1. A semaphore is a signal that indicates the beginning and end of an operation.
2. A named pipe provides a communication conduit for processes when the sending or receiving programs don't know, or don't care, where their data is going to or coming from. Named pipes enable programs to communicate easily over a network.
3. A queue is a collection of data organized in a list. The data can be accessed from either end of the list.
4. Session queues are only accessible by programs running in the same OS/2 session. Private queues are available to any program running on your OS/2 system.
5. In a multitasking environment, polling can hog system resources.
6. Determine whether you need to use a semaphore in the first place. You must close the semaphore file immediately after creating it, and all programs needing access to the semaphore file must agree on where the file is stored.
7. The named pipe server creates and connects with the pipe. Other programs act as named pipe clients by opening the pipe and exchanging data with the server.
8. `RxQueue` lets you create and delete private queues.
9. The `PUSH` instruction stores data on the front of the queue (in LIFO order) and the `QUEUE` instruction stores data on the back of the queue (FIFO order).
10. You can't create a named pipe using REXX unless you purchase a third-party library.

Using the Enhanced Editor

This appendix is a brief introduction to setting up and using the Enhanced Editor. The Enhanced Editor (or EPM) is a powerful text editor with a surprisingly broad range of features. Enough features are covered here to get you up and running.

Getting Set Up

The defaults used when EPM is first installed don't work well for writing programs. This section explains how you can change some of the defaults so that you will find using the editor a little more comfortable for programming.

Finding the Enhanced Editor

The program object (or icon) for the Enhanced Editor is located in the Productivity folder. You can find the program object by doing the following:

- ☐ Open the OS/2 System folder.
- ☐ Open the Productivity folder in the OS/2 System folder.

You should now have two folders open on the desktop (see fig. G.1). Look for the Enhanced Editor in the Productivity folder. You may need to use the scroll bars to bring the program object into view.

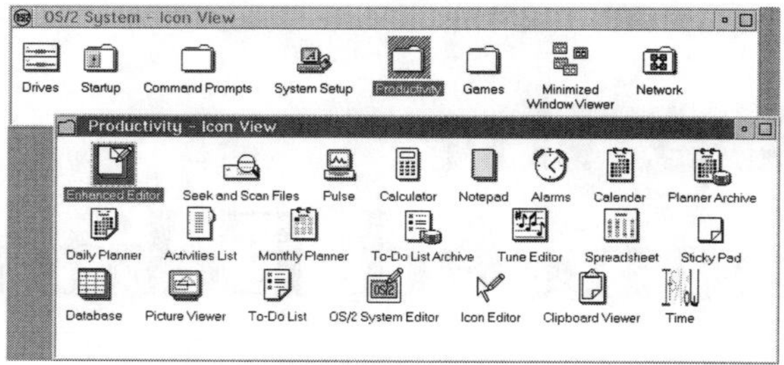

Figure G.1. *Finding the Enhanced Editor in the Productivity folder.*

You can start EPM by double-clicking on the Enhanced Editor icon (or selecting the icon and pressing Enter). This procedure works fine for occasional use. If you are planning to use EPM on a daily basis, however, you may want to create an EPM book on your desktop.

Creating an EPM Book

Creating an EPM book icon gives you quick access to EPM, and it helps EPM start faster. The EPM book is actually the core part of the Enhanced Editor, so the editor stays partially loaded in memory all the time.

To create the EPM book so that it starts every time you boot OS/2, follow these steps:

1. Open the Productivity folder in the OS/2 System folder.
2. Open the Startup folder in the OS/2 System folder.
3. Copy the Enhanced Editor icon from the Productivity folder to the Startup folder. (Put the mouse pointer over the icon, press and hold Ctrl, press the right mouse button, and then drag a copy of the icon to the Startup folder.)
4. Close the Productivity folder.
5. Select the Enhanced Editor icon you created in step 3.
6. Click the right mouse button (or press Shift+F10), select the arrow next to Open (see fig. G.2), and then select Settings.

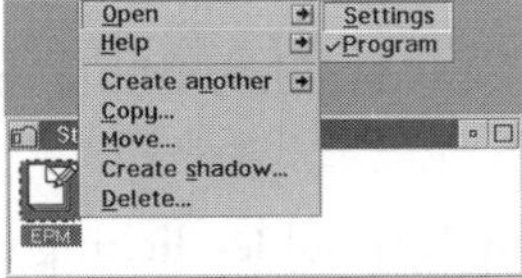

Figure G.2. *Selecting Settings from the pop-up menu.*

A notebook appears on the desktop (see fig. G.3).

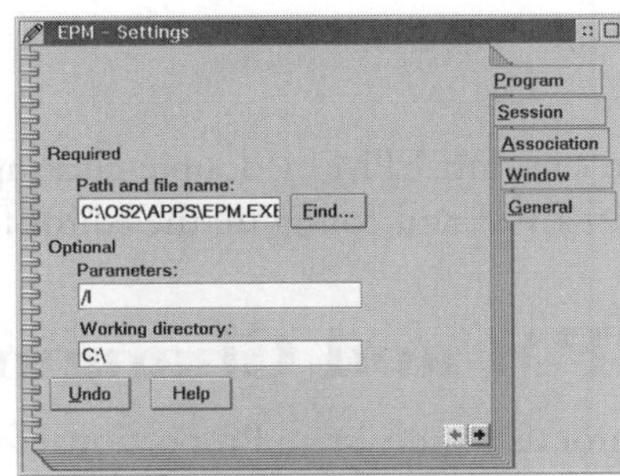

Figure G.3. *The Settings notebook for EPM.*

7. In the Settings notebook, select the Parameters entry box and type `/I`. Your notebook should now have the same information that appears in figure G.3. The `/I` option tells EPM to create a book icon.
8. Select the Window notebook tab.
9. Select the radio button for Minimize window to desktop. The notebook should now look like figure G.4.

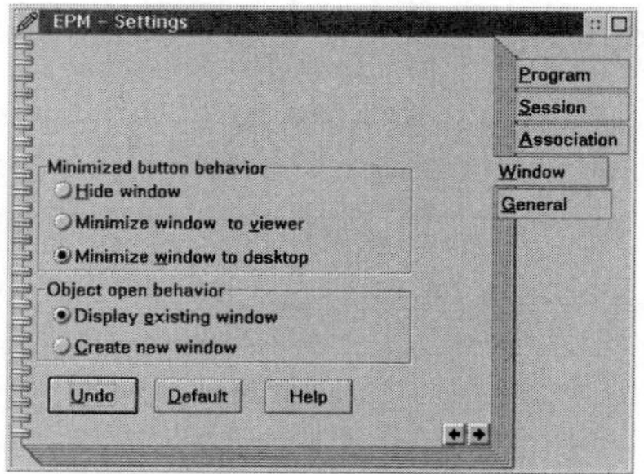

Figure G.4. *The Window page of the EPM notebook.*

10. Close the notebook by double-clicking the icon in the upper-left corner (or press Alt+F4).

You should test your setup by double-clicking the Enhanced Editor icon in the Startup folder. The EPM book icon should appear near the bottom of your screen (see fig. G.5).

Figure G.5. *The EPM book icon.*

From now on, you can start EPM by double-clicking on the book icon. At this point, you're ready to start EPM and configure the editor for programming.

Starting EPM and Changing the Font

The Enhanced Editor uses the System Proportional font by default. A proportional font is good for word processing and general text, but it's not very good for programming

because code and comments don't line up using a proportional font. The best font for writing and viewing programs is a monospace font—each character has the same width. OS/2 includes three monospace fonts: Courier, System Monospaced, and System VIO.

To change the default font, you need to start EPM. Because this is probably the first time you've started EPM, here are the steps:

1. Double-click on the EPM book icon. EPM's Open dialog box then appears on your desktop (see fig. G.6).

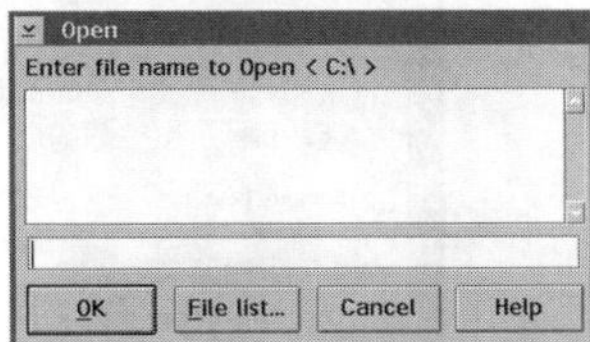

Figure G.6. *EPM's Open dialog box.*

2. Usually, you type a filename in the entry field or select a file by clicking the File list... button. This first time, though, just press Enter or select OK. The Enhanced Editor's main window opens (see fig. G.7).

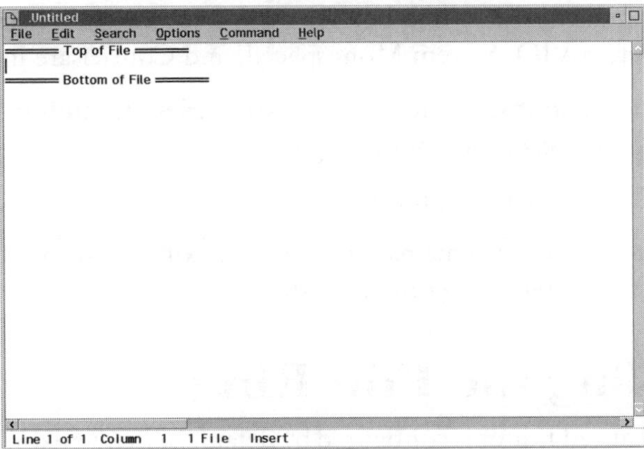

Figure G.7. *The Enhanced Editor's main window.*

The next step is to begin configuring the editor. The first thing to do is to change the default font, as follows:

1. From the Options menu, select Preferences (see fig. G.8). Then select Settings.... The Settings notebook appears.

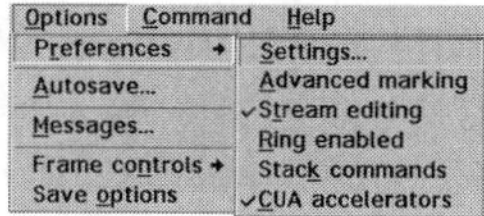

Figure G.8. *The Options menu.*

2. Select the Fonts tab (see fig. G.9).

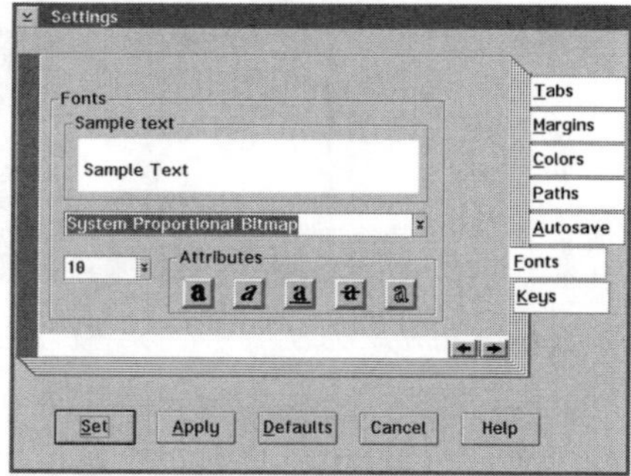

Figure G.9. *The Settings notebook for Preferences.*

3. Pull down the combo box for the font name and select a monospace font. System VIO, System Monospaced, and Courier are included with OS/2.
4. Select a font size. The best font size varies, depending on screen resolution, monitor size, and your eyesight.
5. Select the Set push button.

The font you select remains set until you exit the editor. You learn how to save the settings for posterity after the next step.

Enabling the Edit Ring

The Enhanced Editor is configured by default so that you can edit only one file at a time. To load more than one file into the editor, you need to enable the edit ring.

A ring enables you to load multiple files into the same instance of the editor. The files are loaded so that you can navigate through them as though they are in a circle. Look at figure G.10 to get a better idea of how this process works.

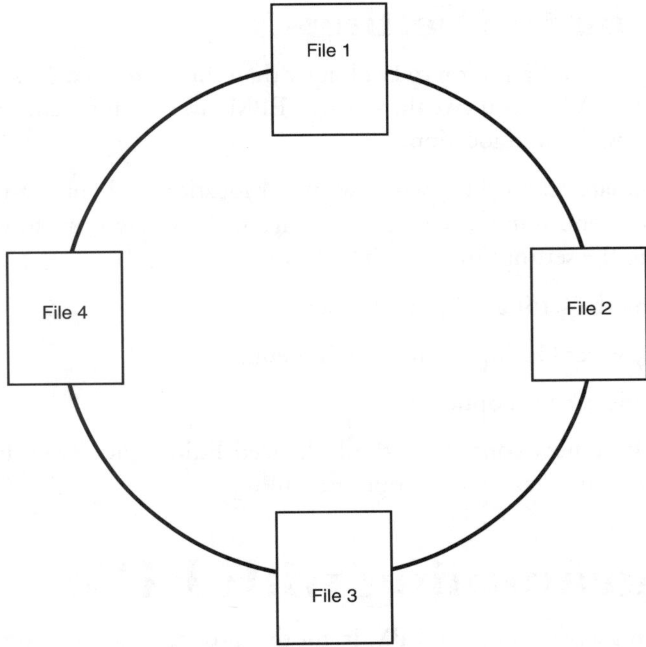

Figure G.10. *Files loaded in an edit ring.*

To enable the edit ring, follow these steps:

1. From the Options menu, select Preferences.
2. Select Ring enabled.

Two buttons appear on the right side of the title bar (see fig. G.11). If you select Options, you also see a new item on that menu, List ring.... Both the buttons and the new menu item remain gray until more than one file is loaded in the edit ring. You can move from file to file in the ring by clicking the ring buttons or by pressing F11 or F12.

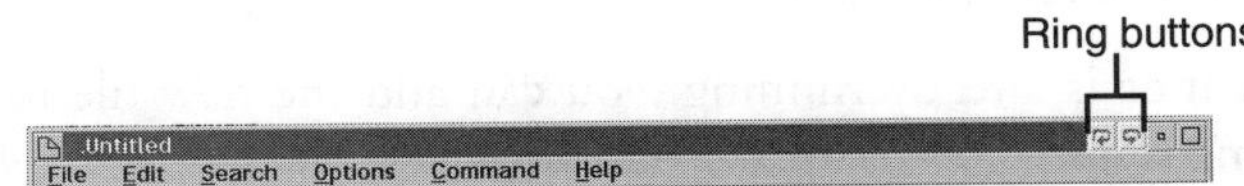

Figure G.11. *The title bar with ring buttons.*

Saving the Settings

For your configuration to last longer than the current edit session, you need to save the settings. When you save the settings, EPM saves the font, current configuration, and the window size and location.

If you later change the window size or location and you want EPM to remember the change, you must save the settings again. You may want to resize the window before saving the settings the first time, however.

Saving the settings is quite simple:

1. Select Options from EPM's menu.
2. Select Save options.

You have now configured the Enhanced Editor and saved the configuration. At this point, you're ready to start programming!

Programming with EPM

Writing a program with EPM is, for the most part, simply a matter of entering text, but some special techniques can speed your use of the editor.

Creating a New File

There are two ways to create a new file, depending on whether you have started the editor yet. If you haven't started the editor, follow these steps:

1. Start the editor from the book icon. The Open dialog box appears (refer to fig. G.6).
2. Type the drive, directory, and new filename into the entry field. For instance, type **`D:\Programs\hello.cmd`**.
3. Press Enter or select OK.

If the editor is already running, you can add the new file to the edit ring using the following steps:

1. From the File menu, select Add file…, or press F8. The Open dialog box appears.

2. Type the drive, directory, and new filename into the entry field. For instance, type **`D:\Programs\hello.cmd`**.
3. Press Enter or select OK.

For either method, a new file is created in memory. The file doesn't exist until you save it to disk.

Loading an Existing File

Loading an existing file works exactly like creating a new file, except that the filename you type should exist on disk.

When you're loading an existing file, you can use an alternative method that can save you some typing. In the Open dialog box, select the File list... button. You can then pick the file you want to load from the list.

Once you have opened a file, the filename is added to the list of files in the top half of the Open dialog box. This list works as a quick recall list of recently edited files. You can select a file from the list instead of typing its name.

Note: You can also load an existing file or create a new file by starting EPM from the command line. For instance, type **`EPM D:\Programs\hello.cmd`** at the command line to start EPM and edit HELLO.CMD.

Saving a File to Disk

You can either save a file using the name that it currently has, or you can save the file using a different name.

To save the file using its current name, select File and then Save, or press F2.

To save the file using a different name, select File and then Save as....

To save the file and quit editing it, select File and then Save and quit, or press F4.

Exiting EPM

To exit from a single file, select File and then Quit, or press F3. If the file is the last one in the edit ring, exiting from the file also exits EPM.

You can also exit from EPM by double-clicking the title bar icon in the upper-left corner or by pressing Alt+F4.

Using Syntax Expansion

Syntax expansion, a feature of the Enhanced Editor, makes the editor type some of your code for you. Syntax expansion is on by default, and it requires a *profile* (see the section on profiles later in this appendix) to shut off permanently.

Syntax expansion relies on the file extension in order to determine what programming language you're using. If the file has a .CMD extension, then EPM assumes you're writing a REXX program. Other file extensions and programming languages that EPM recognizes are .C for the C programming language and .PAS for the Pascal programming language.

With syntax expansion turned on, when you type the first word of an instruction that EPM recognizes, EPM fills in the rest of the code. For example, when you type IF and press the Spacebar, the following appears:

```
IF  then
else
```

The cursor is one space after the `IF`. If you don't want the else, you have to delete it.

Syntax expansion affects several REXX keywords, such as `DO`, `IF`, and `SELECT`.

Entering EPM Commands

The Enhanced Editor includes a Command dialog so that you can issue commands that aren't available from the menu. To open the Command dialog, select Command and then Command dialog..., or press Ctrl+I. The Command dialog then appears (see fig. G.12).

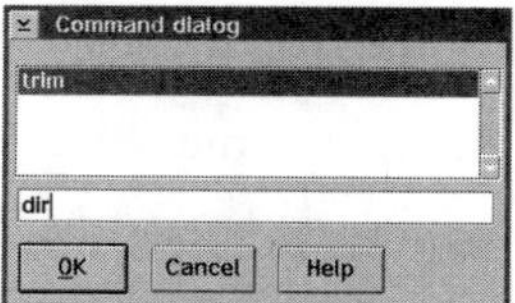

Figure G.12. *The Command dialog.*

In the Command dialog, you can enter a variety of commands. You can change EPM's configuration, search for text in one or several files, save a file with tabs expanded, run

an OS/2 command, change the margins, toggle menu items, and so on. For example, to turn syntax expansion off for the current edit session, type expand off in the Command dialog and press Enter.

For a list of commands, select the Help button on the Command dialog and then select the Editor commands item near the bottom of the help screen.

Creating a Profile

If you want to change a setting permanently and that setting isn't on the menu, you must create a *profile*. The profile is a REXX program that is loaded and run by EPM whenever EPM starts. You can execute most EPM commands from the profile by putting the EPM command in quotation marks. (Creating REXX macros for EPM is covered on Day 20.)

The profile is named PROFILE.ERX, and it must be stored in the \OS2\APPS directory on your OS/2 boot drive. Other than the name, it's just like any other REXX program.

For this example, you turn off syntax expansion. First, create a new file named *x*:\OS2\APPS\PROFILE.ERX (where *x* is your OS/2 boot drive). Then type the following program:

```
/* EPM profile */
'expand off'
EXIT
```

Press F2 to save the file.

You must now tell the Enhanced Editor to use the profile. Do the following:

1. Open the Command dialog by pressing Ctrl+I.
2. Type **`profile on`** and press Enter.
3. Save the profile setting by selecting Options and then Save options.

EPM then runs the profile every time you open the editor. In this case, it has the effect of permanently turning off syntax expansion. As you develop your own preferences, you can add or change commands in the profile.

EPM Keys Mini-Reference

Table G.1 is a short reference for some of the keys you may find immediately useful as you're just starting to use EPM. You can get a full listing of the keys that are used by EPM by selecting Help and then Quick reference.

You should also read the information available by selecting the other topics under Help, especially the General help item.

Table G.1. A mini-reference for EPM keys.

Key	What It Does
F2	Saves the current file
F3	Closes the current file; closes the editor if no more files
F4	Saves and closes the current file
F7	Renames the current file
F8	Edits a file
F9	Undo
F11	Goes to the previous file in the edit ring
F12	Goes to the next file in the edit ring
Left Arrow	Moves the cursor one character left
Right Arrow	Moves the cursor one character right
Up Arrow	Moves the cursor one line up
Down Arrow	Moves the cursor one line down
Page Up	Moves the cursor up one screen of text
Page Down	Moves the cursor down one screen of text
Home	Moves the cursor to the beginning of the line
End	Moves the cursor to the end of the line
Ctrl+Home	Moves the cursor to the beginning of the file
Ctrl+End	Moves the cursor to the end of the file
Enter	Inserts a new line; splits text at the current cursor position
Alt+J	Joins the current line with the following line, separated by a space
Del	Deletes the character at the current cursor position.

Key	What It Does
Ctrl+Backspace	Deletes the current line
Ctrl+E	Deletes text from the cursor to the end of the line
Ctrl+F1	Converts the current word to uppercase
Ctrl+F2	Converts the current word to lowercase
Alt+1	Edits the filename on the line at the current cursor position
Ctrl+I	Displays the EPM Command dialog

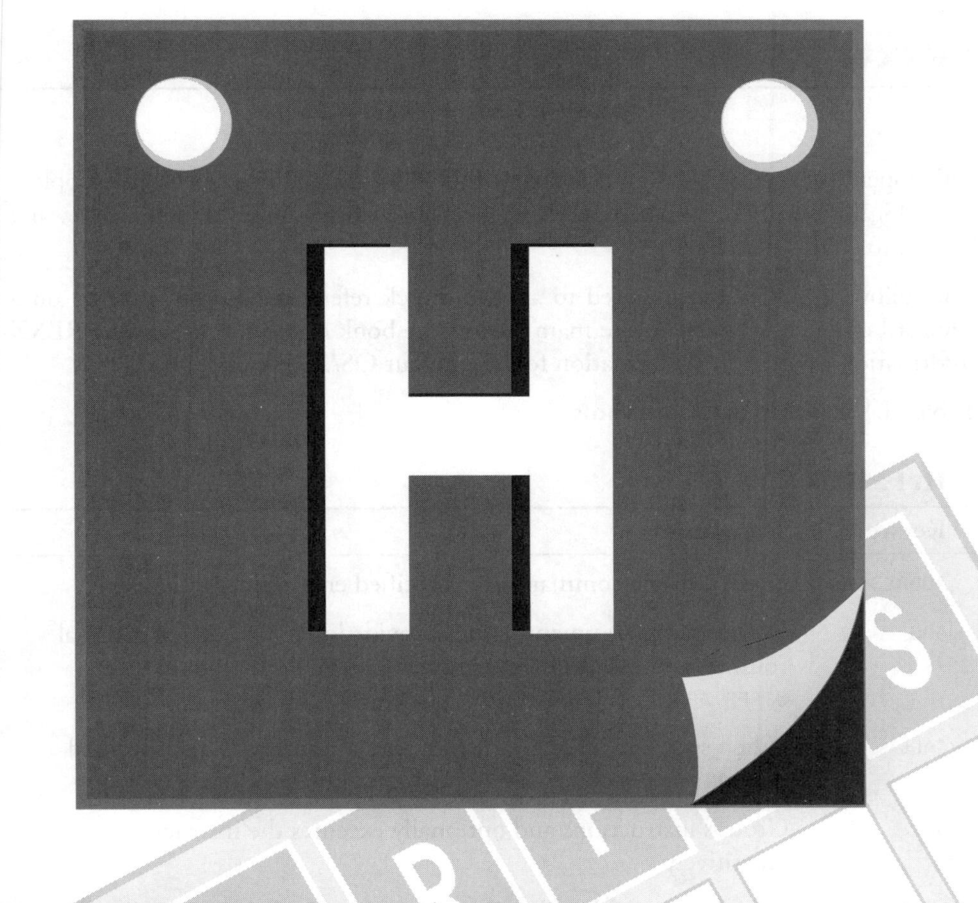

REXX Keyword and Function Reference

REXX Keyword and Function Reference

This appendix lists the functions available within OS/2 and within the libraries supplied with OS/2. Plenty of third-party REXX libraries are available, many of them shareware; be sure to check them out!

The following tables are intended to act as a quick reference. For more detail on a keyword or function, refer to the main part of the book or look in the online REXX Information book in the Information folder on your OS/2 desktop.

Table H.1 lists the REXX keywords.

Table H.1. REXX keywords.

Keyword	Description
`ADDRESS`	Sends a single command to a specified environment.
`ARG`	Retrieves the argument strings provided to a program or internal routine, and assigns them to variables; the short form of `PARSE UPPER ARG`.
`CALL`	When specified with a name, invokes a routine. When specified with `ON` or `OFF`, controls trapping of certain conditions.
`DO`	Groups instructions and optionally executes the instructions repetitively.
`DROP`	Unassigns variables (that is, sets variables to their uninitialized state).
`EXIT`	Leaves a program unconditionally.
`IF`	Conditionally processes an instruction or group of instructions depending on the evaluation of an expression.
`INTERPRET`	Processes instructions by evaluating an expression.
`ITERATE`	Alters the flow within a repetitive `DO` loop.
`LEAVE`	Causes an immediate exit from one or more repetitive `DO` loops.
`NOP`	A dummy instruction that has no effect.
`NUMERIC`	Changes the way in which arithmetic operations are carried out.
`OPTIONS`	Passes special requests or parameters to the language processor.
`PARSE`	Assigns data from various sources to one or more variables according to a template.

H

Keyword	Description
PROCEDURE	Protects existing variables by making them unknown within a subroutine or function.
PULL	Reads a string from the head of the currently active REXX data queue, or from standard input if no data is in the queue; short form of the PARSE UPPER PULL instruction.
PUSH	Stacks a string in *last in, first out* format onto the currently active REXX data queue.
QUEUE	Appends a string in *first in, first out* format onto the currently active REXX data queue.
RETURN	Returns control from a REXX program or internal routine to the point of its invocation.
SAY	Writes the result of an expression to standard output.
SELECT	Conditionally processes one of several alternative instructions. Each alternative instruction is introduced by a WHEN clause or the OTHERWISE clause.
SIGNAL	Causes an abnormal change in the flow of control. Controls trapping of conditions if ON or OFF is specified.
TRACE	Controls the tracing action taken during execution of a program (used for debugging).

Table H.2 lists the REXX built-in functions. Functions discussed in this book are marked with an asterisk (*).

Table H.2. REXX built-in functions.

Function	Syntax
*Abbrev	Abbrev(*information, info [,length]*)

Returns 1 if *info* is equal to the leading characters of *information* and the length of *info* is not less than *length*.

Function	Syntax
Abs	Abs(*number*)

Returns the absolute value of a number.

continues

Table H.2. continued

Function	Syntax
`Address`	`Address()`

Returns the name of the environment to which host commands are currently being submitted.

`*Arg`	`Arg([n [, option]])`

Returns an argument string, or information about the argument strings, to a program or internal routine.

`*Beep`	`Beep(frequency, duration)`

Sounds the speaker at *`frequency`* (Hertz) for *`duration`* milliseconds.

`BitAnd`	`BitAnd(string1 [, string2 ] [, pad ] )`

Returns a string composed of the two input strings logically compared, bit by bit, using the `AND` operator.

`BitOr`	`BitOr( string1 [, string2 ] [, pad ] )`

Returns a string composed of the two input strings logically compared, bit by bit, using the `OR` operator.

`BitXor`	`BitXor( string1 [, string2 ] [, pad ] )`

Returns a string composed of the two input strings logically compared, bit by bit, using the exclusive `OR` operator.

`B2X`	`B2X( binary_string )`

Converts *`binary_string`* to an equivalent string of hexadecimal characters.

`*Center`	`Center( string, length [, pad ] )`
	`Centre( string, length [, pad ] )`

Returns a string of a specified *`length`* with a string centered in it.

`*CharIn`	`CharIn( [name] [, start, length ] )`

Returns the characters read from the character input stream *`name`*.

`*CharOut`	`CharOut( [name] [, string, start ] )`

Returns the number of characters remaining after attempting to write a string to the character output stream *`name`*.

H

Function	Syntax

`*Chars` `Chars( [name] )`

Returns the number of characters in the character input stream *name*.

`Compare` `Compare( string1, string2 [,pad] )`

Checks to see whether two strings are identical. If not, it returns the position of the first character that does not match.

`Condition` `Condition( option )`

Returns information associated with the current trapped condition.

`*Copies` `Copies( string, n )`

Returns concatenated copies of a string.

`*C2D` `C2D( string [, n] )`

Returns the decimal value of the binary representation of a string.

`*C2X` `C2X( string )`

Converts a character string to its hexadecimal representation.

`*Datatype` `Datatype( string [, type ] )`

Determines whether the data is numeric or alphabetic and returns a result of `NUM` or `CHAR`. If *type* is specified, returns `1` or `0` indicating whether *string* is that *type*.

`Date` `Date( [option] )`

Returns the local date in the format *dd mon yyyy*, or when *option* is given, in the format specified.

`DelStr` `DelStr( string, n, [, length] )`

Deletes a substring beginning at character number *n*, for a specified length.

`DelWord` `DelWord( string, n [, length] )`

Deletes a substring of *string* beginning at word *n* and removing *length* words.

`Digits` `Digits()`

Returns the current setting of `NUMERIC DIGITS`.

continues

Table H.2. continued

Function	Syntax
*D2C	`D2C(number)[,n]`

Returns a character string that is the ASCII representation of a decimal number, specified to length *n*.

D2X	`D2X(number[, n])`

Returns a string of hexadecimal characters from a decimal number, specified to length *n*.

*Directory	`Directory([newdirectory])`

Returns the current directory, after changing it to *newdirectory* if an argument is supplied and if the directory exists.

*ErrorText	`ErrorText(n)`

Returns the error message associated with error number *n*.

*EndLocal	`EndLocal()`

Restores the drive, directory, and environment variables in effect before the last `SetLocal` function was executed.

FileSpec	`FileSpec(element, filespec)`

Returns a selected element of a file specification. Valid values for *element* are `Drive`, `Path`, and `Name`.

Form	`Form()`

Returns the current setting of `NUMERIC FORM`.

*Format	`Format( number , [before [, after [, expp] [,expt] ]])`

Returns a number rounded and formatted.

Fuzz	`Fuzz()`

Returns the current setting of `NUMERIC FUZZ`.

Insert	`Insert( new, target [, [n] [, [length] [,pad]]])`

Inserts one string into another.

LastPos	`LastPos( needle, haystack [,start])`

Returns the position of the last occurrence of one string in another.

Function	Syntax
*Left	`Left( string, length [,pad] )`

Returns a string containing the leftmost characters of another string.

*Length	`Length( string )`

Returns the length of a string.

*LineIn	`LineIn( [name] [, [line] [, count] ] )`

Returns *count* (0 or 1) lines read from the character input stream *name*.

*LineOut	`LineOut( [name] [, [string] [,line]] )`

Returns the number of lines remaining after attempting to write a string to the character output stream *name*.

*Lines	`Lines( [name] )`

Reports whether a read action performed by `CharIn` or `LineIn` will succeed.

Max	`Max( number [, number ...] )`

Returns the largest number from a list.

Min	`Min( number [, number ...] )`

Returns the smallest number from a list.

Overlay	`Overlay(new, target [, [n] [, [length] [,pad]]])`

Returns a string that is overlaid with another string, padded or truncated.

*Pos	`Pos( needle, haystack [, start] )`

Returns the position of one string in another.

*Queued	`Queued()`

Returns the number of lines remaining in the currently active REXX data queue.

Random	`Random([min], [max] [, seed])`
	`Random(max)`

Returns a quasi-random, nonnegative whole number.

*Reverse	`Reverse( string )`

Swaps a string, end for end.

continues

Table H.2. continued

Function	Syntax
`*Right`	`Right( string, length, [,pad] )`

Returns a string containing the rightmost characters.

`*RxFuncAdd`	`RxFuncAdd( name, module, procedure )`

Registers the external function *name*, making it available to REXX procedures.

`RxFuncDrop`	`RxFuncDrop( name )`

Removes (deregisters) the function *name* from the list of available functions.

`*RxFuncQuery`	`RxFuncQuery( name )`

Queries the list of available functions for a registration of the *name* function.

`*RxQueue`	`RxQueue( Get )`
	`RxQueue( Set, newqueuename )`
	`RxQueue( Delete, queuename )`
	`RxQueue( Create [, queuename] )`

Used to create and delete external data queues, and to set and query queue names.

`*SetLocal`	`SetLocal()`

Saves the current working drive and directory and the current values of the OS/2 environment variables.

`Sign`	`Sign(number)`

Returns a value that indicates the sign of *number*.

`*SourceLine`	`SourceLine([n])`

Returns the line number of the last line in a source file. If *n* is specified, returns the text from line *n* in the source file.

`*Space`	`Space( string [, [n] [,pad]] )`

Formats blank-delimited words so that there are *n pad* characters between each word.

Function	Syntax
*Stream	Stream(*name*, 'C', *streamcommand*)
	Stream(*name*, 'D')
	Stream(*name*, 'S')

Returns a string describing the state of, or the result of an operation upon, the character stream *name*. The second parameter may also be Command, Description, or State.

*Strip Strip(*string* [, [*option*] [, *char*]])

Removes leading and/or trailing characters from a string.

*Substr Substr(*string*, *n* [, [*length*] [, *pad*]])

Returns a substring of *string* beginning at character *n*.

SubWord SubWord(*string*, *n* [,*length*])

Returns a substring starting at word *n*.

Symbol Symbol(*name*)

Returns the state of a symbol, that is, BAD, VAR, or LIT.

Time Time([*option*])

Returns the local time in the 24-hour clock format *hh:mm:ss* by default. Returns the time in the specified format when *option* is supplied.

Trace Trace([*option*])

Returns trace actions currently in effect.

*Translate Translate(*string*, [[,*tableo* [,*tablei* [, *pad*]]]])

Translates characters in a string to other characters.

Trunc Trunc(*number* [,*n*])

Returns the integer part of *number*, with *n* decimal places.

Value Value(*name*, [, [*newvalue*] [,*selector*]])

Returns the value of the symbol named by *name*, and optionally assigns it a new value.

continues

Table H.2. continued

Function	Syntax
Verify	Verify(*string, reference [, [option] [,start]]*)
Returns the position of the first character in *string* that is or is not also in *reference* (as specified in *option*).	
Word	Word(*string, n*)
Returns word *n* from *string*.	
WordIndex	WordIndex(*string, n*)
Returns the position of the first character of word *n* in *string*.	
WordLength	WordLength(*string, n*)
Returns the length of word *n* in *string*.	
WordPos	WordPos(*phrase, string* [,*start*])
Searches *string* for the first occurrence of the sequence of blank-delimited words *phrase*, and returns the word number of the first word of *phrase* in *string*.	
Words	Words(*string*)
Returns the number of blank-delimited words in a string.	
*XRange	XRange([*start*] [, *end*])
Returns a string of one-byte codes between and including the values *start* and *end*.	
X2B	X2B(*hexstring*)
Converts a string of hexadecimal characters to a string of binary digits.	
*X2C	X2C(*hexstring*)
Converts a string of hexadecimal characters to ASCII characters.	
X2D	X2D(*hextring* [,*n*])
Converts a string of hexadecimal characters to decimal.	

Table H.3 lists the functions in the RexxUtil library. Functions discussed in this book are marked with an asterisk (*). The description of the purpose of each function follows each element.

Table H.3. Functions in the RexxUtil library.

Function	Syntax
*RxMessageBox	*action* = RxMessageBox(*text*, [*title*], [*button*], [*icon*])
Displays a message box from a REXX program running in an OS/2 PM session.	
*SysCls	CALL SysCls
Clears the screen.	
*SysCreateObject	*rc* = SysCreateObject(*classname*, *title*, *location* [,*setup*] [,*option*])
Creates a new instance of an object class.	
*SysCurPos	*pos* = SysCurPos([*row*, *col*])
Optionally moves the cursor to the specified row and column. Returns the previous cursor position.	
*SysCurState	CALL SysCurState *state*
Hides or displays the cursor. The value of state may be either `ON` or `OFF`.	
SysDeregisterObjectClass	*rc* = SysDeregisterObjectClass(*class*)
Deregisters an object class definition from the system.	
*SysDestroyObject	*result* = SysDestroyObject(*name*)
Destroys an existing Workplace Shell object.	
*SysDriveInfo	*info* = SysDriveInfo(*drive*)
Gives drive information.	
*SysDriveMap	*map* = SysDriveMap([*drive*], [*opt*])
Reports accessible drives in the form `'C: D: E:...'`, based on the option specified.	
SysDropFuncs	CALL SysDropFuncs
Drops all the loaded RexxUtil functions.	
*SysFileDelete	*rc* = SysFileDelete(*file*)
Deletes the specified file. Does not support wildcards.	

continues

Table H.3. continued

Function	Syntax
*SysFileTree	*rc* = SysFileTree(*filespec, stem*, [*options*], [*tattrib*], [*nattrib*])

Finds all files and/or directories that are equal to the specified *filespec* and places their descriptions in a *stem* variable.

*SysFileSearch	CALL SysFileSearch *target, file, stem,* [*options*]

Finds all lines in specified file that contain a specified target string and places those lines in a *stem* variable.

*SysGetEA	*result* = SysGetEA(*file, name, variable*)

Reads a named extended attribute from a file.

*SysGetKey	*key* = SysGetKey([*opt*])

Gets the next key from the keyboard buffer or waits for one if none exists. The value of *opt* is either ECHO or NOECHO.

SysGetMessage	*msg* = SysGetMessage(*num*, [*file*] [*str1*],...[*str9*])

Gets a message from a message file.

*SysIni	*result* = SysIni([*inifile*], *app, key, val*)
	result = SysIni([*inifile*], *app, key*)
	result = SysIni([*inifile*], *app, key*, 'DELETE:')
	result = SysIni([*inifile*], *app*, ['DELETE:'])
	result = SysIni([*inifile*], *app*, 'ALL:', '*stem*')
	result = SysIni([*inifile*], 'ALL:', '*stem*')

Allows limited editing of .INI file variables.

*SysMkDir	rc = SysMkDir(*dirspec*)

Makes a directory.

SysOS2Ver	ver = SysOS2Ver()

Returns the OS/2 version information.

Function	Syntax
*SysPutEA	`result = SysPutEA(`*`file, name, value`*`)`

Writes a named extended attribute to a file.

*SysQueryClassList	`CALL SysQueryClassList `*`stem`*

Retrieves the complete list of registered object classes.

SysRegisterObjectClass	*`rc`*` = SysRegisterObjectClass(`*`class, module`*`)`

Registers a new object class definition to the system.

*SysRmDir	*`rc`*` = SysRmDir(`*`dirspec`*`)`

Deletes a specified directory.

SysSearchPath	*`filespec`*` = SysSearchPath(`*`path, filename`*`)`

Searches the specified path for the specified file and returns the full *`filespec`* of the file if found. The *`path`* is specified as an environment variable.

*SysSetIcon	*`rc`*` = SysSetIcon(`*`filename, iconfilename`*`)`

Associates an icon file with a specified file.

*SysSetObjectData	*`rc`*` = SysSetObjectData(`*`name, setup`*`)`

Changes the settings of an existing object or opens an instance of an object.

*SysSleep	`CALL SysSleep `*`secs`*

Sleeps a specified number of seconds.

SysTempFileName	*`file`*` = SysTempFileName(`*`template`*`, [`*`filter`*`])`

Returns a unique file or directory name given a certain template.

SysTextScreenRead	*`string`*` = SysTextScreenRead(`*`row, col`*`, [`*`len`*`])`

Reads a specified number of characters from a specified location of the screen.

SysTextScreenSize	*`result`*` = SysTextScreenSize()`

Returns the size of the screen as `row col`.

*SysWaitNamedPipe	*`result`*` = SysWaitNamedPipe(`*`name`*`, [`*`timeout`*`])`

Performs a timed wait on a named pipe. The *`timeout`* value is in microseconds.

Index

Symbols

A

B

SAMS
PUBLISHING

D

E

F

G

H

I-J

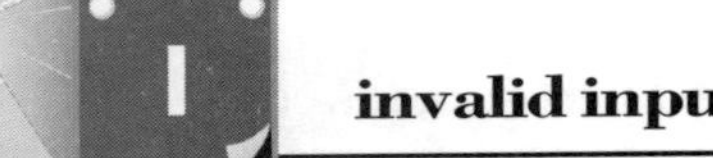

M

N

O

P

Q-R

S

T

Book ISBN 0-672-30529-1